U.S.-Habsburg Relations from 1815 to the Paris Peace Conference

Sovereignty Transformed

This study provides the first book-length account of U.S.-Habsburg relations from their origins in the early nineteenth century through the aftermath of World War I and the Paris Peace Conference. By including not only high-level diplomacy but also an analysis of diplomats' ceremonial and social activities, as well as an exploration of consular efforts to determine the citizenship status of thousands of individuals who migrated between the two countries, Nicole M. Phelps demonstrates the influence of the Habsburg government on the integration of the United States into the nineteenth-century Great Power System and the influence of American racial politics on the Habsburg Empire's conceptions of nationalism and democracy. In the crisis of World War I, the U.S.-Habsburg relationship transformed international politics from a system in which territorial sovereignty protected diversity to one in which nation-states based on racial categories were considered ideal.

Nicole M. Phelps is assistant professor of history at the University of Vermont. She won the Austrian Cultural Forum Dissertation Prize in 2010 and an honorable mention for SHAFR's Unterberger Dissertation Prize in 2009.

U.S.-Habsburg Relations from 1815 to the Paris Peace Conference

Sovereignty Transformed

NICOLE M. PHELPS

University of Vermont

CAMBRIDGE
UNIVERSITY PRESS

CAMBRIDGE UNIVERSITY PRESS
Cambridge, New York, Melbourne, Madrid, Cape Town,
Singapore, São Paulo, Delhi, Mexico City

Cambridge University Press
32 Avenue of the Americas, New York, NY 10013-2473, USA

www.cambridge.org
Information on this title: www.cambridge.org/9781107005662

© Nicole M. Phelps 2013

First published 2013

Printed in the United States of America

A *catalog record for this publication is available from the British Library.*

Library of Congress Cataloging in Publication Data
Phelps, Nicole M.
U.S.-Habsburg relations from 1815 to the Paris peace conference : sovereignty
transformed / Nicole M. Phelps, University of Vermont.
pages cm
ISBN 978-1-107-00566-2 (hardback)
1. United States – Foreign relations – Austria.   2. Austria – Foreign relations – United
States.   3. Diplomatic and consular service, American – History.   4. Diplomatic and
consular service, Austrian – History.   5. Citizenship – United States – History.   6. United
States – Race relations – History.   7. Immigrants – United States – History – 19th
century.   8. Immigrants – United States – History – 20th century.   I. Title.
E183.8.A9P54   2013
327.730436–dc23   2013004471

ISBN 978-1-107-00566-2 Hardback

For the Welkes and the Goods

Contents

Acknowledgments   *page* ix

Abbreviations   xi

Introduction: The Habsburg Empire and the United States
in Transnational Perspective   1

1 Community and Legitimacy: The Diplomatic Culture
   of the Great Power System   13

2 Becoming a Great Power: U.S.-Habsburg Diplomatic
   Relations and the Integration of the United States into the
   Great Power System   39

3 Protection and the Problems of Dual Citizenship: U.S. Consuls
   in the Habsburg Empire   103

4 The Limits of State Building: Habsburg Consuls in the United
   States and the Protection of Lives and Property   147

5 Racial Identity and Political Citizenship: American Challenges
   to Habsburg Sovereignty   197

6 Giving Up on Austria-Hungary: The End of the Great Power
   System and the Shift to the Nationalist Successors   219

7 Establishing Sovereignty: The Process of Aligning Race, Place,
   and Citizenship   258

   Conclusion: After the Peace   275

Index   283

Acknowledgments

So many people to thank, and yet the word count tells me that I have very little space; emotion will have to follow my beautifully constructed citations to the chopping block. Let me start then with the two people who have had the greatest impact on this project, my advisors at the University of Minnesota, David Good and Barbara Welke. I thought they were terrific advisors when I was a graduate student, but as I moved into my own faculty position, I realized how many other demands there were on their time, and they have come to look even more terrific to my more experienced eyes. I am extremely grateful that they allowed me to be a part of their lives.

This project would not have been possible without the general intellectual foundation and love for learning that was nurtured by my parents, Dan and Ginny Phelps, as well as by a number of excellent, inspirational teachers and professors, including Bruce Secker, Jude Ellis, Linda Levy Peck, Hugh Agnew, Joe Hoffmann, Inge Lehne, and Attila Pók. I can trace a more direct line to this project from two papers I wrote while an undergraduate at The George Washington University; my sincere thanks to Charles Herber and Steve Phillips for creating those opportunities. While working on my Ph.D. at Minnesota, I had the great good fortune to work with Gary Cohen, Erika Lee, Kirsten Fischer, J. B. Shank, Martin Sampson, and Colin Kahl.

Friends and colleagues from high school, college, and graduate school have offered invaluable advice and support over the years. My thanks to Dave Morris, Dan Dinero, Jessica Logue, Dan Bouk, Angie Giancarlo, Jaimie Hoops, Alane Kochems, Dave Mitchell, Rachel Foote, Ellen Arnold, Brie Arnold, Marisa Brandt, Nikki Bruin, Susan Graham, Dave

La Vigne, Matt Lungerhausen, Lisa Peschel, Annett Richter, Evan Roberts, and Todd Rowlatt. I am delighted to have landed at the University of Vermont, where I have been pleased to find the line between colleague and friend pleasantly hazy. Everyone in the History Department has done something that has been invaluable to the project, from offering advice on the revisions to commiserating over the less pleasant aspects of life as an academic.

The staff of the U.S. National Archives in College Park, Maryland, and the Haus-, Hof- und Staatsarchiv in Vienna, Austria, helped me navigate their respective collections, and the staff of the University of Minnesota and University of Vermont libraries provided invaluable assistance in helping me acquire materials for my research. A Doctoral Dissertation Fellowship from the University of Minnesota Graduate School supported my writing. Barbara Reiterer, Silke Stern, and Annett Richter very kindly confirmed several of my German translations. Steve Hausmann, Brandon Moblo, and Phillip Moore helped me tame my reference software and kept my office from being engulfed in library books. The editorial and production staff at Cambridge has shown me tremendous patience, for which I am exceptionally grateful.

Portions of Chapters 3, 4, and 6 appeared, respectively, in the following publications: "State Sovereignty in a Transnational World: U.S. Consular Expansion and the Problem of Naturalized Migrants in the Habsburg Empire, 1880–1914," *German Historical Institute Bulletin Supplement* 5 (2008): 41–59; "Securing Sovereignty, Loyalty, and Property: Habsburg Consuls in the United States, 1880–1917," *Europa Orientalis* 6 (2008): 131–52; and "'A Status Which Does Not Exist Anymore': Austrian and Hungarian Enemy Aliens in the United States, 1917–1921," *Contemporary Austrian Studies* 19 (2010): 90–109.

Abbreviations

AHR	*American Historical Review*
AHY	*Austrian History Yearbook*
AQ	*American Quarterly*
AR	Administrative Registratur
BWV	Berichte, Weisungen, Varia
DH	*Diplomatic History*
DOS	Department of State
HHStA	Haus-, Hof- und Staatsarchiv, Vienna, Austria
FRUS	*Foreign Relations of the United States*
JAH	*Journal of American History*
JAEH	*Journal of American Ethnic History*
JGAPE	*Journal of the Gilded Age & Progressive Era*
K	Karton
MFA	Imperial and Royal Ministry of the Imperial and Royal House and Foreign Affairs
NARA	United States National Archives and Records Administration, College Park MD, General Records of the Department of State, Record Group 59, Decimal File 1910–29
NYT	*New York Times*
PA	Politische Archiv
PHR	*Pacific Historical Review*
SecState	Secretary of State

Introduction

The Habsburg Empire and the United States in Transnational Perspective

This is a book about the relationship between two of the world's most famously diverse countries: the United States and the Habsburg Empire. That relationship has not received much scholarly attention, in large part because the two countries did not have the kind of relationship that has traditionally attracted diplomatic historians.[1] There are very few treaties

[1] On U.S.-Habsburg relations before World War I, see Rudolf Agstner, "From Apalachicola to Wilkes-Barre: Austria(-Hungary) and Its Consulates in the United States of America, 1820–1917," *AHY* 37 (2006): 163–80; Merle Eugene Curti, "Austria and the United States, 1848–1852: A Study in Diplomatic Relations," *Smith College Studies in History* 11, 3 (1926): 137–206; Harry Hanak, "Die Einstellung Grossbritanniens und der Vereinigten Staaten zu Österreich(-Ungarn)," in *Die Habsburgermonarchie in System der Internationalen Beziehungen*, vol. 6/part 2, *Die Habsburgermonarchie, 1848–1918*, ed. Adam Wandruszka (Vienna, 1993), 539–85; Alison Frank, "The Petroleum War of 1910: Standard Oil, Austria, and the Limits of the Multinational Corporation," *AHR* 114, 1 (2009): 16–41; Nicole Slupetzky, "Austria and the Spanish-American War," in *European Perceptions of the Spanish-American War*, ed. Sylvia L. Hilton and Steve J. S. Ickringill (Bern, 1999), 181–94; Donald S. Spencer, *Louis Kossuth and Young America: A Study of Sectionalism and Foreign Policy, 1848–1852* (Columbia, 1977); and the document collection by Erwin Matsch, *Wien-Washington: Ein Journal diplomatischer Beziehungen, 1838–1917* (Vienna, 1990). Studies related to World War I and the Paris Peace Conference include Victor S. Mamatey, *The United States and East Central Europe, 1914–1918: A Study in Wilsonian Diplomacy and Propaganda* (Princeton, 1957); Betty Miller Unterberger, *The United States, Revolutionary Russia, and the Rise of Czechoslovakia* (Chapel Hill, 1989); Gerald H. Davis, "The Diplomatic Relations between the United States and Austria-Hungary, 1913–1917" (Ph.D. diss., Vanderbilt University, 1958); Carol Jackson Adams, "Courting the 'Vassal': Austro-American Relations during World War I" (Ph.D. diss., University of Alabama, 1997); Arthur J. May, "Woodrow Wilson and Austria-Hungary to the End of 1917," in *Festschrift für Heinrich Benedikt*, ed. Hugo Hantsch and Alexander Novotny (Vienna, 1957), 213–42; Jon D. Berlin, "The Burgenland: The United States and the Burgenland, 1918–1920," *AHY* 8 (1972): 39–58;

between the two governments, trade between them was relatively small, and, with the exception of World War I, they never went to war with one another. What they did have was a series of conflicts over diplomatic norms, a multitude of legal problems stemming from the migration of several million people back and forth between the two countries between the 1870s and World War I, and, of course, the crisis of the war itself. These conflicts had a dramatic effect on both American and Habsburg political culture, and the clashes between their contrasting approaches to managing their diverse populations contributed decisively to the transition in international politics from the post-1815 Great Power System to the post-1919 nation-state system. Their relationship demonstrates the international and transnational aspects of the construction of sovereignty.

Historical accounts of both countries offer long-standing narratives about the domestic sources of their governments' sovereignty. For the United States, a Lockean conception of natural rights and a social contract is written into the Declaration of Independence, bolstering the claim that the U.S. government derives its legitimacy exclusively from the consent of the governed. For the Habsburg Empire, the conventional wisdom for decades was that the empire collapsed because the government oppressed the empire's constituent national groups, which could not get along and actively sought the independence that was eventually achieved via the 1919 Paris Peace Conference.[2] More recently, scholarly accounts have stressed the importance of the Habsburg government's inability to provide basic services during the strain of World War I in decisively eroding domestic support for Habsburg sovereignty.[3]

These domestically focused narratives do tell us a great deal about American and Habsburg sovereignty, but they do not tell the whole story. Sovereignty does indeed derive in part from the consent of the governed, but it also comes from the recognition of its legitimacy from other governments in the international system; governments look to ensure their survival not only through domestic support, but through

---

Frederick Dumin, "Self-Determination: The United States and Austria in 1919," *Research Studies* 40, 3 (1972): 176–94; and James M. Smallwood, "Banquo's Ghost at the Paris Peace Conference: The United States and the Hungarian Question," *East European Quarterly* 12, 3 (1978): 289–307.

[2] Classic accounts of domestic collapse that are still in scholarly use include Oscar Jászi, *The Dissolution of the Habsburg Monarchy* (Chicago, 1929); and A. J. P. Taylor, *The Habsburg Monarchy, 1809–1918* (Chicago, 1948).

[3] Maureen Healy, *Vienna and the Fall of the Habsburg Empire: Total War and Everyday Life in World War I* (New York, 2004).

international support as well.[4] This study focuses on these international aspects, concerning itself primarily with how the Habsburg government first gained and then lost U.S. recognition of its legitimacy. When the U.S. government and its allies withdrew their support for Habsburg sovereignty during World War I and transferred it to new Central European governments that had been conceived in racial-national terms, a fundamental change in the nature of the international political system occurred.

The Habsburg Empire, commonly known as Austria-Hungary after its dramatic reorganization in 1867, was home to a population whose members conversed in German, Magyar (Hungarian), Czech, Slovak, Polish, Italian, Romanian, Ukrainian, various South Slavic idioms (Serbo-Croatian, Slovene), and Yiddish. Multilingualism was common, and recent scholarship has clearly demonstrated that language use was not equivalent to identification with the racial-national community.[5] Catholics, Protestants, Jews, Orthodox and Uniate Christians, and Muslims abounded. Each of the dozens of territories that made up the empire brought its own history, political traditions, and economic system. In addition to seeking the support of its citizens and subjects, the Habsburg government bolstered its legitimacy by carefully cultivating international support.[6] At the Congress of Vienna in 1815, the Habsburg government led the way in creating the Great Power System, in which member governments were recognized as legitimate by all of the other governments in the system. The five Great Powers in the system – Austria, Prussia (later Germany), Russia, France, and Britain – were supposed to use their

[4] Stephen Krasner, *Sovereignty: Organized Hypocrisy* (Princeton, 1999); see also James J. Sheehan, "The Problem of Sovereignty in European History," *AHR* 111, 1 (2006): 1–15.

[5] See, among numerous others, Pieter M. Judson, *Guardians of the Nation: Activists on the Language Frontiers of Imperial Austria* (Cambridge MA, 2006); and Jeremy King, "The Nationalization of East Central Europe: Ethnicism, Ethnicity, and Beyond," in *Staging the Past: The Politics of Commemoration in Habsburg Central Europe, 1848 to the Present*, ed. Maria Bucur and Nancy M. Wingfield (West Lafayette, 2001), 112–52.

[6] On the political culture of the empire, see Gary B. Cohen, "Neither Absolutism nor Anarchy: New Narratives on Society and Government in Late Imperial Austria," *AHY* 29 (1998): 37–61; Cohen, "Nationalist Politics and the Dynamics of State and Civil Society in the Habsburg Monarchy, 1867–1914," *Central European History* 40, 2 (2007): 241–78; Waltraud Heindl, "Bureaucracy, Officials, and the State in the Austrian Monarchy: Stages of Change since the Eighteenth Century," *AHY* 37 (2006): 35–57; Lothar Höbelt, "Parliamentary Politics in a Multinational Setting: Late Imperial Austria," working paper, *Center for Austrian Studies*, University of Minnesota, 1992; and Daniel L. Unowsky, *The Pomp and Politics of Patriotism: Imperial Celebrations in Habsburg Austria, 1848–1916* (West Lafayette, 2005). For a brief but persuasive assessment of Habsburg success in the international community, see Paul W. Schroeder, "The Luck of the House of Habsburg: Military Defeat and Political Survival," *AHY* 32 (2001): 215–24.

power to guarantee the territorial integrity of the smaller states and to resolve any conflicts that developed, tasks at which they were largely successful.[7] Citizenship was based on territory: all the people living on the land within a government's jurisdiction were citizens or subjects of that government. At Vienna, representatives also articulated a new set of diplomatic rules and norms that were designed to facilitate the maintenance of the system; key to this arrangement was the division of tasks among central foreign ministry staff, diplomatic corps, and consular services. The Habsburg government used the Great Power System and its diplomatic culture to protect its claims to sovereignty over the diverse range of individuals who resided on its territory. The Habsburg central government also used the system to create and maintain the politically based citizenship categories of "Austrian" and "Hungarian" that facilitated the goal of uniform application of the law to the empire's inhabitants, and the Habsburg central government – especially the emperor – enjoyed widespread loyalty and support.[8] As other governments engaged in practices that upheld Habsburg sovereignty, they reaffirmed the Habsburg government's authority to categorize its citizens in political terms.

The United States was not a participant in the Congress of Vienna, and so it was not invested in the diplomatic culture of the Great Power System. Indeed, many Americans throughout the nineteenth century rejected as un-American the diplomacy and especially the specific ceremonies, protocols, and practices that characterized the Great Power System. It became increasingly clear to U.S. officials, however, that they were going to have to participate in the system if they wanted to achieve American economic and political goals. Over the course of the nineteenth century, the United States gradually became integrated into the Great Power System, and conflicts with the Habsburg government about the rules of the system helped to further that integration. Until Woodrow Wilson's administration began in 1913, the Habsburg government was successful in these conflicts, knitting the United States more thoroughly into the system and thus securing

---

[7] Paul W. Schroeder, *The Transformation of European Politics, 1763–1848* (New York, 1994).

[8] On Habsburg citizenship categories, see Benno Gammerl, "Subjects, Citizens and Others: The Handling of Ethnic Differences in the British and the Habsburg Empires (late Nineteenth and Early Twentieth Century)," *European Review of History* 16, 4 (2009): 523–49. On loyalty to the crown, see King, "Nationalization"; Unowsky; and Laurence Cole and Daniel L. Unowsky, eds. *The Limits of Loyalty: Imperial Symbolism, Popular Allegiances, and State Patriotism in the Late Habsburg Monarchy* (New York, 2007).

continued American recognition of legitimate Habsburg sovereignty. In the United States, characterizations of diplomacy as un-American were gradually – although not fully – eclipsed by the idea that compliance with diplomatic norms was civilized behavior.

Like the Habsburg Empire, the United States had a diverse population, and it only became more so as the nineteenth century progressed. In addition to native-born whites, there were multiple waves of immigrants from Europe, the British dominions, and Asia, plus Native Americans, African slaves and their descendants, and former citizens of Mexico and Spain. The founding principle of the United States, of course, is that all men are created equal, but the arrival of more and more people, whether as slaves or as voluntary migrants, prompted many Americans to rethink that promise of equality in an effort to hold on to their own political power. Americans began to develop their own language of racial difference, first to justify taking land from Native Americans and enslaving Africans and then to exclude a wide variety of immigrants from entering the country or becoming naturalized U.S. citizens, prevent newly freed African Americans from exercising full citizenship, and, later, justify overseas colonization.[9] These conceptions of racial difference were increasingly expressed in scientific terms, naturalizing them and imbuing them with significant cultural power. Racial categories were also tied to political culture, with contemporary thinkers arguing that certain biological groups, through genetics and acquired habit, had an innate propensity to liberty and democratic institutions, whereas others were made to be dependent, continually bowing to authority. In this line of thinking, a homogeneous national community of people capable of self-government was a prerequisite for the successful functioning of democracy.[10] By the 1890s, a key, powerful group of Americans adopted these ideas and came to see the United States as an Anglo-Saxon nation that needed to be homogeneous for its superior government to function.

---

[9] For an overview, see Barbara Young Welke, *Law and the Borders of Belonging in the Long Nineteenth Century United States* (New York, 2010); see also Chapter 5.

[10] See, among numerous others, Matthew Frye Jacobson, *Barbarian Virtues: The United States Encounters Foreign Peoples at Home and Abroad, 1876–1917* (New York, 2000); Reginald Horsman, *Race and Manifest Destiny: The Origins of American Racial Anglo-Saxonism*, rev. ed. (Cambridge MA, 1986); Paul Gordon Lauren, *Power and Prejudice: The Politics and Diplomacy of Racial Discrimination* (Boulder, 1996); Rogers M. Smith, *Civic Ideals: Conflicting Visions of Citizenship in U.S. History* (New Haven, 1997); Lloyd E. Ambrosius, "Woodrow Wilson and The Birth of a Nation: American Democracy and International Relations," *Diplomacy & Statecraft* 18, 4 (2007): 689–718; and John S. Haller, *Outcasts from Evolution: Scientific Attitudes toward Racial Inferiority, 1859–1900*, rev. ed. (Carbondale, 1995).

Through their experiences at home and abroad, private American citizens and officials of the U.S. government gradually worked out what it meant to be white, and they were aided in their efforts by European colonial powers and, especially, by similar processes occurring in the settler colonies of Australia, New Zealand, South Africa, and Canada.[11] Working out the narrower definition of Anglo-Saxon, however, was done through contact with the millions of European migrants who came to the United States, and a significant number of these came from the Habsburg Empire.[12] In dealing with European migrants, Americans worked out new categories that later would be considered ethnicities, but which they articulated in terms of race, putting as much distance between, for example, a Pole and a German as there was between an African and an American Indian. These categories were directly at odds with the political citizenship categories that the Habsburg government applied to its citizens.

Had Habsburg migrants to the United States stayed in their new home, those categories of racial nationalism might not have held as much salience back in Europe. However, the late nineteenth and early twentieth century was a time of massive international movement, driven by changes in technology and the economy that made such movement more accessible to a wide range of people. Some Austrian and Hungarian citizens were truly immigrants, making permanent homes in the United States, but approximately half returned to the empire. Short-term travel was also more affordable, prompting a rise in the number of people who were traveling for brief visits to relatives, to conduct business, for educational purposes, or merely for recreation.[13] Most of the travel between the United States and Europe was done without passports or visas, which meant that an individual's citizenship status was not clearly marked and was thus open to question whenever he or she crossed an international border.[14] U.S. officials in the Bureau of Immigration, where scientific categories of racial nationalism had a firm institutional hold, used those categories to

---

[11] Marilyn Lake and Henry Reynolds, *Drawing the Global Colour Line: White Men's Countries and the International Challenge of Racial Equality* (Cambridge, 2008); and Paul A. Kramer, "Power and Connection: Imperial Histories of the United States in the World," *AHR* 116, 5 (2011): 1348–91.

[12] Specific numbers are difficult to determine, due to the statistical categories the Bureau of Immigration used. See Chapter 5 and Mark Wyman, *Round-trip to America: The Immigrants Return to Europe, 1880–1930* (Ithaca, 1993).

[13] Christopher Endy, "Travel and World Power: Americans in Europe, 1890–1917," *DH* 22, 4 (1998): 565–94.

[14] John Torpey, *The Invention of the Passport: Surveillance, Citizenship and the State* (Cambridge, 2000).

mark people from the Habsburg Empire, rather than using the political citizenship categories employed by the Habsburg government. Racial-nationalist ideas in the United States had considerable power, and they could manifest in economic and social discrimination or in actual violence, as well as in everyday public discourse. These ideas and experiences shaped migrants' understanding of race, citizenship, and identity, often sharpening their association with and acceptance of racial-nationalist categories. The movement of people from the Habsburg Empire to the United States and back again provided a conduit for ideas about racial nationalism and the specific categories adopted by the U.S. government to make their way back to the Habsburg Empire, where they contributed to the development of national identities at the expense of Habsburg political citizenship. By the time World War I began, those categories had gained considerable salience in the Habsburg Empire, although the desire for independent national states was confined to a relatively small number of activists.[15]

Neither the American acceptance of Great Power diplomatic culture nor the increasing salience of racial-nationalist categories in the Habsburg Empire was produced exclusively by the U.S.-Habsburg relationship, but they were significantly influenced by that relationship; they were certainly not purely domestic phenomena. However, the specifics of the U.S.-Habsburg relationship were crucial to the end of the Great Power System and the transition to the post-1919 Paris system. Whether he intended it or not, U.S. President Woodrow Wilson became the figure most closely associated with the idea of "self-determination" during World War I and the Paris Peace Conference, and the hopeful national activists of Central Europe made their appeals for recognition of their sovereign claims in terms they thought he would accept. Polish, Czechoslovak, and Yugoslav groups presented their claims to sovereignty to Wilson, his staff of postwar planners, and the American public in racial-national terms, arguing for the biological homogeneity and clearly defined borders of the community they claimed to represent and stressing the fitness of that community for democratic self-government. These groups were not alone in doing so: nationalist leaders from all over the world converged on Wilson in Paris to make similar claims.[16] At the time, however, it was only in Central Europe that such claims were successful. Their success signaled to other hopeful leaders that

---

[15] See, among others, Jeremy King, *Budweisers into Czechs and Germans: A Local History of Bohemian Politics, 1848–1948* (Princeton, 2002).

[16] Erez Manela, *The Wilsonian Moment: Self-determination and the International Origins of Anticolonial Nationalism* (New York, 2007).

the key to international recognition lay in claims to represent clearly defined racial-national communities. Existing governments also received a push to articulate their legitimacy in racial-national terms, facilitating shifts from state-protected individual rights to the identification of majorities and minorities as distinct and quite likely permanent groups within the population.[17] With the Paris Peace Conference, the norms of the international political system shifted: in the earlier Great Power System, the internal structure of governments could vary while the international community protected governmental legitimacy and territorial claims. In the post-1919 Paris system, the legitimate governments in the system needed to be democratic, capitalistic, and representative of a single national community.[18]

The Central European nationalists who were successful in obtaining Wilson's recognition and support were able to do so for two reasons. First, a key aspect of the Great Power System's diplomatic culture had been shut down. In that culture, it was normal for countries at war to break diplomatic relations with one another, suspending the ongoing process of legitimizing sovereignty by removing members of the diplomatic corps from their posts in enemy countries. That is what happened during World War I. As diplomatic channels closed down, the last remaining connection among the warring states was between the United States and the Habsburg Empire. Before the United States entered the war, Wilson made the decision not to receive the newly arrived Habsburg ambassador, Count Adam Tarnowski. With that choice, the aspect of Great Power diplomatic culture that perpetuated mutual recognition of legitimate sovereignty was gone, and the Habsburg government lost its ability to communicate with the Wilson administration and to make a case there for its continued existence. Nationalists then had a monopoly on Wilson's attention.

Second, when determining the details of his peace proposal – the Fourteen Points – and during negotiations in Paris, Wilson chose to circumvent the State Department and instead use The Inquiry, an independent team of experts, to inform his decision making. The State Department

---

[17] Eric D. Weitz, "From the Vienna to the Paris System: International Politics and the Entangled Histories of Human Rights, Forced Deportations, and Civilizing Missions," *AHR* 113, 5 (2008): 1313–43; and Carole Fink, *Defending the Rights of Others: The Great Powers, the Jews, and International Minority Protection, 1878–1938* (New York, 2004).

[18] For decades, scholarship on the Paris Peace Conference focused on Western efforts to block the spread of communism in the wake of the war. The classic study is Arno J. Mayer, *Politics and Diplomacy of Peacemaking: Containment and Counterrevolution at Versailles, 1918–1919* (New York, 1967).

had developed in tandem with the Great Power System, and its personnel and methods were largely committed to the norms of that system. By going around it, Wilson had greater freedom of action. His team of experts was primarily made up of academics, the preponderance of whom were geographers. The most important qualification for membership was enthusiasm for Wilson's publicly stated ideas, and so it was a group in favor of radical change. Many of them were quite young, and although they all had advanced degrees, none of them had made the Habsburg Empire a focus of study.[19] If the State Department was the American institutionalization of the Great Power System, the Inquiry was a group that had thoroughly internalized – or, in some cases, developed – the teachings of scientific racism, and they sought to apply those ideas in Central Europe. They operated on the problematic assumption that each individual person had a single racial identity that was manifested in the language he or she spoke; this way of thinking did not leave space for grappling with the reality of multilingualism in Central Europe, and it suggested that neatly corralling individuals into their proper national communities would be relatively simple.[20] By selecting the Inquiry over the State Department, Wilson's eventual support for ending Habsburg sovereignty in favor of nationalist successor states was almost guaranteed.

Securing international recognition and actually exercising sovereignty on the ground are two different things, however, and the successor governments had their work cut out for them, especially because the homogeneous, nationally conscious, and united populations they claimed to represent did not exist, nor were the physical boundaries of their sovereignty clear.[21] The new states did not spring immediately into existence when Emperor Karl abdicated in November 1918. The U.S. government was important in bolstering the successor governments' sovereign claims and reinforcing their social and physical borders in the years immediately after the war, although it took some time for various agencies of the U.S. government to reach a consensus on those borders. The crucial action

---

[19] Lawrence E. Gelfand, *The Inquiry: American Preparations for Peace, 1917–1919* (New Haven, 1963); and Neil Smith, *American Empire: Roosevelt's Geographer and the Prelude to Globalization* (Berkeley, 2003).

[20] My understanding of this process is informed by the discussion of simplification and legibility in James C. Scott, *Seeing Like a State: How Certain Schemes to Improve the Human Condition Have Failed* (New Haven, 1998).

[21] On the uncertainty of borders, see, among others, Peter Haslinger, *Nation und Territorium im Tschechischen Politischen Diskurs, 1880–1938* (Munich, 2010); and Andrea Orzoff, *Battle for the Castle: The Myth of Czechoslovakia in Europe, 1914–1948* (New York, 2009).

came from the State Department. Although the diplomatic channels of the Great Power System had been shut down with the war, the consular channels, through which governments protected the lives and property of their citizens abroad, remained open, albeit in modified form. Neutral countries took over consular protection duties in belligerent countries. For most of the war, the United States was the neutral power with the largest consular presence, and its representatives assumed many of these duties, operating ten countries' consular services in all belligerent countries, in addition to protecting its own citizens.

The undertaking was massive because the war had left thousands of people stranded away from home as transportation networks shut down. Dealing with the myriad issues that arose made it very clear to State Department employees that unregulated international movement could become an administrative nightmare in a time of crisis. Although consuls had worked hard to determine legal citizenship status for those who claimed U.S. citizenship before the war and to provide protection to them if they were entitled to it, the war demonstrated that it would be much easier for consuls to do their work if people who crossed borders had passports and visas. Such paperwork would clearly mark an individual's citizenship status. The consul's task would be simplest if each individual's political citizenship aligned with his or her racial identity, making a visual assessment of the individual's citizenship claims significantly easier. Getting a passport would add a hurdle to international travel, keeping more people at home, where their physical location would align with their citizenship and racial identity, too. For those who still aimed to travel, visas would regulate the length of their stays, again urging people back home and helping consuls determine cases of expatriation. Passports had been introduced as a wartime measure in Europe, and the State Department successfully advocated for their continued use after the war. By requiring passports, the U.S. government helped the new successor states – as well as preexisting governments – more thoroughly define their social and territorial borders.

Finally, the U.S. Bureau of Immigration had an important role to play in reinforcing the borders of the new nations.[22] As the Paris Peace Conference and then the treaty ratification process dragged on, the Bureau of Immigration was busy sending people back to Europe, deporting people considered dangerous and repatriating prisoners of war and civilian internees. At first, Immigration actions muddied the waters,

[22] The bureau was replaced with the Immigration and Naturalization Service in 1933.

because, ironically, they did not consistently adhere to the racial-national categories that had been propagated in Paris, despite their crucial role in creating those categories in the first place. In determining where to send these people, Swedish consuls – embodying the continued sovereignty of the Habsburg Empire for almost three years after the emperor had abdicated – pressed the U.S. government for a statement of clear and consistent borders, prompting the departments of State, Justice, and Labor to reach a consensus. In the wake of the war and the peace conference's affirmation of racial-nationalist categories, the U.S. Congress also passed emergency immigration quotas in 1921 and regularized that system via the Immigration Act of 1924. These laws privileged Anglo-Saxons above all, then classified other European groups as white, privileging them over nonwhites, whose ability to immigrate and become naturalized citizens was dramatically curtailed or, in many cases, entirely prohibited.[23] The U.S. immigration quota system helped to reinforce categories of racial nationalism, and the border controls it involved helped to discourage international movement, contributing to the desired alignment of citizenship, race, and place.

By tracing the U.S.-Habsburg relationship from its early nineteenth-century origins through its final end in 1921, we can see the mutual influence the two countries had on one another, as well as the impact of their relations on international politics writ large. Understanding the process of change requires thinking about forces beyond the purely domestic, but it also requires us to refrain from thinking about the Habsburg and U.S. governments as unitary actors. In the Great Power System, diplomats, consuls, and foreign ministry staff each had different roles to play. Diplomats in the field engaged in ceremonial and social activities that continually reinforced intergovernmental recognition of legitimacy. The first two chapters of the book focus on this aspect of the Great Power System and Habsburg successes in drawing the United States into the system. Consuls dealt with the legal problems faced by citizens abroad, and their work focused first on determining citizenship status and then on exercising their governments' sovereign rights in aid of those who had a legitimate claim on their protection. Chapter 3 deals with U.S. consular efforts in the Habsburg Empire; Chapters 4 and 5 focus on Habsburg experiences in the United States and their efforts to challenge the application of racial-nationalist categories to Austrian and Hungarian citizens there.

[23] Mae M. Ngai, "The Architecture of Race in American Immigration Law: A Reexamination of the Immigration Act of 1924," *JAH* 86, 1 (1999): 67–92.

During the war, regular diplomatic channels between the United States and the Habsburg Empire were shut down, shifting activity to politicians, specialized wartime agencies, and central foreign ministry staff. As Chapter 6 details, this shift resulted in the American pursuit of several unconnected policies that, when combined, made U.S. support for the creation of nationalist states in Central Europe the only possible outcome. When Emperor Karl abdicated in November 1918, however, the transition to successor states was neither quick nor smooth. Chapter 7 examines the lengthy process of securing U.S. and other international support for the territorial and social boundaries of the successor states. That process was affected not only by events on the ground in Central Europe, but by the actions of delegates at the peace conference and through the decisions taken by various branches of the U.S. government as they attempted to sort out the citizenship status of Austrian and Hungarian enemy aliens who had spent all or part of the war on U.S. soil.

I

Community and Legitimacy

The Diplomatic Culture of the Great Power System

The period from 1815 until World War I was a unique era in European international politics; the Great Power System, which regulated European interaction in this period, was markedly different from the Westphalian system of the seventeenth and eighteenth centuries and the post-1919 international system. What made it so unique was the specific purpose assigned to diplomats in the system: through their participation in ceremonial and social activities, diplomats maintained a fundamental sense of community in the system that limited the severity of international conflicts and reinforced the legitimacy of the sovereign governments in the system. The Great Power System was created at the Congress of Vienna in 1815 in an attempt to limit the incidence of warfare among European states on European soil after the devastating and almost continuous warfare of the seventeenth and eighteenth centuries. By reducing warfare and establishing a system that reinforced international recognition of sovereignty, governments could spend their time and resources coping with the effects of industrialization and increased demands for public participation in government. For all governments in the system, this external support was an important source of legitimacy, but the extent of diversity in the Habsburg lands placed a special premium on such support. On the whole, the Great Power System was successful: European-wide warfare was almost entirely avoided for a century, until the outbreak of World War I.[1]

---

[1] The Crimean War (1853–56) was the exception, but many European countries – including the Habsburg Empire – managed to stay out of the conflict, and its effects and scope were very small when compared with the Napoleonic Wars or World War I.

In 1815, when European statesmen gathered in Vienna at the end of the Napoleonic Wars, they aimed to create a new system for managing international politics.[2] According to historian Paul W. Schroeder, the new system, above all, was supposed to reduce the frequency of war among European states. This goal was understandable, given the turbulence of the seventeenth and eighteenth centuries. From the outbreak of the Thirty Years' War in 1618, most of Europe was more or less at war until 1815.[3] The Thirty Years' War was primarily a religious conflict, pitting Protestants against Catholics. At its conclusion in 1648, European leaders agreed to the Peace of Westphalia, which articulated new norms for international interaction, just as later statesmen would do at Vienna in 1815 and Paris in 1919. The foundational concept of the Westphalian system was territorial sovereignty: Europe was perceived as divided into mutually exclusive territorial units, and each unit had only one sovereign, be it a monarch, a republican government, or some other wielder of authority.[4] The type of government was far less important than the idea that one particular government had complete authority over a specific piece of land. Citizenship and subjecthood were derivatives of territorial sovereignty: a sovereign's citizens or subjects were those people who lived on the land the sovereign controlled.

Although there was consensus on the basic concept of territoriality, the Westphalian system was prone to conflict. Territoriality was supposed to govern the system, but the borders of the constituent territories were far from clear. Accurate maps of Europe were rare, and verbal definitions of borders were open to differing interpretations. These uncertainties prompted the gradual development of more accurate maps and land surveys, and they also prompted disputes and wars as sovereigns sought to define their

[2] On the Congress of Vienna, see Paul W. Schroeder, *The Transformation of European Politics, 1763–1848* (New York, 1994). See also Harold Nicolson, *The Congress of Vienna: A Study in Allied Unity, 1812–1822* (New York, 1946); Edward Vose Gulick, *Europe's Classical Balance of Power: A Case History of the Theory and Practice of One of the Great Concepts of European Statecraft*, reprint ed. (Westport, 1982); and Tim Chapman, *The Congress of Vienna: Origins, Processes, and Results* (London, 1998).
[3] On the almost continuous warfare of the period, see Schroeder, *Transformation*; Jeremy Black, *British Diplomats and Diplomacy, 1688–1800* (Exeter, 2001); and Paul M. Kennedy, *The Rise and Fall of the Great Powers: Economic Change and Military Conflict from 1500 to 2000* (New York, 1989).
[4] Stephen Krasner, *Sovereignty: Organized Hypocrisy* (Princeton, 1999); and Daniel Philpott, *Revolutions in Sovereignty: How Ideas Shaped Modern International Relations* (Princeton, 2001). The Dutch Republic was the notable nonmonarchy in Europe at the time.

territories clearly.[5] The adoption of the concept of territorial sovereignty also contributed to the value of territory: sovereigns sought not just to define their territory, but to expand it as well.[6] The acquisition of specific territories was often the cause or stated goal of military actions, and territory changed hands frequently and was the common reward for military success. Acquisitions could go so far as to erase independent states from the map, with the partitions of the Polish and Lithuanian Commonwealth being perhaps the best known example.[7] In the Westphalian system, diplomats contributed more to conflict than to peace. They were used to signal independence in the system, rather than cooperation, and they were also used to maintain alliances, rather than to negotiate peace or prevent the outbreak of war.[8] As a result, they embodied the conflict of the system.

Modern diplomatic corps had their roots in fifteenth-century Italy, when various Italian city-states such as Venice and Milan began the practice of sending representatives to neighboring polities to report on local conditions there. The main purpose of these representatives was to gather information.[9] There were few rules about how the information was to be collected, however, and many diplomats were essentially engaged in espionage. These early practices gave rise to the common association of diplomacy with "intrigue" and clandestine political maneuverings, an image that has persisted in some circles to the present day, despite subsequent changes in diplomatic practice and the creation of separate espionage institutions.[10]

---

[5] David Buisseret, *Monarchs, Ministers, and Maps: The Emergence of Cartography as a Tool of Government in Early Modern Europe* (Chicago, 1992); and James C. Scott, *Seeing Like a State: How Certain Schemes to Improve the Human Condition Have Failed* (New Haven, 1998).

[6] The predominant economic theory of the time, mercantilism, contributed to this emphasis on territory. Mercantilism posited that the world was a finite collection of resources and that sovereigns should attempt to control as many of those resources as possible. See, among others, Lars Magnusson, *Mercantilism: The Shaping of an Economic Language* (New York, 1994).

[7] The country was reduced by partition in 1772 and 1793, then eliminated entirely in 1795. Russia and Prussia acquired land on all three occasions; the Habsburg Empire participated in the first and third partitions.

[8] On diplomats' role in alliance maintenance, see especially Black.

[9] Matthew Smith Anderson, *The Rise of Modern Diplomacy, 1450–1919* (London, 1993), 2–7.

[10] On diplomacy and "intrigue," see Black; and Warren Frederick Ilchman, *Professional Diplomacy in the United States, 1779–1939: A Study in Administrative History* (Chicago, 1961).

In addition to these early permanent representatives, sovereigns employed other devices for international dealings. If two sovereigns wanted to conduct negotiations on a specific topic, they might meet in person, or they might send a representative who was charged with negotiating on only that particular topic.[11] After negotiations were completed, the representative would return home. These short-term negotiators were good for reaching concrete agreements because they could be given specific instructions about how to handle possible situations that might arise; it was easier to think of possible contingencies when the mission was of limited scope. Short-term negotiators also typically had the trust of the sovereign because they were personal acquaintances, and they were up to date on conditions at home and thus more responsive to their sovereign's immediate needs. This contrasted with permanent representatives, who often stayed abroad for ten years or more, making them experts on the host country yet distancing them from the political pulse of the home country.[12]

To be a permanent representative or a special negotiator in this early system, citizenship and ethnicity were unimportant. It was not uncommon in early modern Europe for "foreigners" to be active in government. To give just a few examples, the Russian service aristocracy contained many German, French, and Scottish names, as people were recruited from abroad because of their skills, expertise, or financial power. The Habsburg Empire's greatest military hero was Prince Eugene of Savoy, who came from outside the empire. The English government employed people from Switzerland and other European countries as diplomats.[13] What was important for holding these offices was the trust of the sovereign in the office holder's loyalties and abilities. For diplomatic office, social standing was important for making connections, as were linguistic abilities, among other traits. Citizenship and ethnicity did not become widely salient factors for diplomatic employment until the mid nineteenth century, and, even then, they typically extended only to the actual ambassador; junior staff members and consular personnel continued to include foreign citizens throughout the nineteenth century, and many countries continue to use them in clerical and lower-level positions today.

---

[11] On the basics of this practice, see Anderson, *Rise*, 12–13.
[12] See Raymond A. Jones, *The British Diplomatic Service, 1815–1914* (Waterloo, 1983), 196–97; and Erwin Matsch, *Der Auswärtige Dienst von Österreich (-Ungarn) 1720–1920* (Vienna, 1986).
[13] See John P. LeDonne, *Ruling Russia: Politics and Administration in the Age of Absolutism, 1762–1796* (Princeton, 1984); Charles W. Ingrao, *The Habsburg Monarchy, 1618–1815* (Cambridge, 1994); and Black.

The Italian use of permanent, officially sanctioned representatives signaled a shift in European culture. Sending an ambassador was a sign of the independent sovereignty of the sending government. Italian city-states' claims to sovereignty undermined the concept of a unified European Christendom and contributed to the development of a conflictual international political culture in the Westphalian system. Gradually, by the seventeenth century, the right to send and receive ambassadors became one of the rights associated with sovereignty. Governments worked to make sure that sovereign states were the only entities that were allowed to send and receive ambassadors and conduct international affairs.[14] By monopolizing certain kinds of international interaction, governments strengthened their claims to sovereignty and also bolstered the claims of the other recognized sovereigns in the system.

Building on Italian developments, the French took important steps toward institutionalizing diplomacy and changing its methods. Under Louis XIV (r. 1648–1715), sending permanent diplomats became more common across Europe. Diplomacy was no longer supposed to be about espionage and intrigue; it was supposed to be governed by honesty, good faith, and personal decorum.[15] As historian Harold Nicolson has described it, the French system "was courteous and dignified; it was continuous and gradual; it attached great importance to knowledge and experience; it took account of the realities of existing power; and it defined good faith, lucidity and precision as qualities essential to any sound negotiation."[16] In the French system, diplomacy was about cultivating trust. That trust could be broken or misplaced, but for a violation of trust to be an effective technique, trust and honesty had to be expected. Other European states gradually adopted French practices: French began to replace Latin as the language of a cosmopolitan European community, and diplomats gradually began to conform to certain accepted behaviors.[17]

---

[14] See Anderson, *Rise*, viii, 4; and Black, 6.

[15] Black; Anderson, *Rise*, 45; Jones; and Harold Nicolson, *The Evolution of Diplomatic Method* (London, 1953).

[16] Nicolson, *Evolution*, 72.

[17] On the European adoption of French practices, see Black; and Anderson, *Rise*. Some Habsburg diplomats before 1848 opted to communicate with their superiors in Vienna in French, rather than the traditional administrative language of German. See the "Nordamerika" folders in HHStA, AR, Fach 7 – Fremde Missionen, K. 22 – Staaten B-P 1830–49; and Erwin Matsch, *Wien-Washington: Ein Journal diplomatischer Beziehungen, 1838–1917* (Vienna, 1990).

Although the French system did promote trust and community, it did so in a particular way that did not prevent widespread warfare. In the French system, sovereigns did not send diplomats to countries they were at war with in hopes of finding peace; they only sent them to their allies or those with which they hoped to be allied. Alliances were critical for fighting the systemic wars of the seventeenth and eighteenth centuries, and those alliances were achieved and maintained by diplomats.[18] Those diplomats were personally trusted by the king, queen, or foreign minister, and they were given a significant amount of latitude to make decisions without instructions. There was little or no diplomatic communication across alliances, however, and so diplomats were not helpful in achieving or maintaining systemic peace.

The warfare engendered by this system ultimately prompted the creation of a second type of life-threatening enemy for European governments: not only did they have to worry about being destroyed by their neighbors, they now had to worry about attacks from within based on emerging natural rights theories of sovereignty and government. These theories were a response to the state-building process that was necessitated by the dynamics of a territoriality-based international system.[19] Sovereigns wanted to know the value of land and the resources contained in or on it, including its human inhabitants. They ordered land cadastres, population censuses, and geological surveys. To conduct these investigations, they needed qualified surveyors and administrators, so they hired them, creating bureaucratic institutions. When there were not enough qualified personnel, sovereigns created and reformed educational systems to produce them. Sovereigns also expanded their armies and navies to control and acquire territory more successfully. All of this required money: the administrators, teachers, and soldiers all had to be paid. To do that, sovereigns raised taxes and, perhaps more importantly, sought to tax more efficiently. They used the cadastres and censuses to determine what resources were out there and how the state could extract them most effectively. Improved education also helped, as it was supposed to lead to more economically and socially productive citizens and subjects.[20]

[18] Black, 4.
[19] On the relationship between war and the state-building process, see, among others, Kennedy, *Rise and Fall*; Mark R. Brawley, *Liberal Leadership: Great Powers and Their Challengers in Peace and War* (Ithaca, 1993); and Hendrick Spruyt, *The Sovereign State and Its Competitors* (Princeton, 1994).
[20] On state building, see, among many others, Ingrao; Waltraud Heindl, *Gehorsame Rebellen: Bürokratie und Beamte in Österreich 1780 bis 1848* (Vienna, 1991);

State building brought the government into the daily lives of its citizens and subjects in new and unexpected ways, and those citizens and subjects did not always accept state expansion. Most European states operated on a divine-right theory of domestic sovereignty – that is, the monarch had been chosen by God to rule – and people were supposed to obey their sovereign because he or she was channeling the will of God.[21] This theory of government worked best when a sovereign's subjects felt that God's policies were consistent with their personal interests. When calls for obedience came up against the practical dissatisfactions of the state-building process, some people began to reconsider the relationships among God, government, and subject. In the face of increased state demands, Thomas Hobbes, John Locke, Jean-Jacques Rousseau, and numerous others began to posit the ultimate, natural sovereign authority of each individual person or "the people" collectively.[22] These theories contributed to the idea that "the government" or the state and "the people" were distinct and at odds, and they were deployed in efforts to reduce the power of the government or, in some cases, to overthrow the government entirely.

The rhetoric of natural rights and popular sovereignty contributed significantly to the obfuscation of the sources of sovereignty, thus creating subsequent confusion and conflict. In practice, the sovereignty of any government has both domestic and international components. A government can exist as a legitimate sovereign only when it has the consent of a critical mass of the people it exercises authority over *and* the consent of a critical mass of other governments in the international system that it

James Van Horn Melton, *Absolutism and the Eighteenth-Century Origins of Compulsory Schooling in Prussia and Austria* (Cambridge, 1988); Derek Beales, *Joseph II* (Cambridge, 1987–2009); Franz A. J. Szabo, *Kaunitz and Enlightened Absolutism, 1753–1780* (Cambridge, 1994); John Brewer, *The Sinews of Power: War, Money and the English State, 1688–1783* (Cambridge MA, 1994); Scott; John Torpey, *The Invention of the Passport: Surveillance, Citizenship, and the State* (Cambridge, 2000); Steven Skowronek, *Building a New American State: The Expansion of National Administrative Capacities, 1877–1920* (Cambridge, 1982); Brian Balough, *A Government Out of Sight: The Mystery of National Authority in Nineteenth-Century America* (New York, 2009); and Margot Canaday, *The Straight State: Sexuality and Citizenship in Twentieth-Century America* (Princeton, 2009).

[21] The quintessential statement of this theory is James I of England's 1609 "Divine Right of Kings."

[22] Important statements of these theories include Thomas Hobbes, *Leviathan* (1651); John Locke, *Second Treatise on Government* (1690); Jean Jacques Rousseau, *On the Social Contract* (1762); Thomas Paine, *Common Sense* (1776); Abbe Sieyès, *What Is the Third Estate?* (1789); and Olympe De Gouges, "Declaration of the Rights of Woman" (1791).

exercises authority alongside.[23] Divine right theories of sovereignty were not incompatible with the idea of international approval because all the appointed sovereigns had been designated by the same Christian God; Europe was at the same time a single community of Christians and a set of distinct, territorial sovereignties. Natural rights theories of sovereignty, such as that of John Locke, stressed that the sole source of governmental legitimacy was the consent of the governed, thus leaving the international out of the story entirely; a Lockean state could exist in a vacuum – or it could be a truly universal world state because all individuals could theoretically consent to the same government. Natural rights theories could therefore contribute significantly to the outbreak of violent conflict: they could be deployed to overthrow a domestic government, they could foster a sharp sense of self-interest and lack of concern for those outside the domestic social contract, and they could feed an effort to absorb one's neighbors into a universal state.[24]

The 1688–89 Glorious Revolution in Britain and especially the American and French revolutions took up the idea of government by the people, and the Napoleonic Wars helped spread variants of those ideas throughout Europe. Governments across Europe recognized the need to deal with popular sovereignty ideas. Ignoring them would invite revolution and therefore the removal of the government from power, and complete suppression of these ideas was impossible – the states were simply not strong enough at the time. Governments therefore embarked on programs of gradual reform and accommodation. To engage in those domestic political reforms, to rebuild materially after the Napoleonic Wars, and to ensure their own survival in the face of revolutionary rhetoric, European governments were interested in international peace – they wanted to worry about domestic problems without the added complications of foreign wars. This desire for peace was widespread in Europe, but no more so than among Austrian government officials.

Under any circumstances, governing the Habsburg Empire was difficult. It was a collection of numerous territories with distinct political traditions. Each territory had a linguistically and religiously diverse population. There was no easy way to align religious, linguistic, and other cultural factors with territorial boundaries, and Habsburg officials rarely tried to accomplish that kind of alignment. To maintain the loyalty of their subjects, the

<hr />

[23] Krasner.
[24] On liberalism's ability to cause conflict with its contradictory rhetoric, see John Gray, *Two Faces of Liberalism* (New York, 2000).

Habsburgs allowed much of the distinctiveness and diversity to remain in place.[25] The royal authority of the Habsburg dynasty was the main commonality across the various territories at first, but, over time, the state-building process brought more commonalities in the form of empire-wide institutions, particularly the bureaucracy and the military.[26]

Habsburg rule brought many benefits to the people of the various territories, especially the economic and security benefits that derived from belonging to a larger country. Habsburg rule was not universally welcome or entirely secure, however, and central officials had to work to maintain the loyalty and compliance of the population – just as their counterparts in other countries did. They did that by providing services, maintaining some local political traditions, extending the rule of law and equality before the law across all territories, and, at times, by playing one interest group against another. Because of the extreme complexity of the country, Habsburg officials typically found it more effective to govern through the bureaucracy rather than a parliament, but the laws and policies enforced by the bureaucracy were usually informed by parliamentary and public debate.[27] Consensus, rather than majority rule, and

---

[25] Notable exceptions include the persecution of Protestants during the Counter-Reformation, policies to restrict the movement and other activities of Roma and Jews, and the use of the German language as the language of administration throughout the country. All of these policies were rescinded over time – religious toleration was guaranteed from 1781, and, over the course of the nineteenth century, other languages were allowed in administration; they had always been allowed for private use. See, among others, Ingrao; and Beales. On religion, see Grete Klingenstein, "Modes of Religious Tolerance and Intolerance in Eighteenth-Century Habsburg Politics," *AHY* 24 (1993): 1–16.

[26] See, for example, Heindl, *Gehorsame Rebellen*; István Deák, *Beyond Nationalism: A Social and Political History of the Habsburg Officer Corps, 1848–1918* (New York, 1990); and Ernst Bruckmüller, "Was There a 'Habsburg Society' in Austria-Hungary?" *AHY* 37 (2006): 1–16. MFA personnel also took a pro-imperial position. See William D. Godsey, Jr., *Aristocratic Redoubt: The Austro-Hungarian Foreign Office on the Eve of the First World War* (West Lafayette, 1999); and James Allan Treichel, "Magyars at the Ballplatz: A Study of the Hungarians in the Austro-Hungarian Diplomatic Service, 1906–1914" (Ph.D. diss., Georgetown University, 1972).

[27] See, among others, Heindl, *Gehorsame Rebellen*; Lothar Höbelt, "Parliamentary Politics in a Multinational Setting: Late Imperial Austria," working paper, Center for Austrian Studies, University of Minnesota, 1992; John W. Boyer, *Political Radicalism in Late Imperial Vienna: Origins of the Christian Social Movement: 1848–1897* (Chicago, 1981); Gary B. Cohen, "Neither Absolutism nor Anarchy: New Narratives on Society and Government in Late Imperial Austria," *AHY* 29, part 1 (1998): 37–61; Cohen, "Nationalist Politics and the Dynamics of State and Civil Society in the Habsburg Monarchy, 1867–1914," *Central European History* 40, 2 (2007): 241–78; and Peter Urbanitsch, "Pluralist Myth and Nationalist Realities: The Dynastic Myth of the Habsburg Monarchy – A Futile Exercise in the Creation of Identity?" *AHY* 35 (2004): 101–41.

temporary compromises that were meant to be renegotiated in the future developed as key aspects of Habsburg political culture over the course of the nineteenth century.

In 1815, Emperor Franz II/I was on the Austrian throne.[28] His reign had been marked by warfare, invasion, and the Napoleonic destruction of the historic Holy Roman Empire, which had been an important source of Habsburg power. Together with his chief minister, Prince Metternich, the emperor hoped to preserve what remained of the Habsburg realm, the authority of the crown, and many of the reforms introduced by his predecessor, Joseph II (r. 1780–90).[29] Franz II/I and Metternich were decidedly conservative, but they often aimed to conserve many of the liberal reforms of Joseph II, including religious toleration and the bureaucracy's commitment to the rule of law. Metternich served as the primary Austrian representative at the Congress of Vienna, and he was a key figure in shaping the policies and ideals articulated at the conference.[30] He aimed to secure the empire's international position so its government could concentrate on maintaining Habsburg rule of the country's diverse population.

Previous end-of-war treaties in the seventeenth and eighteenth centuries had often been nothing more than ceasefires, and the signatories had realized that.[31] At the Congress of Vienna, however, the representatives aimed at establishing a long-term solution. Britain, Prussia, Austria, and Russia had defeated Napoleonic France, and, as victors, they were in a position to set the terms of the settlement. However, Metternich and his counterparts in Britain, Prussia, and Russia were aware of the fact that the success of the peace and the subsequent international system depended on the inclusion of defeated France. The French – and particularly the newly restored French monarchy – were invited to participate fully in the conference; French Foreign Minister Talleyrand was an active shaper of the new Great Power System.[32] All five major powers were content with the system in 1815 – and for quite a long time afterward – and the fact that none felt

---

[28] Franz was the second Holy Roman Emperor named Franz, hence his title as Franz II; he stopped using this when the Holy Roman Empire was dissolved in 1806. He adopted the title of Emperor of Austria – of which he was the first – in 1804. See Robert A. Kann, *A History of the Habsburg Empire, 1526–1918* (Berkeley, 1974).

[29] Leopold II, a younger brother of Joseph II, ruled briefly from 1790 to 1792.

[30] Paul W. Schroeder, *Metternich's Diplomacy at Its Zenith, 1820–1823* (Austin, 1962); and Henry Kissinger, *A World Restored: Metternich, Castleregh and the Problems of Peace, 1812–22* (Boston, 1957).

[31] Schroeder, *Transformation.*

[32] Guglielmo Ferrero and Theodore R. Jaeckel, *The Reconstruction of Europe: Talleyrand and the Congress of Vienna, 1814–1815* (New York, 1941).

cheated or punished contributed significantly to the longevity of the system.[33]

At Vienna, territorial sovereignty was reaffirmed as the foundation of the international system, but the representatives at the congress added other aspects to the system that altered the meaning of this basic concept. The new system was to be openly hierarchical. There would be five Great Powers: Austria, Britain, France, Prussia, and Russia. The Great Powers recognized each other's right to exist as independent, sovereign states, and they agreed not to interfere in one another's domestic affairs. They also agreed to cooperate to maintain the peace: they would communicate among each other to reach solutions to whatever problems occurred, and the Great Powers would use their influence in the smaller states to assure the compliance of those governments. The smaller states did not enjoy the same rights of noninterference or direct participation in the international handling of conflicts and crises. However, the Great Powers guaranteed their territorial integrity and took responsibility for finding nonviolent solutions to international problems, which meant that the smaller states did not have to deal with these issues and could use their resources for other purposes. In 1815, the smaller states of Europe also consented to the Vienna system.[34]

At its inception in 1815, the Great Power System applied strictly to Europe and European affairs. The restraints that the signatories accepted for European politics did not apply to countries or affairs in other parts of the world, and, as the events of the nineteenth century demonstrate, European powers had few qualms about infringing upon or even entirely destroying governmental structures in Africa and Asia. The United States did not send representatives to the conference, nor did other non-European states. Over the course of the nineteenth century, the Great Power System gradually expanded to accommodate the United States, the independent countries of Latin America, and Japan. That process of expansion was not always smooth, but states could join the system and be recognized as legitimate sovereigns if they conformed to the behavioral norms of the system.

---

[33] The desire of dissatisfied powers to revise international political systems has been identified by numerous political scientists and other scholars as a significant contributor to the outbreak of war; the victors-only approach taken at the Paris Peace Conference in 1919 has been especially criticized for fostering discontent and leading to the outbreak of World War II. See, for example, Brawley; Klaus Schwabe, *Woodrow Wilson, Revolutionary Germany, and Peacemaking, 1918–1919: Missionary Diplomacy and the Realities of Power* (Chapel Hill, 1985); and Randall Schweller, "Bandwagoning for Profit: Bringing the Revisionist State Back In," *International Security* 19, 1 (1994): 72–107.

[34] On the process of reaching this consensus, see Schroeder, *Transformation*.

So, at the Congress of Vienna, all the states of Europe recognized each other's right to exist and to exercise sovereignty over mutually recognized territories and the people that resided therein. They agreed on the rights and responsibilities of different types of states in the system, and they agreed to attempt to solve international problems without resorting to violence. In other terms, they proposed a shift away from what constructivist theorist Alexander Wendt would characterize as the Hobbesian culture of the Westphalian system, in which states perceive each other as enemies and are willing to fight to the death, to a Lockean culture, in which states perceive each other as rivals, rather than enemies.[35] Such a perception allowed states to temper their conflicts with a sense of community that prevented the "death" of the system's states. It was truly a transformation of European politics, as historian Paul Schroeder has dubbed it.[36]

Agreeing to all these new principles over the course of a few weeks in 1815 and maintaining the system over time were two different things, however. Realizing this, the representatives at Vienna went a step further and established an apparatus for maintaining the Great Power System. They took advantage of the developing institutions of diplomatic corps and central foreign ministries – and the potential for change caused by the chaos of the war – and opted to adjust the purpose and practice of diplomacy to serve the needs of the Great Power System. Although central foreign ministry personnel would be the chief decision makers regarding foreign policy and international conflict, diplomats in the field would provide an expression of the underlying community of the system.

The split between central office personnel and diplomats in the field is crucial for understanding how the Great Power System operated. Over the course of the eighteenth century, diplomatic practice shifted in many European countries, and diplomats served less as personal servants of the monarch and more as state employees under the direction of developing foreign ministries. The French had again led the way in the development of an institution for international affairs: there was one minister devoted solely to external affairs from 1589. The Habsburg foreign ministry was created in 1720.[37] The British had two secretaries of state who also dealt

---

[35] Alexander Wendt, "Anarchy Is What States Make of It: The Social Construction of Power Politics," *International Organization* 46, 2 (1992): 391–426.

[36] See Schroeder, *Transformation*.

[37] The Habsburg foreign ministry changed forms and titles often. The title "foreign minister" was really only used after 1866. In 1895, the ministry adopted its last official title: the Imperial and Royal Ministry of the Imperial and Royal House and Foreign Affairs. Its name derived from the fact that, in addition to dealing with foreign relations, the ministry

with internal issues until 1782, when a foreign ministry was created.[38] The capital city–based staff of these ministries was typically very small, with one or two clerks assisting the foreign minister. With such an arrangement, plus the slow pace of communications, diplomats in the field played a key role in policy formation and implementation in the Westphalian system. As the state-building process continued across Europe, however, the central office staff began to grow slowly in size and to wrest more power away from the diplomats in the field. Some contemporaries thought – or hoped – that changes in communication technology would eliminate the need for diplomats in the field entirely, as foreign ministry personnel could communicate directly with their counterparts abroad.[39] Central office personnel and diplomats in the field performed different functions in the Great Power System, however, and the presence of both was necessary for the maintenance of the system.

Whereas diplomats in the Great Power System were for cooperation and ceremony, central office personnel were about conflict and practical business. Central office personnel were more responsive to domestic politics than diplomats were. They were also more vulnerable to domestic calls for civil service reform, and so their ranks became more open to the middle classes while diplomatic corps remained decidedly aristocratic.[40] As communications technology changed and became more efficient over the course of the nineteenth century, foreign ministers moved to shift as much decision-making power as possible away from diplomats in the field and to central office personnel. This was done in the hope of having a more consistent foreign policy. Gradually, it was common practice for diplomats to refrain from acting in political matters without specific instructions from

---

also handled various legal issues for the ruling house. See Matsch, *Auswärtige Dienst*; Godsey, 9; and Adam Wandruszka, ed., *Die Habsburgermonarchie in System der Internationalen Beziehungen*, vol. 6, *Die Habsburgermonarchie, 1848–1918* (Vienna, 1989, 1993).

[38] On the British, see Black; Jones; Zara S. Steiner, *The Foreign Office and Foreign Policy, 1898–1914* (Cambridge, 1969); and Anderson, *Rise*.

[39] Jones, 172.

[40] On the aristocratic nature of European diplomatic corps vis-á-vis central office personnel, see Jones; Godsey; and M. B. Hayne, *The French Foreign Office and the Origins of the First World War* (Oxford, 1993). Although the United States did not have a formal aristocracy, it did have a class structure in practice, and U.S. diplomats were typically drawn from the upper echelons, whereas Washington-based DOS staff were more apt to be from the middle classes. See Robert D. Schulzinger, *The Making of the Diplomatic Mind: The Training, Outlook, and Style of United States Foreign Service Officers, 1908–1931* (Middletown, 1975); Ilchman; and Graham H. Stuart, *The Department of State: A History of its Organization, Procedure, and Personnel* (New York, 1949).

their government. By stripping diplomats of their policy-making power, the importance of their ceremonial and social functions was amplified. The actual policy being made was the product of domestic politics and was therefore often belligerent and short-sighted. Diplomats and their adherence to form blunted the hostility of central office actions and slowed the pace of international politics, creating time for conflicts to subside. As one former diplomat put it, "The envoy ... should be someone who is capable of getting things done if that is indicated, or alternatively, keeping the lid on if need be, adroitly doing nothing of consequence."[41]

Diplomats contributed to the peace of the system in part by obscuring the difference between interpersonal and international affairs. A diplomat was both a human being and a representative of his country. A foreign minister might sit in his office and launch a war against some distant country without really considering the consequences, but he could not shoot an ambassador standing in his office with the same detachment. When international affairs were mixed with interpersonal interactions, the restraint of good manners could trump or at least curb the aggression of international politics.

Diplomats built those interpersonal relationships while participating in social activities such as dinners, receptions, balls, hunts, and house parties that allowed diplomats to form personal relationships of trust with local elites and officials, as well as with diplomats representing other countries. Those relationships could be used for official purposes in times of crisis. Social gatherings could also be opportunities for acquiring information. Information gathering and contextualization were definitely part of a diplomat's job, but it appears that the information that diplomats passed along to their colleagues at home was rarely utilized when central office personnel were constructing policy, in large part because the amount of information sent from the field was far too great for the small central office staffs to process.[42] Because the ceremonial and social activities of diplomats were so important, countries looked to appoint people to these

---

[41] Henry E. Mattox, *The Twilight of Amateur Diplomacy: The American Foreign Service and Its Senior Officers in the 1890s* (Kent, 1989), 133.

[42] For example, U.S. representatives in Vienna sent reports to Washington between 1838 and 1906 that comprise fifty-one rolls of microfilm, whereas messages from the department to the legation in Vienna in that same period take up only four rolls. See *T157: Despatches from United States Ministers to Austria, 1838–1906*, 51 vols. (Washington, 1959); and *M77: Diplomatic Instructions of the Department of State, 1801–1906. Austria*, 4 vols. (Washington, 1946). Habsburg records are comparable. See HHStA, PA XXXIII – Vereinigten Staaten.

positions who were comfortable engaging in these elite social activities and who would be accepted in elite circles abroad. As a result, most diplomatic corps were staffed by aristocrats through World War I; even the United States, which did not possess a titled nobility, appointed the very wealthy and well-connected to diplomatic posts.[43]

This use of aristocrats as diplomats began in the French-led Westphalian system for symbolic, political, and financial reasons. A government signaled its high regard for another government by sending a diplomat with a high social rank. For example, if the British government wanted to convey that it attached the highest importance to its relationship with, say, Prussia, it would send a diplomat who was a duke, the highest rank in the British aristocracy. Even republican countries, such as the Dutch Republic, expected other countries to send noble diplomats to them as a sign of respect.[44] For political reasons, sending aristocrats was also important. Because of their noble status, they could expect – or demand – access to the host monarch and therefore their opinions would be heard.[45]

Besides these symbolic and political imperatives, aristocrats also occupied diplomatic posts for financial reasons. In France, diplomatic posts were technically salaried positions, but the financial problems faced by the government meant that diplomats were often paid quite late – years after their service – or not at all.[46] In other countries, diplomats were not salaried, or their state salaries were extremely small. The costs of being a diplomat, however, were very high.[47] Because social and ceremonial aspects were so important, diplomats had to perform them properly, and that meant having the right clothes, home, and transportation, as well as hosting one's own dinners and receptions. In addition to these costs, diplomats had to have servants and an office staff. All of these expenses, plus transportation to and from the post and rent on an office,

---

[43] See Lamar Cecil, *The German Diplomatic Service, 1871–1914* (Princeton, 1976); Godsey; Hayne; Jones; Ilchman; Schulzinger; and Rachel West, *The Department of State on the Eve of the First World War* (Athens, 1978).

[44] On republican demands, see Anderson, *Rise*, 12; and Black, 7, 40.

[45] On this right of presentation, see Black, 2.

[46] Hayne, 15–20.

[47] On costs, see, among others, Hayne; Jones; Mattox; and Catherine Allgor, "'A Republican in a Monarchy': Louisa Catherine Adams in Russia," *DH* 21, 1 (1997): 15–43. As one example, even in 1900 – when diplomatic salaries had been augmented considerably – the costs of being the U.S. envoy in Rome were approximately $75,000 a year, whereas the chief of mission's official salary was only $12,000.

were typically covered by the diplomat out of his own pocket.[48] His government might reimburse him to a limited extent later, but he could not count on that. Because of the high costs of service, aristocrats were often the only people who could afford to be diplomats. Well into the nineteenth century, most governments – including that of the United States – required that applicants for diplomatic posts have a minimum annual private income.[49] Ironically, most nineteenth-century criticism of diplomats centered on the accusation that they were burdens on tax-payers and did nothing important, but, in reality, diplomats essentially financed themselves, giving their countries the benefit of their services while costing the public relatively little.

Although diplomats have often been criticized by contemporaries and scholars for being frivolous, too concerned with form, and for being useless attenders of cocktail parties, in the nineteenth-century Great Power System, their ceremonial and social activities were the glue that held the system together.[50] They were charged with signaling their government's recognition of other governments' legitimate sovereignty, and they did that by engaging in ceremonies that reaffirmed the underlying community of the system. The maintenance of the system was an ongoing process, not a one-time acknowledgment. Diplomatic ceremonies came in two major forms: the presentation of credentials, which occurred in some form every time there was a change in the host government, the sending government, or the leadership of the legation or embassy; and daily "linguistic ceremonies," in which a diplomat engaged every time he

---

[48] Before World War I, it was uncommon for countries to own property abroad. An embassy was a group of people, not a building. Typically, the location of the office changed with the diplomat, or even more frequently, depending on local real estate conditions. For example, the U.S. legation in Vienna occupied at least seven different locations between September 1897 and May 1908. See nos. 42381, 34949, 74477, 39962, and 39130, various U.S. chiefs of mission to Gołuchowski, all in HHStA, AR, Fach 7, K. 46 – BWV 1906–7. On the development of embassies as buildings, see Ron Theodore Robin, *Enclaves of America: The Rhetoric of American Political Architecture Abroad, 1900–1965* (Princeton, 1992).

[49] Godsey, 6; Black, 3, 4–5, 110; Jones, 20, 171; Ilchman, 74; Hayne, 8.

[50] Black's study is a key scholarly attempt to explore the importance of diplomatic ceremonial and social functions; other important works include Allgor, "Republican in a Monarchy"; Molly M. Wood, "Diplomatic Wives: The Politics of Domesticity and the 'Social Game' in the U.S. Foreign Service, 1905–1941," *Journal of Women's History* 17, 2 (2005): 142–65; and Wood, "'Commanding Beauty' and 'Gentle Charm': American Women and Gender in the Early Twentieth-Century Foreign Service," *DH* 31, 3 (2007): 505–30. It is not a coincidence that these aspects of diplomacy are of particular interest to scholars studying the role of women in diplomacy; wives and daughters were key in these areas. Anderson is at the other end of the spectrum, criticizing ceremony in favor of professionalization; see *Rise*, 56, 80.

employed the stylized language of the system in his written correspondence with the host government and his foreign ministry at home. Together, these ceremonies continually reinforced the underlying community of the Great Power System.[51]

The ceremony for the presentation of credentials occurred every time a head of state or the diplomats empowered to represent him or her changed. After a diplomat had been selected for a particular post by whatever method his[52] country employed, he traveled to the capital of the host country and called on the foreign minister or secretary of state. The foreign minister then set about arranging an audience for the newly arrived diplomat with the sovereign, be it the monarch or the president.[53] The diplomat could not officially begin his duties until that audience had taken place because he had not yet officially been recognized as the legitimate representative of his sovereign in the host country.

On the day appointed for the audience, the diplomat would don his formal uniform. Permissible attire varied from country to country and person to person, but it was typically a military-style dress uniform or the country's court dress, and it included any awards, orders, or decorations the diplomat had received from his sovereign. American diplomatic costume was the subject of much heated debate in the United States, but, basically, it was a formal black suit consistent with the predominant men's fashion of the day.[54] Once dressed, the diplomat would get into an appropriately fashionable carriage and drive to the palace or White House, where household officials would conduct him to the head of state.

Once the diplomat and the head of state were in the same room, the diplomat was announced, and he was welcomed by the head of state. The diplomat typically made a statement – often a memorized speech – that expressed his pleasure at being in the host country and extended the good

---

[51] My interpretation of international politics as a continuous process is indebted to Alexander Wendt, *Social Theory of International Politics* (New York, 1999).

[52] Women were not appointed to head diplomatic missions or foreign ministries in the Great Power System and were typically not allowed to enter foreign services in nonclerical capacities until after World War I. Women did, however, have an important role to play. See note 61.

[53] On the arrangement of audiences, see HHStA, AR, Fach 7, K. 46. For one early example of the whole process, see Muhlenberg to Forsyth, 13 November 1838, in *T157*, roll 1.

[54] Robert Davis, "Diplomatic Plumage: American Court Dress in the Early National Period," *AQ* 20, 2, part 1 (1968): 164–79; David Paull Nickles, "US Diplomatic Etiquette during the Nineteenth Century," in *The Diplomat's World: A Cultural History of Diplomacy, 1815–1914*, ed. Markus Mösslang and Torsten Riotte (New York, 2008), 287–316; and Ilchman.

wishes of his sovereign for continued friendly relations between the two countries.[55] This statement affirmed that relations between the two countries were indeed friendly. Even if there was some sort of dispute under way, the statement of friendship indicated that the sending country still believed in the host government's right to exist, even if they were not happy with a specific action or policy of that government.

After the diplomat's statement, the head of state typically returned the good wishes. Then the pair usually abandoned the formal script and engaged in some small talk. For example, the head of state might inquire about the diplomat's journey or the health of his sovereign. Although this small talk was normal, it was not absolutely required, and leaving it out might be a signal of the host government's dissatisfaction with the sending government. A particularly jovial conversation might be taken as a sign of the head of state's approval of the sending government or of the diplomat himself.[56] The main point of this conversation was to inject a personal element into the ceremony, thereby reinforcing the blend of international and interpersonal that diplomats brought to the Great Power System.

The small talk was also often a chance for either the diplomat or the head of state to show off their abilities in the other's language, if they had such abilities. If they did not, translators were available, but the verbal aspects of credentials ceremonies were typically conducted in a language shared by the two individuals, with French, English, and German being the most common. One of the privileges of holding ambassadorial rank in the Great Power System was the ability to address the host government in the diplomat's native language – thereby shifting the burden of translation to the host government – but it would appear that the members of the various diplomatic corps and European sovereigns usually spoke enough languages that they could find at least one common tongue in which to communicate.[57]

After the diplomat's speech and the unscripted small talk, the diplomat presented his letter of credence to the head of state. This was a physical piece of paper – it was a letter from the sending sovereign to the host sovereign introducing the diplomat and stating that he had permission to represent the sending sovereign. These letters had a set format. The 1913

---

[55] See, for example, Muhlenberg to Forsyth, 13 November 1838.

[56] For a positive example, see ibid. For a negative example, see Konstantin Dumba, *Memoirs of a Diplomat*, trans. Ian F. D. Morrow (Boston, 1932).

[57] On the importance of language and the burden of translation in diplomacy, see James H. Merrell, *Into the American Woods: Negotiators on the Pennsylvania Frontier* (New York, 1999).

letter of credence from Woodrow Wilson to Franz Joseph regarding Ambassador Frederick Courtland Penfield provides an example. The letter began, "To His Majesty Franz Joseph, Emperor of Austria, Apostolic King of Hungary, King of Bohemia, etc., etc., etc."; the salutation demonstrated the U.S. government's concurrence in the titles of sovereignty Franz Joseph claimed.[58] This formal introduction was followed by the less formal and more amiable greeting, "Great and Good Friend." This more informal statement affirmed a personal relationship between Wilson and Franz Joseph and Wilson's recognition that Franz Joseph was the representative holder of Austro-Hungarian sovereignty, again mixing the interpersonal and the international.

In the brief body of the letter, Wilson introduced Penfield and announced that he was the representative of the United States to Franz Joseph's government, thereby affirming Penfield's legitimate representational role. Wilson closed his letter with a statement of his desire to continue the friendly relations between the two countries, and he signed himself, "Your Good Friend." This conclusion again stressed the idea of personal friendship between the two heads of state. It also placed Wilson on equal footing with Franz Joseph. A typical closing for much other contemporary correspondence was "Your obedient servant," which implied some sort of hierarchy. There were no servants among the sovereigns, however, only friends or relatives. The head of state of the host government accepted the letter, and it was later filed in the foreign ministry archives.[59]

With the letter handed over, the diplomat took his leave, now officially empowered to embark upon his duties. After this audience, the diplomat typically began to pay calls on an assortment of other people in the capital, including members of the royal family, government officials and members of the legislature, and other diplomats. These calls could take several weeks to complete.[60] Sometimes they involved actual conversations; at other

---

[58] This rendering of Franz Joseph's titles was normal: he had a great many, and it was standard practice to use just the main three and "etc." The U.S. government did not always get this right. For example, Theodore Roosevelt's letter of credence for Charles Francis listed the Bohemian title ahead of the Hungarian, which undoubtedly raised some eyebrows in Vienna – and Budapest. See Roosevelt to Franz Joseph, in HHStA, AR, Fach 7, K. 46, folder Francis.

[59] See, for example, no. 22229, Taft to Franz Joseph, 30 December 1909; and no. 66563, Wilson to Franz Joseph, 29 July 1913, both in HHStA, AR, Fach 7, K. 46. See also Muhlenberg to Forsyth, 13 November 1838; and no. 1, Hengelmüller to Kálnoky, 1 January 1895, in HHStA, PA XXXIII, K. 35 – USA BWV 1895, folder Berichte 1895.

[60] For a detailed account of this procedure – and numerous complaints about it – see Muhlenberg to Forsyth, 13 November 1838.

times, the diplomat simply left his card. If the diplomat was married and his wife was in town with him, she had her own round of calls to make on other official wives.[61] Paying all these calls established official and social relationships that would develop at official meetings and public and private social events during the course of the diplomat's stay. Such calls were not exclusive to diplomats: they were common practice in European and American cities, and they served the same function of initiating and maintaining relationships everywhere.[62]

When a diplomat left his post, he was obliged to repeat the process. He paid his calls, closing relationships he had opened upon his arrival. He also had a farewell audience with the head of state, in which he went through the same basic process of a formal speech, informal small talk, and the presentation of paperwork that made his departure official. The farewell audience reaffirmed continuing positive relations between the two countries, even if there would be no head of mission present in the immediate future to symbolize that relationship on a daily basis. The departing diplomat also informed the head of state and foreign minister in writing of who would be in charge of the legation or embassy until the next chief of mission arrived.[63]

In addition to these ceremonies for arriving and departing diplomats, there also had to be ceremonies for presenting new credentials if the host or sending governments changed. For example, when Franz Joseph died in 1916, President Wilson, through the State Department, had to send Ambassador Penfield another letter, this one addressed to the new emperor, Karl. Penfield had to have another audience to present his credentials to the

---

[61] Wives could be important assets or serious liabilities, and they were closely regulated by European and American foreign ministries. In the Habsburg Empire, applicants for the diplomatic corps had to be unmarried, in large part because local hostesses often looked to the low-ranking diplomatic staff as a socially useful pool of bachelors to even numbers and provide amusement at social events. When a Habsburg diplomat did wish to marry, both the foreign minister and the emperor had to approve the match. The Habsburg government did view wives as an asset later in life, and they especially approved of marriages to foreign women, which furthered the creation of useful transnational personal networks. The Germans, on the other hand, largely insisted on German wives. See Godsey, 85–92. The French actively encouraged their diplomats to marry, and a wife was a prerequisite for an ambassadorial post; Hayne, 26. In the United States, wives were mentioned on their husbands' performance evaluations until well into the twentieth century. See Wood, "Commanding Beauty."

[62] On the importance of paying calls in Washington, see Catherine Allgor, *Parlor Politics: In Which the Ladies of Washington Help Build a City and a Government* (Charlottesville, 2000).

[63] Diplomats also had to inform the host country's foreign minister when they went on vacation. See correspondence in HHStA, AR, Fach 7, K. 46. See also no. 22, Buchanan to Jenifer, 18 April 1845, in M77, roll 13.

new head of state.[64] As another example, when President McKinley was assassinated, the U.S. envoy in Vienna remained the same, but he had to present new credentials that stated that he represented the Roosevelt administration, rather than the McKinley administration. Reaccreditations were important because they symbolized that the sending government recognized and approved the change in sovereignty of the host government, or that the diplomat had the approval of the new sovereign or head of state in the sending country. Reaccreditations made sure that the lines of communication and recognition were clear, accurate, and mutually recognized.

Ceremonies surrounding credentials happened at changes in leadership, but diplomats engaged in smaller linguistic ceremonies that reaffirmed the system on a daily basis. When addressing a communication to the foreign ministry of the host government – a *note verbalé* in diplomatic parlance – a diplomat employed a stylized salutation and closing. For example, a U.S. diplomat writing to the Habsburg foreign minister opened his letter with the salutation, "Your Excellency," which acknowledged that the diplomat was aware of and approved the foreign minister's societal rank. The body of the letter usually began, "I have the honor to inform Your Excellency ..."[65] *Honor* was an oft-invoked word in the ceremonies of the Great Power System and in contemporary interpersonal relationships. In Great Power System diplomatic correspondence, writers using the word implied that their service for their ministry, sovereign, country, and the system as a whole was a privilege. The formality of each *note verbalé* reflected the formality of the letter of credence on a smaller scale – one more appropriate to a foreign minister and diplomat as opposed to that used between two heads of state.

After the salutation, the diplomat stated his business. He tried to be as clear as possible, mentioning previous correspondence by date and file number so the relevant documents could be easily located, or mentioning the date of a personal conversation on which he was following up. After stating his business, he concluded his letter with more prescribed language: "I avail myself at the same time of this opportunity to renew to Your Excellency the assurances of my highest consideration and personal Esteem."[66] With this conclusion, the diplomat was reinforcing both interpersonal and international connections. These introductions and

---

[64] Ad. Z. 7431, in HHStA, AR, Fach 7, K. 46, folder 1917.
[65] See, for example, Tower to Gołuchowski, 30 April 1898, in HHStA, PA XXXIII, K. 36 – BWV 1897–98, folder Varia 1898.
[66] Ibid.

conclusions appear in every single piece of written correspondence between diplomat and foreign ministry. Every time they communicated in writing, they reinforced the norms of the system and the mutual recognition of legitimacy those norms protected. Diplomats in training often spent most of their time copying correspondence, and, as a result, the linguistic forms of the system became deeply ingrained habits.[67] Ironically, when diplomatic correspondence was reprinted, either in the newspaper or in governmental collections, the salutations and closings were often omitted, downplaying their true importance to the maintenance of the international system.

Comparable language was used in despatches from diplomatic and consular personnel to the foreign minister or department of state, thus reinforcing the chain of command in these institutions. U.S. diplomats wrote to "the Honorable Secretary of State" that they had the honor to report on a particular issue, and they signed themselves "Your obedient servant."[68] Habsburg forms were more varied depending on the personal rank of the foreign minister, but all salutations and conclusions were appropriately deferential in formal correspondence. This formality was used in all official correspondence, regardless of the private personal relationship between diplomat and foreign minister.

There was, however, some room for more informal correspondence. State Department and Habsburg Ministry of Foreign Affairs archives also contain some letters that show more personal relationships. For example, Ambassador Hengelmüller wrote numerous personal letters to Foreign Minister Aehrenthal in which he addressed the minister as "Lieber Freund," or "dear friend," a very familiar salutation.[69] Although many people at the ministry might see such letters, they were not intended for publication. Diplomats could be less formal – and more open – in these quasi-official letters, which drew more on interpersonal rather than institutional relationships. These personal letters were arguably more important than regular despatches from the field because they were far more likely to be read in a timely fashion.

[67] French diplomats reported that the practice of copying was useful to them. See Hayne.

[68] The formal salutation "To the Honorable Secretary of State" was preprinted on diplomatic stationery in the second half of the nineteenth century. For this reason, I have opted to list the office, rather than a specifically named individual, as the recipient of these formal communications in the footnotes.

[69] Hengelmüller to Aehrenthal, [n.d., 1910], in HHStA, PA XXXIII, K. 49 – USA, BWV 1910, folder Varia. See also the various personal letters from Hengelmüller to Aehrenthal, in HHStA, PA XXXIII, K. 47 – BWV 1908, folder Varia.

Diplomatic credential ceremonies and the repetitious formalities of their correspondence thus reinforced the cooperation and mutual recognition of legitimate sovereignty that formed the foundation of the Great Power System. The diplomatic culture of the system had another aspect to it, however: it preserved and reinforced the power hierarchy that was also part of the system's underpinnings. In the forty years before the Congress of Vienna, the issue of diplomatic ranks had been very much in flux, and there was no generally accepted set of practices besides the notion that a diplomat with a high aristocratic rank symbolized the sending government's respect for the host government. The advent of the United States and republican France had introduced ambiguities and conflicts into the diplomatic ranking process, however, because their representatives did not have personal titles of nobility. The Congress of Vienna provided an opportunity to create a consensus that would not only clarify these issues, but allow diplomatic rank to be a mechanism for reinforcing the Great Power System.

The key document in this process was known as the Regelmént of 1815; it was signed at the Congress of Vienna. The Regelmént established five ranks for the heads of diplomatic missions. From lowest to highest, they were agent, resident, minister, envoy, and ambassador. Agents, residents, ministers, and envoys headed legations, while ambassadors headed embassies. It was up to each country to determine the titles of the lower ranking staff of legations and embassies, but most employed the title *secretary* for mid-ranking personnel who drew a (small) salary from the state and *attaché* for unpaid, entry-level personnel.[70] When the head, or chief, of a diplomatic mission was away from his post, the person left in charge was called a *chargé d'affaires*. Representatives at the Congress of Vienna also affirmed that two countries were supposed to exchange diplomats of the same rank to avoid both social and political awkwardness. For example, if Britain was going to send an envoy to Austria, Austria should also send an envoy, rather than an ambassador or a minister. Equality of rank signaled that two countries had a mutual understanding of the nature and relative importance of their relationship.

Shortly after the Congress of Vienna, in 1818, this ranking system was clarified further. The question of what to do when two diplomats at the

---

[70] On staffing these lower ranks, see Godsey, 14; Hayne, 23; and Ilchman. Ilchman argues that the changes surrounding the secretarial rank in the U.S. diplomatic corps over the course of the nineteenth century were the key to the gradual professionalization of U.S. diplomats.

same place held the same title – for example, a British and a Russian ambassador in Paris – had long been debated. Which should have precedence at official occasions? The Portuguese court had pioneered the idea of seniority in 1760. According to this principle, precedence would be awarded to the individual diplomat who had been at that post longest. In 1818, it was officially adopted throughout Europe.[71] One effect of the seniority rule was that it encouraged keeping people at one post for long periods of time to increase their prestige.

Perhaps most importantly, the delegates at Vienna reached both explicit and tacit decisions about the meaning and use of the highest diplomatic rank, that of ambassador. The Regelmént assigned special rights and obligations to the ambassadorial rank. Only ambassadors were given the right of presentation, or personal access to the sovereign to whom they were accredited. Envoys and other lesser diplomats could have access to the sovereign, but only if the sovereign invited such contact; these lesser diplomats only had guaranteed access to the foreign minister and his staff. This rule heightened the prestige and political power connected with the ambassadorial rank. It also fostered the continued presence of the aristocracy in diplomatic ranks. Most European courts had specific rules about who could be presented at court. In Austria, for example, an individual had to establish his or her "sixteen quarterings," or the noble status of his or her parents, grandparents, great-grandparents, and great-great-grandparents. Technically, a person with the rank of ambassador was guaranteed access to the sovereign regardless of his ancestry, but to force such a person on a royal court could create tensions, and so most European diplomatic corps found people to be ambassadors who also met the court's requirements for presentation, which meant that they selected members of the titled nobility.[72]

Representatives at Vienna also agreed that the ambassadorial rank should be reserved only for the Great Powers and that it should be used sparingly. Indeed, several relationships among the Great Powers themselves were maintained by envoys until the 1850s.[73] The costs to the state of paying the higher salaries of ambassadors acted as a conservative force in this regard. The limited use of the ambassadorial rank reinforced the

---

[71] Anderson, *Rise*, 6–7.

[72] Hayne, 24; Black, 21. See also Godsey.

[73] See Jones, 173; and Godsey, 13. After Franz Joseph came to the throne, there was a redistribution of ranks in the Habsburg Empire; the first ambassadors of this period went to the Holy See and France in 1856.

established hierarchy of the Great Power System because it reflected the actual distribution of political, military, and economic strength of the states in the system.

In the 1860s, however, a newly united Italy demanded the right to send and receive ambassadors. Britain and France complied, largely because of short-term political concerns. The Habsburg government, demonstrating its commitment to the maintenance of the Great Power System, resisted until 1877.[74] The Spanish government quickly followed the Italian lead and demanded ambassadors, and, again, the British and French governments complied; this time, the Habsburg government put off such recognition until 1888. Although the Italian and Spanish governments sent and received ambassadors and demanded that they be called Great Powers, the five original Powers rarely treated them as equals. At this point, the symbolic and ceremonial practices of the Great Power System began to undermine the system rather than reinforce it; the symbolism no longer accurately reflected the underlying power structure of the system.

After granting Italy and Spain the use of the ambassadorial rank, the European Great Powers opened no more embassies until the 1890s, when the United States was first admitted to the ranks of the Great Powers. Adding the United States to the system as a Great Power was certainly controversial, in part because it meant the extension of the ceremonial and social aspects of diplomacy. Although these aspects of the system were vital to maintaining the basic peace of the system, the ceremonies and rigid form of Great Power diplomacy had a great many critics in nineteenth-century Europe. British reformers called the diplomatic corps a "system of outdoor relief for aristocratic families," and an Austrian critic observed that diplomats were "born to eat fruit."[75] But nowhere were the critics of diplomacy more vociferous than across the Atlantic in the United States. Congressman Benjamin W. Stanton of Ohio was expressing a common sentiment when he said in 1859 that he "knew of no area of the public service that is more emphatically useless than the diplomatic service – none in the world."[76] Despite American attempts to remain out of European politics and to stay true to their republican and democratic

---

[74] The Habsburg embassy to the Vatican symbolized the special relationship between the empire and the Catholic Church, but the Habsburg government did not view the Holy See as a fellow Great Power.

[75] Cited in Jones, 215; and Godsey, 16. See also Black, 52.

[76] Cited in Ilchman, 24–25.

roots, American statesmen increasingly found themselves trapped between domestic criticism of diplomacy and European demands for conformity with the rules of the Great Power System. The history of U.S.-Habsburg relations provides a window for examining the U.S. government's gradual adoption of Great Power System diplomatic norms and its subsequent inclusion in the system as a Great Power.

2

Becoming a Great Power

U.S.-Habsburg Diplomatic Relations
and the Integration of the United States
into the Great Power System

To be a part of the Great Power System was to follow the norms of acceptable diplomatic behavior. The integration of the United States into the system was a long and contentious process because of long-standing American aversion to European diplomatic forms, which many in the United States characterized as profoundly un-American. There was always a vocal group of Americans who wanted to ignore or openly reject diplomacy, a position most commonly held by Democrats of all pre-World War I varieties, including Jeffersonians, Jacksonians, and post-Civil War Democrats. Nevertheless, the realities of international interactions and partisan politics created opportunities for a pro-integrationist perspective to form and gain important footholds that eventually propelled the United States into the Great Power System. In the mid nineteenth century, American party politics were such that when one party took a stand, the other party reflexively took up the opposite point of view.[1] Thus, as Democratic expansionists applauded filibusters and cavalier war-mongering in mid century, Whigs and then Republicans took up a pro-diplomacy position. However, while the Republican Party held the White House for almost the entire fifty years between the Civil War and World War I, they were gradually able to change the pro-diplomacy rhetoric from merely a knee-jerk reaction to Democratic opposition into a positive argument: conforming to diplomatic norms was civilized

---

[1] Curti makes this point about parties taking opposite views exclusively for the 1848–52 period, but it has much greater applicability. See Merle Eugene Curti, "Austria and the United States, 1848–1852: A Study in Diplomatic Relations," *Smith College Studies in History* 11, 3 (1926): 137–206.

behavior, and it would result in European powers treating the United States with the respect and status it deserved.

By some measures, the handful of diplomatic conflicts occurring between the United States and the Habsburg Empire from the 1830s until World War I were insignificant in that they never resulted in wars and very seldom resulted in treaties or economic agreements.[2] However, because these conflicts were primarily about diplomatic form, they had great importance in that incidents between the United States and the Habsburg Empire created opportunities for American debates on the topic, which in turn created opportunities for the U.S. government to adopt practices that were compliant with the norms of the system, thus furthering U.S. integration into the Great Power System. Habsburg officials actively pursued policies in these incidents that they believed would result in U.S. adherence to the norms of the Great Power System, and, until 1913, they were largely successful. When the United States was compliant, it was recognizing and reinforcing Habsburg legitimacy, and U.S. legitimacy was mutually reinforced by the Habsburg Empire.

ECONOMICS AND THE AMERICAN CASE AGAINST DIPLOMACY

Between 1776 and 1829, the United States and the Habsburg Empire had very little to do with one another, a state of affairs that reflected domestic developments in both countries and the diplomatic culture of the larger Westphalian system. During the American Revolution, the U.S. government sent a handful of diplomats to various European capitals in an effort to secure international political and material support for the new country. The most famous of these advocates was Benjamin Franklin, and his effort to gain French support was the only true success story of the various missions. Most other European governments, including that of the Habsburg Empire, were wary of provoking Britain by recognizing U.S. independence. They were also cool toward endorsing revolution and republicanism because that could set a dangerous precedent for their own subjects. Even when the war officially ended in 1783, most European states were unconvinced that U.S.

---

[2] Virtually all U.S.-Habsburg interaction prior to World War I is treated as insignificant in the two main studies of the relationship: Gerald H. Davis, "The Diplomatic Relations between the United States and Austria-Hungary, 1913–1917" (Ph.D. diss., Vanderbilt University, 1958); and Carol Jackson Adams, "Courting the 'Vassal': Austro-American Relations during World War I" (Ph.D. diss., University of Alabama, 1997).

independence would last, and so they minimized their involvement with the new republic, again preferring to safeguard their relationship with Britain. The Habsburg government did, however, send an official observer to the United States in 1783; Baron de Beelen-Bertholff stayed until 1790 and provided reports on the development of American institutions.[3]

Beelen-Bertholff apparently did not have official diplomatic status; he was merely an observer and was not empowered by the Habsburg government to represent the emperor or enter into any agreements on behalf of the empire. In addition to their concern for their relationship with Britain, Habsburg officials might have worried that an official diplomatic representative would not be safe in the United States. Under the Articles of Confederation, the U.S. federal government was very weak vis-à-vis the various state governments, and it could not guarantee the safety of foreign diplomats on U.S. soil or that the individual states that made up the country could be compelled to follow international legal norms. This was made extremely clear in 1784, when a French consul, Barbé de Marbois, was assaulted on the streets of Philadelphia by a French citizen, Longchamps. Pennsylvania state authorities refused to allow Longchamps's extradition, despite demands from both the French government and the U.S. legislature. The incident provided a concrete example to American leaders of the danger of noncompliance with international norms, and, as historians G. S. Rowe and Alexander Knott have demonstrated, it provided a key group of American state builders with a strong argument for the creation of a more robust central government. Without a federal government that could ensure American compliance with the most basic rules of diplomatic interaction, the United States risked ostracism by European countries and possibly even war and the loss of its independence.[4]

There were many Americans who would have considered European ostracism a good thing. This viewpoint was articulated by departing President George Washington in his 1796 "Farewell Address." Washington, thinking of then-recent French efforts to influence American domestic politics, maintained that the United States should stay out of European politics. Washington's speech was later invoked by generation after generation of Americans who advocated an isolationist position. It is important to realize, however, that Washington's speech contained a second

---

[3] On Beelen-Bertholff, see Ernest Wilder Spaulding, *The Quiet Invaders: The Story of the Austrian Impact upon America* (Vienna, 1968), 41.
[4] G. S. Rowe and Alexander W. Knott, "The Longchamps Affair (1784–86), the Law of Nations, and the Shaping of Early American Foreign Policy," *DH* 10, 3 (1986): 199–220.

directive regarding international affairs: while arguing against political involvement, Washington also advocated the expansion of U.S. commerce abroad. For Washington and many other Americans, there was no contradiction between the two goals: the United States could easily expand economically while remaining politically aloof, since politics and economics were, to their way of thinking, two different things.

To the European powers, however, politics and economics were not so easy to separate. Europeans also controlled most of the places where Americans wanted to trade, including the Caribbean and, of course, Europe itself. To break into colonial economies in general and then to break through the British blockade and into Napoleon's Continental System during the French Revolutionary and Napoleonic Wars, the U.S. government had to send negotiators abroad. They were frequently rotated out of office, in large part because it was feared that long exposure to the European milieu was harmful to good, republican Americans.[5]

Gradually, the United States began to develop a diplomatic corps, posting people to Paris and Madrid in 1790, Lisbon in 1791, and London and The Hague in 1792; diplomatic missions to St. Petersburg and Stockholm followed in 1808 and 1813, respectively.[6] These early diplomats were generally very competent and quite accomplished.[7] Their ranks included James Monroe, John Quincy Adams, Thomas Pinckney, and Gouverneur Morris.[8] These men generally embraced European diplomatic norms because they believed that following the prevailing rules would earn the young United States the respect of the European powers and thus bolster its claims to independent sovereignty. It is no coincidence that many of these early U.S. diplomats were Federalists and then Whigs: the structures and hierarchies of European diplomacy were more palatable to these people than to their Anti-Federalist or Democratic Republican counterparts, who

[5] On the allegedly corrupting nature of life abroad, see Warren Frederick Ilchman, *Professional Diplomacy in the United States, 1779–1939: A Study in Administrative History* (Chicago, 1961), 26.

[6] The next wave of diplomatic post openings occurred in 1823, when the Monroe administration opted to recognize the governments of many recently independent Latin American states. See U.S. DOS, *Principal Officers of the Department of State and United States Chiefs of Mission, 1778–1990* (Washington, 1991).

[7] Charles Stuart Kennedy, *The American Consul: A History of the United States Consular Service, 1776–1914* (New York, 1990); and Catherine Allgor, "'A Republican in a Monarchy': Louisa Catherine Adams in Russia," *DH* 21, 1 (1997): 15–43.

[8] Monroe was posted to Paris (1794–96); Quincy Adams served at The Hague (1794–97) and then in St. Petersburg (1809–14); Pinckney was in London (1792–96); and Morris was in Paris (1792–94).

placed great emphasis on the social equality of all (white) men.[9] This desire for European acceptance was especially important prior to the War of 1812, in which the Americans defeated the British a second time and put their independence on much surer footing.

The need to address economic questions through diplomatic channels led to the establishment of diplomatic relations between the United States and the Habsburg Empire. In the confusion of the French wars, the U.S. government had established a consular post at the busy Austrian Adriatic port of Trieste in 1800. The consul was perfectly capable of facilitating existing trade and aiding seafarers from his post in Trieste, but when the U.S. government charged him with expanding U.S. trade with the Habsburg Empire, he was helpless.[10] The consul, having no diplomatic rank or personal title of nobility and being located far from the capital in Vienna, was unable to do anything to get the Habsburg government to liberalize its trade policies and therefore benefit the United States. In an attempt to address this problem, the U.S. government negotiated a treaty of commerce and navigation with the empire in 1829. The treaty entered into force in 1831 and served as the first instance of official mutual recognition between the U.S. and Habsburg governments. As part of the treaty, the United States opened a consular post at Vienna in 1830; the consul was charged with lobbying the government for freer trade policies. Despite the consul's physical proximity to the seat of the Habsburg government, he possessed no ranks or titles that would allow him access to those top-level ministers who actually made economic policy, and so his lobbying efforts were ultimately as useless as those of the Trieste consul.

In the 1830s, a group of Southern politicians and plantation owners held a special conference to discuss possibilities for Southern economic growth and particularly how they might expand tobacco exports. One method they decided on was to request the U.S. government to send "special tobacco agents" to gather information about tobacco production and consumption abroad and note potential markets. They were also supposed to meet with foreign policymakers to establish trade policies

[9] See, among others, Saul Cornell, *The Other Founders: Anti-Federalism and the Dissenting Tradition in America, 1788–1828* (Chapel Hill, 1999); David Waldstreicher, *In the Midst of Perpetual Fetes: The Making of American Nationalism, 1776–1820* (Chapel Hill, 1997); Alan Taylor, *Liberty Men and Great Proprietors: The Revolutionary Settlement on the Maine Frontier, 1760–1820* (Chapel Hill, 1990); and Jack N. Rakove, *Original Meanings: Politics and Ideas in the Making of the Constitution* (New York, 1996).

[10] On Trieste, see *T242: Despatches from U.S. Consuls in Trieste, Italy, 1800–1906*, 13 vols. (Washington, 1962).

that would be favorable to American tobacco. The State Department complied and sent several of these quasi-official agents overseas. The Habsburg Empire was the recipient of one such agent. He did acquire plenty of information about Hungarian tobacco production, but he noted that the central government held a monopoly on tobacco sales that it was unlikely to relinquish.[11] The agent, again possessing no diplomatic credentials, did not have access to the relevant high-ranking policymakers, including Prince Metternich.

For many Americans, Metternich was synonymous with Austria, and he did not enjoy a favorable image in the United States. To most Americans, he was not the architect of a cooperative and peace-promoting Great Power System. Instead, he was an arch-conservative opponent of liberal revolution and free trade. But what incensed Americans most was Metternich's involvement in the creation of the Holy Alliance. The Holy Alliance, in many ways, was more symbolic than practical. It was an 1815 agreement among the Austrian, Russian, and Prussian governments to come to each other's defense in the event of liberal revolution. Not only was it anti-republican, it was couched in Christian terms, obfuscating the line between church and state that American rhetoric revered. Metternich and the Habsburg Empire were also commonly associated with Catholicism, which was unpopular with many Americans.[12] In the United States, the dominant perception of the Habsburg Empire was caught up in visions of Metternich, the Holy Alliance, and conservative anti-republicanism, thus making the establishment of relations with the empire and participation in Metternich's type of diplomacy difficult to achieve.[13]

The demand to expand U.S. exports was pressing, however, and finally, in 1838, the U.S. government broke down and established a diplomatic mission at Vienna. The government in Vienna reciprocated by sending Baron Wenzel von Mareschall to Washington in April 1838. The U.S. diplomatic representative, Henry Muhlenberg of Pennsylvania, presented his credentials as the U.S. Envoy Extraordinary and Minister Plenipotentiary

---

[11] On his mission, see *T157: Despatches from United States Ministers to Austria, 1838–1906*, 51 vols. (Washington, 1959); and *M77: Diplomatic Instructions of the Department of State, 1801–1906. Austria*, 4 vols. (Washington, 1946).

[12] On American anti-Catholicism, see John C. Pinheiro, "'Religion Without Restriction': Anti-Catholicism, All Mexico, and the Treaty of Guadalupe Hidalgo," *Journal of the Early Republic* 23, 1 (2003): 69–96; Jody M. Roy, *Rhetorical Campaigns of the 19th Century Anti-Catholics and Catholics in America* (Lewiston, 2000); and Linda Gordon, *The Great Arizona Orphan Abduction* (Cambridge MA, 1999).

[13] On Metternich's U.S. reputation, see Spaulding, esp. 42.

to Emperor Ferdinand I on 7 November 1838. As an envoy, he did have access to Metternich and other officials, and he used the opportunity to explain the mutually beneficial aspects of free trade – and especially U.S. tobacco imports – to the prince. Muhlenberg reported that change would be slow to come, as the tobacco monopoly was lucrative for the Habsburg government.[14]

Muhlenberg also observed that Metternich, other Habsburg officials, and the Austrian population in general knew little about the United States, its commerce, or its republican institutions. For an American citizen used to thinking of his country as an exemplary "city on a hill" and the American Revolution as an event of global significance, this ignorance – or, more likely, indifference – was quite a shock. While insisting that the U.S. government adhered strictly to a policy of noninterference, Muhlenberg spent much of his time explaining republican government and free trade to anyone in Vienna who would listen. Such behavior did nothing to endear him to the Habsburg government, whose members found it easier to believe that he wanted to promote the spread of republicanism than to accept his claims of noninterference.[15] The exchange between Washington and Vienna of diplomats holding the relatively prestigious rank of envoy was short-lived. Muhlenberg left his post in September 1840. His replacement, Daniel Jenifer, was not appointed until almost a year later, and he did not present his credentials in Vienna until March 1842.

In the meantime, the Habsburg envoy, Mareschall, left his Washington post in June 1841. Finding a Habsburg diplomat willing to serve in Washington was exceptionally difficult. Any post outside Europe was considered undesirable – bordering on exile – by most diplomats in all Great Power diplomatic corps.[16] Habsburg officials therefore decided to leave Mareschall's assistant, Johann von Hülsemann, in charge of the post. Since he had not served in the diplomatic corps long, Hülsemann was kept at the rank of chargé d'affaires until 1853.[17]

---

[14] Muhlenberg to Forsyth, 15 February 1839, in *T157*, roll 1.
[15] Ibid.
[16] On this perception, see William D. Godsey, Jr., *Aristocratic Redoubt: The Austro-Hungarian Foreign Office on the Eve of the First World War* (West Lafayette, 1999); Raymond A. Jones, *The British Diplomatic Service, 1815–1914* (Waterloo, 1983); M. B. Hayne, *The French Foreign Office and the Origins of the First World War* (Oxford, 1993); and D. C. M. Platt, *The Cinderella Service: British Consuls since 1825* (London, 1971).
[17] Technically, this was a temporary title in the Great Power System. However, in the 1840s and '50s, especially, it was often used instead of *agent* for the lowest ranking heads of diplomatic missions.

TABLE 2.1 *Personnel of U.S.-Habsburg Diplomatic Relations, 1838–1917*

U.S. Presidents	U.S. Secretaries of State	U.S. Diplomats in Vienna
Martin Van Buren	John Forsyth	Henry A. Muhlenberg
William Henry Harrison	Daniel Webster	Daniel Jenifer
John Tyler	Abel P. Upshur	William H. Stiles
James K. Polk	John C. Calhoun	James Watson Webb
Zachary Taylor	James Buchanan	Charles J. McCurdy
Millard Fillmore	John M. Clayton	Thomas M. Foote
Franklin Pierce	Daniel Webster	Henry R. Jackson
James Buchanan	Edward Everett	J. Glancy Jones
Abraham Lincoln	William L. Marcy	J. Lothrop Motley
Andrew Johnson	Lewis Cass	Henry M. Watts
Ulysses S. Grant	Jeremiah S. Black	John Jay
Rutherford B. Hayes	William H. Seward	Godlove S. Orth
James A. Garfield	Elihu B. Washburne	Edward F. Beale
Chester A. Arthur	Hamilton Fish	John A. Kasson
Grover Cleveland	William M. Evarts	William Walter Phelps
Benjamin Harrison	James G. Blaine	Alphonso Taft
Grover Cleveland	Frederick T. Frelinghuysen	John M. Francis
William McKinley	Thomas F. Bayard	Alexander R. Lawton
Theodore Roosevelt	James G. Blaine	Frederick D. Grant
William Howard Taft	John W. Foster	Bartlett Tripp
Woodrow Wilson	Walter Q. Gresham	Charlemagne Tower
	Edwin F. Ulh	Addison C. Harris
	Richard Olney	Robert S. McCormick
	John Sherman	Bellamy Storer
	William R. Day	Charles S. Francis
	John Hay	Richard C. Kerens
	Elihu Root	Frederick Courtland Penfield
	Robert Bacon	
	Philander C. Knox	
	William Jennings Bryan	
	Robert Lansing	

By lowering the rank of the Habsburg official in Washington, the Habsburg government introduced an inequality into the system: the United States had an envoy in Vienna, whereas the empire only had a chargé in Washington. The U.S. government, typically unconcerned with diplomatic form, did not complain; indeed, its members did not notice the situation for several years. The Habsburg foreign minister compensated for this reduction in rank by keeping Hülsemann in Washington for a total of twenty-five years. This long service in one place reflects a major difference in the approaches to diplomacy adopted by the empire and the United

Becoming a Great Power 47

TABLE 2.1 *(continued)*

Habsburg Diplomats in Washington	Habsburg Foreign Ministers	Habsburg Emperors
Wenzel Mareschall	Friedrich Ferdinand Beust	Ferdinand I
Johann von Hülsemann	Julius Andrássy	Franz Joseph I
Nikolaus Giorgi	Heinrich Haymerle	Karl
Ferdinand Wydenbruck	Gustav Kálnoky	
Karl Franckenstein	Agenor Goluchowski	
Karl Lederer	Alois Aehrenthal	
Wilhelm Schwarz-Senborn	Leopold Berchtold	
Ladislaus Hoyos	Stephen Burián	
Ernst Mayr	Ottokar Czernin	
Ignaz Schaeffer	Stephen Burián	
Ernst Schmit von Tavera		
Ladislaus Hengelmüller		
Konstantin Dumba		
Erich Zwiedinek		

* Because the titles of nobility for Habsburg personnel often changed during their lifetimes – or even during their service – I have omitted them entirely. The overwhelming majority were barons and/or counts. For titles and biographical sketches, see Erwin Matsch, *Der Auswärtige Dienst von Österreich (-Ungarn) 1720–1920* (Vienna, 1986).

States: the Habsburg government valued long service, whereas the U.S. government preferred rotation in office.[18]

In the Habsburg Empire, the relationship between the foreign ministry and the emperor fostered lengthy service in one post. Foreign ministry personnel, including members of the diplomatic corps and consular service, served at the discretion of the emperor, and there was not much turnover on the Austrian throne, especially after Franz Joseph came to power in 1848; he ruled for sixty-eight years, until his death in 1916. Even with the development of political parties and a parliamentary culture in the second half of the nineteenth century, foreign ministry personnel were not attached to the various parties. Loyalty to the emperor was the requirement for service, and most diplomats actively rejected political or nationalist affiliations in favor of loyalty to their sovereign and a supranational

[18] On rotation in the Habsburg and U.S. corps (in addition to Table 2.1) see Godsey; and Ilchman. On the issue more generally, see Jeremy Black, *British Diplomats and Diplomacy, 1688–1800* (Exeter, 2001). Republican governments were more apt to rotate their officials than monarchies were; Matthew Smith Anderson, *The Rise of Modern Diplomacy, 1450–1919* (London, 1993), 7.

pro-Habsburg identity. Patronage and familial connections did play a role in getting positions in the ministry and securing specific posts in the field, but Habsburg diplomats generally enjoyed long-term job security.[19]

By leaving a diplomat in one place for a long time, the government reaped several important benefits. The diplomat became an expert on that country, so he could provide an analysis of particular events in the context of the host country. He could also master the language and therefore the nuances of word choice and tone that were essential to diplomatic communications. His sovereign and the foreign minister could develop a strong bond of trust with him. Perhaps more important, he was able to build long-term relationships with local elites and reap the benefits of the trust and interpersonal networks established.[20] For a country as unpredictable as the United States at mid century, such experience was invaluable, and Hülsemann was particularly skilled at building these relationships. Historian Merle Curti – one of the very few people who has examined any aspect of U.S.-Habsburg relations in any depth – noted that Hülsemann "took his mission very seriously, and consciously made more political and personal friends than was customary or possible for most diplomats whose terms of residence at Washington were usually short."[21]

The American approach to diplomatic service was rather different, especially in the period from 1829 until 1877 – that is, from the Jackson administration to that of Ulysses S. Grant. Rotation in office ruled the day during these decades, when the diplomatic corps was most responsive to the political patronage system. When Jackson was elected in 1828, he ran on a platform that advocated wider participation in government. Not only should more people be able to vote, but more people should hold government offices. Jackson's faith in the common man's abilities and his understanding of government employment led him to believe that anybody could hold any government office without any training or education beyond what they got on the job. Jackson's presidency coincided with a general proliferation of government offices, including an expansion of the consular service and diplomatic corps,[22] and loyal Democrats were rewarded for

[19] Godsey; and James Allan Treichel, "Magyars at the Ballplatz: A Study of the Hungarians in the Austro-Hungarian Diplomatic Service, 1906–1914" (Ph.D. diss., Georgetown University, 1972).
[20] Black, 58–60.
[21] Curti, "Austria and the United States," 144.
[22] Harry L. Watson, *Liberty and Power: The Politics of Jacksonian American* (New York, 1990); and Donald C. Cole, *The Presidency of Andrew Jackson* (Lawrence, 1993). The

their support by being granted salaried offices. In terms of diplomacy, this meant that many people with no real experience in international relations and no linguistic abilities were appointed to serve overseas. As historian Warren Ilchman observed, an American diplomat who was acquainted with a foreign language or the history of the country to which he was posted was "purely fortuitous."[23] The stereotype of American diplomats as cavalier or incompetent amateurs dates to this period, and, in many cases, the stereotype was accurate.[24] Diplomats were also rotated out of office with considerable frequency, in part to give others a chance to serve and in part because electoral results allowed new presidents to reward their friends and supporters.

The proliferation of offices under Jackson and his successors gave rise to calls for economy in government and civil service reform – calls that typically came from the party not occupying the White House.[25] It was this call for retrenchment on the part of the federal government and a change in administration that brought to light the disparity between the rank of the Habsburg diplomat in Washington and the U.S. diplomat in Vienna. In 1844, Democrat James K. Polk was elected president, and he took office in March 1845. His secretary of state was James Buchanan, who had previously served as the U.S. minister to Russia, as well as having been elected to multiple terms as a congressman and then a senator.[26]

The question of the rank of the American chief of mission in Vienna came up in a meeting of the Finance Committee of the U.S. Senate in which the appropriations bill for the State Department was under consideration. Congress exercised considerable power over U.S. foreign relations through its control of the budget. In terms of diplomatic posts, the Finance

United States opened and operated approximately 166 consular posts prior to 1828; 58 new posts were opened during the Jackson administration (1829–36). See National Archives and Records Administration, *Diplomatic Records: A Select Catalog of National Archives Microfilm Publications* (Washington, 1986).

[23] Ilchman, 11. Ilchman says this of the entire 1787–1888 period, but I would argue that it only applies to the shorter 1829–77 period.

[24] This stereotype is the basis for several institutional histories, including Robert D. Schulzinger, *The Making of the Diplomatic Mind: The Training, Outlook, and Style of United States Foreign Service Officers, 1908–1931* (Middletown, 1975); Ilchman; Henry E. Mattox, *The Twilight of Amateur Diplomacy: The American Foreign Service and Its Senior Officers in the 1890s* (Kent, 1989); and Richard Hume Werking, *The Master Architects: Building the United States Foreign Service, 1890–1913* (Lexington, 1977).

[25] Calls for such reform were not exclusive to the United States. On the British, see Jones; and Platt.

[26] After serving as secretary of state, Buchanan served as U.S. minister to Britain and was later elected president.

Committee, on an annual basis, reviewed the appropriation for each legation member drawing a government salary, as well as contingent, fixed, and extraordinary expenses for each post.[27] In the case of the State Department's 1845 budget, the Finance Committee proposed reducing the budget by reducing the titles of the chiefs of mission in Austria and Brazil from envoys to chargés, thus reducing the salary the government had to pay out. The transcript of the meeting – which the Habsburg representative in Washington made sure to send to the foreign ministry in Vienna – reflects a number of trends in U.S. diplomacy in general and U.S. relations with the Habsburg Empire in particular.[28]

Buchanan, newly in office, was able to make a strong case on the spot for maintaining the rank of the U.S. representative in Brazil. He said that "there was but one mission more important" to the United States – presumably in London – and that "our commercial relations with that country [Brazil] are extensive." Invoking substantial commerce with Brazil was enough to quiet the Finance Committee, whose members quickly agreed to leave the Brazilian mission at the original rank. Commerce was, of course, allegedly the only legitimate realm of international interaction for the United States, and it had to be protected and expanded.[29]

When it came to Austria, however, Buchanan admitted that he "knew little or nothing," other than that relations were friendly and had originated over the tobacco question. He wanted to keep the appropriation, at least until he had time to visit the State Department and find out what U.S. relations with Austria were.[30] Buchanan's attitude reflects the fact that there were few matters of substance in the U.S.-Habsburg relationship at the time. However, that Buchanan did not want to risk an international

---

[27] Fixed expenses could include salaries; rent payments for office space; the costs of providing each post with copies of U.S. treaties, laws, and congressional proceedings; and certain operating expenses, such as a fixed amount of stationery and other office supplies. Each post also had a "contingent account," which the chief of mission could spend with considerable discretion. It was usually used to aid Americans in peril and for office maintenance and other necessary but unforeseeable expenses. Finally, there were extraordinary expenses. For example, if the workload was such that an additional staff member was needed, or if the staff had to go into mourning for an American or local official, the chief of mission typically paid those expenses himself, then requested reimbursement from Congress. DOS records are full of despatches on these subjects. On finances in general and Congressional power, see Ilchman, 31–32.

[28] The transcript from the session – probably clipped from the *Congressional Globe* – is enclosed in no. 8 C, Hülsemann to Metternich, 5 March 1845, in HHStA, AR, Fach 7: Fremde Missionen, K. 22 – Staaten B-P 1830–49.

[29] Ibid.

[30] Ibid.

incident over a ceremonial question without full information suggests that he understood the importance of the symbolism of diplomacy in the contemporary international system.

Another senator on the committee, George McDuffie, a Democrat from South Carolina, interrupted Buchanan's statement to ask about the annual volume of commerce between the United States and Austria. Buchanan did not know, and the chair of the committee said that he did not know either, but he knew "that the amount was not great." Since substantial commerce was not involved, McDuffie took the opportunity to voice his opinion of the diplomatic corps:

> [I regard] many of these foreign missions, as very much like some of our army and naval establishments, intended rather for the benefit of persons, than of the government which supported them. If [I understand] the commercial relations between this country and Austria, that country, considering its extent and power in Europe, was least of all other powers to be regarded by us. [I feel] sure that a minister of a lower grade than we now kept in Austria would be sufficient for all our purposes, and that an embassy of a higher grade than a chargeship was a mere sinecure.[31]

McDuffie's comments reflected the common idea that diplomatic posts provided unnecessary jobs for the benefit of individuals and not the state; they were products of the spoils system, rather than useful undertakings. They also suggested that economics was the only acceptable justification for posting U.S. representatives abroad.

Buchanan let the matter drop after McDuffie's comments, and the U.S. mission to Austria was reduced to the lowest possible level, that of chargé d'affaires.[32] Affairs with the empire in 1845 were unimportant enough to allow a sense of economy to prevail. William H. Stiles, a former congressman from Georgia, was sent to Vienna as chargé, where he remained throughout the Polk administration and into the Taylor administration. By the time he left his post in August 1849, the Habsburg government was in the midst of a serious domestic crisis, and relations between the United States and the empire were precarious and worsening quickly.

THE HUNGARIAN REVOLUTION AND LAJOS KOSSUTH

In the 1840s and 1850s, neither the Habsburg Empire nor the United States were at their best. In the United States, a sense of reckless invincibility permeated a significant portion of the public and the government, resulting

[31] Ibid.
[32] Ibid.

in the expansionist Mexican War (1846–48) and filibuster action and rhetoric that aimed at further territorial expansion into Latin America, the Caribbean, and British-controlled Canada. All of this agitation was caught up in the slavery question, as filibusters typically hoped to gain territories that would support a plantation economy based on slave labor.[33] The Democrats – where most of the pro-slavery elements found their political home – enjoyed an advantage because the Whigs were faltering at the polls and abolitionists were just beginning to come together to embrace direct political action and form the Republican Party.[34]

In Europe, the 1840s saw the development of assorted political reform movements, many of which culminated in revolutionary outbreaks in 1848. The Habsburg government was threatened on multiple fronts: the Frankfurt Parliament pondered the creation of a new German constitutional monarchy that might have included some or all of the Habsburg territories; liberals in Vienna took up arms to achieve political and economic reforms and oust Prince Metternich; Italian nationalists revolted in Venice; and Hungarian liberals throughout the country declared Hungarian independence and the formation of a republican government – a movement that was only put down after months of fighting and the eventual intervention of the Russian army.[35] The empire in the 1850s was

---

[33] On expansionism in this period, see Reginald Horsman, *Race and Manifest Destiny: The Origins of American Racial Anglo-Saxonism*, revised ed. (Cambridge MA, 1986); Robert E. May, *Manifest Destiny's Underworld: Filibustering in Antebellum America* (Chapel Hill, 2002); and Amy S. Greenberg, *Manifest Manhood and the Antebellum American Empire* (Cambridge, 2005).

[34] On partisan politics in this period and the development of the Republican Party, see, among numerous others, Jean H. Baker, *Affairs of Party: The Political Culture of Northern Democrats in the Mid-Nineteenth Century*, 2nd ed. (New York, 1998); William Gienapp, *The Origins of the Republican Party, 1852–1856* (New York, 1987); and Joel H. Silbey, *The American Political Nation, 1838–1893* (Stanford, 1991).

[35] On events in the Habsburg Empire, see, among others, R. J. W. Evans, "1848–1849 in the Habsburg Monarchy," in *The Revolutions in Europe, 1848–1849: From Reform to Reaction*, ed. Hartmut Pogge von Strandmann and R. J. W. Evans (Oxford, 2000), 181–206; Alice Freifeld, *Nationalism and the Crowd in Liberal Hungary, 1848–1914* (Washington, 2000); Alan Sked, *The Decline and Fall of the Habsburg Empire, 1815–1918* (New York, 1989); Pieter M. Judson, *Exclusive Revolutionaries: Liberal Politics, Social Experience, and National Identity in the Austrian Empire, 1848–1914* (Ann Arbor, 1996); and Dominique K. Reill, *Nationalists Who Feared the Nation: Adriatic Multi-Nationalism in Habsburg Dalmatia, Trieste, and Venice* (Stanford, 2012).

in its "neoabsolutist" period, in which liberal rhetoric was largely suppressed, but liberal policies – especially economic policies – were implemented.[36]

From his vantage point in Washington, Habsburg chargé Hülsemann viewed American and European problems as closely interconnected. He repeatedly warned the foreign ministry in Vienna and other European governments to consider the United States when making foreign policy decisions, even though U.S. representatives consistently claimed that U.S. policy was one of noninvolvement in European affairs. Some European powers – Britain in particular – were considering intervening in the war between the United States and Mexico in order to protect their own economic interests and to limit U.S. expansion.[37] Hülsemann insisted that such intervention was a bad idea because it could very likely lead to a complete rejection of George Washington's traditional nonintervention policy and then to U.S. involvement in European revolutions. Hülsemann also apprised Vienna of American designs on British Canada, which might affect the Great Power System by deflecting British interest from Europe to North America. Hülsemann's reports created the impression in Vienna that the American government and public were reckless and aggressive and thus should be given a wide berth. According to Hülsemann, "The adventurous spirit of this country will lead to trouble with everyone."[38]

With the Hungarian declaration of independence in 1848, many of Hülsemann's admonitions proved to be well founded. The U.S. government embarked on a diplomatic course that had grave implications for the sovereignty of the Habsburg government and, thus, the very fabric of the Great Power System. Hülsemann had the unenviable task of trying to convince various members of the U.S. government that they should comply with the norms of Great Power diplomacy and stay out of Habsburg domestic affairs.

---

[36] See David F. Good, *The Economic Rise of the Habsburg Empire, 1750–1914* (Berkeley, 1984); and Jeffrey T. Leigh, "Public Opinion, Public Order and Press Policy in the Neoabsolutist State: Bohemia, 1849–52," *AHY* 35 (2004): 81–99.

[37] See, for example, Sam W. Haynes, "Anglophobia and the Annexation of Texas: The Quest for National Security," in *Manifest Destiny and Empire: American Antebellum Expansionism*, ed. Sam W. Haynes and Christopher Morris (College Station, 1997), 115–45; and Charles Soutter Campbell, *From Revolution to Rapprochement: The United States and Great Britain, 1783–1900* (New York, 1974).

[38] Curti, "Austria and the United States," 144–49; no. 3D, Hülsemann to Buol-Schauenstein, 5 January 1853, in HHStA, PA XXXIII – Vereinigten Staaten, K. 14 – USA BWV 1853. See also Erwin Matsch, *Wien-Washington: Ein Journal diplomatischer Beziehungen, 1838–1917* (Vienna, 1990). Curti's account is based on Habsburg and U.S. archival sources and provides a document-by-document account of what occurred between 1848 and 1852. It contains little analysis of the significance of the events he chronicles, however.

Through the conflicts of the 1848–52 period, the Habsburg government learned valuable lessons about the role U.S. party politics and the press could play in securing American compliance with Great Power norms. Habsburg foreign ministry personnel were also provided with another example of the important role specific individuals could play in helping or hindering international cooperation; Americans had not yet fully grasped that concept, even after their experiences in this period. Although the two countries made it through these years of crisis without actually going so far as to sever their diplomatic relations, the period had a profound, negative impact on subsequent U.S.-Habsburg relations. Many Americans developed a pro-Hungarian position at this time – a stance that persisted in American popular and official opinion until the creation of a Hungarian communist government under Belá Kun, in 1919, at which point American anticommunist sentiment overpowered the long-standing U.S. pro-Hungarian stance.[39] American support for an independent Hungary undermined Habsburg claims to sovereignty over the Kingdom of Hungary and thus the integrity of the empire as a whole.

The Hungarian revolutionaries, often known as '48ers, advocated the creation of an independent, constitutional, republican Hungary. Like their American, French, and Viennese revolutionary predecessors, they spoke in universalist, Enlightenment terms, but, in reality, they envisioned a state governed by a particular group of like-minded people.[40] In the Hungarian case, the Magyar-speaking middle classes and gentry advocated their control of the new state at the expense of the Habsburgs, the higher aristocracy, and the Slovaks, Romanians, Croats, and other non-Magyars who made up more than half the kingdom's population. The '48ers were led by a group that included several lawyers, writers, and journalists; one of the most important of this circle was the journalist

---

[39] On American support for Hungary, see John Komlos, *Louis Kossuth in America, 1851–1852* (Buffalo, 1973); and Donald S. Spencer, *Louis Kossuth and Young America: A Study of Sectionalism and Foreign Policy, 1848–1852* (Columbia, 1977). On anticommunism and the Paris settlements, see Arno J. Mayer, *Politics and Diplomacy of Peacemaking: Containment and Counterrevolution at Versailles, 1918–1919* (New York, 1967).

[40] See, for example, Taylor, *Liberty Men*, which illustrates the concept through a case study; Judson, *Exclusive Revolutionaries*; Freifeld; Robert Nemes, "Associations and Civil Society in Reform-Era Hungary," *AHY* 32 (2001): 25–45; Andrew C. Janos, *The Politics of Backwardness in Hungary, 1825–1945* (Princeton, 1982); András Gerő, *The Hungarian Parliament, 1867–1918: A Mirage of Power* (Boulder, 1997); Keith Michael Baker, *Inventing the French Revolution: Essays on French Political Culture in the Eighteenth Century* (Cambridge, 1990); and William Sewell, "A Rhetoric of Bourgeois Revolution," in *The French Revolution: Recent Debates and New Controversies*, ed. Gary Kates (London, 1998), 143–56.

Lajos Kossuth, who was unquestionably skilled at mobilizing the population with convincing rhetoric.[41]

Kossuth and the '48ers cultivated the idea that their revolution was closely akin to the American Revolution. Invoking that parallel played to the popular U.S. assumption that the American revolution was indeed "the shot heard 'round the world" that would prompt others to throw off monarchical government and step into the self-evident enlightenment of the American republican system. In early 1849, the '48ers, now engaged in a military struggle against the Habsburgs, pushed the Americans to do something more than serve as ideological brethren or mentors: they approached the American chargé in Vienna, William Stiles, and asked him to negotiate a truce between the revolutionaries and the Habsburg government. Stiles was faced with a serious dilemma. Because the situation was too changeable for him to wait to act until he had received instructions from his superiors in Washington, he had to decide which American tradition was more important: encouragement for American-style revolution or noninvolvement in European political affairs.[42]

Stiles opted for the revolutionary tradition, and he agreed to try to negotiate an agreement between the two parties. He approached the Habsburg government and offered to mediate, but his offer was refused. That the Habsburg government turned Stiles down is unsurprising; to involve him would have been a default acceptance of the idea of Hungarian independence. After the Habsburg refusal, Stiles let the matter drop, knowing that to do more without specific instructions would very likely be going too far. He wrote to Secretary of State Buchanan to apprise him of developments and explain his actions. Buchanan approved Stiles's decisions retroactively, but did not encourage him to take any further action.[43]

The matter might have ended there, with the Habsburg government being displeased with Stiles's actions but not unhappy enough to sever relations with the United States. However, 1848 was an election year in the United States, and in March 1849, a new administration took office. Whig Party candidate General Zachary Taylor was victorious, having defeated the Democratic candidate, Senator Lewis Cass of Michigan. Taylor's

---

[41] On the '48ers, see István Deák, *The Lawful Revolution: Louis Kossuth and the Hungarians, 1848–1849* (New York, 1979).

[42] Curti, "Austria and the United States," 151. See also the correspondence in *M77*, roll 13; and *T157*, roll 1.

[43] Curti, "Austria and the United States"; and no. 26, Buchanan to Stiles, 2 February 1849, in *M77*, roll 13.

military experience worked in his favor during the election,[44] but because both Whigs and Democrats were fairly bellicose, Taylor's election spelled trouble for U.S.-Habsburg relations.

Fighting between the Habsburg government and the '48ers continued through the spring of 1849, and, in June, Secretary of State John M. Clayton felt the time was right to take serious action. He wrote to A. Dudley Mann, an attaché at the U.S. legation in Paris, and instructed him to go to Hungary. Mann was supposed to evaluate the situation and see if Hungary was "able to maintain the independence she had declared." If Mann determined that Hungarian independence was viable, he was empowered to recognize the Hungarian government on behalf of the United States, conclude a commercial treaty with the new government, and generally "hail with a hearty welcome her entrance into the family of nations."[45] This was serious, indeed. The U.S. government was prepared to be the first country to recognize Hungarian independence, which would grant the '48ers an important claim to legitimacy that would be difficult for the Habsburg government to overcome. The power to set these events in motion was vested in just one person: Mann alone was to decide whether Hungary was a viable independent state or not.

Mann left Paris for Budapest, planning to stop in Vienna on the way. Before he arrived in Budapest, however, the Habsburg government, with the help of the Russian army, had defeated the Hungarian revolutionaries. Thus, Mann never had to make his crucial decision. Disaster was not entirely averted, however: while Mann was in Vienna, Stiles was on vacation, and he had left Mr. Schwarz, the U.S. consul in Vienna, in charge of the legation. Schwarz was an Austrian citizen – a situation that was not uncommon for U.S. consuls at the time – and he apparently obtained a copy of Mann's instructions and turned them over to the Austrian foreign ministry.[46] The Habsburg government was therefore aware of how far the Americans had been willing to go, and they were far from pleased. American recognition of Hungarian independence would directly contradict Habsburg claims to sovereignty over the Kingdom of Hungary and

---

[44] On the election of 1848, see William Freehling, *Road to Disunion: Secessionists at Bay* (New York, 1990).

[45] Curti, "Austria and the United States," 152–53, citing Clayton to Mann, 18 June 1849, Senate Documents, 31st Congress, 1st Session, vol. X, Executive Documents, no. 43, Pt. 11.

[46] It is possible that the staff of the ministry found out from another source. They were reputed for obtaining and deciphering messages. See Black; and Hayne. In "Austria and the United States," Curti argues that it was likely Schwarz (154–55).

violate the Great Power System's norm of mutual recognition of legitimate sovereignty. It also violated the frequently voiced U.S. policy of noninvolvement in European affairs.

In a process that remains mysterious and shrouded in the passive voice, Mann's instructions were published in the *London Times* on 7 September 1849, making the whole affair public and thus turning it into a full-fledged international incident. Newspapers on both sides of the Atlantic offered editorial opinion on both American actions and Austrian possession of Mann's confidential instructions. In the United States, Senator Cass, the defeated Democratic presidential candidate, took up the pro-Hungarian cause in an effort to appeal to immigrant voters. He was assisted by Francis Grund, a Bohemian-born immigrant with a passionate hatred of monarchical government, who also owned several important American newspapers. On 24 December 1849, Cass took the major step of proposing a Senate resolution that would suspend U.S. diplomatic relations with the Austrian government because of its treatment of the Hungarian revolutionaries.[47]

The severance of diplomatic relations in the Great Power System was an accepted practice, but it was also serious business. It was typically used to signal one government's dissatisfaction with a specific action of another government. Direct relations between the two countries – always the most desirable because they were the least complicated – were suspended, but indirect relations persisted. In the Great Power System, the financial and personal interests of private citizens living, working, or traveling abroad were significant enough to require states to continue to protect them, even when diplomatic relations were severed. Governments therefore turned to neutral countries to ask them to take over the protection of such private interests.[48] In this way, countries could continue to interact with one another on certain issues through neutral intermediaries. The expectation was that regular, direct relations would resume when the specific disagreement had been resolved. The mutual recognition of each other's right to exist that diplomats had built was supposed to last through those periods of conflict when diplomats were not around to signal that recognition on a daily basis; in a sense, the relationship existed on reserves of good will.

---

[47] Ibid., 153–56. A later speech was printed for public circulation: Lewis Cass, "Diplomatic Relations with Austria. Speech of Hon. Lewis Cass, of Michigan, in Senate of the United States, Friday, January 4, 1850, on Suspending Our Diplomatic Relations with Austria" (Washington, 1850).

[48] David D. Newsom, *Diplomacy Under a Foreign Flag: When Nations Break Relations* (Washington, 1989).

The danger was that those reserves might not outlast the conflict. Although neutral powers protected individuals' interests, they did not perform the ceremonial or social functions that contributed to mutual recognition of legitimate sovereignty. If the conflict lasted too long or was too severe, these reserves could run out, creating an opportunity for the dissatisfied government to withdraw its recognition entirely and recognize a competing sovereignty. This actually happened between the United States and the Habsburg Empire during World War I, and it was this state of affairs that Cass was threatening with his proposal to cut diplomatic ties with the Habsburg government in 1849. Breaking those relations was a necessary first step toward recognizing an independent Hungarian sovereignty.

Fortunately for the Habsburg government, the observance of the Christmas holiday season bought Hülsemann some time to maneuver before the Senate took any decisive action on Cass's 24 December proposal. Hülsemann and his superior in Vienna, Prince Schwarzenberg, wanted an official disavowal of the Mann mission from President Taylor, as well as an apology for it. Hülsemann thought that the Southern senators would likely prevent Cass's resolution from passing, in part because most U.S.-Austrian commerce involved the sale of Southern raw materials to Austria, and in part out of sectional resistance to Northern proposals. If the South failed to come through, Hülsemann believed that the Austrian government could take two steps to make sure relations were not broken: publicly, they could threaten to suspend the U.S.-Austrian Treaty of Commerce. Attacking the Americans' precious trade agreements would certainly prompt sufficient opposition to Cass because he would have to justify his call to overturn Washington's policy of noninvolvement in European political affairs, while his opponents could say they were upholding Washington's economic expansion mandate. In addition to this public threat, Hülsemann thought it could be mentioned privately to certain members of the U.S. government that it was not entirely proper for a nation of slaveholders to tell the alleged "despots" of Europe what to do in a matter concerning freedom.[49]

Cass's resolution never made it out of the Senate, but the controversy did not die there because Taylor refused to disavow the Mann mission publicly. In fact, in his annual message to Congress, the president openly affirmed Clayton's directions to Mann.[50] Since relations were so fragile,

---

[49] Curti, "Austria and the United States," 156.
[50] See Zachary Taylor's Annual Message to Congress, 4 December 1849, in *A Compilation of the Messages and Papers of the Presidents*, vol. 5, part 1, *Presidents Taylor and Fillmore*, ed. James D. Richardson (Washington, 1902).

Hülsemann did not want to take decisive action on Taylor's speech without clear instructions from Vienna. He took a moderate, symbolic step instead: he stopped attending social functions at the White House. The administration and the press had no problem interpreting Hülsemann actions.[51] That he chose to express his displeasure by curtailing his social and representational functions, and that his actions were interpreted as having clear and important political meaning, demonstrates the importance of social action in the Great Power System.

Meanwhile, the government in Vienna was trying to determine the best course of action. Schwarzenberg advocated pressing for an apology, but the rest of the cabinet was inclined to let the matter drop. General Webb, the new U.S. chargé in Vienna and a member of the Whig Party, encouraged moderation on the Austrians' part. He argued that a major international incident – as this was shaping up to be – could discredit the Whigs and hurt their future electoral power. If they were defeated in the elections, that would mean a Democratic administration, and Webb warned that the passionate and aggressive Democrats were more likely to act decisively in ways that would hurt Habsburg interests – after all, Cass was a Democrat. Foreign ministry personnel also thought a serious clash between the United States and Great Britain was in the offing, and they wanted to avoid taking sides now in an effort to keep their options open in that anticipated conflict.[52] Ruled by the cabinet, Schwarzenberg instructed Hülsemann to back down and encourage a return to normal, friendly relations between the two countries. The Vienna government's position was to blame specific individuals, particularly Secretary of State Clayton, rather than the whole country, and therefore breaking diplomatic relations was no longer a punishment that fit the crime.[53]

Once again, this could have been the end to the conflict, and, once again, an individual chose to extend and escalate it instead. This time, it was President Taylor. In an effort to outmaneuver Cass, on 18 March 1850, Taylor chose to send all of the correspondence relating to the Mann mission to the Senate; in effect, he published it.[54] Schwarzenberg and the Vienna government were angry that the situation was apparently not closed and that the transatlantic public might resume speculation and

[51] Curti, "Austria and the United States," 160.
[52] On Anglo-American relations, see Campbell; and Kathleen Burk, *Old World, New World: Great Britain and America from the Beginning* (New York, 2008).
[53] Curti, "Austria and the United States," 158–61.
[54] Ibid., 159–61.

debate on how the Habsburg government had obtained Mann's instructions. They instructed Hülsemann to protest strongly. Hülsemann drafted a less virulent protest than Schwarzenberg probably would have liked, but, before he could deliver it formally, Taylor died. The traditions of mourning had to be observed; the Habsburg protest had to wait, but it was not forgotten.[55]

With Taylor's death, the constellation of actors involved in the conflict changed, bringing new opportunities and challenges. The new president was Millard Fillmore, and he selected Daniel Webster for his secretary of state, replacing Clayton, whom the Habsburg government considered responsible for the Mann mission. Hülsemann hoped he could deal with Webster more effectively than he had with Clayton, and he met with the new secretary on 27 July 1850. At that meeting, Hülsemann informally mentioned his government's displeasure over the publication of the Mann correspondence. He hoped that conversation would result in an official apology and therefore a successful resolution of the issue. Webster took no action, however, and Hülsemann was therefore obligated to issue a formal protest, which he sent to the State Department on 30 September 1850.[56]

Webster was in a bind. Personally, he felt that the Habsburg government was justified in its complaint, but he also felt that it was the fault of the previous administration – Fillmore and Webster should not have to apologize for their predecessors' mistakes and therefore be made to appear weak before their fellow Americans. Webster let domestic political demands rule the day: he went public with the conflict, publishing a very forceful reply to Hülsemann's protest. The Habsburg chargé received a copy of Webster's polemic on 24 December 1850. This time, Christmas did not stand in the way of congressional action, and, by 30 December the Senate – whose members had read the statement in the papers – was clamoring to see all U.S.-Habsburg correspondence relating to the issue. Several members wanted to publish the correspondence, which would inform – that is, agitate – the public and hopefully produce a clear mandate for the government to take further action.[57]

Senator Henry Clay urged his colleagues to let the matter drop. He tied the issue to U.S. domestic politics: "It would be well . . . were we to act with the delicacy we should like from others if one of our states revolted and an

[55] Ibid., 161–62.
[56] Ibid., 162–63.
[57] Ibid., 164–66.

agent was sent by a foreign government."[58] Given the climate of agitation over slavery and states' rights, the revolt of a U.S. state was a distinct possibility. Clay's reasoning failed to persuade, however, and the Senate voted to print five thousand copies of the U.S.-Habsburg correspondence at government expense for public circulation. With this action, the journalists of Europe and America waited with bated breath to see if relations between the two countries would be severed, and, if they were, which side would take the decisive action.[59] With the Democrats and their allies at sympathetic newspapers calling for a severance of relations, the Whigs and their papers took up the opposite perspective, arguing that the United States should let the matter rest. By letting it drop, they argued, they would be reaffirming Habsburg sovereignty in the hopes that the Habsburgs would do the same in the future, should a U.S. state try to leave the union. The divided nature of editorial opinion on the matter kept the U.S. government from taking anti-Habsburg action, even if the specific arguments the Whigs put forward were not sufficiently persuasive.[60]

By going to the partisan press, Webster had maintained U.S.-Habsburg relations while managing to avoid making an apology for the Mann mission. The Habsburg government – and Hülsemann in particular – had also learned a valuable lesson about American politics; namely, that they could count on the parties to take up opposing positions out of sheer spite. The U.S. government had been brought to maintain U.S.-Habsburg relations – even over the American desire to support liberal revolutions – by the dynamics of partisan politics: a pro-diplomacy position had been created out of a desire to oppose the other party, and Habsburg officials were hopeful that they might use this same strategy in the future.

Although the conflict over the Mann mission had been resolved, a related issue was simmering and would again challenge those who would maintain a U.S.-Habsburg diplomatic relationship. When the Hungarian revolution was put down in the summer of 1849, Lajos Kossuth and several other '48ers had avoided prosecution – and likely execution – by escaping to the Ottoman Empire. The Ottoman government reached an agreement with the Habsburg government that the Ottomans would keep the revolutionaries in their empire; if the '48ers wanted to leave, they

---

[58] Ibid., 167. By 1850, the European revolutions had become more politically divisive in the United States. See Timothy M. Roberts, "'Revolutions Have Become the Bloody Toy of the Multitude': European Revolutions, the South, and the Crisis of 1850," *Journal of the Early Republic* 25, 2 (2005): 259–83.

[59] Curti, "Austria and the United States," 167–68.

[60] See Silbey, *The American Political Nation*.

would have to secure the approval of the Habsburg government. The British and French governments immediately protested to the Ottoman government for making this agreement, and they repeatedly pointed out that their cooperation with the Ottomans rested on public opinion, which would not tolerate support for an overly despotic regime – and detaining the Hungarian revolutionaries was too despotic. The U.S. government was also involved: in January 1850, when President Taylor was still alive and Clayton was still secretary of state, Clayton had sent a U.S. representative to Constantinople to encourage the Ottoman government to release the Hungarians. The Ottoman government began to succumb to the combined force of British, French, and American pressure, and they reached an agreement with the Habsburg government to release all the Hungarians except one: Lajos Kossuth. Kossuth was the most prominent of the revolutionaries held in the Ottoman Empire, and Habsburg officials were concerned that he would go to Britain or the United States and provoke revolution from there.[61]

Just as the conflict over the Mann mission correspondence was dying down, the U.S. government took decisive action on the Kossuth question and reopened their conflict with the Habsburg government. The two houses of Congress passed a joint resolution that called for sending a U.S. naval vessel to pick up Kossuth and transport him to the United States. On 3 March 1851, President Fillmore approved the resolution and ordered the USS *Mississippi* to sail; he also made a commitment to Hülsemann that the U.S. government would not officially welcome Kossuth to the United States or do anything in connection with Kossuth that could be interpreted as official support for Hungarian independence. Members of the Habsburg government, still expecting a U.S.-British clash, opted to overlook the American decision to send the ship, but they did publicly point out that, if Kossuth caused problems, they would hold the U.S. and Ottoman governments responsible. Prince Schwarzenberg also gave Hülsemann permission to leave Washington – but not U.S. soil – if the situation became too difficult and to make a formal protest if the U.S. government took any further official pro-Kossuth action.[62]

The U.S. naval vessel brought Kossuth to New York City via Marseilles and Liverpool. Apparently, Kossuth was a rather difficult passenger – he

---

[61] Curti, "Austria and the United States," 169–74. This was a realistic concern, as those two countries were the favorite havens of political exiles because they were allowed to continue to give voice to their opinions and political programs.

[62] Ibid., 170–77. See also Matsch, *Wien-Washington*, 125–41.

complained constantly about the conditions on board the ship and succeeded in seriously irritating the captain. The captain wrote several unfavorable letters about Kossuth to various members of the U.S. government, and Hülsemann hoped these letters would find their way into the American papers. A few papers did print the negative reviews, and the Catholic Church was quick to denounce Kossuth from the pulpit and in its papers, but on the whole, the media was silent, waiting to pass judgment until Kossuth actually arrived in the United States.[63]

Although they remained silent about the Kossuth affair, some papers were printing stories about an alleged argument between Hülsemann and Webster. The papers reported that Hülsemann was upset that private communications between the two men were being published by the press. Although Hülsemann was indeed concerned, the papers – especially those owned by Grund, who had helped Cass stir up immigrant feeling over the Hungarian Revolution in 1849 – painted Hülsemann in a particularly negative light. In hopes of fixing his relationship with Webster, Hülsemann visited President Fillmore, with whom he had developed a good relationship through his attendance at Washington social events. Hülsemann left a written complaint to Webster with Fillmore at the White House and discussed the situation with the president, hoping Fillmore would take care of the situation. Fillmore did bring the matter up with Webster.[64]

Webster was not happy that Hülsemann had gone to Fillmore, and he announced that any future communication between Hülsemann and himself would have to be in writing. This was a massive affront in a diplomatic culture that put such a high premium on interpersonal interaction. At virtually the same time as Webster's announcement, the U.S. Navy fired cannons as part of a welcoming ceremony for Kossuth in New York harbor. This was an official action, exactly the kind of thing Hülsemann was supposed to protest. Hülsemann went to see Fillmore again, opting to fight only one of the battles: he stayed silent on the cannons, but said he would undoubtedly be called home by the government in Vienna if the ban on verbal communications with Webster remained in place. Fillmore interceded with a reluctant Webster, and the conflict was briefly suspended.[65]

---

[63] Curti, "Austria and the United States," 177–78.
[64] Ibid., 179–80.
[65] Ibid., 181.

Hülsemann had not forgotten the cannons, however. They were hard to forget, being simply one early instance of an outpouring of public and private American support for Kossuth. The revolutionary leader toured the country amid banquets, toasts, and speeches in favor of Hungarian independence.[66] On 13 December 1851, Hülsemann decided the time was right to address Kossuth's reception on behalf of his government, and he put his official protest in writing and sent it to Webster, who chose to ignore it. From Vienna, Webster heard from Charles McCurdy, the current U.S. chargé there, that the Habsburg government would not break relations over the Kossuth issue. McCurdy did not mention that Hülsemann still had Schwarzenberg's standing approval to leave the capital, however.[67]

With McCurdy's analysis and his continued annoyance with Hülsemann over the correspondence issue still very much in mind, Webster, who planned to run for president in the 1852 election, decided to tap into American support for Kossuth for his own political ends. Members of Congress hosted a banquet for Kossuth on 7 January 1852, and Webster attended, allegedly in his capacity as a private American citizen and a former congressman and senator, not as secretary of state. At the banquet, Webster gave a speech that called for Hungarian independence, saying that the nation of Hungary could govern itself more effectively than Austria could.[68] This was strong stuff, especially coming from one who happened to be the U.S. secretary of state and was thus in a position to potentially turn his words into actions.

On reading Webster's speech – it was published in the newspapers, of course – Hülsemann wrote to President Fillmore to ask if Webster's statement was the official U.S. government position. If it was, Hülsemann warned, diplomatic relations would surely be suspended. While Hülsemann was communicating with Fillmore, Webster was writing to McCurdy, instructing him to go to the foreign ministry and read Webster's speech verbatim to Schwarzenberg. McCurdy was then told to insist that Webster had been speaking as a private citizen – as if private citizens could force officials of foreign governments to listen to a recitation of their opinions.[69]

---

[66] On Kossuth's visit, see Komlos; and Spencer.
[67] Curti, "Austria and the United States," 182–85. For more on the Kossuth issue, see Spaulding, 46.
[68] *Writings and Speeches of Daniel Webster*, XIII, 452–62; cited in Curti, "Austria and the United States," 184–85.
[69] Curti, "Austria and the United States," 186. See the correspondence in M77, roll 13; and T157, roll 1.

Webster also met with Fillmore and took up the matter of diplomatic protocol. Webster reminded the president that, as a mere chargé, Hülsemann should have no right to talk with Fillmore.[70] Webster instructed McCurdy to bring up the presentation issue with Schwarzenberg in Vienna, too, implying that Hülsemann was overstepping his bounds. Webster observed to Schwarzenberg via McCurdy that "a marked disrespect of ordinary forms implies disrespect to the Government itself."[71] Although Schwarzenberg was undoubtedly glad that a U.S. secretary of state had finally grasped this basic point about diplomatic norms, he was incensed that he would bring it up after having violated so many diplomatic norms himself. In response to Webster's messages, Schwarzenberg got Emperor Franz Joseph to award Hülsemann the Chevalier's Cross of the Order of the Iron Crown to symbolize the crown's support for Hülsemann and his actions.[72]

Back in Washington, Fillmore summoned Hülsemann to the White House to discuss the situation. In an action that Schwarzenberg would latter approve, Hülsemann announced that either Webster must step down as secretary of state or Hülsemann and the Russian minister would leave the United States in protest, thereby severing American diplomatic relations with both the Habsburg Empire and Russia.[73] The Russian minister was then able to negotiate between Fillmore and Hülsemann for Fillmore's verbal disavowal of Webster's speech. Hülsemann was not sure that this would satisfy Schwarzenberg, however, so he decided to leave Washington until instructions could arrive from Vienna. He timed his departure for maximum effect: he left on 22 January 1852, just in time to miss a large White House diplomatic dinner. The significance of his action was not lost on an irritated Fillmore.[74]

On 4 February, Schwarzenberg wrote to Hülsemann with more instructions. The verbal disavowal was not enough, as Hülsemann had suspected. Schwarzenberg ordered Hülsemann to have no interaction with Webster and to inform Fillmore that Webster must step down or else the Habsburg government would publish his disavowal of Webster's speech, which had

---

[70] If Webster was demanding Fillmore's strict adherence to the norm of presentation, no diplomat posted to Washington could speak to the president. The first ambassador from any country did not arrive in the United States until 1890.

[71] Webster to McCurdy, 8 June 1852, in M77, roll 13.

[72] Curti, "Austria and the United States," 186–88. The Iron Crown was the crown of Lombardy, of which the Habsburgs were dukes.

[73] No. 13, Hülsemann to Schwarzenberg, 22 January 1852, in HHStA, PA XXXIII, K. 13 – USA, BWV 1852.

[74] Curti, "Austria and the United States," 188–89.

so far remained confidential.[75] At the same time, the Russian and Prussian ministers were working to smooth things over in Washington. The Russian minister was in contact with Fillmore, while the Prussian minister talked with Webster; after the two ministers talked with each other, they felt confident enough in their efforts to write to Hülsemann in early April to tell him to come back to Washington.[76]

When Hülsemann arrived, however, the February instruction from Schwarzenberg was waiting for him, undoing much of what the Russian and Prussian ministers had accomplished. Shortly after Hülsemann's return, matters reached an impasse: Webster refused to recant his speech, Fillmore refused to fire Webster, and Schwarzenberg had ordered Hülsemann not to deal with Webster. Again, Hülsemann wrote to Schwarzenberg for instructions. In the meantime, he had to buy some time while not giving the impression of backing down. He opted for another symbolic gesture: at the end of April, he advertised in a Washington newspaper that he was selling his furniture.[77] This suggested that he was about to be called back to Vienna, and readers were left to assume that he would likely be leaving because the Habsburg government had severed relations with the United States.

When a letter next arrived from Vienna, it brought no instructions. Instead, it contained news that complicated the issue still further. Prince Schwarzenberg had died. In terms of U.S.-Habsburg relations, his death meant that nothing could be accomplished until a new minister was installed in Vienna and the prescribed period of mourning had been observed. Hülsemann put off his departure while the Russian minister went back to mediating. He was on his way to getting Webster to agree to a written apology when events took another turn and negotiations ceased. By this point, Fillmore was angry with everyone, and he refused to help find a solution. Hülsemann announced that he would leave the United States but that the consul general in New York City would stay, thus moderating the harshness of the severance. Hülsemann sailed shortly thereafter, and Webster wrote to McCurdy that he hoped to be able to say shortly that Hülsemann would not be welcomed back to the United States at any point in the future.[78]

---

[75] See correspondence in Matsch, *Wien-Washington*, 126–36.
[76] Curti, "Austria and the United States," 190–91.
[77] Ibid., 191–93.
[78] Ibid. See also Webster and McCurdy's correspondence in *M77*, roll 13; and *T157*, roll 1.

On his way home, Hülsemann stopped in London, where instructions from the new minister, Buol-Schauenstein, were waiting to be put on a ship bound for the United States. In those instructions, Buol-Schauenstein ordered Hülsemann to stay in Washington. But Hülsemann was already in London, and Webster was moving to have him declared persona non grata, which meant that he could not go back. Hülsemann wrote a long defense of his actions to Buol-Schauenstein, who accepted Hülsemann's explanation.[79] Just then, McCurdy announced that he was leaving Vienna for personal reasons. Buol-Schauenstein doubted that this was the real cause, and he told McCurdy to tell his government that it was not at all clear that a new U.S. representative would be welcomed in Vienna.[80]

At this point, a third and final death occurred to add further upset to the tumultuous history of this period of U.S.-Habsburg relations. In October 1852, Daniel Webster died, and the major opponent of a U.S.-Habsburg reconciliation was no longer part of the equation. Four years of intense conflict suddenly evaporated as Edward Everett became secretary of state. He had no personal stake in Webster's previous actions – or those of Clayton and Taylor – and so he could help put relations back on a normal footing. A new U.S. chargé, Thomas Foote, was sent to Vienna, and Hülsemann returned to Washington. Democrat Franklin Pierce won the 1852 presidential election, further changing the personnel involved in U.S.-Habsburg relations. In 1853, the U.S. and Habsburg governments agreed to raise their chargés to minister residents, an action that signaled not only cooperation, but also the mutual recognition that their relationship was more important than the chargé rank signified.

The 1848–52 period was pivotal in shaping subsequent U.S.-Habsburg relations. The Mann mission and the U.S. hosting of Kossuth signaled the pro-Hungarian – and therefore anti-Habsburg – stance of a significant portion of the U.S. population that viewed the Hungarians as fellow progressive, republican, Protestant revolutionaries and the Habsburgs as backward, arbitrary, Catholic despots. With the arrival of subsequent Hungarian immigrants to the United States, the creation of voluntary associations that celebrated Kossuth and other '48ers, and

---

[79] See Hülsemann, "Historische Darstellung der Umstände, welche den kaiserlichen Geschäftsträger, Herrn Hülsemann, veranlaßten, seinen Posten zu verlassen," 20 June 1852, in HHStA, PA XXXIII, K. 13.
[80] Curti, "Austria and the United States," 184–97. See also Webster and McCurdy's correspondence in *M77*, roll 13; and *T157*, roll 1.

ceremonies and commemorations on the event of Kossuth's death in 1894, the memory of these turbulent years was kept very much alive on both sides of the Atlantic.[81] Habsburg government officials learned how far the U.S. government might be willing to go in support of Hungarian sovereignty, which in turn convinced them that U.S. compliance with the diplomatic norms of the Great Power System was essential to Habsburg security. Habsburg officials also learned that American party politics could create public debate that could either move U.S. policy toward full compliance with the system or give renewed support to the anti-diplomacy position.

MOTLEY, MEXICO, AND THE CROWNING OF THE KING OF HUNGARY

After the conflict over the Hungarian Revolution at mid century, U.S.-Habsburg relations remained fairly calm and routine for approximately thirty-five years. In 1858, diplomatic representatives in the two countries were raised to the rank of envoy. In 1863, the long-serving Hülsemann finally retired, to be succeeded by three different envoys who served for very short periods until Baron Karl von Lederer was appointed in 1868. Lederer was the first in a series of envoys who served approximately six-year periods before the next long-serving chief was appointed in 1894.[82]

On the U.S. side, one diplomat served as envoy in Vienna from the fall of 1861 until the summer of 1867. J. Lothrop Motley was a renowned American historian from Massachusetts, and he ably maintained the Habsburg government's recognition of the Union government throughout the U.S. Civil War. That job was not nearly as difficult as those faced by Union diplomats in Britain, France, and Spain, who worked in direct competition with representatives of the Confederacy. Although Confederate diplomats would have welcomed Habsburg recognition, they did not actively seek it because they knew it would be extremely

---

[81] On immigration and voluntary associations, see Chapter 4; and Julianna Puskás, *Ties that Bind, Ties that Divide: 100 Years of Hungarian Experience in the United States*, trans. Zora Ludwig (New York, 2000). On Hungarian memory of the revolutionary period, see Freifeld. On U.S. events at Kossuth's death, see, for example, no. 9B, Tavera to Kálnoky, 24 March 1894; no. 10B, Tavera to Kálnoky, 31 March 1894; and no. 11, Tavera to Kálnoky, 7 April 1894, all in HHStA, PA XXXIII, K. 35 – BWV 1895–96.

[82] See Table 2.1; and Erwin Matsch, *Der Auswärtige Dienst von Österreich (-Ungarn) 1720–1920* (Vienna, 1986).

difficult to come by – the government in Vienna was not likely to support anyone's revolution.[83]

Motley's challenge in Vienna in the 1860s was not to protect the Union against the Confederacy, but rather to defend one of the main pillars of U.S. foreign policy, the Monroe Doctrine. Issued by President James Monroe in 1823 and backed up in practice by the British Navy, which wanted to protect British economic interests in Latin America, the doctrine essentially forbade all European political involvement in the countries of the Western Hemisphere.[84] With the United States preoccupied with the Civil War, however, the French government – once again a monarchy, this time ruled by Louis Napoleon – decided the time was right to exert its influence in Mexico. Mexico had been an independent country since 1821, and it had a republican government. The government was chronically unstable, however, and, as a result, the country as a whole had fallen behind with payments on the debts it owed to various European institutions. The French government, with limited support from the governments of Spain and Britain, decided to install a Catholic monarchy in Mexico. Discussion of the plan began in 1861, and, by 1863, Louis Napoleon had found a candidate for the Mexican throne: Archduke Maximilian, a younger brother of Habsburg Emperor Franz Joseph.[85]

The dominant American perception of the situation was that the French were to blame for the whole Mexican monarchical project. That perception certainly worked to the advantage of the Habsburg government, which did not want to get involved in another conflict with the United States, especially because it was dealing with serious problems with Prussia. Maximilian was part of the imperial family, however – a fact that anti-diplomacy factions in the United States believed to be of utmost significance. The Habsburg government, therefore, was not spared all involvement.

Motley was under strict instructions from Secretary of State William Seward and President Abraham Lincoln not to speak officially about the situation in Mexico, but that did not stop Motley from having several conversations about the issue with members of the Habsburg government. When reporting on these conversations to Seward, Motley repeatedly

---

[83] See Joseph A. Fry, *Dixie Looks Abroad: The South and U.S. Foreign Relations, 1789–1973* (Baton Rouge, 2002); and Henry Blumenthal, "Confederate Diplomacy: Popular Notions and International Realities," *Journal of Southern History* 32, 2 (1966): 151–71.

[84] Mark T. Gilderhus, "The Monroe Doctrine: Meanings and Implications," *Presidential Studies Quarterly* 36, 1 (2006): 5–16.

[85] On Maximilian in Mexico, see Patrick J. McNamara, *Sons of the Sierra: Juárez, Díaz, and the People of Ixtlán, Oaxaca, 1855–1920* (Chapel Hill, 2007).

stressed that, before he discussed the subject, he made sure that the listener understood that he was speaking as a private citizen, not as a representative of the U.S. government. One of his accounts of such a conversation was repeatedly published in American newspapers; the *New York Times* observed, "We do not remember to have seen the arguments against any attempt on the part of European Powers to overthrow republican institutions, and establish a monarchy in Mexico, at any time set forth with such clearness and force, and the policy of the United States in that event laid down with such distinctness, as we have found in a dispatch from our able Minister to Austria, the eminent historian, Mr. Motley."[86]

Journalists might not always have the best memory in cases such as these, but Motley's defense of the Monroe Doctrine was undoubtedly compatible with popular sentiment in both the Union and the Confederacy. When asked what American reaction was likely to be if Maximilian accepted the Mexican throne, Motley replied: "I thought the opposition would be universal and intense. . . . I gave two reasons: first, the American people, abstaining from European politics, have always had a strong feeling in regard to European interference with political arrangements on the North American Continent. Secondly, the republican form of Government was the hereditary one over the greater part of our Continent, and attempts to supersede it by monarchical forms, by means of force, would be regarded both by the lovers of progress, and by more conservative parties, as revolutionary, unphilosophical and mischievous."[87] Motley's words invoked Washington's policy of noninterference in European politics and the antithetical relationship between a republican New World and a monarchical Old World. He also claimed unanimity in American public opinion, with both "lovers of progress" and the "more conservative" opposing European involvement in Mexico. His comments were quintessential American foreign policy rhetoric.

Despite Motley's cautions as a private citizen, Maximilian did accept the Mexican throne, and he was supported primarily by French troops. The Habsburg government largely managed to stay out of the situation until 1866, when Maximilian's government and his life were in jeopardy and the U.S. Civil War was over, thus allowing the U.S. government to turn its attention to the Mexican situation. Most official U.S. correspondence on the subject was directed to the French government, but Motley was instructed to deliver copies to the Habsburg government and keep them

---

[86] "Napoleon's King for Mexico," *NYT*, 22 March 1863, p. 4.
[87] Ibid.

apprised – and hopefully out – of the conflict. In the spring of 1866, approximately one thousand Austrian subjects formed a volunteer legion planning to go to Mexico to fight for Maximilian. The Habsburg government insisted to Motley that these men were strictly volunteers, that they had already completed their obligatory military service in Austria, and that they were in no way affiliated with the Habsburg government. Motley passed this news on to Seward, who did not care that they were volunteers – they were foreign troops, and that violated the Monroe Doctrine.[88]

Immediately before the Austrian volunteers were set to depart, the U.S. government managed to secure French agreement to the withdrawal of their troops from Mexico. Seward did not want Habsburg troops to replace the French, and he instructed Motley to inform the Habsburg government officially of the U.S. position. Motley complied, sending a *note verbalé* to Count Mensdorff on 6 May 1866. The note is a classic example of Great Power System diplomatic correspondence. Motley had something very serious to say – stay out of Mexico – but he couched his government's threat in terms that tried to preserve not only U.S.-Habsburg relations, but his own relationship with Mensdorff: "An imperative duty is now placed upon me of again most respectfully calling your Excellency's attention to the general and growing uneasiness throughout the United States on the subject of foreign troops in Mexico. In so doing I wish to use the most courteous and becoming terms that are compatible with a faithful execution of the task just committed to me by my Government."[89] Motley used language to distance himself personally from the orders of his government, which would not be agreeable to his audience; in short, he was asking that Mensdorff not shoot the messenger. Motley's rather lengthy letter spelled out official U.S. opinion on the sanctity of the Monroe Doctrine, which was, according to him, "a matter of history and known to mankind."[90]

Mensdorff's reply, which was printed alongside Motley's letter in U.S. newspapers, was another classic diplomatic text. Mensdorff wrote: "The undersigned, although not sharing all the points of view developed in Mr. Motley's note, is, nevertheless, in a position to announce to him that in consequence of the above-mentioned consideration [of the U.S. position]

---

[88] See correspondence in the "Austria" section of U.S. DOS, *Executive Documents Printed by Order of the House of Representatives, During the Second Session of the Fortieth Congress, 1867–68*, vol. 1 (Washington, 1867–68), 548–73.

[89] Motley to Mensdorff, 6 May 1866, in "The Monroe Doctrine," *NYT*, 17 June 1866, p. 3.

[90] Ibid.

the necessary measures have been taken in order to suspend the departure of the newly enlisted volunteers for Mexico."[91] Mensdorff agreed not to allow the troops to sail, which is what the U.S. government wanted, but he also stressed that the Habsburg government was not in full agreement with the U.S. government as to *why* the troops would not go. Mensdorff was not sanctioning the Monroe Doctrine in general; he was merely agreeing not to send troops in this particular instance. Such a distinction was crucial because it allowed future members of the Habsburg government to reject the doctrine if they wanted or needed to, thus aiming to assure future freedom of action.

After his successful defense of the Monroe Doctrine and the Union, Motley, as a loyal Republican, a prominent American, and a competent diplomat, could have expected to remain in Vienna as long as he wanted. This was especially true because the Republican Party was the undisputed victor in American politics after the Civil War, with almost uninterrupted control of the White House and the federal patronage system. However, Motley ended up departing from office in 1867 in a storm of controversy. The U.S. legation in Vienna was without an envoy for more than a year as domestic American politics foiled the Andrew Johnson administration's attempts to secure a replacement for Motley. Unfortunately for the Habsburg government, the American conflict prevented American participation in Franz Joseph's Hungarian coronation ceremony, an event that had great significance for Habsburg sovereignty.

In the fall of 1866, a letter signed by a George M'Crackin arrived at the White House. In it, the author made a great number of complaints and accusations about various U.S. officials serving overseas, including Motley. Subsequently, many people questioned the actual existence of a person named M'Crackin, but on receipt of the letter, President Andrew Johnson did with it what most other presidents would have done; namely, he sent it to the secretary of state.[92] Seward wrote to Motley and several others among the named officials asking them to comment on M'Crackin's charges. For Motley – and for many of his friends, including his biographer, Oliver Wendell Holmes, Sr. – the fact that Seward had even asked him to address the charges was a massive insult. As a man of good social standing and reputation, to be doubted even to that degree was a serious

[91] Mensdorff to Motley, 20 May 1866, in "Monroe Doctrine."
[92] There are a number of complaints – and letters of commendation – from the public in DOS records. See file no. 123.2 in NARA.

affront. Holmes, in his unique style, wrote that, to Motley, Seward's questions "stung like the thrust of a stiletto."[93]

Motley wrote to Seward to affirm that all the allegations were false and that M'Crackin was "absolutely unknown to me; that to the best of my knowledge, memory and belief he never saw me nor heard the sound of my voice."[94] Motley was so upset at Seward's questions that he resigned his post. He could not leave Vienna, however, until his resignation had been accepted by Seward and Johnson.

Seward was a busy man, though. In addition to negotiating his famous purchase of Alaska from the Russian government, he was dealing with a major crisis in Mexico and ongoing, fragile negotiations with Britain stemming from the Civil War. Not to mention that President Johnson was under attack on numerous political fronts and would soon be facing impeachment. Because of all this, it took Seward almost six months to write back to Motley to accept his resignation. Even then, Motley still could not leave Vienna – the letter to Emperor Franz Joseph that Motley needed in order to take leave of the Habsburg government was not included in Seward's letter.[95]

Motley complained in writing and later in person to a number of his friends about his treatment. Chief among them was Senator Charles Sumner, the chair of the Senate Foreign Relations Committee. Under Sumner's leadership, the Senate rejected Johnson's nominee for Motley's replacement, former Senator Edgar Cowan.[96] Members of the Senate indicated that they would gladly reinstate Motley, but they were not likely to approve any other nomination. For more than a year, the Senate rejected nomination after nomination, turning down at least eight, a singular occurrence in U.S. history. Finally, in late July 1868, the Senate approved

[93] Oliver Wendell Holmes, Sr., *John Lothrop Motley: A Memoir* (Boston, 1879), part XVIII. For the full set of exchanges between Seward and Motley, see *M77*, roll 13; and *T157*, roll 1.

[94] "The Motley Correspondence," *NYT*, 6 December 1867, p. 5. Holmes quotes a letter from Motley to him that echoes similar sentiments in extremely similar language.

[95] There is some question of who wrote the letter Motley received accepting his resignation. Holmes suggests that Seward's actual letter – in which the secretary refused to accept Motley's resignation and apologized for the questions – was replaced at the last possible moment by a much sharper letter, which was actually penned by the "paranoid" President Johnson. For a brief account of Seward's tenure as secretary of state, see Graham H. Stuart, *The Department of State: A History of its Organization, Procedure, and Personnel* (New York, 1949).

[96] "Washington," *NYT*, 13 March 1867, p. 5.

the appointment of "staunch Republican" Henry Watts of Pennsylvania as envoy in Vienna.[97]

To the detriment of the Habsburg government, Motley's precarious position in the spring of 1867 prevented him from representing the United States at a major event in the empire: Franz Joseph's coronation as king of Hungary. Almost twenty years after the revolutions of 1848, the Habsburg government was making major internal reforms and altering its relationship with the Kingdom of Hungary. In 1867, the entire empire was reorganized through the Ausgleich, or Compromise, creating what was popularly termed "Austria-Hungary." The empire was divided into two halves, the Kingdom of Hungary, and everything else, or "Austria." Austria and Hungary each had their own governments, including separate parliaments. The two halves were joined in a personal union: Franz Joseph was the emperor in Austria and the king in Hungary. There were also three joint ministries – war, finance, and foreign affairs – that had jurisdiction over both halves of the country. The Austrian half received a new constitution from the emperor that spelled out the basic rights all citizens possessed, and the Hungarian government passed a number of laws that granted many of these same rights, regardless of language, nationality, or religion. Under this new system, all Habsburg subjects were now citizens of either Austria or Hungary, depending on the half of the country in which they had been born. The agreement was renegotiated every ten years, and that renegotiation gave the Hungarian government considerable power over the affairs of the country as a whole.[98]

The symbolic confirmation of these new arrangements was Franz Joseph's coronation as King of Hungary. Although the Habsburg government had been ruling Hungary since the end of the revolution in 1849 – and for centuries before that – Franz Joseph had never officially been

---

[97] The U.S. Senate has rejected more nominations for Vienna than for any other diplomatic post to date, primarily due to this incident. The rejections appear to be about wanting Motley reinstated, rather than being tied up in Reconstruction or other political questions. See the *NYT* "Washington" column on 26 March 1867, 29 March 1867, 10 April 1867, 14 April 1867, 18 April 1867, 16 January 1868, 8 July 1868, 21 July 1868, 26 July 1868 (quotation); and "Minor Topics," 21 July 1868; see also U.S. DOS, *Principal Officers*. Motley's name was cleared relatively quickly after Sumner requested the publication of the related correspondence.

[98] For detailed accounts of this structure, see Sked; A. J. P. Taylor, *The Habsburg Monarchy, 1809–1918* (Chicago, 1948); and Robert A. Kann, *A History of the Habsburg Empire, 1526–1918* (Berkeley, 1974). Some scholars blame the Hungarians for weakening the Habsburg government through their demands for privileges; In *The Quiet Invaders*, Spaulding presents a particularly forceful example of this argument.

crowned. The ceremony symbolized not only Franz Joseph's right to rule, but also the Hungarian aristocracy's right to consent to his rule. The coronation was supposed to put relations between the Hungarians and the Habsburgs back on a positive footing. It was a major ceremonial event, not just for domestic politics, but for international politics as well. The diplomatic corps – and special representatives from European royal families – were invited to attend; their presence signaled the approval of their countries for Habsburg rule in Hungary.

Because Motley had officially resigned but had not yet been relieved of his duties when the ceremony took place, he informed the foreign minister that he could not attend the coronation.[99] Because U.S.-Habsburg relations were disrupted, the Habsburg government did not benefit from an official American sanction of Habsburg sovereignty in Hungary and of the Ausgleich. The foreign minister and Franz Joseph understood Motley's position, but they were no doubt disappointed that the United States – the main proponent of Hungarian independence in 1848 – would not be represented at the coronation.

ANTHONY KEILEY AND THE *AGRÉMENT* CONTROVERSY

Motley had been Abraham Lincoln's nominee for the Vienna legation, and he was the first in a long line of Republican appointees to serve at that post. Indeed, the Republican Party controlled the White House, and therefore the federal patronage system, for almost the entire period from 1861 until 1913; the exceptions were Grover Cleveland's two nonsequential terms in 1885–89 and 1893–97. Although the Republican administrations between 1869 and 1885 – especially the Grant administration – have been criticized by contemporaries and subsequent scholars for their corrupt officials, appointments made to the diplomatic corps during this period were not that bad.[100] Those appointed were able to maintain positive relations with most countries, including Austria-Hungary. Arguments over diplomatic form were largely absent during this period, and the United States typically

---

[99] "Motley Correspondence."

[100] On the patronage system and its critics, see Robert H. Wiebe, *The Search for Order* (New York, 1967); Margaret Susan Thompson, *The "Spider Web": Congress and Lobbying in the Age of Grant* (Ithaca: Cornell University Press, 1985); and Leslie Butler, *Critical Americans: Victorian Intellectuals and Transatlantic Liberal Reform* (Chapel Hill, 2007). A survey of U.S. DOS, *Principal Officers* reveals that, for diplomats, a significant number held multiple diplomatic posts over the years, so that although they were not officially "professional" diplomats, they did bring some relevant experience to the job.

complied with Great Power System expectations. The period of Republican rule from 1861 to 1885 was one of relative stability, and it established a strong precedent for compliance with Great Power System norms. When Cleveland came to office in 1885, that stability and compliance were interrupted and the traditional Democratic disregard for diplomatic form resurfaced. As a result, a significant conflict erupted in U.S.-Habsburg relations.

President Cleveland and his secretary of state, Thomas F. Bayard, viewed diplomatic appointments as a function of domestic politics. They were patronage positions – some of the few such positions that remained after considerable reform in the civil service, and that made them all the more valuable.[101] In the opinion of Cleveland and Bayard, the tradition of amateur diplomacy and the idea of an American society without social classes were sacred, and they chose for their representatives men of "intelligence and standing" who did not necessarily possess any special skills that would make them good diplomats.[102] They also believed that one diplomatic post was basically the same as any other and that none was particularly important, so it did not really matter whom they sent where; as representatives selected and approved by the U.S. government, these diplomats would be accepted wherever they went. Being able to send anyone anywhere was a vital aspect of national sovereignty to Cleveland, Bayard, and many other members of the Democratic Party.[103]

European foreign ministry personnel did not usually share this view of diplomatic assignments. They recognized that diplomacy was not simply about office work; it also encompassed essential social aspects. To be an effective diplomat, a person had to be able to operate in the host society, particularly at that society's highest levels. The European tradition was typically to follow the path of least resistance when it came to diplomatic appointments. They considered the specifics of each post and each available diplomat and tried to make the best possible matches. European foreign ministries usually sent people with private social credentials that would allow them to be presented at court without having to invoke their

---

[101] With the 1883 Pendleton Act, the president could remove certain government positions from the patronage system and make them civil service positions, but the act did not apply to the diplomatic corps. See Kennedy, *American Consul*, 178. Cleveland was known for fighting corruption in government and embracing civil service reform in general, but his changes did not extend as far as the diplomatic corps. See Stuart, 164.

[102] See Bayard to Schaeffer, 20 May 1885, in HHStA, AR, Fach 7, K. 45 – Staaten J-N 1880–1918; and Stuart.

[103] On Cleveland and Bayard, see Stuart, 164–71.

diplomatic title. They also considered questions of image and prestige. For example, the French government always sent aristocrats to St. Petersburg – rather than someone from the growing number of bourgeois diplomats employed at the Quay d'Orsay – because the French were anxious to impress the Russian government and secure the Franco-Russian alliance.[104] European foreign ministry personnel also considered other issues that could make for awkward situations and made their staffing decisions accordingly. For example, the Habsburg Ministry of Foreign Affairs did not send ethnic Poles to Berlin or St. Petersburg. The British always sent one of their three best men to Washington because the post was "less important but most sensitive."[105] There was no point in making relationships that were already complex and fragile any more complicated.

In some cases, European foreign ministers secured an *agrément* before they sent a diplomat to a particular post. An *agrément* was the potential host government's formal approval of the diplomatic candidate. This approval was sought confidentially and before any appointments were made. It is not clear how often *agréments* were sought before the 1880s, but they could be used in cases of uncertainty to avoid serious problems later. The norm was to accept the potential candidate; to be rejected, there had to be something seriously wrong with the candidate, and usually foreign ministry personnel knew enough about the members of their diplomatic corps to know if there might be something objectionable about their service at particular posts.

Prior to 1885, it was not common practice in the United States to secure *agréments* for U.S. diplomats.[106] European governments usually accepted whomever the U.S. government sent, even if not entirely thrilled with the American choice. The U.S. government was unpredictable enough that a refusal could provoke a huge controversy, and most European governments did not want to spend their time dealing with such an issue.

Everything changed in 1885, when Cleveland and Bayard nominated Anthony Keiley of Virginia to be the U.S. envoy to Rome.[107] Keiley had

---

[104] Hayne.

[105] On the Habsburgs, see Godsey; on the British, see Jones, 127, 174.

[106] According to Bayard, a search of DOS records in 1885 produced no evidence of *agréments*. My own research confirms this for the Vienna post, specifically. See Bayard to Schaeffer, 20 May 1885.

[107] See James H. Bailey, "Anthony M. Keiley and 'The Keiley Incident,'" *Virginia Magazine of History and Biography* 67, 1 (1959): 65–81; Luigi Caltagirone, "Il Doppio Affare Keiley," *Storia e Politica* 4, 3 (1965): 428–39; and numerous articles by Joseph P. O'Grady, especially "Religion and American Diplomacy: An Incident in Austro-American Relations," *American Jewish Historical Quarterly* 59, 4 (1970): 407–23.

been active in the Democratic Party in Virginia, and, in the typical pattern for the time, his patron, Congressman Randolph Tucker, approached Bayard and Cleveland about Keiley's appointment to a diplomatic post in recognition of that service.[108] Newspapers identified him as a "Bayard man." His was clearly a political patronage appointment.

Keiley's appointment to Rome was confirmed by the Senate, and, shortly thereafter, he set sail for Europe. Although an *agrément* had not been sought from the Italian government, they were informed that Keiley was on his way. Unbeknownst to Cleveland, Bayard, or the Senate, members of the Italian government knew a significant amount of information about Keiley. They knew, likely from earlier reports made by their representative in Washington, that Keiley had made at least one public speech in Virginia hostile to the Italian government. The speech was made in 1871, when the Italian government under King Victor Emmanuel and the Vatican were embroiled in a number of disputes. Keiley, himself a Catholic, had made comments in his speech that were hostile to the Italian government and favorable to the Catholic Church. Fourteen years later, the Italian government refused to receive Keiley as the envoy to Rome because of that speech.[109]

Bayard and Cleveland found the Italian rejection difficult to swallow. Bayard wrote that, "it seems difficult to imagine the basis for such an objection to a gentleman who has as yet never been in Europe nor held official relations to any foreign State."[110] He and Cleveland decided not to press the issue with the Italians, however, and instead they quickly nominated Keiley for the post at Vienna – all while Keiley was still en route to Europe. Again, no *agrément* was sought. When Keiley's new destination was announced, the Italian representative in Vienna went to Count Kálnoky, the foreign minister, and encouraged him not to accept Keiley either. Kálnoky took the Italian position into consideration, and he learned more about the U.S. nominee.[111] Kálnoky discovered that Keiley had been married in a civil ceremony to a woman who was "a Jewess." Although it is

---

[108] "About Mr. Keiley," *New York Herald*, [1885], enclosed in no. 47, Schaeffer to Kálnoky, 20 June 1885, in HHStA, AR, Fach 7, K. 45.

[109] Bayard to Francis, 1 July 1885, enclosed in Francis to Kálnoky, 25 July 1885 in HHStA, AR, Fach 7, K. 45; and "A Friend of Mr. Keiley Explains," *NYT*, [1885], enclosed in no. 47, Schaeffer to Kálnoky, 20 June 1885.

[110] Bayard to Schaeffer, 15 June 1885, enclosed in no. 45, Schaeffer to Kálnoky, 17 June 1885, in HHStA, AR, Fach 7, K. 45.

[111] Kálnoky's telegram to Bayard via Schaeffer, 8 May 1885, in HHStA, AR, Fach 7, K. 45; and Schaeffer to Bayard, 11 June 1885, enclosed in no. 45, Schaeffer to Kálnoky, 17 June 1885.

not entirely clear whether Kálnoky thought the civil union or Mrs. Keiley's Jewishness – be it religious or racial – was the bigger problem, he felt that the Keileys would not be readily accepted in Viennese social circles.[112] Although the Habsburg government insisted on religious toleration, both religious and racial anti-Semitism were on the rise in Austria-Hungary and in Europe more generally – it was hardly unknown in the United States, either.[113] Viennese society was also deeply attached to the idea of church-sanctioned marriages, and, indeed, Austrian law prohibited marriages between Christians and Jews.[114] Kálnoky recognized that part of the U.S. representative's duties would involve active participation in Viennese social events and that his "domestic situation" was going to make that extremely difficult.[115]

Kálnoky telegraphed the Habsburg representative in Washington, Baron Ignaz von Schaeffer, and asked him to bring the matter up with Bayard. Kálnoky instructed Schaeffer to "direct in the most friendly way the attention of the American Government to the generally existing Diplomatic practice to ask previously to any nomination of a foreign minister the *agrément* of the Government to which he is accredited." He also observed that "the position of a foreign Envoy wedded to a Jewess by civil marriage would be untenable and even impossible in Vienna."[116]

From Kálnoky's perspective, the issue was the *agrément*. The United States should have checked with the government in Vienna to see if Keiley would be acceptable, particularly after one European government had already refused to receive him. He also felt it was his responsibility to

---

[112] Kálnoky's telegram to Bayard via Schaeffer, 8 May 1885.
[113] On anti-Semitism, see, among numerous others, Ivar Oxaal, Michael Pollak, and Gerhard Botz, eds., *Jews, Antisemitism and Culture in Vienna* (London, 1987); John W. Boyer, *Political Radicalism in Late Imperial Vienna: Origins of the Christian Social Movement: 1848–1897* (Chicago, 1981); Steven Beller, *Vienna and the Jews, 1867–1938: A Cultural History* (Cambridge, 1989); Marsha Rozenblit, *The Jews of Vienna, 1867–1914: Assimilation and Identity* (Albany, 1983); Robert S. Wistrich, *The Jews of Vienna in the Age of Franz Joseph* (Oxford, 1989); Leonard Dinnerstein, *Antisemitism in America* (New York, 1994); David A. Gerber, *Anti-Semitism in American History* (Urbana, 1986); Eric L. Goldstein, *The Price of Whiteness: Jews, Race, and American Identity* (Princeton, 2006); and Frederic Cople Jaher, *A Scapegoat in the New Wilderness: The Origins and Rise of Anti-Semitism in America* (Cambridge MA, 1994).
[114] Gerald Stourzh, "The Age of Emancipation and Assimilation: Liberalism and Its Heritage," in *Österreich-Konzeptionen und jüdisches Selbstverständnis. Identitäts Transfigurationen im 19. Und 20. Jahrhundert*, ed. Hanni Mittelmann and Armin A. Wallas (Tübingen, 2001), 11–28.
[115] Schaeffer to Bayard, 11 June 1885.
[116] Kálnoky's telegram to Bayard via Schaeffer, 8 May 1885.

alert foreign governments to potential problems before new diplomats arrived in order to prevent those problems from occurring.[117]

Bayard did not see it this way. In a lengthy letter to Schaeffer – and thus to Kálnoky – Bayard attempted to shift the debate away from diplomatic practice to the question of religious freedom. His interpretation was that the Austrian government was refusing to accept a member of the Jewish faith as a representative of the United States. Bayard's response was a polemic on the virtues and practices of the United States, one that was heavily critical of the Habsburg government. It demonstrated that Bayard held the popular American view of Austria-Hungary; namely, that it was a backward, oppressive, arbitrary, despotic monarchy. He was attempting to force the Habsburg government to adopt American-style policies, specifically those regarding religious toleration, the separation of church and state, and the rule of law, which he apparently believed Austria-Hungary lacked.[118]

Bayard insisted that the U.S. government had no right to inquire after the religious beliefs of its citizens, especially proposed office holders and their families. He observed that "the supreme law of this land expressly declares 'that no religious test shall ever be required as a qualification to any office or public trust under the United States,'" and that "religious liberty is the chief corner-stone of the American system of government, and provisions for its security are imbedded in the written character and interwoven in the moral fabric of its laws." In a one-sentence paragraph that made his words stand out as especially significant to the reader, Bayard went on to assert that "This is a government of laws, and all authority exercised must find its measure and warrant thereunder."[119] The implication was that Austria-Hungary was not a "government of laws," but rather an arbitrary autocracy. This was a common perception in the United States, but it was not an accurate reflection of Austro-Hungarian political culture.

In addition to extolling religious freedom, Bayard argued that Mrs. Keiley should be exempt from any objection because she was an American woman. He wrote, "in harmony with this essential law [of religious freedom] is the almost equally potential unwritten law of American society that awards respect and delicate consideration to the women of the United States and exacts deference in the treatment at home

---

[117] Schaeffer to Bayard, 11 June 1885.
[118] Bayard to Schaeffer, 18 May 1885, in HHStA, AR, Fach 7, K. 45.
[119] Ibid.

and abroad of the mothers, wives and daughters of the Republic."[120] Bayard was not only criticizing the Austro-Hungarian government as arbitrary, but as unchivalrous to women, an offense that was at least as bad, if not worse.

Finally, Bayard played the civilization card. He wrote, "it is not believed by the President that a doctrine and practice so destructive of religious liberty and freedom of conscious, so devoid of catholicity and so opposed to the spirit of the age in which we live, can for a moment be accepted by the great family of civilized nations, or be allowed to control their diplomatic intercourse."[121] Bayard's play on the word *catholicity* was likely not missed by the Habsburg government, which was staffed by large numbers of Roman Catholics, not to mention the fact that members of the royal family had always been ardent supporters of the Catholic Church. More important, Bayard was saying that Austria-Hungary was uncivilized and backward, an insult of growing severity in the race-conscious transatlantic culture of the late nineteenth century.[122]

Bayard had called Austria-Hungary intolerant, arbitrary, unchivalrous, backward, and uncivilized because he believed the issue was Habsburg intolerance of Mrs. Keiley's religious beliefs. Only at the end of his missive did he address the issue of the practice of *agrément*, saying that he and the president "fully [recognized] the highly important and undoubted right of every government to decide for itself whether the individual presented as the Envoy of another State is or is not an acceptable person – and, in the exercise of its own high and friendly discretion, to receive or not the person so presented." However, Bayard wanted the Habsburg government to reconsider its stance on Keiley and find him an acceptable envoy.[123]

Before Schaeffer or Kálnoky could respond to the serious charges leveled at them in this communication, Bayard sent Schaeffer another polemic, just two days after the first, this one focusing on the issue of the *agrément*. Bayard had ordered the staff of the State Department to go to the records to see if they could find any previous *agréments*, and they could not. Bayard argued that such a practice was an infringement on national sovereignty because foreign governments could refuse to accept diplomats of a particular political party and thereby render a president's foreign

[120] Ibid.
[121] Ibid.
[122] Gail Bederman, *Manliness and Civilization: A Cultural History of Gender and Race in the United States, 1880–1917* (Chicago, 1995).
[123] Bayard to Schaeffer, 18 May 1885.

policy impotent. He stated that "our system of frequently recurring elections at regular and stated periods, provides – and was intended to provide – an opportunity for the influence of public opinion upon those to whom the administration of public affairs has been entrusted by the people."[124] Bayard's lesson in the basics of the American government suggests that he did not think the monarchical Austro-Hungarian government had any idea how elections worked or that public opinion should play a role in determining policy.

Kálnoky was not at all pleased by Bayard's letters, which framed the conflict in terms of a debate about the nature of government. In a "personal and confidential" letter to Bayard, Schaeffer passed along Kálnoky's opinion that this was not the time to embark on "a discussion with the Government of the United States upon religious liberty."[125] Schaeffer pointed out that "in Austria-Hungary as well as in the United States the Constitution grants entire liberty to all forms of religious worship." He stated that the objection to Keiley's service was Keiley's "want of political tact" – a reference to the Italian government's refusal to receive him – and "that his domestic relations preclude that reception of him by Vienna Society which we judge desirable for the representative of the United States."[126] That Habsburg correspondence kept mentioning "domestic relations" rather than Judaism suggests that the most fundamental problem was the civil marriage.

Although the official correspondence between the U.S. and Habsburg governments over Keiley's appointment had not been made public, the press was aware that there was some question of Keiley's suitability for the Vienna post. In June 1885, before any of the correspondence had been published, the American press debated the issue largely in terms of Keiley's anti-Italian comments. The *New York Times* interviewed an acquaintance of Keiley's to get details about his 1871 speech about the Italian government, and that acquaintance insisted that the speech was the only reason Keiley was objectionable; he did not mention Mrs. Keiley at all.[127] Other papers hostile to the Cleveland administration pointed out that, if Keiley was unacceptable in Rome, he would be unacceptable in all European posts and that the governments of Europe were perfectly justified in refusing to receive a person who had made politically tactless statements that

---

[124] Bayard to Schaeffer, 20 May 1885.
[125] Schaeffer to Bayard, 11 June 1885.
[126] Ibid.
[127] "A Friend of Mr. Keiley Explains."

undermined the legitimacy of their governments.[128] Some papers went after Bayard personally, noting that he had no knowledge of foreign affairs.[129] Others criticized the patronage system as a whole and pointed out that the allegedly corrupt Republican administrations of recent years had never faced such problems.[130] Of the numerous clippings on the issue collected by the Austro-Hungarian legation staff in Washington, only one made any reference at all to Mrs. Keiley, noting that Keiley had "a family alliance which would be a source of grave embarrassment, owing to the peculiar race prejudices which are yet so all-powerful in Eastern Europe."[131] The use of the word *yet* suggested that the United States had progressed past race prejudice. Ironically, this was from a Southern paper, and, of course, race prejudice was hardly peculiar in the South, or indeed anywhere in the United States.

With all the attention the issue was receiving in the press, Bayard finally broke down and wrote to the current U.S. envoy in Vienna, Charles Francis, enclosing more information about the situation to be passed along to Kálnoky. In this letter, he met the Habsburg points in greater detail, and his tone suggests that he was struggling to comprehend what was so wrong with the whole situation. The most startling piece of information to come out of this letter was that Mrs. Keiley was not a practicing member of the Jewish faith. Bayard informed Francis that "Mrs. Keiley, although of Hebrew ancestry, has never professed ... the Jewish faith." He added that "the marriage had the sanction of the highest ecclesiastical Roman Catholic authorities in the United States, many of whom, moreover, joined most warmly in commending Mr. Keiley's appointment."[132] Bayard's earlier comments about religious freedom and his defense of practicing Jews as some of "the most honoured and valued citizens of the United States" were now rendered largely irrelevant.[133] And to find this out, Bayard had had to inquire about Mrs. Keiley's religious practices, which went against the law he had invoked in his first statement.

Bayard also apparently thought that Keiley's lack of diplomatic experience was of concern to the Habsburg government. In his 20 May letters to

[128] Clipping from the *Southern Press*, [1885]; and "The Austrian Mission," *The Tribune*, [1885], both enclosed in no. 47, Schaeffer to Kálnoky, 20 June 1885.
[129] "The Austrian Mission."
[130] "About Mr. Keiley"; "The Austrian Mission."
[131] Clipping from the *Southern Press*.
[132] Bayard to Francis, 1 July 1885.
[133] Bayard to Schaeffer, 18 May 1885.

Schaeffer and to Francis, Bayard stressed that the United States did not have a professional diplomatic corps, and he defended the practice because he felt it was a reflection of American society, which, in Bayard's opinion, was free of social class distinctions. He did, however, admit that the American preference for nonprofessional diplomats "may not invariably have been wise." A member of the Austro-Hungarian Ministry of Foreign Affairs staff underlined that passage and marked it with an exclamation point, suggesting that the Austrian government had never been thrilled with this American practice.[134] However, they had not raised this as an issue in opposing Keiley's arrival. It was not that he was not a professional diplomat, but rather that the U.S. government had not sought the Habsburg government's previous approval of the appointment after the Italian government had rejected him. Whatever the Austro-Hungarian government's objections, Bayard wrote to Francis that "The President is exceedingly desirous for the continuation and promotion of the closest and most friendly relations with Austria-Hungary, and to comply in all things with the wishes and interests of that Government as indicated by its agents, – but not to an extent involving the slightest forfeiture of our national self-respect, or the respect and sense of friendly duty which – to exist at all between two equals – must be mutually guarded and maintained."[135]

Kálnoky and the rest of the Habsburg government refused to change their minds about Keiley, and he arrived in Vienna only to turn around and return to the United States. In December 1885, several months after Keiley returned, the whole situation came up again, likely because Keiley complained publicly about not receiving another diplomatic post from the Cleveland administration. In their own defense, Cleveland and Bayard had "the Keiley correspondence" printed for public circulation, which initiated a new round of editorial comment in American newspapers.[136]

Included in the correspondence was Bayard's letter to Keiley on his return from Vienna. Bayard wrote that "the President and his Cabinet are completely satisfied with your attitude and action throughout this remarkable episode in our diplomatic history." In a statement undoubtedly aimed at the public in the United States and Europe, he added, "I will not believe that the people of the United States will ever consent to the creation or enforcement

[134] Bayard to Schaeffer, 20 May 1885.
[135] Bayard to Francis, 1 July 1885.
[136] See no. 62, Weissenfeld to Kálnoky, 24 December 1885; and no. 61, Weissenfeld to Kálnoky, 18 December 1885, both in HHStA, AR, Fach 7, K. 45.

of such tests as have been insisted upon by the government of Austria-Hungary. Such action must naturally awaken widespread amazement coupled with indignation and resentment when the history of the case is made public, nor do I believe that these sentiments will be confined to our own country, but that wherever religious liberty is valued and respected a common judgment will be formed." Again, Bayard was framing the situation as a question of religious freedom and implying that Austria-Hungary was beyond the pale of civilization. Bayard and Cleveland could offer Keiley no other government post because they had all been filled by that point; instead, Bayard offered noble words: "I congratulate you that your name is honorably associated with the maintenance and vindication of principles which constitute the very soul of personal liberty, and which lie at the foundation of our government. To be allied with such principles is honor at all times, with success as a certain finality."[137]

In this second newspaper debate over the Keiley situation, the Washington papers generally took a pro-Bayard position. One ran Bayard's letter to Keiley in full under the headlines "Austrian Bigotry Denounced" and "No Foreign Dictation," lauding American toleration and national sovereignty. The article included comments from Francis in Vienna, who insisted "Austria is tolerant and liberal in respect of religious matters."[138] Another Washington editorial also backed Bayard, saying that Keiley's "rejection by Italy is immaterial." They took Bayard's position that the controversy was about Austrian racial and religious prejudice. The writer noted that "our own Constitution and laws emphatically forbid the recognition of the different races and religions of our people." Even if the government discovered a person's racial or religious identity, the author argued, such information "would be pertinent to nothing."[139] This was, of course, the letter of the law in the United States, but it was hardly observed in practice, as segregationists and nativists continually gained ground in popular opinion.

Other papers were not as kind to the administration. The German-language papers took a pro-Habsburg position.[140] The *New York*

---

[137] "The Keiley Incident," *Washington Post* [?], [1885], enclosed in no. 61, Weissenfeld to Kálnoky, 18 December 1885.

[138] Ibid.

[139] "The Keiley Case," *Washington Post*, [1885], enclosed in no. 61, Weissenfeld to Kálnoky, 18 December 1885.

[140] Clippings from the *New Yorker Staatszeitung* and the *New Yorker Oesterreichisch-Amerikanischen Zeitung*, enclosed in no. 61, Weissenfeld to Kálnoky, 18 December 1885.

Evening Post ran an editorial that was undoubtedly music to the ears of Austro-Hungarian Ministry of Foreign Affairs personnel. The *Post* observed that "we cannot, and never could, send any kind of men we pleased to be consuls or ministers in foreign countries. The Emperor of Austria is not bound to grant the enormous social privileges and legal immunities with which international usage surrounds diplomatic representatives in his own capital, to anybody whom we choose to pick out for the purpose," and added that "The notion that it makes no difference whether they are agreeable or not, and that foreigners ought to like anybody we send, has a flavor of the nursery about it." The author spelled out the social realities of diplomatic life and lauded Kálnoky for doing his duty:

> In all European capitals the foreign Ministers form, ex-officio as it were, part of the best society of the place. Everybody connected with the Government, from the sovereign down, is expected to invite them to balls, dinners, and receptions, on a footing of equality with the highest class in that community. If these civilities were not offered in any particular case, it would be considered, and justly considered, a slight to the country which the Minister represented, as well as to him personally. In European capitals, too, and in Vienna above all capitals, this official society has prejudices and requirements and notions of various sorts, which we here either know nothing of or consider absurd, but which there are very important and have, in fact, for social purposes the force of fundamental rules. . . . When the Foreign Minister of any government has reason to believe that an envoy is being sent to him whose family the society of the place will not tolerate, it is not simply his right, but his duty to do what Count Kálnoky did in this case – refuse to receive him.[141]

The *Post* also identified another crucial issue, noting that "it would do a great deal towards preventing diplomatic rows of this character if we were to abandon the notion that it is our business to reform, or purify, or elevate European society, or that our ministers are sent out as in any sense missionaries."[142] Here, the *Post* was offering a position that was consistent with Washington's command to stay out of European politics, but now the correct way to achieve that goal was to comply with European diplomatic norms. Again, a partisan desire to disagree with the other side made compliance with diplomatic rules a politically viable policy option for the U.S. government.

In his initial telegram, when he had asserted that *agréments* were "generally observed Diplomatic practice," Kálnoky had been on shaky ground. Formal *agréments* were not common, but thinking about the realities of life

---

[141] "The Keiley Correspondence," *The New York Evening Post*, [1885], enclosed in no. 61, Weissenfeld to Kálnoky, 18 December 1885.
[142] Ibid.

at particular posts was normal behavior when making diplomatic appointments. The United States, with its glorified tradition of amateur diplomacy articulated by the Democratic Party, did not often make such considerations. Whether this was his intended goal, Kálnoky scored a major victory through the Keiley affair: every subsequent U.S. diplomat considered for the mission to Austria-Hungary – including those proposed by Democrats – was confirmed by *agrément* prior to leaving the United States to take up his duties.[143] Kálnoky had succeeded in bringing the United States further into the Great Power System by requiring it to make the same kinds of considerations that European states did when making diplomatic appointments.

HENGELMÜLLER, PENFIELD, AND THE HEIGHT OF U.S.-HABSBURG RELATIONS

The last phase of U.S.-Habsburg relations before the outbreak of World War I began in 1894, when Ladislaus Hengelmüller von Hengervár – later Baron Hengelmüller – was appointed to head the Austro-Hungarian legation in Washington. He stayed until 1913, ending a forty-four-year diplomatic career with almost twenty years of service in the United States. Hengelmüller's time in Washington corresponded with a period in the Great Power System when the processes set in motion earlier in the century largely came to fruition: the shift in policy-making from diplomats in the field to central office personnel was essentially complete, thanks to the telegraph and telephone.[144] As a result, the ceremonial and social functions of diplomats were at their greatest level of importance, and the diplomatic corps of Europe and the United States had largely converged in terms of their social composition, level of professionalization, and overall quality.[145] The process of U.S. integration into the Great Power System

---

[143] See no. 3, Weissenfeld to Kálnoky, 4 February 1886, in HHStA, AR, Fach 7, K. 45; File Francis (II); no. 64.567, Hale to Gołuchowski, 23 September 1902; no. 6696, Ambrózy's telegram to MFA, 13 March 1909; no. LXXIX-B, Dumba to MFA, 7 July 1913, all in HHStA, AR, Fach 7, K. 46 – BWV 1906–7; and no. 17, Ambrózy to Aehrenthal, 17 May 1909, in HHStA, PA XXXIII, K. 48 – USA, BWV 1909, folder Berichte.

[144] The French diplomatic corps was an exception; diplomats with the ambassadorial rank continued to hold considerable policy-making power because of the frequent turnover in foreign ministers, which was a result of the volatility of the Third Republic's political culture; see Hayne. On shifts in diplomatic practice, see Schulzinger; Ilchman; Mattox; Werking; Godsey; Lamar Cecil, *The German Diplomatic Service, 1871–1914* (Princeton, 1976); and Jones.

[145] To prove this conclusively requires its own study, but a survey of existing scholarly and amateur works on the various diplomatic corps, as well as an examination of DOS chief of mission records, bears out the basic point that American as well as European diplomats

had also progressed considerably, with its period of closest integration coming during the Theodore Roosevelt and Taft administrations (1901–13). The integration of the United States was symbolized by the sending and receiving of ambassadors by the U.S. government, a phenomenon that began in the 1890s.

When Hengelmüller was first appointed to head the Austro-Hungarian legation in Washington, he was less than thrilled. According to historian William Godsey, Hengelmüller "attributed his American exile to the dislike of Foreign Minister Kálnoky," and his continued service there to similar feelings on the part of Kálnoky's successor, Gołuchowski.[146] The sense that the Washington post was an exile was, of course, common among European diplomats. Hengelmüller made the most of his situation, however, and he provided long and well-appreciated service. He was vital in the maintenance and improvement of U.S.-Habsburg relations. Hengelmüller's departure from Washington coincided with the beginning of the Wilson administration. Although Wilson's choice of Frederick Courtland Penfield as U.S. ambassador to Vienna was a positive one in terms of maintaining the Great Power System and U.S. recognition of Habsburg legitimacy, Wilson's overall contempt of Great Power diplomacy – in keeping with Democratic tradition – contributed decisively to the removal of the Habsburg Empire from the international political system and the creation of a new, conflictual diplomatic culture in the post-1919 world.

Hengelmüller was a Hungarian, and, when he left Europe in 1894, he was fluent in both German and Magyar, as well as several other languages, including English. His attachment to the Habsburg state was far stronger than his attachment to Hungary – as befitted a Habsburg diplomat – and his Magyar got very rusty while he was in Washington, although he did maintain his German. The Habsburg diplomatic corps generally remained a bastion of the old aristocracy, but Hengelmüller himself was a product of the nineteenth-century service nobility. His grandfather had been a butcher in Upper Austria, and his father had entered the civil service. Hengelmüller completed the family's transition to the nobility by marrying Countess Albertine Borkowska, a member of an old noble family from Galicia.[147]

---

were partially but imperfectly professionalized and drew their ranks predominantly from the most affluent segment of society before World War I.

[146] Godsey, 174.

[147] Ibid., 144–45, 20, 95. Godsey's main thesis throughout his book is the persistence of the old aristocracy in the ministry.

In Godsey's account, he states that Hengelmüller and his wife were not noted for their "social gifts," but they seem to have done extremely well in Washington.[148] On their final departure in 1913, the *Washington Post* observed that "Official and social Washington will greatly regret the departure of Baron Hengelmueller, the Ambassador of Austria-Hungary, and Baroness Hengelmueller. During a residence of eighteen years in Washington the Ambassador and Ambassadress have constantly widened their circle of friends, and the news of their final leave-taking will be heard with a sense of personal loss in Washington."[149] Secretary of State Philander Knox wrote to Hengelmüller in 1912 that "You and the Baroness have been here so long that we have come to claim a proprietary interest in you and have adopted you as American citizens in every except the technical sense."[150] In addition to their time in Washington, Hengelmüller and his wife summered with American and European elites in various New England summer communities, especially Bar Harbor, Maine. In their summer residences, they further expanded their social circle to include a number of prominent private American citizens.[151] Most important was Hengelmüller's close friendship with Theodore Roosevelt; that personal relationship was essential in strengthening a positive official relationship between the United States and Austria-Hungary.[152]

Hengelmüller's long service in Washington also meant that he was the senior member of the city's diplomatic corps for several years. His lengthy stay at the top of the diplomatic corps brought attention and prestige to himself, his government, and his country. The *Washington Post* observed that "His high character, great ability, and dignified bearing made it peculiarly appropriate that he should stand at the head of the body of

[148] Ibid., 98.
[149] "Departure of Baron Hengelmuller," *Washington Post*, [1912], enclosed in 12.9.12, Hengelmüller to Berchtold, 24 August 1912, in HHStA, PA XXXIII, K. 50 – USA, BWV 1912, folder Varia 1912.
[150] Knox to Hengelmüller, 14 August 1912, enclosed in 12.9.12, Hengelmüller to Berchtold, 24 August 1912.
[151] "Austrian Ambassador, Now at Bar Harbor, Has Spent 20 Years in the U.S.," 23 August 1912, enclosed in 12.9.12, Hengelmüller to Berchtold, 24 August 1912.
[152] See, for example, no. 33 A-C, Hengelmüller to Gołuchowski, 30 December 1902, in HHStA, PA XXXIII, K. 42 – BWV 1902. On Roosevelt's personal diplomacy, see Nelson M. Blake, "Ambassadors at the Court of Theodore Roosevelt," *Mississippi Valley Historical Review* 42, 2 (1955): 179–206; and Aaron Forsberg, "Ambassador J. J. Jusserand, Theodore Roosevelt, and Franco-American Relations," in *Theodore Roosevelt – Many-Sided American*, ed. Natalie A. Naylor, Douglas Brinkley, and John Allen Gable (Interlaken, 1992), 329–40.

men who represent the nations at the American capital," and added that "because of the tactfulness and charm of the Ambassador and Ambassadress, ... the geniality and spirit of the entire diplomatic corps have been enhanced."[153]

Hengelmüller did his job well. In conjunction with the consular service, he took an active role in dealing with citizenship and protection cases arising from the movement of people back and forth between Austria-Hungary and the United States, which was the most important aspect of his office work. He reported on domestic and American political conditions, as well as on U.S. foreign policy and discussions that took place among the diplomatic corps in Washington.[154] Often, there was not much to say. One summer, he reported to Foreign Minister Gołuchowski that "Feuilleton Artikel hätte ich Euer Excellenz diesen Sommer über Amerika schreiben können, politische Berichte nicht."[155] His one major foray into the traditional realm of international politics came in the 1890s, when the United States and Spain were on the brink of war over Cuba. Hengelmüller attempted to use his influence in Washington on behalf of the Spanish government to avoid a war, but he obviously was unsuccessful. He did manage to avoid bad publicity over his involvement for himself, his government, and Austria-Hungary generally, which was perhaps as much as he could have realistically hoped for.[156]

The few conflicts occurring between the United States and Austria-Hungary during Hengelmüller's tenure were primarily about diplomatic form. There was a small tempest in the U.S. press over Austrian reaction to President McKinley's assassination. In the Great Power System, on the occasion of the death of a member nation's leader, it was customary for the other governments in the system to express their condolences. Although this could take several different forms, one common practice was for the

[153] "Departure of Baron Hengelmuller."

[154] Matsch, *Wien-Washington.*

[155] "This summer I could write feature articles about America, but not political reports." No. 13, Hengelmüller to Gołuchowski, 27 August 1906, in HHStA, PA XXXIII, K. 46 – BWV 1906–7, folder Berichte 1906. The *feuillton* was a special Viennese literary institution, whose most noted practitioners include Theodore Herzl and Karl Kraus.

[156] On Hengelmüller's efforts, see Matsch, *Wien-Washington;* no. 4 B, Hengelmüller to Gołuchowski, 4 February 1902, in HHStA, PA XXXIII, K. 42 – BWV 1902; and Nicole Slupetzky, "Austria and the Spanish-American War," in *European Perceptions of the Spanish-American War,* ed. by Sylvia L. Hilton and Steve J. S. Ickringill (Bern, 1999), 181–94. On the war, see Kristin Hoganson, *Fighting for American Manhood: How Gender Politics Provoked the Spanish-American and Philippine-American Wars* (New Haven, 1998).

sympathetic legislature to vote to send a message of condolence to the legislature in the afflicted country. When McKinley died in September 1901, the Austrian Reichsrat was not in session, and so condolences were sent through other agents of the Habsburg government. When the Reichsrat did convene again in November, its members did not acknowledge McKinley's death, and a storm of protest arose in American newspapers.[157] There were, however, two more significant conflicts in U.S.-Habsburg relations during Hengelmüller's tenure that demonstrated integration of the United States into the Great Power System, but also the limits of that integration: the decision to raise U.S.-Austro-Hungarian relations to the ambassadorial rank, and the events surrounding the questionable conduct of the first U.S. ambassador in Vienna, Mr. Bellamy Storer, and his wife.

The question of the use of the ambassadorial rank was already a contentious one in the Great Power System, with the Habsburg government stalling for years before appointing ambassadors to Italy and Spain. As previously discussed, the use of this rank was supposed to coincide with Great Power status and thus reinforce the basic hierarchy of the system, but the extension of the ambassadorial rank to Italy and Spain began to destabilize the system because actual power and symbolism were no longer in sync. The United States had stayed out of the issue for much of the century; its rhetorical tradition of noninvolvement in European affairs kept U.S. leaders from pushing for the extension of the rank to American diplomats.

In the late 1880s – during the one Republican presidency between Cleveland's two nonconsecutive terms – some Americans began to push for the United States to be recognized as a Great Power, with the right to exchange ambassadors. They argued that the United States was at least as powerful as the European Great Powers and deserved to be recognized as a premier world power. They drew on the rhetoric of racialist thinking – particularly Anglo-Saxonism – and "civilization" that was helping to overcome the Old World-New World dichotomy in American thinking and to replace it with the idea of a transatlantic white civilization.[158] They were able to connect civilized behavior and Great Power status with U.S. compliance with European diplomatic norms, thus overcoming many –

---

[157] No. 26 C, Hengelmüller to Gołuchowski, 12 November 1901, in HHStA, PA XXXIII, K. 41 – BWV 1901.
[158] Bederman; and Paul Kramer, "Empires, Exceptions, and Anglo-Saxons: Race and Rule between the British and U.S. Empires, 1880–1910," *JAH* 88, 4 (2002): 1315–53.

but certainly not all – of the objections to an allegedly frivolous and un-American diplomacy.

The first victory for these "civilization" proponents was the establishment of a British embassy in Washington; a reluctant Queen Victoria approved it in 1889, and the first ambassador arrived the following year.[159] Congressional debates slowed the approval process in the United States considerably, and the U.S. government was not able to reciprocate by sending an ambassador to London until 1893. U.S. embassies were also opened that year in Paris, Berlin, and Rome, and an ambassador was sent to St. Petersburg in 1898.

Austria-Hungary was conspicuously absent from this list, and Hengelmüller began to lobby the Habsburg government for an embassy in Washington. He argued that, not only was the United States an increasingly important country that affected the European system by engaging with Great Powers in other parts of the world, but also that the Habsburg government should consider its image in American opinion.[160] With Theodore Roosevelt's assumption of the presidency following McKinley's assassination in 1901, the American press began to agitate for an Austro-Hungarian embassy in Washington. That this call came on the heels of McKinley's death is no coincidence: the funeral observances were a huge ceremonial event, and the status of the Habsburg representative would have been widely noticed because of press coverage of diplomatic participation in the funeral ceremonies.[161] In 1902, the U.S. and Habsburg governments agreed to raise their representatives to ambassadors. Hengelmüller was promoted as of 1 January 1903 – the same day that the new U.S. ambassador, Bellamy Storer, presented his credentials in Vienna. Roosevelt was enthusiastic about the change for both political and personal reasons. Yet another country was recognizing U.S. importance, which pleased the president, and he wrote to Hengelmüller that "This elevation of the rank of your mission is the more gratifying to me in as much as the agreeable personal associations of the past eight years are thus continued."[162]

---

[159] Jones. That the British were first to accept Italy, Spain, the United States, and Japan into the circle of ambassadors reflects British strength and security in their isolated geographic position. They could afford a destabilization of the system more than the Habsburg government.

[160] Godsey, 175.

[161] See Nicole Phelps, "The Deaths of European Monarchs and American Perceptions of the International System, 1870–1920" (MA thesis, University of Minnesota, 2003).

[162] No. 33 A-C, Hengelmüller to Gołuchowski, 30 December 1902.

The incorporation of the United States into the Great Power System through the exchange of ambassadors made a great deal of sense. The United States was a large and powerful country, and its economic and political interests throughout the world brought it into frequent contact with European governments at home and in the colonies. It was a significant actor in international politics generally and in the European Great Power System, notwithstanding the persistent rhetorical tradition that proclaimed American isolation.

Even as the U.S. government conformed to common diplomatic practices, however, many U.S. officials were not fully committed to the underlying principles of the Great Power System, including the spirit behind the use of the ambassadorial rank. They bought into the trappings of the system, but not into the underlying sense of community in the Great Power System. In 1898, the U.S. government began using the ambassadorial rank outside Europe. The government sent ambassadors to Mexico City in 1898, Rio de Janeiro in 1905, Santiago and Buenos Aires in 1914, and Guatemala City in 1916.[163] In some ways, these embassies were consistent with the meaning attached to embassies in the Great Power System – they symbolized that the relationship between the two countries was important. In the Great Power System, however, an ambassador meant that the sending government viewed the host government as a legitimate equal, and the exchange of ambassadors was also an affirmation of the system's norm of noninterference. The U.S. government did not adopt this spirit of equality and nonintervention in Latin America; embassies were instead used to project U.S. power into the host countries, which few U.S. officials considered equal to the United States.[164] Instead of demonstrating true equality and respect, embassies were on their way to becoming, at best, "empty shells" and, at worst, tools of hegemony or imperialism.[165]

The first American ambassador appointed to Vienna initially appeared to represent the qualities and practices that had come to be expected of Great Powers. Bellamy Storer was typical of U.S. diplomats serving in Europe between the Civil War and World War I in terms of his education, political connections, and previous diplomatic experience.[166] An Ohio

---

[163] A U.S. embassy in Madrid opened in 1913 as well.
[164] See Ron Theodore Robin, *Enclaves of America: The Rhetoric of American Political Architecture Abroad, 1900–1965* (Princeton, 1992).
[165] Jones refers to twentieth-century embassies as "empty shells" (174).
[166] This claim is based on a survey of U.S. DOS, *Principal Officers*; it is supported by Mattox.

native, he had graduated from Harvard in 1867 and gone on to practice law in Cincinnati. Storer was a well-connected Republican: his father had been a congressman and an important Ohio judge, and he was also related to the Longworth family, which was powerful in Republican politics. Because of his connections and his party affiliations, Storer did well in terms of patronage appointments, beginning with a position as an assistant U.S. attorney. When the Democrats briefly held the White House in the early 1890s, he served two terms in the House of Representatives. With McKinley's election in 1896, and the subsequent Republican return to power, Storer began a career as a diplomat: he served briefly in Washington as assistant secretary of state in 1897 before being appointed U.S. envoy to Belgium (1897–99) and then to Spain (1899–1902). In 1902, he was appointed to head the embassy in Vienna. Given his previous diplomatic experience, Storer should have known how to behave when representing the United States abroad.

In March 1906, the troubles began. In the preceding weeks, President Roosevelt had received a series of troubling communications from and about Storer. The ambassador had telegraphed the White House in code to request that his wife be given official authorization to represent the United States at the Vatican, where she wanted to discuss the appointment of a second cardinal in the United States. According to other communications, Mrs. Storer had apparently encouraged her husband to translate his official status in Vienna into a private mission to the Vatican. She was also allegedly working with a network of elite, Catholic, European women to arrange a marriage between Princess Klementine of Belgium and Prince Victor Bonaparte, who together would then overthrow the French Third Republic and restore a Catholic monarchy in France. As these allegations reached the president and his secretary of state, Elihu Root, they tried to contact Storer for an explanation, but Storer ignored their letters and telegrams and cut off all correspondence with Washington.[167]

To say the least, this was not the kind of behavior Roosevelt expected from any U.S. diplomat, especially one of Storer's experience. Roosevelt was faced with a dilemma. Clearly, the Storers had the potential to become a huge political liability for Roosevelt if news of their activities reached the press. On a personal level, the gender-conscious Roosevelt was not at all

---

[167] No. 8, Hengelmüller to Gołuchowski, 23 April 1906; no. 7832, Hengelmüller's telegram to MFA, 19 March 1906; and no. 7C, Hengelmüller to Gołuchowski, 9 April 1906, all in HHStA, AR, Fach 7, K. 46. See also no. 19 A-C, Széchenyi to Aehrenthal, 17 December 1906, in HHStA, PA XXXIII, K. 46, folder Berichte 1906.

pleased that Ambassador Storer was apparently not in control of his wife.[168] That concern was likely exacerbated by the fact that Storer's nephew, Congressman Nicholas Longworth, had just married Roosevelt's daughter, Alice, in February, making the connection between Roosevelt and Storer closer and more personal. More important were larger political concerns. Anti-Catholicism had a long tradition in the United States, and many people particularly feared the expansion of the Church hierarchy's influence in the United States, which was exactly what Mrs. Storer was out to achieve.

Finally, Roosevelt was on a mission to improve the position of the United States in the world, to have the United States treated with the respect he felt it deserved – that is, as a Great Power of equal stature with Britain, France, Germany, Russia, and Austria-Hungary.[169] Roosevelt understood that the inclusion of the United States in world affairs as a Great Power hinged on its ability to behave in a manner acceptable to the existing, recognized Great Powers. That meant adhering to the rules and norms of diplomacy put in place at the 1815 Congress of Vienna. Roosevelt faced significant challenges to his program; for the entirety of U.S. history, a significant and vocal part of the U.S. population criticized diplomacy as "intrigue," an immoral European monarchical practice antithetical to the republican United States.[170] These critics had blocked the development of an American diplomatic corps and the country's integration into the Great Power System whenever possible. Mrs. Storer's clandestine efforts to expand the Catholic Church's influence and regain the French throne through a strategic royal marriage fit the negative stereotype of diplomacy perfectly and were therefore dangerous to Roosevelt's integrationist plans.

Roosevelt ultimately decided that Storer would have to be recalled from his post – in layman's terms, he would have to be fired. Roosevelt and Root hoped to keep the whole situation out of the papers as much as possible,

---

[168] See no. 8, Hengelmüller to Gołuchowski, 23 April 1906. On Roosevelt and gender roles, see, among numerous others, his famous 1900 speech, "The Strenuous Life"; and Hoganson.

[169] On Roosevelt's ambitions, see Raimund Lammersdorf, *Anfänge einer Weltmacht: Theodore Roosevelt und die transatlantischen Beziehungen der USA, 1901–1909* (Berlin, 1994); John Milton Cooper, *The Warrior and the Priest: Woodrow Wilson and Theodore Roosevelt* (Cambridge MA, 1983); Richard H. Collin, *Theodore Roosevelt, Culture, Diplomacy, and Expansion: A New View of American Imperialism* (Baton Rouge, 1985); and Howard K. Beale, *Theodore Roosevelt and the Rise of America to World Power* (Baltimore, 1956).

[170] On the tradition of opposition to diplomacy, see Ilchman.

and so they opted to telegraph Storer quietly and tell him to step down from his post and come home. They also agreed that Storer should be replaced by Charles Francis, who had previously been in charge of the U.S. legation at Athens, and they made arrangements for Francis to proceed to Vienna: if Storer ignored the telegram, he would still have to deal with Francis in person.[171]

Roosevelt and Root put their plan in motion, but they had neglected one crucial element: they had given the Austro-Hungarian government no indication that Storer's recall was in progress. Proper form would have been to tell the Austro-Hungarian ambassador in Washington so he could quietly inform the Ministry of Foreign Affairs in Vienna. Roosevelt and Root certainly had opportunities to mention it: Ambassador Hengelmüller was a fixture in Washington society, and he was personal friends with Roosevelt. He had spent several weekends at the president's estate in Oyster Bay, and he was also a frequent guest at White House events.[172] Hengelmüller's relationship with Root was not as close, but he regularly visited Root's office at the State Department, and Root could easily have brought the matter up at such a meeting. In fact, Root and Hengelmüller had met just three days before Storer's recall became public, and Root had mentioned nothing about the situation.[173]

On 22 March 1906, news of Storer's recall and his replacement by Francis appeared in the Washington evening newspapers; no reason for the recall was printed. On reading the news, a surprised and affronted Hengelmüller telegraphed the Ministry of Foreign Affairs in Vienna to report the recall and to say that he had had no prior warning or explanation, despite his recent meeting with Root.[174] He was in an awkward position: he was ignorant about an extremely important development involving his country, and that lack of knowledge would look bad to his superiors in Vienna. After all, one of the main points of posting diplomats abroad was to gather information about events in the host country. Hengelmüller was also offended for himself and for his country. The

---

[171] It never came to that. Storer stepped down quietly. He returned briefly to the United States, then he and his wife moved to France, where he died in 1922.

[172] See Hengelmüller to Gołuchowski, 13 August 1904, in HHStA, PA XXXIII, K. 42; the various personal letters from Hengelmüller to Aehrenthal in HHStA, PA XXXIII, K. 47 – USA, BWV 1908, folder Varia; and no. 111, Francis to Root, 6 December 1906, in *M862: Numerical and Minor Files of the Department of State, 1906–1910, roll 315, Cases 3381–3388* (Washington, 1972), case no. 3388.

[173] No. 7832, Hengelmüller to MFA, 19 March 1906.

[174] Ibid.

norms of the diplomatic culture of the Great Power System called for the sharing of such information, and interpersonal norms should have led Roosevelt to inform his friend of the news.

The personnel of the Ministry of Foreign Affairs in Vienna were also placed in an awkward position because they did not know how Storer's recall should be interpreted. Had Storer personally done something to injure the Austro-Hungarian government or abuse his position? If so, the president or some other member of the U.S. government should have informed the ministry in case Austro-Hungarian officials needed to take steps to repair the damage. If it was not a personal action on Storer's part that prompted his recall, then the other interpretation open to Ministry of Foreign Affairs personnel was that the U.S. government as a whole was symbolically indicating its displeasure with something the Austro-Hungarian government had done. Typically, in the Great Power System, that was what a recall meant, and it was a serious event. A recall could indicate a severance of diplomatic relations, and that could serve as a prelude to war.

Foreign ministry staff were at a loss to determine what specific grievance the United States government might have against Austria-Hungary in March 1906, and so they opted to take the pragmatic course of waiting for Hengelmüller to send them more information before they took action. Three days after he sent his telegram containing the initial news, Hengelmüller spoke to Root and was able to send a bit more information to Foreign Minister Gołuchowski. According to Root, "Mr. Storer's recall had absolutely nothing to do with his administration as ambassador or with mutual relations [between Austria-Hungary and the United States], but was necessary because of the indiscretions of his spouse."[175]

Hengelmüller and Gołuchowski were inclined to trust Root's basic explanation, but they still needed to decide how to handle the Roosevelt administration's failure to inform the Austro-Hungarian government of Storer's recall before it became public knowledge. One choice would have been for Hengelmüller to deliver a formal, written protest to Secretary of State Root. Such an action was perfectly acceptable in contemporary diplomatic culture, and it would have signaled strong, serious dissatisfaction on the part of the Austro-Hungarian government. It also would have been a public action: undoubtedly, the text of the protest would have ended up in American, Austro-Hungarian, and other European

---

[175] No. 6488, Hengelmüller's telegram to Gołuchowski, 22 March 1906, in HHStA, AR, Fach 7, K. 46.

newspapers. If the press became involved, the subject would be open to public commentary in newspapers on both sides of the Atlantic, and it would have received attention in the U.S. House and Senate and possibly in the Austrian Reichsrat and Hungarian parliament. With public discussion, the situation could quickly spiral out of executive branch control and become far more serious than necessary. Debates over diplomatic form in the American press usually included criticism of diplomacy in general and would likely also include criticism of Austria-Hungary as being frivolous enough to care about form. Austro-Hungarian foreign ministry personnel undoubtedly also considered that a serious dispute with the Roosevelt administration could reduce Republican credibility with the American public and result in an undesirable Democratic take-over of the executive branch at the next election. All this rhetoric would hurt the Habsburg goal of American compliance with Great Power System norms and contribute to a negative image of Austria-Hungary in the United States.

Given the risks involved in issuing a formal protest, the Austro-Hungarian government opted to pursue a different, equally permissible course of action: they would have Hengelmüller discuss the matter privately with Roosevelt at a social gathering. Using this strategy, the Austro-Hungarians hoped to translate the personal friendship between Hengelmüller and Roosevelt into future American compliance with diplomatic norms. Because the discussions would be carried out in private, the stakes for Roosevelt would be lower, and the Austro-Hungarian government would therefore be more likely to obtain his compliance. A social event was more desirable than a scheduled meeting at the White House because, in the event of a formal meeting, the press would speculate on the cause and content, but the mutual attendance of the president and the ambassador at a dinner or reception was so commonplace as to be unworthy of the label "news."[176]

Roosevelt opted to cooperate with the Austro-Hungarian strategy. According to Hengelmüller, the two men discussed "the Storer Affair" several times at various Washington social events, and Hengelmüller noted that Roosevelt was eager for these private conversations. Because of their years of friendship, Hengelmüller was able to speak "with deliberate frankness," and he told Roosevelt in no uncertain terms that Roosevelt and Root had erred when they neglected to inform Hengelmüller or the Ministry of Foreign Affairs of Storer's imminent recall. Although he could

---

[176] No. 8, Hengelmüller to Gołuchowski, 23 April 1906.

not undo what was already done, Roosevelt accepted Hengelmüller's criticism and responded by giving Hengelmüller the full details of Mr. and Mrs. Storer's transgressions, including details that he had managed to keep from the press.[177] Roosevelt was by no means obligated to accept Hengelmüller's words or share such information: he could have done what some of his predecessors had done in similar situations; namely, go to the press and thereby rally American public indignation over Austro-Hungarian criticism. Instead, Roosevelt and Hengelmüller were able to use tactics accepted in the Great Power culture of diplomacy to resolve the conflict successfully and with relatively little damage to either individual, either government, or U.S.-Habsburg relations in general. In the Storer case, the Austro-Hungarian government achieved its goal of maintaining a positive relationship with the United States that conformed to the norms of Great Power diplomacy and therefore reaffirmed the legitimate sovereignty of the Habsburg government.

Ambassador Hengelmüller ended his long career in Washington in 1913, just weeks before Woodrow Wilson became president. His replacement was Dr. Konstantin Dumba, who proved a disaster for U.S.-Habsburg relations. Wilson had a marked contempt for diplomacy and the Great Power System, and his first secretary of state, William Jennings Bryan, very much shared that opinion. Wilson failed to see the cooperative and community-building aspects of Great Power diplomatic culture and instead viewed it as slavish devotion to a balance of power and to national self-interest, with diplomats engaged in meaningless or even harmful frivolity and intrigue. Since diplomats were unimportant to Wilson, political patronage concerns were paramount when he selected diplomats. Earlier Republican efforts to achieve a modicum of professionalization of the diplomatic corps and the State Department staff limited to a degree the extent of damage Wilson and Bryan could do. Also, Wilson and Bryan followed a tradition established by the Republicans and appointed several people who had served abroad during the Cleveland administration, thus bringing some experienced men into the system. On the whole, however, the cavalier attitude with which these men and many of their appointees approached diplomacy did more to undermine the system than to maintain it.[178]

---

[177] Ibid.
[178] On Wilson and Bryan, see Seward W. Livermore, "'Deserving Democrats': The Foreign Service Under Woodrow Wilson," *South Atlantic Quarterly* 69, 1 (1970): 144–60; Rachel West, *The Department of State on the Eve of the First World War* (Athens,

Despite the contempt Wilson and Bryan felt for European diplomacy, they managed to appoint an ambassador to Vienna who excelled at his job. Frederick Courtland Penfield was very much a product of a New England-based transatlantic elite. Born in Connecticut in 1855, he attended a prestigious military academy and later attended Princeton. He also studied abroad in Germany, where he became fluent in German.[179] He worked as an editor of a newspaper in Hartford for five years before President Cleveland appointed him to serve as a vice consul-general in London in 1885. During Cleveland's second term, Penfield was the U.S. diplomatic agent in Cairo for four years. His elite familial connections, his diplomatic service, his private travels, and his writings contributed to the collection of a set of credentials that rivaled those of a good many European diplomats.[180]

In 1908, he added to his achievements by marrying Mrs. Anna Weightman Walker, the widow of a Philadelphia entrepreneur who had made a considerable fortune in the chemical industry.[181] Her fortune – which, of course, became Penfield's – was estimated to be at least $30 million.[182] With those millions, the Penfields gave a considerable amount to both the Democratic Party and Wilson's 1912 campaign fund; their goal was to get an embassy if Wilson was elected. Having studied in Germany, Penfield originally preferred Berlin, but Wilson gave him Vienna instead, which turned out to be a good match.[183] In addition to being wealthy, cosmopolitan speakers of German, the Penfields were devoutly Catholic. They fit extremely well into Viennese society. Mrs. Penfield became a particular favorite of Emperor Franz Joseph, and, during the war, she

1978); and Stuart. On Republican reform efforts, see Ilchman; Schulzinger; Mattox; Werking; and Stuart. Professionalization measures included the introduction of entrance examinations, foreign language requirements, and the establishment of an inspection team that conducted regular reviews of personnel. These measures were not strictly enforced. Similar trends and lax enforcement could be found in most other European diplomatic corps. See Jones; Hayne; and Godsey.

[179] On the importance of study in Germany on shaping American society at the turn of the century, see Daniel T. Rodgers, *Atlantic Crossings: Social Politics in a Progressive Age* (Cambridge MA, 1998).

[180] See Penfield's entry in *Who Is Who in America for 1913*, in no. LXXIX-B, Dumba to MFA, 7 July 1913.

[181] Mrs. Walker was Penfield's second wife. From 1892 until her death in 1905, he was married to Catherine Albert McMurdo.

[182] No. LXXIX-B, Dumba to MFA, 7 July 1913. See also no. 4658, Dumba's telegram to MFA, 29 June 1913, in HHStA, AR, Fach 7, K. 46.

[183] On his campaign contributions and his desire for Berlin, see West.

and her niece received prestigious decorations from the emperor for their volunteer work with local nursing services.[184]

Penfield took the routine office duties of his job very seriously as well. Many diplomats serving both European countries and the United States worked very short hours, sometimes limiting office hours to as little as four hours a day. This was not Penfield's style: the U.S. embassy was typically open from nine in the morning until six in the evening, and Penfield and his staff often stayed later to complete the day's work, which focused primarily on citizenship and protection cases. He repeatedly asked for a larger staff so that he could devote more time to the social aspects of his job. In December 1913, he wrote to the secretary of state:

> But with the cooperation of the Secretary of the Embassy, who on occasions worked with me until midnight, neither the routine office work nor the strict observance of the outside etiquette has suffered. But the work was at times extremely onerous. So busy have I been since coming to Vienna that I have been not once to theatre or opera, dined out not once, had little time to look for a residence, and given but one formal dinner – that of Thanksgiving night, when I entertained the Embassy staff, the Consul-General and family, the officials of the American Medical Association in Vienna, and members of the American colony.[185]

He also added that "No other Embassy at this capital is run with a staff as small as this Embassy of the United States of America."[186] He could afford to pay another man himself – he had told the secretary of state that "It has been a pleasure to pay from my own pocket for a great many services accruing to the benefit of the Embassy" – but to do a secretary's job properly, he needed an official title and a salary paid by the U.S. government and approved by Congress.[187]

Penfield's dedication to his job was much appreciated by the Habsburg government, but the fact that Penfield had become the main center of stability, friendship, and mutual recognition in the U.S.-Habsburg relationship after Hengelmüller's departure from Washington was very dangerous for the Habsburg government. Although Penfield did his job very well, sending a multitude of reports home to Washington, such reports were rarely taken into consideration by the overworked State Department

---

[184] Mrs. Penfield received the Order of Elizabeth First Class; Miss Georgia Penfield received the Order of Elizabeth Second Class. See 77.645/1, Berchtold to Franz Joseph, 28 September 1914; and 82.221/1, Berchtold to Franz Joseph, 6 October 1914, both in HHStA, AR, Fach 7, K. 46.

[185] No. 38, Penfield to SecState, 10 December 1913, file no. 124.63/-, in NARA.

[186] Ibid.

[187] Ibid.

staff, and Penfield's were no exception. What the Habsburg government needed to ensure continued American recognition of its legitimate sovereignty was a well-liked advocate in Washington who could minimize the impact of the anti-diplomacy Democratic administration on the Great Power System in general and Habsburg sovereignty in particular. Ambassador Dumba was not up to this task, although he had performed well at his earlier, European posts. With the outbreak of fighting in World War I, the diplomatic structures of the Great Power System that helped bind the United States and Austria-Hungary fell away one by one, creating an opportunity for American recognition of alternative sovereignties in Central Europe.

3

Protection and the Problems of Dual Citizenship

U.S. Consuls in the Habsburg Empire

Charles Moerser was born in Krakow, Galicia, Austria in 1858.[1] His parents had previously lived in England for a time, and the family appears to have spoken both German and English at home.[2] In 1859, his father went to the United States to find work, and the next year Charles, his mother, and his six older siblings joined their father in the United States. Seven years later, Charles and his parents returned to Krakow. Nine years after that, in 1874, a sixteen-year-old Charles "borrowed" 500 marks from his employer to make a journey to America – borrowed without permission. What Charles did in the United States for the next several years is uncertain, but, in February 1881, he enlisted in the U.S. Army and fought the Apaches in Arizona and New Mexico. He started going by the name

---

[1] Galicia became part of Poland after World War I. Charles Moerser's case can be found in no. 353, Grant to Gresham, 9 April 1893, in *T157: Despatches from United States Ministers to Austria, 1838–1906*, 51 vols. (Washington, 1959). The despatch contains thirteen enclosures, including correspondence among Charles, his father, the U.S. legation in Vienna, and various personnel of the Habsburg Ministry of Foreign Affairs. The enclosures also include two personal accounts of Moerser's life story, which, when compared, reflect minor differences (or possibly just unintentional errors made while the author was writing).

[2] From the details available about Moerser's life in DOS files, it seems very likely that his family was Jewish, but that is never explicitly mentioned. I base this assumption primarily on Moerser's ability to speak German and English, his inability to speak Polish, and the family's ability to travel as early as the 1850s. That he did not speak Polish suggests that he was a minority in the predominantly Polish-speaking province of Galicia, and Jews in the Habsburg Empire were often German speakers. That the family had the financial means to travel to England and the United States in the 1850s suggests that they were more prosperous than many Galicians and likely involved in trade, rather than agriculture; Jews played a prominent role in the empire's commerce.

Charles Mercy, most likely to appear more "American" – that is, Anglo-Saxon and Christian. After his military service, he moved to Newark, New Jersey, where his naturalization as a U.S. citizen was finalized in November 1884. Two years later, he was married, and he and his wife went on to have three American-born children. In Newark, Charles opened a hat factory, and, by 1893, it was a successful operation with approximately 150 employees. Charles also owned real estate in New Jersey. He was flourishing.

Although we do not know much about the fate of Charles's parents and siblings, we do know that his father was living in Krakow in 1893, as was one of Charles's sisters, who had married a Polish-speaking man there. At some point prior to 1893, Charles sent money to this brother-in-law – money that was supposed to be used to pay back the 500 marks Charles had taken when he left Austria in 1874. Unbeknownst to Charles, his brother-in-law pocketed at least half the money.

Not yet aware that his brother-in-law was not entirely trustworthy, Charles traveled to Krakow in early 1893 to visit his family and pursue a potentially lucrative business opportunity. The plan was to give his brother-in-law the capital to start a business that would process rabbits for use in Charles's New Jersey hat factory. When Charles arrived in Krakow and met his brother-in-law, he realized that the man was neither a good potential business partner nor a good husband to his sister. Charles changed his plan: he would take his sister back to the United States and set her up with a dress-making shop, leaving her husband to fend for himself in Austria.

On 24 February 1893, as Charles was waiting for the train in Krakow to begin the first leg of his journey back to the United States – it is unclear whether or not his sister was with him – his brother-in-law came to the train station to demand that Charles give him money. Charles refused; his brother-in-law called for the police. When they arrived, the man spoke to them in Polish, which Charles did not understand, telling them that Charles was using an alias to hide his identity, that his real name was Saul Moeser (not Moerser), and that, back in 1874, he had stolen 500 marks. Charles, uncertain of what was going on because of the language barrier, was arrested and jailed. The authorities confiscated the papers Charles was carrying, which included his naturalization papers, the only documents in his possession that could prove his U.S. citizenship.

Charles's father contacted the U.S. legation and consulate in Vienna to alert them to the situation. His sense of the details was not very good – for example, he said that Charles had served in the Mexican War, which had actually occurred ten years before Charles's birth – and the legation advised him to have Charles himself write and provide the details of the situation.[3] While this was occurring, Charles paid back the entirety of the 500 marks he had taken, and on 4 March, he was able to post his own 1,000-florin bail. Once out of jail, Charles wrote to the legation, providing a biography that stressed his military service and the fact that he had a wife, children, and property in the United States. He complained that the local authorities had confiscated his papers and then asked him to prove his U.S. citizenship, despite the fact that they held the documents that demonstrated his citizenship. He also wrote that he had been stuck in a "filthy" jail "with a lot of Poles."[4]

Frederick Grant, the head of the U.S. legation in Vienna, wrote to Count Welsersheimb, the chief of the relevant section of the Habsburg Ministry of Foreign Affairs, to ask for the ministry's assistance in sorting out the case and dismissing the charges against Charles. Welsersheimb responded that the legal proceedings had to continue, since Charles had committed a crime prior to his emigration, and the 1870 U.S.-Habsburg naturalization treaty was on the Habsburg government's side on the matter.[5] Grant then took a different tack, going over Welsersheimb's head to Count Kálnoky, the minister of foreign affairs. Rather than focusing on the theft, Grant complained that it was unfair and illogical for the local authorities to "take the responsibility of seizing the identification papers of a citizen of a friendly power, and hold him to prove his foreign citizenship which they have made it impossible for him to prove."[6]

On 15 March, the day after Grant had addressed his communication to Kálnoky, Charles arrived at the legation in Vienna and gave a more formal statement about the situation.[7] Grant advocated the simplest way out: Charles should simply return to the United States before his trial, and the whole mess would go away. Grant wrote, "I said to Mr. Mercy, that if he withdrew from this country before his trial, that such action would be recognized technically as an acknowledgment of his guilt and that he

---

[3] E. F. Moerser's statement to the U.S. legation at Vienna, enclosure 1 of no. 353, Grant to Gresham, 9 April 1893.

[4] Mercy to Grant, 7 March 1893, enclosure 7 of no. 353, Grant to Gresham, 9 April 1893.

[5] Welsersheimb to Grant, 1 March 1893, enclosure 5 of no. 353, Grant to Gresham, 9 April 1893.

[6] Grant to Kálnoky, 14 March 1893, enclosure 10 of no. 353, Grant to Gresham, 9 April 1893.

[7] Mercy's 15 March 1893 statement to legation, paraphrased and quoted in no. 353, Grant to Gresham, 9 April 1893.

would not only forfeit his bail by such action, but would also be liable to arrest if he ever returned to this country." The record of the case ends with a letter Grant wrote to the State Department in mid April 1893, informing them of all the details and telling them that he presumed that Charles had returned to the United States to stay.[8]

Charles Mercy's story provides an example of several important nineteenth-century trends. For economic and financial reasons, he crossed the Atlantic at least five times in his life, an activity that became increasingly common among an ever-broader segment of the European and North American population as the century progressed. He maintained connections with his family in Europe while he was in the United States, and his plan had been to use those transatlantic family ties to achieve a more prosperous economic position for himself and his family. To gain acceptance in the United States, he changed his name, served in the army, got married, had children, purchased property, and became a naturalized citizen. That he put down so many roots in the United States undoubtedly made him more successful there than many of his fellow immigrants, who planned to work for a few years to earn money and then return to Europe.[9]

His story also reflects another key trend: as a naturalized U.S. citizen returning to his native land, he got into trouble with local authorities who questioned his U.S. citizenship, and he called on the U.S. Consular Service for help.[10] The consular service was gradually expanding, both in the number of posts it maintained and the types of issues with which it dealt. U.S. representatives in the Habsburg Empire attempted to get the charges against Charles Mercy dropped by claiming jurisdiction over him as a U.S. citizen. Habsburg authorities countered with a claim to territorial sovereignty and existing international law – regardless of his citizenship, Charles had committed a crime on Habsburg soil, giving the Habsburg authorities jurisdiction. In addition, the 1870 naturalization treaty – made when mass transatlantic travel was only beginning and its implications were not well known – supported the Habsburg position. Rather than making an attempt to solve the conflicting sovereign claims more systematically, U.S. officials offered a nonsolution: Charles should flee to the

[8] No. 353, Grant to Gresham, 9 April 1893.
[9] The classic work on return migration is Mark Wyman, *Round-trip to America: The Immigrants Return to Europe, 1880–1930* (Ithaca, 1993).
[10] For a study of problems faced by naturalized U.S. citizens who returned to Germany, see Luciana R. W. Meyer, "German-American Migration and the Bancroft Naturalization Treaties, 1868–1910" (Ph.D. diss., City University of New York, 1970).

United States and stay there, where he was protected by U.S. territorial sovereignty.

By the end of the nineteenth century, American and European consular services had undergone major transformations, and the American consular service was leading the way. The duties of a consul had expanded over the course of the century from trade facilitation to trade promotion and, finally, to the protection of citizens abroad. This last function developed in conjunction with changing notions of sovereignty. Although territorial sovereignty had been sufficient for delineating the subjects of state authority in the past, the massive international movements of people in the decades preceding World War I undermined that system. In addition to jealously guarding their own territorial sovereignty, states now began to claim jurisdiction over their citizens anywhere in the world, and they expected their claims to sovereignty over the bodies of their citizens to trump territorially based claims to jurisdiction. Although these claims over citizens abroad were rarely expressed in racial-national terms, they did further the connection between a state and a group of people that was not explicitly connected to a particular territory, thus make a racial-national community easier to imagine. Expanding consular services were vital in furthering claims to sovereignty over citizens abroad. The coexistence of territorial and population-focused claims before World War I could create problems such as those faced by Charles Mercy – especially since documents proving citizenship were not required for international travel at the time. Consuls were the people who attempted to sort out competing claims, and, by the end of World War I, they were ready to implement changes in the international legal order that would clearly define a person as a citizen of only one country and limit his or her ability to cross international borders.

Consular services have existed since the sixth century BCE, when the Egyptians and Greeks developed them as a system for regulating interaction between the Egyptian government and the local Greek merchant population in Egypt.[11] They still exist today, although common practice is for a country to have a foreign service that combines diplomatic and consular activity; these combined foreign services are post-World War I creations.[12] For the purposes of my argument, I am interested in European

---

[11] See Charles Stuart Kennedy, *The American Consul: A History of the United States Consular Service, 1776–1914* (New York, 1990), 1.
[12] The U.S. Foreign Service was created via the Rogers Act in 1924, and the British service came into existence in 1943.

108 *Sovereignty Transformed*

and American consular services as they existed in the eighteenth and nineteenth centuries, until their incorporation into twentieth-century combined foreign services. These consular services were products of the economic and state-building conditions of the eighteenth century. The Habsburgs began their service in 1718, and the U.S. service started in 1783. The British lagged behind in creating a formal service, which began in 1825, but they had various people performing consular duties in the eighteenth century. Information on other European countries is lacking, as consular services have not been a popular subject of inquiry among professional historians.[13]

European and American consular services followed a common trend from the eighteenth century through World War I. They began with the same, rather limited agenda: to facilitate international trade and to assist merchants and sailors. In this capacity, they invoiced cargo and certified its contents and value for tariff purposes, assisted in legal actions relating to piracy and seizure, informed merchants and ship captains of local conditions and regulations, and provided legal and financial assistance to sailors in peril. British consuls also provided the British navy with intelligence about foreign shipbuilding and naval movements.[14] Given the nature of these duties, consular posts were primarily based at ports.

Over time, trade promotion was added to the list of duties – not only were consuls supposed to assist with extant trade, but they were supposed to actively seek out opportunities for expanding trade, reporting local conditions and potential opportunities to businessmen and merchants at home. Consuls also assisted in lobbying for legal changes that would result in increased trade, such as reductions in tariffs. The United States pioneered this promotional aspect of the consular agenda because it needed to break into British and French mercantile empires after its independence.[15]

---

[13] The French also had a consular service, which began either in the late seventeenth or early eighteenth century. Histories of the American, British, and Habsburg consular services have been written by former consuls turned amateur historians. Their contributions are extremely valuable and reflect extensive archival research, but they do not place the histories of the services in a broader context. See Jörg Ulbert and Lukian Prijac, eds., *Consuls Et Services Consulaires Au XIXe Siecle = Die Welt Der Konsulate Im 19. Jahrhundert = Consulship in the 19th Century* (Hamburg, 2010); Kennedy, *American Consul*; Platt; and Rudolf Agstner, "From Apalachicola to Wilkes-Barre: Austria (-Hungary) and Its Consulates in the United States of America, 1820–1917," *AHY* 37 (2006): 163–80.

[14] D. C. M. Platt, *The Cinderella Service: British Consuls since 1825* (London, 1971), 7.

[15] On the British consular service's failure to adopt a trade promotion agenda, see ibid., 108, 113.

Finding new markets for its exports remained an important aspect of U.S. foreign policy as well. With this extension of the consular agenda, the number of consular posts expanded, often opening offices in inland industrial and manufacturing centers.

Until the mid nineteenth century, consular services were almost exclusively occupied with trade and commerce. With the introduction of railroads, steamships, and other new technology that continually reduced transportation costs, however, international affairs changed fundamentally, and countries were obliged to adapt their consular services accordingly. People began to cross international borders in unprecedented numbers. They traversed the Atlantic to further their business interests, find work, pursue their education, improve their health, visit friends and relatives, and see the world.[16] Almost all of this international movement was done without passports, visas, or other documents that would mark a person's citizenship status. As a result of this new, frequent, high volume of unregulated movement, individuals faced legal problems that were rare or unheard of a few decades earlier. Among other things, people whose citizenship status was in question were impressed into the armed forces of the countries they visited; people working abroad were killed or injured on the job, raising questions about who was responsible for caring for them and their dependents; spouses deserted each other and had separate families, one on each side of the Atlantic; and people were arrested for spreading unwelcome political ideas in foreign countries. The consular agenda expanded to deal with all these issues, and protecting citizens abroad became a vital aspect of consular work. The number of consulates expanded again, this time to provide services in areas where a country's citizens concentrated abroad.

U.S.-Habsburg relations reflect this broad trend of consular expansion. Trade between the United States and the Habsburg Empire was modest, expanding over the course of the nineteenth century as U.S. consuls stationed in the empire worked to find new commercial opportunities. Still, commercial relations between the two countries were not particularly significant.[17] U.S.-Habsburg relations expanded massively with the rise of transatlantic migration, however. Millions of the Habsburg Empire's

---

[16] Christopher Endy, "Travel and World Power: Americans in Europe, 1890–1917," *DH* 22, 4 (1998): 565–94; and Wyman.

[17] Finding U.S.-Habsburg trade statistics is difficult. The two countries did have a small number of economic disputes over tobacco, pork, and cotton seed oil. See file 611.633 in NARA; and Gerald H. Davis, "The Diplomatic Relations between the United States and Austria-Hungary, 1913–1917" (Ph.D. diss., Vanderbilt University, 1958).

citizens went to the United States, primarily for economic reasons; they made up large numbers of the "New Immigrants" arriving in the United States from Central, Eastern, and Southern Europe between approximately 1880 and World War I.[18] Although some of these people stayed in the United States, and a smaller number became American citizens, a significant number remained only temporarily in the United States, working to earn money and then returning to Europe to establish themselves permanently. Some people migrated back and forth multiple times, following trends in the international economy.[19]

The massive movements of people between the United States and the Habsburg Empire raised vital questions about sovereignty and citizenship, and the solutions gradually worked out had a decisive impact on the international political system in the aftermath of World War I. American and Habsburg consular officials were key in this process. At the root of almost all U.S.-Habsburg protection cases was the question of how to prove an individual's citizenship status – a question made all the more difficult by the lack of passports or other identifying documents. For U.S. officials in the Habsburg Empire, the issue was dual citizenship: how could naturalized U.S. citizens born in the Habsburg Empire be correctly identified by local authorities as U.S. citizens? From approximately 1880 until the outbreak of World War I in the summer of 1914, there were few decisive victories. American officials dealt with the Habsburg authorities on a case-by-case basis without making significant efforts to negotiate a new treaty that would close dual citizenship loopholes in the existing naturalization treaty of 1870.[20] U.S. officials in Austria-Hungary usually won their cases, but it could take months to achieve results in any one case; in consequence, they became increasingly frustrated with both the Habsburg government – especially its Hungarian component – and with the international regime of undocumented travel more generally.

Then the war began. The transatlantic movement of people came to a sudden, grinding halt as borders closed for war and civilian transportation was stopped or converted to military use. Millions of people were caught out of place, stuck in foreign countries, sometimes without financial resources, and often with newly acquired "enemy alien" status. The United States was officially neutral at the start of World War I, and it maintained diplomatic

---

[18] On "New Immigrants," the classic study is John Higham's 1955 study, *Strangers in the Land: Patterns of American Nativism, 1860–1925* (New Brunswick, 2002).

[19] For statistics, see Wyman.

[20] On the negotiation attempts, see Davis, "Diplomatic Relations," 8–23.

relations with the Habsburg Empire until 9 April 1917, shortly after the U.S. declaration of war against Germany. With the outbreak of war, U.S. officials in the Habsburg Empire suddenly became far more powerful – and far more overworked. In keeping with the norms of the Great Power System, belligerent states asked neutrals to protect their interests in enemy countries – in other words, to operate their consular services for them.[21] In the Habsburg Empire, U.S. consuls were not only assisting U.S. citizens, they were also protecting the interests of the citizens of ten other countries. In five countries, U.S. officials represented Habsburg interests. In short, a huge portion of the world's consular work was being conducted by the U.S. Consular Service. In the short term, U.S. officials were able to get their way with the Habsburg government more often and more efficiently because Habsburg officials did not want to do anything that might make the United States enter the war as a belligerent. In the longer term, U.S. consulates improved markedly in efficiency, giving them an edge after the war. More important, however, it was U.S. consuls who were in charge of sorting out the identity and citizenship of huge numbers of people, as well as deciding whether they should be transported out of the war zone, and if so, where. The huge volume of work convinced many U.S. consuls and their superiors at the State Department that passports, visas, and border controls should be an important part of the post-World War I world.

In nineteenth-century diplomatic practice, the norm was for all correspondence between foreign governments to be channeled through their foreign ministries. For example, a U.S. Department of Agriculture (USDA) official working on establishing product classifications wanted to ask the relevant Habsburg authorities whether a beer had to be made in the Bohemian town of Pilsen to be officially considered a "Pilsner." Rather than write to the Habsburg commercial authorities directly, the USDA employee wrote to the State Department, which then forwarded the letter on to the U.S. embassy in Vienna. The embassy then addressed a communication to the Habsburg Ministry of Foreign Affairs, where officials passed it along to the relevant domestic authorities. Those officials, claiming the geographical exclusivity of Pilsner beer, drafted a response to the Ministry of Foreign Affairs, and the answer made its way back to the USDA through the same channels that it had originally traveled.[22] The

---

[21] See David D. Newsom, *Diplomacy Under a Foreign Flag: When Nations Break Relations* (Washington, 1989).

[22] Acting Secretary of Agriculture to SecState, 6 April 1911, file no. 611.634/3, in NARA.

point of this process was to make sure that all international correspondence was properly formal – no one wanted an incident or even a war
because two officials, likely not hired for their tact, were thrown into
contact with one another.

This method of communicating through embassies and foreign offices
resulted in a different relationship between the U.S. embassy and consulates in the Habsburg Empire and that which existed between the
Austro-Hungarian embassy and consulates in the United States.
Because Habsburg consuls dealt primarily with workers' compensation
issues and the settlement of estates, both of which were local government
issues handled by private attorneys, they did not have to communicate
through their embassy very often. Instead, they communicated with the
U.S. government in the courtroom, through American attorneys. U.S.
consuls in the Habsburg Empire dealing with military service cases and
the arrest of U.S. citizens by Austrian or Hungarian authorities for
political crimes, however, were required to speak to the Austrian or
Hungarian governments through the U.S. embassy or, in some cases,
through the consulate general's office in Budapest, which was the conduit
for certain types of communication with the Hungarian government.
Because of the content of U.S. activity in the Habsburg Empire, the
embassy at Vienna played a major role in consular activity – a role that
made the post unique. Indeed, Ambassador Frederick Penfield observed,
"In few embassies can there be more inquiry as to citizenship, military
service and passports."[23]

Together with the embassy in Vienna, the U.S. consular presence in the
Habsburg Empire expanded in size over the course of the nineteenth
century as the consular agenda diversified from trade facilitation to promotion and then to the protection of U.S. citizens abroad. The number of
U.S.-Habsburg interactions increased significantly over the course of the
century as a fairly meager trade relationship gave way to huge waves of
transatlantic migration. By the outbreak of World War I, the United States
had seven consular posts in the empire: consulates-general at Vienna and
Budapest, and consulates at Trieste, Prague, Reichenberg (Liberec),
Carlsbad, and Fiume (Rijeka). With the exception of Carlsbad, which
primarily served American tourists, all of these posts initially opened for
commercial reasons. Reichenberg alone remained almost exclusively commercial. Emigrants to the United States departed from the ports of Trieste
and Fiume, adding to the consuls' busy commercial agenda there. Prague

[23] No. 38, Penfield to SecState, 10 December 1913, file no. 124.63/-, in NARA.

also maintained a heavy commercial workload, but it was also the post that had to deal most often with the effects of nationalism, which, as we will see, was fostered by travel between the crownland of Bohemia and the United States. The consulates-general at Vienna and Budapest dealt primarily with citizenship matters, which, in the U.S.-Habsburg context, usually meant military service cases.

The United States established its first consular post in the Habsburg Empire in 1800, at the Adriatic port of Trieste.[24] Trieste, whose diverse population spoke Italian, German, and various Slavic idioms, among other languages, was Austria's only major port,[25] making it the hub of U.S.-Habsburg trade. More important, however, it was a key port for Mediterranean trade, and it maintained its importance to the world economy throughout the nineteenth century.[26] By the start of World War I, the British, French, Germans, Italians, Turks, Brazilians, Argentineans, and Greeks not only maintained consulates-general there, but also staffed them with professional consuls, both marks of the post's importance. Indeed, Ralph Busser, the U.S. consul at Trieste during World War I, reported that local businessmen were "astonished" that the United States had only a consulate and not a consulate general there. Busser advocated upgrading the post – and, by implication, his rank and salary – but the State Department denied his request on the advice of Ambassador Penfield in Vienna.[27]

When the Trieste post was originally created, its purpose was to facilitate U.S. trade in the region and assist sailors, who, given the aggressive policies of the Barbary states at sea, were often in need of assistance. The

---

[24] Basic information on consular posts is elusive. The DOS does have statistics on the number of official posts, but not their locations, and honorary consulates are not included. The opening dates I have used are based on information from National Archives and Records Administration, *Diplomatic Records: A Select Catalog of National Archives Microfilm Publications* (Washington, 1986). This publication lists extant consular records by post through 1906; the start date of the records does not necessarily reflect when the post was created by Congress or the DOS or when the first consul arrived, but they are relatively close.

[25] Hungary developed its own port at nearby Fiume later in the nineteenth century.

[26] After World War I, Trieste became part of Italy, until it was occupied by Tito's Yugoslav troops in 1945; although most of the city was officially returned to Italy in 1947, a border dispute persisted between Yugoslavia and Italy over the city until the 1975 Treaty of Osimo.

[27] No. 202, "Recommendations for improvement in ranking and facilities of American Consulate at Trieste," Ralph Busser to SecState, 9 November 1915, file no. 125.9453/36; and no. 943, Penfield to SecState, 12 November 1915, file no. 125.9453/37, both in NARA.

consul also hoped to influence the Habsburg government to liberalize its trade policies. Those efforts shifted to Vienna by 1830, and the consuls at Trieste were free to concentrate on trade promotion among the locals. As Habsburg trade policies gradually changed over the course of the nineteenth century, those efforts proved successful. Vice Consul Orestes de Martini asserted that he was personally responsible for generating $10 million in new U.S.-Habsburg trade between 1902 and 1911.[28]

The commercial nature of the post is also evident from one of Consul Busser's 1916 despatches to the State Department, in which he complains that numerous U.S. publications to which the consulate subscribed were no longer reaching him due to wartime postal conditions.[29] He commented that the absence of these periodicals was "lessening the efficiency of this Office, which should always be informed as to the latest … commercial and industrial situation in the United States." His list included fifty-four items, twenty-one of which he considered especially important. Those key publications included the *National Food Magazine*, *Hardware Dealer's Magazine*, and the *Woman's Home Companion*; of lesser importance were *Concrete and Cement Age*, *Sugar*, and *The Carriage Monthly*.[30] One can imagine the consul slipping a mention of the latest products into casual conversation with local businessmen and allowing locals to use the consulate office as a reading room for the latest trade publications.

After Trieste, the United States opened its second Habsburg consulate in Vienna, in 1830.[31] It was a product of the 1829 Treaty of Commerce and Navigation between the two countries. The Vienna consulate's early story straddles the line between diplomacy and commerce: its purpose was to lobby the central government in Vienna for more liberal – and pro-U.S. – trade policies, especially regarding tobacco. As discussed in Chapter 2,

---

[28] De Martini to Congressman Calder, 7 August 1911, file no. 125.9453/1, in NARA. See also *T242: Despatches from U.S. Consuls in Trieste, Italy, 1800–1906*, 13 vols. (Washington, 1962).

[29] The British were primarily responsible for interruptions in continental mail delivery, as they seized and searched all the postal bags they could find. According to Austrian officials, the British only forwarded regular, personal mail on to the continent. See translation of Z.13169/3, Dr. Kamler (I. R. Court-Counselor of the K. K. Post-und Telegraphen-Direktion für Triest, Küntenland and Krain) to the Consulate of the USA, 5 June 1916, file no. 125.9452/20, in NARA.

[30] No. 265, "American Periodicals addressed to the American Consulate, Trieste," Ralph Busser to SecState, 1 June 1916, file no. 125.9452/20, in NARA.

[31] For U.S. consular despatches from Vienna, see *T243: Despatches from U.S. Consuls in Vienna, 1830–1906*, 20 vols. (Washington, 1958–62).

U.S. consuls lacked the necessary rank to gain access to the relevant Habsburg policymakers, and so the tobacco policy question shifted out of the realm of consuls and into the realm of diplomacy.

On the specific issue of tobacco, change was slow to come but, in some areas, Metternich did advocate a closer U.S.-Habsburg commercial relationship. Metternich, who held a special place in his heart for Bohemia, wanted a U.S. commercial agent – a particular category of consul[32] – to be stationed in Prague, the Bohemian capital. Because Bohemia was the emerging industrial center of the empire, Metternich's request was endorsed by Henry Muhlenberg, the first U.S. minister in Vienna. Muhlenberg also advocated the creation of a consulate in Budapest, and he even went so far as to put forward the name of a Budapest merchant who would be willing to take up the post "for the honor," rather than the potential profit.[33]

Prague and Budapest would have to wait until 1869 and 1876, respectively, before they received official U.S. consulates. At Prague, the work of the consulate was mainly commercial until after the turn of the century, and the consulate conducted its business in both Czech and German, as well as English. Prior to World War I, trade between the United States and Bohemia grew steadily, as many middle-class people emigrated to the United States from the province and then did business with friends and relatives who had remained in Bohemia. The consulate also actively worked to promote trade. In 1911, Consul Joseph Britton reported that the commercial correspondence of the office had increased 50 percent during the four years he had been in office.[34] Consul Frank Deedmeyer, who took over the post in November 1913, reported that the office had sent the State Department 110 trade lists and 152 reports of trade extension possibilities in an eight-month period – one extension for every working day of his tenure.[35] Reports from the Prague consulate

---

[32] The position of "commercial agent" was a uniquely American creation. Essentially, it was the term people like Thomas Jefferson used instead of *consul*, because they wanted to distance the United States from European diplomatic culture. Kennedy, *American Consul*, 9–11.

[33] On Metternich and Bohemia, see Muhlenberg to Forsyth, 14 July 1840, in *T157*, roll 1. On Budapest, see Muhlenberg to Forsyth, 8 August 1839, in *T157*, roll 1. Frederick Kappel was Muhlenberg's nominee.

[34] "Contingent Expense and Clerk Hire," Britton to SecState, 7 February 1911, file no. 125.7334, in NARA.

[35] No. 33, "Trade Extension Work at Prague Consulate from November 10, 1913 to July 1, 1914," Frank Deedmeyer to SecState, 14 July 1914, file no. 125.7336/5, in NARA.

included "Beer Production in Austria," "Demand for Leather in Prague," "Sale of Fresh Fruits in Bohemia," and "Market for Paper of all Classes."[36]

Because Bohemia was the industrial center of the Habsburg Empire, and the United States was keenly interested in trade, Bohemia merited a second commercially focused consular post. The post at Reichenberg (Liberec in Czech) was opened in 1886. To work there, the consul and vice consul would ideally "have had practical business experience, [and] be wholly familiar with the German language, its dialect forms, and with a knowledge of Polish if possible. Otherwise he will be useless."[37] The Reichenberg consulate produced a minimal documentary record, and it appears that the United States was the only country to have an official consulate there.[38] That the U.S. consul was there alone, promoting trade, illustrates the U.S. position on the cutting edge of using consuls to increase trade, rather than simply to facilitate existing commerce.

Consuls at Trieste, Vienna, Prague, Budapest, and Reichenberg, in addition to those at Fiume and Carlsbad, performed myriad duties in the service of their fellow Americans. They were involved in various transatlantic legal transactions, including extraditions, the transmission of letters rogatory, and the collection of depositions for criminal and civil cases, with divorce proceedings and patent investigations being the most common.[39] As mentioned earlier, these consuls handled the paperwork necessary for U.S.-Habsburg trade and looked for potential commercial opportunities that would benefit the United States. They also answered quite a number of random commercial questions. As one such example, in 1913, the U.S. Treasury Department received a letter from Congressman W. J. Stone, transmitting an inquiry from one of his constituents, a Mr. W. C. Grubbs, who was the manager of the Hawkeye Pearl Button Company of Canton, Missouri. Mr. Grubbs was

---

[36] "Range of Trade Reports from Prague, Austria, Consulate. From November 10, 1913-July 1, 1914. Made by Consul, Frank Deedmeyer, Vice Consul, John L. Bouchal," enclosure to no. 33, "Trade Extension Work at Prague Consulate." For additional consular despatches from Prague, see *T663: Despatches from U.S. Consuls in Prague, 1869–1906*, 13 vols. (Washington, 1962).

[37] No. 33, "Nomination of Vice and Deputy Consul at Reichenberg," William J. Pike to SecState, 8 July 1912, file no. 125.7574/15, in NARA.

[38] For U.S. consular despatches from Reichenberg, see *T664: Despatches from U.S. Consuls in Reichenberg, 1886–1906*, 3 vols. (Washington, 1962).

[39] See file 081.63, in NARA.

under the impression that "buttons imported from Austria are manufactured by convict labor," and he wanted to know if this was true.[40] The Assistant Secretary of the Treasury wrote to the Secretary of State, who forwarded the inquiry on to Vienna. The U.S. Consular Service swung into action. Within six weeks, the consul at Fiume reported that no buttons were made at all in his district, whereas Trieste noted that no buttons had been exported to the United States; similarly, Prague reported that no buttons had been exported, but those that were made were not made by convicts. From Budapest, word came that "there are no buttons manufactured in Hungary in whole or in part by convict labor, and that during the last year there has been no export from Hungary to the United States of buttons of any kind." Vienna's buttons had not been made by convicts for fifteen years. Carlsbad's buttons, some of which were exported, were not made by convicts. And in the Reichenberg consular district, where button-making was actually a significant enterprise, no convict had made a button in ten years.[41] As a button manufacturer, Mr. Grubbs might have been disappointed that he could not claim that his buttons were morally superior to Austrian buttons, but as an American businessman, he surely could not have been dissatisfied with the resources marshaled by the consular service to answer his inquiry.

Although the presence of commercially focused consulates at Trieste, Prague, and Reichenberg reflects the importance of commerce and industry in the Austrian half of the empire, the posts at Budapest and Fiume, both in the Kingdom of Hungary, reflect Hungarian nationalist efforts toward achieving sovereignty independent of the rest of the empire. The Budapest consulate general was essentially an embassy in disguise, in recognition of the Hungarian government's extensive but incomplete sovereign activity.[42] To strengthen the Hungarian economy, the Hungarian government wanted its own trade and its own industry, and so it began to develop its own port at Fiume. Like Trieste, Fiume was located on the Adriatic, and its population was predominantly Italian- and Croatian-speaking – indeed,

---

[40] Assistant Secretary of the Treasury to SecState, 24 October 1913, file no. 611.636/2, in NARA.

[41] For consular responses, see file no. 611.636/2, in NARA.

[42] This use of consuls as diplomats in disguise had its origins in the Ottoman Empire, as U.S. and European governments looked for ways to interact effectively with the diverse and physically widespread population that was under Ottoman sovereignty. See Kennedy, *American Consul*; Platt; and Ruth Kark, *American Consuls in the Holy Land, 1832–1914* (Detroit, 1994). For U.S. consular despatches from Budapest, see *T531: Despatches from U.S. Consuls in Budapest, 1876–1906*, 4 vols. (Washington, 1961).

the port was less than fifty miles from Trieste, but it was "Hungarian," and that was what mattered.

While race-conscious Americans in the United States launched Americanization programs to assimilate immigrants and achieve a "100 percent American" population, the Hungarian government had similar concerns and somewhat similar programs, which promoted "Magyarization." The Hungarian government wanted the inhabitants of the Kingdom of Hungary to be as Magyar as possible, despite the fact that ethnic Magyars made up only about half of the kingdom's population. Speakers of Romanian, German, Slovak, and other Slavic languages living in the kingdom were encouraged – and, over time, required – to learn Magyar in an effort to create a more homogeneous population.[43]

That efforts at Magyarization were at least partially successful is evident from reports from the U.S. consulate at Fiume. Although it is unclear when the post first opened, an honorary consular agency was in place by 1903, and the post became an official consulate at some point between 1906 and 1908.[44] Originally, much of the business of the consulate was conducted in German and Italian, with German being used with government officials and Italian being more common among private citizens engaged in commerce. Even by 1910, no one at the consular agency was conversant in Magyar, despite requests for a staff member who knew the language. In July 1910, Consul Clarence Rice Slocum asked again for someone who knew Magyar, noting that, "with the continued growth of the port, the use of the Hungarian language locally becomes much more general among the commercial people and the necessity of at least one of the Government's

---

[43] On Americanization, see, for example, Rogers M. Smith, *Civic Ideals: Conflicting Visions of Citizenship in U.S. History* (New Haven, 1997); Matthew Frye Jacobson, *Barbarian Virtues: The United States Encounters Foreign Peoples at Home and Abroad, 1876–1917* (New York, 2000); Gary Gerstle, *American Crucible: Race and Nation in the Twentieth Century* (Princeton, 2002); and Christopher Capozzola, *Uncle Sam Wants You: World War I and the Making of the Modern American Citizen* (New York, 2008). On Magyarization, see Andrew C. Janos, *The Politics of Backwardness in Hungary, 1825–1945* (Princeton, 1982); and Marius Turda, "The Biology of War: Eugenics in Hungary, 1914–1918," *AHY* 40 (2009): 238–64.

[44] On the general uncertainty of the dates of consular posts, see note 24. We know that Fiorello LaGuardia was the consular agent from 1903 to 1906. The *Diplomatic and Consular Service* list of 14 February 1912 lists the consul serving at the post at the time as having been appointed in June 1908. The difficulty in dating the Fiume post is compounded by the fact that the DOS had a temporary and largely impenetrable filing system for the 1906 to 1910 period.

employees at this post being conversant with the language much more apparent."[45]

One effect of Magyarization's language policies and economic development plans was to increase the number of people emigrating permanently or temporarily to the United States. Serving at the Habsburg Empire's two major ports, the U.S. consuls at Trieste and Fiume processed an increasing number of emigrants each year. Consul Busser at Trieste had to write to the State Department to request additional copies of U.S. immigration laws, as "one copy . . . is not sufficient for the needs of this Consulate."[46] At Fiume, Consul Slocum requested an additional staff member for the consulate who was "proficient in Hungarian, Croatian, German and English."[47] The request for a knowledge of Croatian was a direct product of an increase in emigration because many Croats were recruited by U.S. companies for work in mines and other labor-intensive enterprises in the American West.[48]

Whereas U.S. consuls at Trieste and Fiume were indeed witnessing rising levels of emigration, only a fraction of Austrian and Hungarian emigrants actually traveled through those ports because they were located far to the south of the empire. Departure from north German ports was far more popular. Approximately 20,000 people emigrated through Fiume in the period between 1903 and 1906, when transatlantic travel was well established and the number of people traveling was large. By contrast, the north German ports of Hamburg and Bremen had processed 20,000 emigrants each in 1870, when the "New Immigration" was just barely getting started.[49] Those northern ports continued to be the primary site of departure to the United States.

Although the number of emigrants at Fiume was relatively small, an innovation in immigrant processing developed there is perhaps the best known legacy of the U.S. consular presence in the Habsburg Empire. It is famous not only because it changed the way the U.S. government processed immigrants, but because of its originator. Undoubtedly the most historically prominent person to have served as a U.S. representative in the Habsburg Empire, Fiorello LaGuardia, later mayor of New York City, was

---

[45] No. 113, Slocum to SecState, 5 July 1910, file no. 125.381–1786/104, in NARA.
[46] No. 21, Busser to SecState, 16 March 1914, file no. 125.9452/11, in NARA.
[47] No. 175, Slocum to SecState, 17 August 1911, file no. 125.3813/1, in NARA.
[48] For a brief overview of Croatian immigration, see Stephan Thernstrom, ed. *The Harvard Encyclopedia of American Ethnic Groups* (Cambridge MA, 1980).
[49] For statistics, see Kennedy, *American Consul*, 143–44, 212–13.

the U.S. consular agent in Fiume from 1903 to 1906, having first served for four years as a clerk in the Budapest consulate general.[50]

Prior to LaGuardia's reforms, entrants arriving at U.S. ports were given medical examinations. If they did not pass – because they had a contagious disease or because their health made them "likely to become a public charge" – they were sent back to their country of origin. This was a politically charged process. Although many European countries, including the Habsburg Empire and especially its Hungarian half, did not want their citizens to emigrate, they did not want those who did emigrate to be rejected by U.S. officials. They thought rejection reflected poorly on the sending government and the nation it represented. To save time and embarrassment, LaGuardia began the process of having steamship lines provide medical examinations at the point of embarkation, so that any unfit people were stopped from making the transatlantic journey in the first place. This system also benefitted the U.S. government, which saved money on medical personnel by shifting the costs to the steamship lines, who were profiting significantly from heavy transatlantic travel.

While many people who went through Trieste and Fiume were leaving the empire, the seventh U.S. consular post in Austria-Hungary existed primarily to serve tourists coming from the United States. The United States opened a consulate in 1902 in the Bohemian town of Carlsbad, "the best known and most popular cure city of the world."[51] According to Consul Charles Hoover, "Several thousand Americans visit this resort every year, to say nothing of the great number of leading people from all over Europe who come here and with whom the members of the consular force are frequently thrown in contact."[52] Hoover's predecessor, Will Lowrie, mentioned the presence of a California congressman among approximately fifty of "our American friends" in town in the offseason in 1912.[53]

The exclusive nature of Carlsbad's visitors resulted in extremely high costs of living, which, in turn, produced frequent turnover among the consular staff. Between 1910 and 1917, the post had three different consuls, and all three had to make multiple requests for new vice consuls. Each noted that the vice consul had to be unmarried, because a single man could only

---

[50] On LaGuardia, see ibid., 212–13.

[51] No. 34, "Transfer of Vice Consul George P. Waller, Jr.," Young to SecState, 22 June 1915, file no. 125.2813/44, in NARA. For U.S. consular despatches from Carlsbad, see *T540: Despatches from U.S. Consuls in Carlsbad, 1800–1906*, 1 vol. (Washington, 1962).

[52] No. 30, "Comments upon employment of Vice and Deputy Consul at Carlsbad," Hoover to SecState, 28 December 1913, file no. 125.2813/27, in NARA.

[53] Lowrie's personal letter to Carr, 24 April 1912, file no. 125.2813/12, in NARA.

just support himself on the salary – and that only if he "[spread] it on thin in spots."[54] The need for economy was problematic though, given the social demands of the post. Hoover observed, "If the Vice Consul is even to have friends of the proper kind he must entertain some occasionally and this cannot be done on the salary."[55] Stressing the social demands of the post, Lowrie requested "a pleasant, capable young chap."[56] Consul Wallace Young wrote that "a man accustomed to the usages of good society should be sent."[57] Hoover noted that a vice consul in Carlsbad should be "a person of tact, of good appearance and accustomed to meeting people."[58] All three stressed the importance of being able to speak German.[59]

The ability to speak German – and to speak it with tact and social grace – was absolutely vital to the main duty of the consul and vice consul. Consul Lowrie, who clearly enjoyed and felt comfortable in his high-society post, tactfully observed that "[w]e have many complaints to be investigated and adjusted."[60] Consul Hoover, who was quickly transferred to Prague, a post that seems to have suited him better, described the duties a bit differently: "During the season, hundreds of little disagreements between Americans and the Carlsbad boarding-house keepers, coachmen, and small merchants are brought before the Consulate for mediation. Usually they are so trivial that they are easily settled by a little tact if one knows the German language and they could easily be handled by the Vice Consul while the Consul gives his attention to callers who have more important matters."[61] U.S. consular officials in Carlsbad were there to prevent an international incident arising from the cost of a hotel room in an atmosphere charged with social and national prejudice.

After the war started, Carlsbad was also a unique post because it provided a clear view of the tensions that existed between citizens of Germany and Austria, despite the fact that the two countries were allied. Many of the visitors to the city were German citizens, and Consul Young observed that

---

[54] Ibid.
[55] No. 30, "Comments upon employment of Vice and Deputy Consul at Carlsbad," 28 December 1913.
[56] Lowrie to Carr, Carlsbad, 24 April 1912.
[57] No. 34, "Transfer of Vice Consul George P. Waller, Jr.," 22 June 1915.
[58] No. 30, "Comments upon employment of Vice and Deputy Consul at Carlsbad," 28 December 1913.
[59] Lowrie to Carr, 24 April 1912; no. 30, "Comments upon employment of Vice and Deputy Consul at Carlsbad," 28 December 1913.
[60] Lowrie to Carr, 24 April 1912.
[61] No. 30, "Comments upon employment of Vice and Deputy Consul at Carlsbad," 28 December 1913.

the local Austrian citizens, whom Young found universally "kindly, hospitable, and sympathetic," were less than enthusiastic about the visiting Germans. Young took the Austrians' side and pointed out the strident anti-American feeling displayed by the majority of Germans. Young noted that, "since he lives in a hotel," he had extensive first-hand experience of the German "hatred of things American" and "anyone whose mother tongue is English." When he requested a new vice consul, Young specifically requested "that a so-called 'German American' be not sent here," as that would exacerbate the problems and make it harder to deal with the Austrians.[62]

Indeed, it was at the Carlsbad consulate that the most serious race-based personnel problem among U.S. representatives in the empire arose. The existing correspondence between U.S. diplomats and consuls stationed in the empire and the State Department is almost entirely devoid of any indication that U.S. personnel abroad subscribed to the racialist thinking and prejudices that were popular by the turn of the century. That does not mean, of course, that they did not have those opinions, simply that they did not feel they were appropriate to official correspondence. It is possible, however, that their experiences in the empire did not lead them to believe that such categories were pertinent. The one exception to this lack of racialist sentiment is a letter from George P. Waller, Jr., who was vice consul at Carlsbad from 1913 until July 1915.

During his service at Carlsbad, the war began, and the United States was officially neutral – a policy that U.S. consuls and diplomats in Austria-Hungary took more seriously than many other Americans. Waller – and Consul Young and Ambassador Penfield – repeatedly asked for a transfer. Waller specifically requested a post "in an English speaking country outside of Canada." He said that, despite his best efforts, he was incapable of remaining neutral and expressing the sympathy necessary to deal with the wartime duties of the post. "On the other hand," he wrote, "by heredity, environment and ways of thought, my sympathies are, in the larger sense, fully with the Anglo Saxons and in a time like the present I am quite sure that I should be of vastly greater service among such a people."[63] The State Department gave the matter "its careful attention" for several months until Young, Ambassador Penfield, and Vienna Consul General Halstead all

---

[62] No. 34, "Transfer of Vice Consul George P. Waller, Jr.," 22 June 1915. See also Michael Ermarth, "Hyphenation and Hyper-Americanization: Germans of the Whihelmine 'Reich' View German-Americans, 1890–1914," *JAEH* 21, 2 (2002): 33–58.

[63] "Request for Transfer of Vice Consul George P. Waller, Jr.," Waller to SecState, 13 March 1915, file no. 125.2813/40, in NARA.

wrote and telegraphed again, requesting the transfer.[64] Penfield's telegram referred to Waller's attitude as "seriously embarrassing."[65] Secretary of State Lansing finally responded; he granted Young and Penfield's request for Waller to go, but Waller was likely not particularly thrilled by his new post: Athens.[66]

In Carlsbad, consuls were frequently called on to deal with arguments between American elites and local hotel managers. In Prague, Vienna, and Budapest, the citizen protection cases that U.S. consuls dealt with were far more serious, both for the individuals involved and for international politics more broadly. In Vienna and Budapest, military service cases dominated the citizen protection agenda. In Prague, numerous American citizens were arrested for treasonous or other illegal activity that undermined the authority of the Habsburg state.[67] In both military service and arrest cases, U.S. officials intervened with Habsburg authorities with the intension of claiming jurisdiction over the bodies of U.S. citizens. However, there were limits to how far U.S. authorities would go. If the person asking for release from military service declared his intention of staying in Austria-Hungary, U.S. officials declined to assist him. Similarly, in the Prague arrest cases, the U.S. consulate did not challenge the final decisions of the Austrian courts, letting people whose politics were still Austrian be governed by Austrian territorial sovereignty, even if they were technically U.S. citizens. In both types of case, U.S. officials aimed to align a person's physical location with his political identity.

The case of Zdenek Bodlak provides an example of the forces at work in this type of citizen protection case. Bodlak's Czech-speaking parents – or at least his father – were born in Bohemia, emigrated to the United States, and became naturalized U.S. citizens. Bodlak himself was born in St. Paul,

[64] Carr to Waller, 27 April 1915, file no. 125.2813/40; no. 34, "Transfer of Vice Consul George P. Waller, Jr.," 22 June 1915; no. 109, "Transfer of Mr. Waller," Halstead to SecState, 23 June 1915, file no. 125.2813/43; and Penfield's telegram to SecState, 24 June 1915, file no. 125.2813/42, all in NARA.

[65] Penfield's telegram to SecState, 24 June 1915.

[66] Lansing's telegram to the U.S. Embassy in Vienna, 14 July 1915, file no. 125/2813/44a, in NARA.

[67] There were a large number of reported arrests in Budapest as well. The vice consul reported that an average of three Americans were arrested each week in 1913. The records are incomplete, however, and it is difficult to determine what the charges were in those Budapest arrests. On the number of arrests, see "Memorandum with regard to questions 33 and 36 on pages 7 and 8 respectively, of the inspection return," Mallett to SecState, 6 September 1913, file no. 125.2436/23, in NARA.

Minnesota, in 1893, and was therefore a U.S. citizen. He was fluent in Czech and English, and, in June 1913, the twenty-year-old Bohemian-American[68] went to Prague to study music.

Prague in 1913 was a key theater for the development of Czech nationalism. The crownland of Bohemia, along with neighboring Moravia and Silesia, made up the Kingdom of Bohemia[69]; the Habsburg family had acquired it through marriage in the early sixteenth century. The dominant languages in the province were German and Czech, and a significant portion of the population was bilingual. Although the Kingdom of Bohemia had not always been fully supportive of the Habsburgs, dissatisfaction intensified with the 1867 Ausgleich, which created Austria-Hungary. Many in Bohemia wanted the kingdom to have equal status with Hungary – they wanted a Triple Monarchy, rather than a Dual Monarchy. Very, very few people wanted a fully independent Czech state at this point; in fact, independence as a viable option did not gain much popular support in Bohemia until well into World War I. Many did want the Czech language to be legally equal with German in the kingdom, for civil servants to speak both Czech and German, and for the government to make Czech-language schools more widely available.[70]

Due in part to these dissatisfactions, and because of opportunities for economic advancement in America, many Bohemians emigrated to the United States. The emigrants included a significant number of middle-class people, who reached a greater level of prosperity in the United States more quickly than many of their fellow countrymen.[71] Once in the United States, Czech speakers, like other immigrant groups, banded together for the benefit of the community as a whole. Various Czech communities began publishing their own Czech- and English-language newspapers. Those newspapers included comments on events in Austria,

---

[68] *Bohemian* was the term commonly used by pre-World War I U.S. authorities, including DOS and Immigration personnel, and American newspapers. It referred to both the people and the language we know today as "Czech." *Czech* did not really enter these sources until Tomáš Masaryk and his supporters introduced the idea of a Czecho-Slovak state into the American imagination during the war.

[69] Slovakia, which would later become part of Czechoslovakia, was part of the Kingdom of Hungary.

[70] See, among others, Tara Zahra, *Kidnapped Souls: National Indifference and the Battle for Children in the Bohemian Lands, 1900–1948* (Ithaca, 2008); Jeremy King, *Budweisers into Czechs and Germans: A Local History of Bohemian Politics, 1848–1948* (Princeton, 2002); and Gary B. Cohen, *The Politics of Ethnic Survival: Germans in Prague, 1861–1914*, new ed. (West Lafayette, 2006).

[71] For a brief overview of Czech immigration, see Thernstrom.

as well as reports on conditions there, derived from personal letters exchanged among transatlantic networks of Bohemians.[72] The basic editorial stance of many of these publications was critical of the Austrian government and in favor of Czech nationalism.

Czech nationalist American newspapers frequently found their way to Bohemia, where they were circulated among the local population. They also found their way to the Habsburg authorities, including the Prague police. Charles Hoover, the U.S. consul in Prague from 1913 to 1917, reported that "the authorities are greatly enraged over the articles which appear in the Bohemian papers of Chicago and it is certain for that reason to go hard with any American who transgresses the Austrian law."[73] Hoover went so far as to advocate that the State Department approach these papers: "it would serve the interests of the American citizens of Bohemian origin who travel in this country if these papers were to adopt a more temperate tone regarding affairs in this country, although I am aware that it would be difficult to suggest such a course to them."[74]

To combat the transatlantic nationalist network, the Prague police were especially vigilant, scrutinizing the public statements of American citizens, as well as the letters they wrote to Austrian citizens. Zdenek Bodlak's arrest was a result of this increased police scrutiny, and his was definitely not the only such case. Hoover told the State Department that "the records here are full of instances" of this nature, and that "such convictions are more than daily happenings here."[75]

Bodlak was arrested and incarcerated on 27 November 1914 for "disturbing the public order."[76] That had been a crime in Austria-Hungary before the war, but after the war began, its definition expanded and the sentences were more serious. Over the course of four months, Bodlak sent a series of letters to his family and friends in the United States. When

---

[72] For an example of these transatlantic networks, see "Imprisonment of Zdenek Bodlak," Hoover to SecState, 10 March 1915, file no. 363.112 B63/3, in NARA.

[73] Ibid.; a similar sentiment is expressed in no. 320, Hoover to SecState, 28 December 1918, file no. 363.112 B63/3, in NARA.

[74] "Imprisonment of Zdenek Bodlak," 10 March 1915.

[75] No. 49, "Imprisonment of Zdenek Bodlak," Hoover to SecState, 28 July 1915, file no. 636.112 B 63/8, in NARA. Another well documented case is that of Albert Bohdan, who was arrested for "inciting soldiers to treasonable conduct" by telling them not to "shoot at the Servians," because "they are our brothers." See no. 475, Penfield to SecState, 16 April 1915, file no. 363.11 B63/9; and "Imprisonment of Albert Bohdan, American Citizen," Hoover to SecState, 14 November 1914, enclosed in Grant Smith to Carr, 16 April 1915, file no. B63/10-; and "Imprisonment of Albert Bohdan," 3 August 1915, all in NARA.

[76] Translation of the Trial Transcript for the Bodlak Case, page 6, file no. 363.112 B63/8, in NARA.

mailing them, he marked them "open," which meant that they were not directed exclusively to the addressee. More important, it meant that Austrian authorities were entirely free to open and read the letters, which they did. Bodlak also sent a number of letters to a local girl in Prague that contained news and newspaper clippings from the United States. Bodlak marked these letters "closed," but he did not tell the recipient to destroy or hide them, and the police discovered them when they conducted a voluntary search of her parents' home.[77]

Bodlak's letters are extremely critical of Austria and Germany, and they are dripping with sarcasm. He criticized the Austrian government for drafting eighteen-year-olds for the service – "children," according to Bodlak.[78] He also pointed out the Austrian government's press censorship, writing to his father in America that "quite a number of things you knew in August were first made known to us at the beginning of November."[79] When Turkey entered the war on the side of the Central Powers, Bodlak wrote, "Isn't it just grand to see the peerless German culture shake hands with such a heathenisch [sic] murdering skunk as is Turkey?"[80] He also called the conflict "the war of Kaiser extermination" and wrote that "It should last until Germany and Austria disappear from the map."[81]

The Austrian court determined that "in circulated writings, ... also publicly, [Bodlak] endeavored to stir up hatred and contempt against the Government ... the person of the Kaiser ... the form of government ... [and] the unity of the Empire." Although Bodlak did help himself somewhat by admitting very late in the game that "he had written improper matter in the letters," this was more than offset by the fact that he repeatedly sent such letters and made no attempt to keep them private. On the contrary, the court observed, "he rather wished that they should be circulated, as to be expected of such persons who are so evilly disposed toward the State." Bodlak was sentenced to three years hard labor, "sharpened by one fast day each three months," and, on completion of his

---

[77] Ibid.
[78] Bodlak to Ohl, 26 October 1914, included in Translation of the Trial Transcript for the Bodlak Case. Eighteen-year-olds could enter the U.S. military at the time, but perhaps Bodlak viewed that voluntary service as qualitatively different from conscription.
[79] Bodlak to John Bodlak, 11 November 1914, included in Translation of the Trial Transcript for the Bodlak Case.
[80] Ibid.
[81] Extermination quote: Ibid. Map quote: Bodlak to Junek, 17 November 1914, in Translation of the Trial Transcript for the Bodlak Case.

sentence, banishment from the empire.[82] With the help of Hoover and the embassy, Bodlak appealed the verdict, but it was upheld.[83]

After the initial conviction, Consul Hoover informed the State Department of the case, but the despatch did not arrive, given uncertain wartime mail conditions.[84] The department learned about it from the American Czech population, which was in an uproar over the incident and especially the sentence. Hearing of events from the public and not from U.S. officials overseas was not to the department's liking, and they sent Hoover multiple telegrams asking for a report. Hoover then wrote a number of communications to Washington explaining the case and offering his assessment. He criticized the Austrian legal system for the inclusion of political activities as illegal acts. In a statement that office personnel at the State Department took pains to label as definitely not for publication, Hoover wrote:

This is a conviction for a purely political crime and as such it is entirely impossible to comprehend the logic of the argument upon which the conviction was based when considered from the standpoint of American law. What might under American practice be considered the grossest distortion of fact, trivial, childish, and malicious, might be in entire consonance with the laws of other countries. To take away three years of the life of a human being for having put a little ink on a piece of paper in a certain form when it did not injure any one in the slightest and could not have injured any one if it had been seen by the whole world is not in accord with American ideas of justice.[85]

Hoover also found fault with the methods of the Prague police, commenting that "there is no need for the authorities to go into private letters for statements which have been given no publicity to find sedition for it is rife here and the fact that it is well known to the authorities."[86]

Although Hoover was no fan of the Austrian legal system, he stood by Bodlak's conviction. Hoover wrote that, "when Bodlak came to this

---

[82] Translation of the Trial Transcript for the Bodlak Case.

[83] Hoover and Penfield also contemplated making a direct appeal to Franz Joseph. That had been tried unsuccessfully in earlier cases; the emperor had merely referred the case back to the court, which upheld itself. No. 49, "Imprisonment of Zdenek Bodlak," 28 July 1915. Bodlak was released from prison early – in October 1916 – due to illness; he died in December 1917 while staying with a relative in Bohemia. See Hoover to SecState, 20 October 1916, file no. 363.112 B63/14; and Hoover to SecState, [no date, 1917/18], file no. 363.112 B63/18, both in NARA.

[84] See file 125.2346, in NARA for communications from DOS officials saying which messages they had received and which numbers needed to be sent again because they had not arrived.

[85] No. 49, "Imprisonment of Zdenek Bodlak," 28 July 1915.

[86] No. 320, Hoover to SecState, 28 December 1918.

country he placed himself under its laws and there seems to be no question
of his having committed the acts for which he was convicted under the
Austrian law by a regularly constituted court." Perhaps Hoover was hoping that Bodlak's fate would serve as an example to other members of "that
exasperating class to which danger of imprisonment has the same attrac-
tion that the flame of a candle has for a moth." Bodlak and others like him
seem to have enjoyed taunting the police, putting "every possible tempta-
tion to arrest them in the way of the officials by boasting of their immunity
from arrest" because they were U.S. citizens.[87]

The Austrian government had allowed U.S. consuls and the embassy
to intervene in previous cases and secure lighter punishments for U.S.
citizens, "but now in war time all criticism of the State are punished with
the greatest rigor."[88] Hoover was content to let the Austrian government
have its way. By doing so, he helped align politics and physical location. If
naturalized American citizens were more interested in Austrian politics
than American politics and went so far as to return to Bohemia to
promote nationalist ideologies, then they should not be able to hide
behind the barrier of American citizenship. If their priorities were in
Austria, then their bodies should be there, too – even if those bodies
were in an Austrian jail.

No doubt making the traditional assumption that consuls were about
commerce, Ralph Busser, the U.S. consul in Trieste in 1915, asserted that
"Trieste is undoubtedly the busiest Consulate in Austria."[89] Although he
might have been right when referring to the decades before the 1880s, after
that point, he was definitely wrong. It is difficult to say which post actually
was the busiest, but it was probably Vienna, or, even more likely,
Budapest. Paul Nash, who was consul general in Budapest in 1911,
observed that "The responsibilities of this post are so much greater than
those of the average consulate, principally on account of the complicated
protection cases."[90] Ambassador Penfield also pointed to the high number
of citizenship and military service cases as a mark of the uniqueness of U.S.-
Habsburg relations.[91]

Military service cases dominated the consular agenda at Vienna and
Budapest. Although exact figures regarding the number of cases do

[87] No. 49, "Imprisonment of Zdenek Bodlak," 28 July 1915.
[88] Ibid.
[89] No. 202, "Recommendations," 9 November 1915.
[90] No. 212, Paul Nash to SecState, 21 March 1911, file no. 125.2433/10, in NARA.
[91] No. 38, Penfield to SecState, 10 December 1913.

not exist,[92] we know from the consuls themselves that these cases were time consuming, and the surviving files concerning these cases make up the second largest subset of files in the State Department's U.S.-Habsburg "protection of interests" files.[93] Some concrete statistics are available: the Budapest consulate general alone processed 108 military service cases in the 1912/13 fiscal year, 105 cases between 1 August and 31 December 1914, and an additional 114 cases in the calendar year 1915.[94] Records also indicate that some cases did not come to the attention of U.S. authorities until 1919,[95] after the fighting had stopped, but before all prisoners of

---

[92] The documentary evidence on military service cases – and protection cases in general – is incomplete. Standard record-keeping practice was to record cases in the consulate's log book, and all correspondence relating to a case would be kept in the consulate archives. Correspondence generated by the DOS and the consulate was generally done in triplicate, so there was the copy sent to the designated recipient, a copy retained in the consular archives, and a copy sent to Washington. Once World War I began – and the workload of the consulates skyrocketed – this system could not be maintained. From Budapest, Vice Consul Mallett wrote, "It has been impossible to prepare and transmit confirmation copies of the several thousand telegrams received and sent." In Fiume, Consul Chase observed to the DOS that "Many features of the work, involving much time and labor, cannot be shown by statistics as a record was not kept for such, or any other purpose." Only some items were mailed to Washington at all, and because of the uncertainty of wartime mail, even for diplomatic correspondence, not all of the items mailed arrived and found their way into departmental files. In terms of military service cases, 157 cases from the 1910–22 period appear in Washington files in some form, although most are incomplete. The consular archives themselves were sealed when the United States severed diplomatic relations with Austria-Hungary in the spring of 1917, and most posts in the former Habsburg Empire did not reopen until at least 1921. The keys to the archives were left with Habsburg police authorities. Needless to say, not everything survived. On the closing of consulates, see Lansing's telegram to Penfield, 4 February 1917, file no. 124.63/13a; Young's personal letter to Herbert, 30 June 1917, file no. 125.281/2; and no. 46, "Closing of the Budapest Consulate General," Coffin to SecState, 24 July 1917, file no. 125.2432/54, all in NARA. For the Mallett quote, see "Conduct of the Consulate General at Budapest, Hungary, since July 4, 1914," Mallett to SecState, 14 September 1914, file no. 125.2436/32, in NARA. For the Chase quote, see no. 119, "Activities of Fiume Consulate for Foreign Interests," Fiume, 18 December 1915, file no. 125.3816/20, in NARA.

[93] The largest subset of files are requests from Americans to locate friends and relatives in the empire and report on their welfare during World War I; DOS files contain approximately 3,000 such requests. See file 363.11, in NARA. On the consular workload during the war, see also Katharine Elizabeth Crane, *Mr. Carr of State: Forty-Seven Years in the Department of State* (New York, 1960).

[94] On the 1912/13 year, see "Memorandum with regard to questions 33 and 36," 6 September 1913; for other statistics, see "Work of the Budapest Consulate General during the war," Coffin to SecState, 6 January 1916, file no. 125.2436/42, in NARA.

[95] See file nos. 363.117/532 and 543a, in NARA.

war were released, and at least one case was not successfully resolved until August 1921.[96]

The Habsburg military was based on the idea of universal service. All male Austrian or Hungarian citizens of a certain age could be called for military service, and they were all obliged to attend multiple training sessions and medical examinations.[97] Military service was important to Habsburg authorities. Not only did it help to protect the country in actual wars, but service exposed people to a broad cross-section of the empire's population, thus building supranational identity and loyalty to the emperor.[98] Because of the universal nature of the service and its impor- tance to the state, Habsburg authorities expected all males of the right age who were physically located on Habsburg soil to participate. When a man claimed exemption because he was a U.S. citizen, authorities were less than pleased, and they waited for citizenship to be established through official channels before releasing the man in question. They typically confined men to barracks pending citizenship decisions, rather than assigning them to active duty.[99] During World War I, however, that was not always entirely possible, as fighting was occurring on Austro-Hungarian soil, and several people claiming to be U.S. citizens became prisoners of war in Russia, Serbia, and Italy over the course of the war.[100] Existing records indicate that only one man was actually killed in action: Joseph Tott died in June 1915, six months before his family was able to report his impressment.[101]

---

[96] The case of Chaim Hook, a naturalized U.S. citizen born in Galicia, is the most extreme military service case. Hook traveled to Galicia to visit relatives in the spring of 1914, and, by the time his case was resolved in August 1921, he had been a POW in Russia and Italy and then sent to the new Polish state. See file nos. 363.117/60, 258, 344, 411, 466, 486, 537, H76, in NARA.

[97] The laws regarding military service in Austria and Hungary varied over time and were not always the same in both halves of the empire. By 1910, the laws were brought in line with each other, and, throughout the Habsburg crownlands, a man was liable to be taken for service "after the 1st of January of the calendar year in which the man in question reaches his twenty-first year and ends with the 31st of December in that year in which the man in questions ends his 36th year." This meant a change in the Hungarian law, which had held men between the ages of nineteen and forty-two liable for service. See Flournoy to Van Dyne, 20 October 1910, file no. 363.117/2, in NARA.

[98] See István Deák, *Beyond Nationalism: A Social and Political History of the Habsburg Officer Corps, 1848–1918* (New York, 1990).

[99] No. 135, "Work of the Budapest office since the war commenced," Coffin to SecState, 2 January 1915, file no. 125.2436/35, in NARA.

[100] Examples of POW cases include Max Gelb in Russia, file nos. 363.117/34 and 341; Dusan Ratkovich in Italy, file nos. 363.117/300 and 346; and Robert Fuchs in Serbia, file nos. 363.117/351 and 396, all in NARA.

[101] File nos. 363.117/229a, 262, 271, 277a, 292, 349, in NARA.

While men claiming U.S. citizenship waited, officials at the U.S. embassy and consulate general in Vienna and the consulate general in Budapest took action to investigate citizenship claims and request the release of those holding legitimate U.S. citizenship.[102] There were four categories of military service cases. The first category consisted of cases that were clearly covered by the 1870 naturalization treaty between the United States and Austria-Hungary, and these cases were relatively easy to resolve.[103] The second was cases of incomplete or illegal naturalization, which were equally easy to resolve, if more trying for the people who asked for and were denied assistance. The third category was dual citizenship cases, which fell into a loophole in the 1870 treaty and were therefore far more contentious. American politicians and the public had a clear opinion on these cases, but their opinion was not in keeping with international law. Finally, there were cases in which the man in question had been in Austria-Hungary for more than two years, and, as a result, a presumption of expatriation arose against him. To convince U.S. authorities to help him, he had to provide a good reason for his lengthy stay in his native country. For U.S. consuls, these were the most frustrating cases because they had to make an essentially subjective decision about where an individual's loyalties lay. All of these cases required a significant amount of work by the staff of the Vienna and Budapest consulates-general and the embassy. By the end of the war, U.S. officials were ready to change the international legal system to resolve dual citizenship cases and institute passport and visa systems to mark citizenship more effectively and regulate international movement.

The 1870 U.S.-Habsburg naturalization treaty was supposed to resolve citizenship and military service issues, and, in many cases, it succeeded. The treaty held that properly naturalized citizens were not liable for military service in their native land. In the United States, naturalization

---

[102] After 1867, the Habsburg army was divided into three major parts: the Imperial Army, which served the monarchy as a whole and was under the jurisdiction of the joint war ministry; the Landeswehr, which was for the Austrian half of the country; and the Honvéd, for Hungary. To get someone removed from the military rolls for the Imperial Army or the Austrian Landeswehr, the U.S. embassy in Vienna had to address a communication to the Ministry of Foreign Affairs, which then passed the message on to the war ministry or the Austrian government for investigation and an eventual decision, which would then be transmitted to the embassy via the Ministry of Foreign Affairs. For the Hungarian Honvéd, the Budapest consulate general dealt directly with the Hungarian authorities. There was also an Imperial Navy, but no cases of naval impressment occur in the existing military service records.

[103] The treaty entered into force in 1871.

had been a multistep process since it was first codified in 1790. After a specific period of residence, a man[104] declared his intention to become a U.S. citizen and the court issued his so-called first papers. After another period of residence, the man received his second papers. He was then examined by a judge, and if that interview was a success, he became a naturalized U.S. citizen. When he was naturalized, any minor children he had who had been born abroad but currently resided in the United States also became U.S. citizens.[105] Men who had gone through the whole naturalization process themselves or who were legally U.S. citizens via their father's naturalization were clearly covered by the 1870 treaty, and the Habsburg government released them from service after the embassy or the Budapest consulate general made an official request.[106]

In these clear-cut cases, the Habsburg government trusted U.S. representatives to acquire legitimate proof of citizenship. If the embassy or consulate general was satisfied enough to make an official request for release, the Habsburg government was satisfied. This trust was a product of the diplomatic culture of the Great Power System: it was a further indication that the Habsburg government recognized the sovereign authority of the U.S. government over its citizens, and, by not contesting U.S. claims, the Habsburg government hoped the U.S. government would return the favor.

The burden of proving citizenship was therefore on the embassy or consulate general, and the staff did its best to acquire proper documentary evidence. Consulate general, embassy, or State Department staff needed to see a man's passport or his naturalization papers – or his father's naturalization papers – to be convinced of the man's citizenship. Such documentation was not required for international travel, so many of those asking for assistance could not provide these documents. The consulate general or

---

[104] Citizenship law prior to World War I was patriarchal. An unmarried woman of legal age could go through the process described here. Married women's citizenship status was a function of their husbands' status, and the citizenship status of minor female children was covered by their father's status. When a man became a U.S. citizen, his wife and minor children were automatically naturalized. On citizenship in the United States, see, among others, James H. Kettner, *The Development of American Citizenship, 1608–1870* (Chapel Hill, 1978); Nancy Cott, "Marriage and Women's Citizenship in the United States, 1830–1934," *AHR* 103, 5 (1998): 1440–74; and Barbara Young Welke, *Law and the Borders of Belonging in the Long Nineteenth Century United States* (New York, 2010).

[105] Residency requirements changed over time, but for most of the nineteenth century, it was a total of five years; in 1906, it was raised to seven. See Paul R. Spickard, *Almost All Aliens: Immigration, Race, and Colonialism in American History and Identity* (New York, 2007).

[106] See, for example, Andrew Kanalkiewicz's case, file nos. 363.117/333, in NARA.

embassy would send a telegram to the State Department, which would then attempt to secure the necessary information. If the man had ever had a passport, which required proof of naturalization to obtain, the department would go to its own files to find the application. To get naturalization papers, they wrote to the man's family or the court that had originally issued them. When the department was convinced of the man's citizenship status, they telegraphed the embassy or consulate general, who then wrote to the Ministry of Foreign Affairs to present their case.[107]

Before the war, the Habsburg government could take months or even a year to process such cases, much to the frustration of U.S. officials.[108] One explanation for the slow pace would be that the Habsburg bureaucracy could be a very slow moving, inefficient, and backward entity.[109] It seems more likely, however, that the process was intentionally slow in an effort to send a message to the individual and others like him. That message was, if you are going to leave the country and become a U.S. citizen, don't come back. The Habsburg government, too, was interested in an alignment between citizenship and physical location.

During the war, however, the Habsburg government responded to these cases with much greater speed. Consul General Coffin made sure to mention this progress to the department: "I wish to say that the Hungarian Government has shown a gratifying disposition to give immediate consideration to the claims of naturalized citizens to exemption from military service and the consideration of them has been much prompter than in time of peace."[110] In part, it was out of concern for the individual, as the chances of injury or even death were much greater during wartime. More important, however, the Habsburg government did everything it could to keep the United States out of the war. Irritating Americans over military service cases was not in Habsburg interests.

The second category of military service cases were those that involved incomplete or illegal naturalization, or other false claims to U.S. citizenship. Since U.S. naturalization was a multistep process, there were many people who thought they already were U.S. citizens, or were at least entitled to U.S. consular protection, when, in fact, they had only gone

---

[107] See, for example, John Tulea's case, file nos. 363.117/88 and 153, in NARA.
[108] See file no. 363.117/W181, in NARA. For a complaint from a U.S. official, see Grant-Smith to MFA, 2 August 1914, file no. 363.117/8, in NARA.
[109] See, for example, Waltraud Heindl, *Gehorsame Rebellen: Bürokratie und Beamte in Österreich 1780 bis 1848* (Vienna, 1991); and A. J. P. Taylor, *The Habsburg Monarchy, 1809–1918* (Chicago, 1948).
[110] No. 135, "Work of the Budapest office since the war commenced," 2 January 1915.

through part of the process. The idea that they were already entitled to protection was furthered by the fact that many states allowed noncitizens or those with only their first papers to vote as part of efforts to attract settlers. If they could vote, surely they were entitled to consular protection? Some were even sure to mention that they had voted Democratic, in hopes of winning favor with Wilson administration officials.[111] U.S. consuls had to inform them that they were not eligible for protection.

Other people who asked for protection discovered that their naturalization had been illegal and was therefore invalid.[112] This was most common among people who had been recruited in Europe directly by mining corporations that handled all immigration and citizenship matters in-house. They presented large numbers of immigrants to judges all at once, and the information they provided about length of residence was not always accurate. Those discrepancies came out when men were asked by the consulate to provide an account of their time in the United States, and many did not know that they needed to lie in order to be considered legal U.S. citizens. Like those with incomplete naturalization, U.S. officials declined to assist these illegally naturalized people.

Finally, U.S. officials denied protection to a third group of individuals: children of naturalized U.S. citizens who had never been to the United States themselves.[113] It was common practice for men to travel to the United States to find work while leaving their wives and children at home in Austria-Hungary. If the men became naturalized U.S. citizens, their children could only claim U.S. citizenship if they had resided in the United States. That residency requirement was not always clear to either fathers or their children.

Cases in which a person clearly was not a U.S. citizen or where he clearly was solely a U.S. citizen were easy to resolve. Other cases, however, were far more complicated. The 1870 treaty contained a significant loophole: it did not stipulate how people with dual citizenship should be handled. At the outbreak of the war, R. W. Flourney, chief of the department's Bureau of Passport Control, wrote that he was "afraid that our naturalization … treaty with Austria will be put to a pretty severe test, unless peace is

[111] Congressman Igoe to Lansing, 12 April 1917, file no. 363.117/418; see also Joe Grund's case in file nos. 363.117/43, 44, 46, 47, all in NARA. See also Alexander Keyssar, *The Right to Vote: The Contested History of Democracy in the United States* (New York, 2000).
[112] See, for example, Frank Tadejevic's case, file nos. 363.117/310 and 388, in NARA.
[113] See, for example, Franjo Simac's case, file no. 363.117/261, in NARA.

established in Europe."[114] Dual citizenship cases arose from the conflict between American *jus soli* citizenship laws and Austro-Hungarian *jus sanguinis* laws. U.S. law held that people born on U.S. soil were U.S. citizens, regardless of the citizenship of their parents. Austro-Hungarian law, however, posited that a child born anywhere in the world to a man who held Austrian or Hungarian citizenship was an Austrian or Hungarian citizen. This meant that all male children born on U.S. soil to Austrian or Hungarian immigrants were liable for military service if they went to Austria-Hungary because they held dual citizenship.

U.S. policy was to try to have proven dual citizens released from service. Proving birth in the United States could be more difficult than one might expect, however; not only did people rarely travel with their birth certificates in the nineteenth century, but many jurisdictions did not even issue them. Significantly for U.S.-Habsburg relations, Cook County, Illinois – the county in which Chicago is located – did not begin to issue birth certificates until the first decade of the twentieth century.[115] Chicago natives had to rely on the testimony of parish clergy to prove their place of birth – if the clergyman could still be found.[116]

Once they had proof of U.S. citizenship, U.S. officials would present their claim to the Habsburg government and request the man's release from service. During the war, the Habsburg military wanted every man it could get, and so they asserted their right to claim the dual citizenship status of these men and retain them for military service. Ambassador Penfield, the U.S. consuls, and the staff in Washington all knew that the treaty was ambiguous in these cases and that international law had to be respected. With this in mind, they did not pursue cases after the Habsburg government claimed dual citizenship.[117]

This approach, although perfectly legal, produced significant protest in the United States. The issue was broader than U.S.-Habsburg relations because other countries, notably Italy, had similar laws and similarly ambiguous treaties with the United States. Perhaps the most prominent person to question how U.S. citizens could be held for military service on dual citizenship grounds was Senator Henry Cabot Lodge. In a letter to the State Department requesting action to release a U.S. citizen from the Italian

[114] Flourney to Putney, 31 July 1914, file no. 363.117/51, in NARA.
[115] Petrich to DOS, 5 January 1916, file no. 363.117/226; and County Clerk of Cook County IL to DOS, 12 November 1918, file no. 363.117/487, both in NARA.
[116] See, for example, Joseph Zunic's case, file nos. 363.117/414, 511, in NARA.
[117] See, for example, John Kulusich's case, file nos. 363.117/86, 101, 103, 117, and 131, in NARA.

army, Lodge wrote: "I cannot assent for a moment to the proposition that such a thing as dual citizenship is possible ... and to attempt to retain the right over a boy born in this country of parents not naturalized ... for military service in the country of origin of the parents is absurd on its face and is something to which we should never assent for a moment."[118] Secretary Lansing drafted a lengthy letter detailing the official departmental perspective on the issue in June 1915. The department had to defend its position on dual citizenship so often that the letter was printed and used as a circular, distributed to politicians and people who were denied assistance because they held dual citizenship.[119] The issue received sufficient attention among policymakers so that the post-World War I treaty regime contained provisions that eliminated all previous ambiguities in favor of the U.S. position on sole citizenship. The consuls had upheld international law during the war, but they were undoubtedly in favor of subsequent changes that resolved this issue.

Finally, there were the cases in which a presumption of expatriation had arisen against the man claiming U.S. citizenship. In March 1907, the U.S. Congress had passed a law that declared a person expatriated if he or she had been absent from the United States for two years or more.[120] To retain a claim to U.S. citizenship, a man had to provide evidence to overcome the presumption of expatriation. This issue became increasingly hazy as the war progressed, however. Once the war started, it was difficult and unsafe to travel. Without proper papers, which most people had not brought from the United States, one could not leave the empire, and a short trip to visit relatives could quickly become a two-year stay during the war.

U.S. officials were generally willing to assist people who had clearly come to Austria-Hungary for a fixed amount of time. Such trips to visit relatives, obtain an education, or dispose of property that were begun shortly before the war were easily recognized as cases worthy of intervention. U.S. officials were also willing to accept that people were in the empire for medical reasons. Many women who were ill returned to Austria with their children to recover their health while the father remained in America; some of the children had obtained their majority during their stay in Austria-Hungary and were thus eligible for service. Other men were

---

[118] Robert Lansing, "Status of Persons Born in the U.S. of Alien Parents and of Foreign-Born Persons Naturalized in This Country," 9 June 1915, file no. 363.117/181, in NARA. See also Bahar Gürsel, "Citizenship and Military Service in Italian-American Relations, 1901–1918," *JGAPE* 7, 3 (2008): 353–76.

[119] Lansing, "Status of Persons."

[120] Carr to Busser, 26 June 1916, file no. 363.117/315, in NARA.

there because of their personal health or the health of their wives. Medical practitioners at the time frequently prescribed "a change of air" to restore people to health, and, in many of the cases presented here, the patients had been taking the empire's air for ten years or more.[121]

The State Department instructed U.S. officials in the empire to determine whether the men had taken an oath of allegiance to Austria-Hungary, Emperor Franz Joseph, or the Habsburg flag. Taking such an oath would be a violation of the naturalization agreement because it was a show of loyalty to a state other than the United States and a practical election of foreign citizenship. It was, however, virtually impossible to be on active duty in the Habsburg army without having taken such an oath.[122] Most people claiming U.S. protection swore in an affidavit that they were forced to repeat the oath against their will. Whether someone had taken such an oath was never the exclusive reason why assistance was denied, but it was taken into consideration.[123] In one case, the State Department even argued that applying to the Habsburg government for the travel pass necessary to get to an embassy or consulate to report an impressment case was a profession of Austrian or Hungarian citizenship and therefore a sign of expatriation.[124]

More important than taking an oath or applying for a travel pass was whether the person in question had issued a formal protest to the Austro-Hungarian authorities at the time of their arrest or impressment.[125] Ernest Harris, the American consul general in Vienna after the war, wrote that "According to the 'Wehrgesetz' (National Defense Law) of the Monarchy, there were two appropriate authorities to which cases of this nature, protesting against service in the Austro-Hungarian Army, should have been lodged. After having received the official notification to appear on a certain day before the recruiting board, a protest could have been lodged with either the 'Bezirkshauptmannschaft' or governmental administration authorities or with the recruiting board itself."[126] Many impressed soldiers said that they failed to protest to the Habsburg military officials because they were afraid of being penalized by the authorities. Fred Jaklitsch, a man who applied for the release of himself and his son in Trieste in April

---

[121] See, for example, Joseph Zunich's case, file nos. 363.117/168, 451, 456, and 468, in NARA.

[122] Gerard to DOS, 20 April 1916, file no. 363.117/299, in NARA.

[123] Ibid.; Lansing to the U.S. Legation in Berne, 2 July 1918, file no. 363.117/457, in NARA.

[124] Busser to DOS, 22 December 1916, file no. 363.117/399, in NARA.

[125] U.S. Legation at Berne to DOS, 14 March 1918, file no. 363.117/444, in NARA.

[126] Harris to DOS, 10 December 1929, file no. 363.117/551, in NARA.

1916, testified that "It is war, and one does not know if anything is allowed or not. I have always heard that one must not oppose the military authorities if one does not wish to be punished."[127]

Other factors that affected the U.S. government's willingness to intervene included proof of involuntary service, prior registration as an American citizen, and holding oneself out as an American citizen, rather than as an Austrian.[128] Those who had been in Austria-Hungary for a number of years and who owned property or engaged in business in the empire were often considered expatriated. Owning property was considered a sign of involvement in the country where the property was located, and although owning property in the empire was a detriment to those claiming U.S. citizenship, owning property and having a family in the United States were definitely assets in protection cases.

U.S. officials also wanted to know about the impressed man's plans for returning to the United States. They were uninterested in helping people get out of the army and then stay in Austria. Officials dealing directly with the men and department staff in Washington both recognized that many people were asking for assistance merely to avoid military duty. After getting help, they demonstrated "the greatest disinclination to return to the United States."[129] Ulysses Grant-Smith, the U.S. consul general in Vienna, pointed out that "many naturalized American citizens of Polish, Croatian, Hungarian or other origin, return to their countries of their nationality for the purpose of taking up their permanent abode therein; and when the question of their military service is involved endeavor to obtain protection under the cloak of forfeited American citizenship.... Had it not been for the present war, there is no doubt that many such persons would have continued to reside in their former homes as American citizens without any wellfounded claims as such."[130] In two cases, efforts to secure release were completely dropped when men admitted that they did not plan to return to the United States.[131] State Department officials in Washington instructed U.S. officials in Austria-Hungary to inquire about an impressed man's intent to return and to make every effort to facilitate a speedy departure, either when the case was resolved, or, if possible, after

---

[127] Affidavit of Fred Jaklitsch, in Penfield to DOS, 19 April 1916, file no. 363.117/308, in NARA.

[128] U.S. Legation at Berne to DOS, 3 October 1918, file no. 363.117/475, in NARA.

[129] Penfield to DOS, 26 April 1916, file no. 363.117/290, in NARA.

[130] Grant-Smith to DOS, 31 January 1916, file no. 363.117/H76, in NARA.

[131] Mike Roth's case can be found in file nos. 363.117/222, 242, 246, 280, 293, 311, 314, 348; Eugene Neuwirth's case can be found in file no. 363.117/361, all in NARA.

the man was released, pending a decision.[132] By facilitating a man's return to the United States, the consular service ensured that the case could not be reopened. More important, the man's physical location and citizenship would be in alignment.

The number of military service cases U.S. officials in Austria-Hungary had to deal with naturally increased once World War I began, but this was just the tip of the iceberg in terms of the wartime consular workload. Before the war, the Budapest consulate general already maintained unusually long working hours: it was open to the public from 9 to 4 Monday through Saturday and 9 to 1 on Sundays and holidays, with the staff staying regularly until 6 or 7 in the evening.[133] Once the war started, the Budapest consulate general staff grew to seventeen members, and they "worked every day Sundays included from early in the morning until 7 or 8 in the evening, and every second night from 9 in the evening until 2 or 3 in the morning."[134] U.S. officials were busy helping U.S. citizens, getting them back to the United States, providing relief payments, and tracking people down in Austria-Hungary because people in the United States had inquired about their whereabouts and well-being.

Added to all this, though, was the fact that the United States, as a neutral power, was called on to protect the interests of Britain, France, Italy, Russia, Japan, Serbia, Montenegro, Romania, San Marino, and Belgium in Austria-Hungary.[135] In addition, U.S. officials were protecting Habsburg interests in Britain, France, Japan, Russia, and Belgium, which meant that additional correspondence went through U.S. posts in the Habsburg Empire.[136] On the one hand, the result of this was a very over-worked consular service, which rarely saw increases in pay despite the

---

[132] Crosby to Paris, 17 February 1916, file no. 363.117/238, in NARA.
[133] Such hours were highly unusual and demonstrate the unique nature of U.S.-Habsburg relations. To be open on Sundays and holidays was unheard of, even among most other U.S. posts in the empire. British consulates anywhere in the world were never open for more than six hours a day on working days. The DOS in Washington was open from 9 to 4:30, Monday through Friday. On Budapest, see: "Suggestion that Mr. Kemeny be appointed Deputy," Nash to Assistant SecState, 2 July 1910, file no. 4935/88, in NARA; on the British, see Platt, 104; on the DOS, see Ilchman, 98.
[134] Mallett, "Conduct of the Consulate General at Budapest," 14 September 1914.
[135] No. 46, "Closing of the Budapest Consulate General," 24 July 1917; Mallett, "Conduct of the Consulate General at Budapest," 14 September 1914; and "Work of the Budapest Consulate General during the war," Coffin to SecState, 6 January 1916, file no. 125.2436/42, in NARA.
[136] Penfield's telegram to SecState, 29 December 1915, file no. 124.63/4, in NARA; and Mallett, "Conduct of the Consulate General at Budapest," 14 September 1914.

massive increase in work – and the fact that consuls were often still paying additional clerks out of their own pockets.[137] On the other hand, it made the U.S. Consular Service more efficient in both the short and long term. Wartime consuls found ways to deal with the workload, and Congress began to consider seriously a reorganized and better-funded service. U.S. consuls and the State Department had extensive first-hand experience of how so much could become so complicated so quickly when unregulated international movement came to a stop and millions of people were left stranded and without identification.

The shift in workload can be seen through some statistics compiled at the Budapest consulate general in August 1916. The report broke down the number of certain types of duties it had performed by fiscal year, providing data for the 1913/14, 1914/15, and 1915/16 periods. In 1913/14, the Budapest consulate general certified 1,264 invoices for goods totaling just over $2.3 million. By 1915/16, that had fallen to 55 invoices for $70,794 worth of goods. By contrast, the Budapest office issued only eight passports in 1913/14, but, in 1914/15, it issued 509. Even more telling is the post's volume of correspondence. In 1913/14, 8,562 letters and telegrams were received and sent, up from the previous year's 6,323. The next year, the number was 28,188.[138] From Trieste, Consul Busser reported that, "during the two years from July 31, 1914, to July 31, 1916, [the consulate received] 6,618 incoming letters and telegrams; 8,870 outgoing letters and telegrams; totaling 15,488."[139] At the Vienna embassy, Penfield reported that correspondence performed in the interests of the Austro-Hungarian government alone was "responsible for more than half of the labor of the greatly augmented and costly staff of the embassy, to say nothing of the enormous expenditure for telegrams, cables and postage." In this connection, between 31 July 1914 and 22 October 1915, the U.S. embassy had received "approximately 9,390 communications" and sent another 6,180, just for the Habsburg government.[140]

[137] Penfield's telegram to Lansing, 13 September 1916, file no. 124.63/6; Penfield's telegram to Lansing, 4 January 1917, file no. 124.63/8; Grant-Smith to Phillips, 26 December 1916, file no. 124.63/14–1/2; and Penfield's telegram to Lansing, 25 November 1916, file no. 124.633/58, all in NARA.
[138] "Statistics of Office Work at the Budapest Consulate General during the Fiscal Years of 1913/14, 1914/15 and 1915/16," 22 August 1916, in NARA. The 1912/13 statistics are from "Memorandum with regard to questions 33 and 36," 6 September 1913.
[139] No. 304, Busser to SecState, 20 September 1916, file no. 125.9453/53, in NARA.
[140] No. 3852, Note Verbalé from the U.S. Embassy to MFA, 16 November 1915, enclosed in no. 967, Penfield to SecState, 18 November 1915, file no. 124.636/20, in NARA. Much of this correspondence related to the treatment of Austro-Hungarian POWs in Russia. See

In taking over the protection of foreign interests, the United States was upholding an aspect of the diplomatic culture of the nineteenth-century Great Power System. The practice had emerged earlier in the century as it became clear that the needs and problems of individual citizens would not stop during war; the third plank of the consular agenda – the protection of citizens abroad – was firmly entrenched. The practice signaled that belligerent states still recognized each other's legitimacy; they were putting full diplomatic practice on hold, but with every intention of restoring it as soon as the political problem of the moment was solved. There was a risk, however: without diplomats and consuls to reinforce the Great Power System on a daily basis, it was possible that the reserves of good will and mutual recognition amassed in friendlier times would not outlast the conflict. By accepting the responsibility of protecting foreign interests, the United States demonstrated its full participation in Great Power System diplomacy. After the United States entered the war in 1917, it again played by Great Power rules, arranging for the still-neutral Spanish to take over the protection of its interests in Austria-Hungary.[141]

Once the war started, the types of problem faced by U.S. citizens and the foreign citizens protected by U.S. officials were essentially the same, but the war gave them new urgency – and more serious consequences. The unrestricted flow of people across international borders that had obtained in peacetime came to a sudden halt. Steamship lines shut down, borders closed, and millions of people were stranded in foreign countries. Vice Consul Mallett observed:

There are thousands of persons in Hungary at present, who have resided . . . many years in America, and who have families, property, business and employment in the United States. Most of these persons are women and children whose husbands and parents are in America, and who have come to Hungary this summer to make brief visits. Most of them are bound to the United States by many ties, and have few interests in Hungary, and inasmuch as they came to Hungary provided with funds for a short time only, they are at present either destitute or in a very unpleasant situation. Many of them have checks and letters of credit which they cannot use at present, and nearly all of them have return tickets on the German steamship lines.[142]

Davis, "Diplomatic Relations," 84; and Crane. See also Alon Rachamimov, *POWs and the Great War: Captivity on the Eastern Front* (Oxford, 2002).

[141] See Penfield's telegram to SecState, 29 December 1915; and Lansing's telegram to Penfield, 4 February 1917.

[142] Mallett, "Conduct of the Consulate General at Budapest," 14 September 1914.

These women and children certainly did not have their husbands' or fathers' naturalization papers with them, and so U.S. officials in the empire could not help them or offer them financial assistance. Consul Hoover reported similar problems from Carlsbad, noting that local banks would not cash checks or honor letters of credit, creating financial problems for Americans in the area.[143]

For people who could prove their citizenship, U.S. officials in Austria-Hungary arranged for special ships and trains to send people home. To notify them of the opportunity to leave, the staff of the Budapest consulate general sent a thousand telegrams in a twenty-four-hour period to Americans in Hungary who "had previously expressed a desire to return to America as soon as possible."[144] U.S. consuls then had to issue passports and obtain visas from the countries through which these Americans would be traveling on their way home. Vice Consul Mallett reported that this task was "enormous."[145]

U.S. officials also helped citizens of other countries leave the empire. From Budapest, Consul Coffin reported in January 1915 that "Three parties of Frenchwomen have been organized and repatriated through Italy. Many small parties of Englishwomen have been sent home. More than 1,000 Russian subjects have been repatriated through this office. While such cases do not usually involve financial assistance they require a good deal of time and attention, as information concerning trains and routes, police travel permits, passport visas etc. must be given, and passports issued in cases where the people have none."[146] Finding foreign citizens, providing them with proper paperwork, and arranging for them to go home was a massive undertaking. The work clearly showed consuls how intertwined European and American populations had become, and how valuable passports and visas could be when trying to sort everybody out and return them to their homes.

U.S. officials expected the workload to decrease fairly quickly after the start of the war because they expected foreigners on Habsburg soil, including U.S. citizens, to depart quickly. This was not the case. The Budapest office had repatriated 1,400 Americans by December 1914, and, in 1915, there were 874 more.[147] Mallett observed that "although there was every

[143] Hoover's telegram to SecState, 4 August 1914, file no. 363.11/6, in NARA.
[144] Ibid.
[145] Ibid.
[146] No. 135, "Work of the Budapest office since the war commenced," 2 January 1915.
[147] Coffin, "Work of the Budapest Consulate General during the war," 6 January 1916.

reason to assume that the work would decrease in proportion to the number of Americans relieved and sent en route to America, it has however not decreased, but on the contrary it was increased regularly since the effects of the present war conditions began to become apparent."[148] Since the general belief in Europe and the rest of the world at the start of the war was that it would be of limited scope and short duration, many people did not try to leave in the first months. As the war continued, a steady flow of people trying to leave the country or in need of other assistance was maintained.

For those people who could not return home, foreign governments authorized relief payments, which were organized and distributed through U.S. consulates. In January 1915, Coffin reported that "Nearly 2,000 individual payments of relief to subjects of Russia, Servia, Great Britain and France have been made from the relief funds of the respective governments sent to this office. This work is on the increase and the weekly payments now amount to about two hundred."[149] By the end of 1915, the Budapest office had made more than 8,300 payments totaling almost a half a million crowns.[150] The Fiume consulate made 4,036 payments totaling 114,169.25 crowns between November 1914 and November 1915.[151] Each individual transaction required careful and time-consuming documentation for the records of the consulate, the State Department, and the foreign government making the payment.[152]

U.S. officials in the Habsburg Empire also undertook to find people all over Europe. Although actual statistics on the number of such requests are unavailable, it seems reasonable that, between American requests to find people in Austria-Hungary and Austrian and Hungarian requests to find people in Britain, France, Russia, and Belgium, the number of requests is likely somewhere in the thousands. Answering American requests, which typically arrived through the State Department, received priority.[153] It was often difficult to provide adequate information, however, as fighting was occurring in Hungary and Galicia, which not only disrupted the mail and

---

[148] Mallett, "Conduct of the Consulate General at Budapest," 14 September 1914. Coffin expressed a similar sentiment in no. 135, "Work of the Budapest office since the war commenced," 2 January 1915.

[149] No. 135, "Work of the Budapest office since the war commenced," 2 January 1915.

[150] Coffin, "Work of the Budapest Consulate General during the war," 6 January 1916.

[151] No. 119, "Activities of Fiume Consulate for Foreign Interests," 18 December 1915, file no. 125.3816/20, in NARA.

[152] Most of these records have not survived. See note 92.

[153] These requests can be found in file 363.11, in NARA.

telegraph services, but also forced many people to move, and to do so without leaving a forwarding address.

In Budapest, Vice Consul Mallett, a U.S. citizen, was in charge of the post for several weeks at the start of the war, owing to the illness of Consul Coffin's wife in Paris. Mallett reported that "many requests were made to this Consulate General by Hungarians in the interests of relatives and friends in enemy countries." He found it very difficult to cope with all of these private requests, although he tried, and he gave priority to the many requests that were submitted through the Hungarian government. Mallett believed that this work for the Hungarians was exceptionally important:

The number of these requests has since increased in an extraordinary degree, and it does not appear at present advisable to refuse these requests. By this means the gratitude of the Hungarian Government and of the Hungarian people has been deserved, and at present public opinion in Hungary is very favorable to America, and America holds, with regard to Hungarians, an extraordinary and enviable position. As a direct result, I am enabled to protect those subjects and citizens of enemy countries at present in Hungary in a degree which would be impossible under other circumstances. Every request which I made to the Hungarian Government in behalf of such citizens or subjects has been complied with.[154]

When Consul Coffin returned, however, he significantly reduced the number of such requests the consulate general processed, so that only requests "from Ministers or other prominent officials are given attention."[155] Coffin chose to sacrifice Hungarian public opinion rather than work his harried staff into the ground. Whether his decision resulted in reduced cooperation on the part of the Hungarian government is unclear. Habsburg efforts to keep the United States out of the war likely provided Coffin with an equal or greater power when dealing with the Hungarian government.

In January 1915, Consul Coffin reported that "By far the most exacting and time consuming part of the work has been the task of giving information and advice to innumerable callers. Americans, Hungarians, English, French, Russians, Servians, in fact people of all nationalities, even Germans, have seemed to feel that American representatives could help them and have not hesitated to ask for help."[156] As one of the only functioning consular services in Austria-Hungary and indeed

[154] Mallett, "Conduct of the Consulate General at Budapest," 14 September 1914.
[155] No. 135, "Work of the Budapest office since the war commenced," 2 January 1915.
[156] Ibid.

much of Europe, the Americans were definitely the people to ask for help. Ambassador Penfield was particularly proud of the work he and the embassy and consular staff were doing in the empire. He repeatedly asked for raises for his staff – and for the hiring of additional staff members – and he also wrote letters of commendation for the private U.S. citizens who volunteered their services to help the American representatives.[157]

The ardently neutral work of the U.S. representatives in the empire was not fully appreciated by the State Department staff back in Washington, and Penfield was particularly devastated when Secretary Lansing made the decision to entrust U.S. interests in the empire to Spanish protection when diplomatic relations were severed in 1917. Penfield repeatedly entreated Lansing to allow the Chilean or Swiss consular staffs to take over U.S. interests, noting that the Spanish embassy in Vienna was "no good" and that it "neglects responsibility."[158] A few days later, he observed that allowing the Spanish to take over would "be a mistake for which we could never forgive ourselves," and in a third and final protest, he called the Spanish minister "pro-German" and pointed out that, "To have our interests left with the Spanish Empire would be a sad ending to my hard work."[159] Lansing insisted on the Spanish, however: he had already instructed the U.S. minister in Madrid to ask the Spanish government to take over before Penfield's opinion had been requested, and he refused to change his mind.[160]

When the Spanish took over the protection of American interests in the empire, much of the burden of dealing with those cases shifted to the department staff in Washington, because the Spanish were not as empowered to make independent decisions as the U.S. consular and embassy staff had been. With first-hand experience of the varieties of problems that could arise and the sheer number of people in need of assistance produced by an abrupt cessation in the international movement of people, U.S.

---

[157] For example, Penfield wrote to the department to express his thanks for the volunteer clerking efforts of "Mr. Thomas D. M. Cardeza of Philadelphia and Prof. John Archer Silver of Hobart College." See no. 190, Penfield to Lansing, 7 October 1914, file no. 124.633/11, in NARA.

[158] Penfield's telegram to Lansing, undated [received 7 February 1917], file no. 124.63/14, in NARA.

[159] Penfield's telegram to Lansing, 8 February 1917, file no. 124.63/16, in NARA; and Penfield's telegram to Lansing, 4 April 1917, file no. 124.63/21, in NARA.

[160] Lansing's telegram to Penfield, 5 April 1917, file no. 124.63/21, in NARA; see also Willard's telegram to Lansing, 5 February 1917, file no. 124.63/13, in NARA.

officials were ready to make changes at the Paris Peace Conference that would hopefully minimize this type of problem in the future. By closing dual citizenship loopholes in the Paris peace treaties, keeping passport requirements in place after the war, and developing a visa system and strict immigration quotas, the United States demonstrated that it had learned the hazards of unregulated international travel. That lesson was not lost on the other governments in the system, including the Habsburg government, whose consuls serving in the United States had their own negative impressions of unregulated mobility.

4

The Limits of State Building

Habsburg Consuls in the United States and the Protection of Lives and Property

In 1907, Rudolf Guertelschmied, a citizen of Austria, was working on a construction project in Spokane, Washington. The work was on behalf of the city, and Guertelschmied was being paid by two separate companies that had contracted with the city. As work on the project proceeded, something went wrong, and a 67,000-volt electric current passed through Guertelschmied's body. He was unconscious for several days, and he lost his hands and feet as a result of the incident. He was still alive, however, although his body was useless for future labor. This raised the questions of whether he should be compensated for his injuries and where he should seek long-term financial support.

Despite the presence of large numbers of Austrian and Hungarian citizens in the Pacific Northwest, the closest Austro-Hungarian consulate was in San Francisco, and it was highly unlikely that the consul there ever heard about the incident. Guertelschmied probably used an American lawyer or an immigrant mutual aid society to help him seek restitution from his employers. Guertelschmied might have sought their assistance, or they might have contacted him to offer their help; either is a distinct possibility. What is clear is that Guertelschmied sought compensation from both companies and the city of Spokane.

The results of his three suits varied. The court dismissed the case against the city, so Guertelschmied received no compensation from that quarter. The first company went to court in an effort to avoid paying Guertelschmied, but they were unsuccessful; the court awarded Guertelschmied $500 for his injuries. The second company opted to settle out of court. They gave Guertelschmied $750, but they insisted that he return to Austria and promise never to make any other claims against the company.

At some point between receiving his injuries in 1907 and early 1911, Guertelschmied did return to Austria. There, he became the financial responsibility of the Austrian government because he was no longer able to support himself. On the one hand, the Habsburg government was pleased that he had returned because it wanted to retain as large a population as possible: at the turn of the century, a large population was often considered a sign of strength in the international community, and it could easily be interpreted as reflecting popular support for the government. On the other hand, Guertelschmied was now a financial liability for the Habsburg state.

Austrian government officials asked Guertelschmied about what compensation he had received; they thought it was unreasonably low, given that the man would never be able to work and therefore earn his own living again. Austrian domestic authorities asked their foreign ministry to survey the Austro-Hungarian consuls in the United States about what typical compensation was in such cases. The consuls reported that, in cases they had been involved in, settlements of $3,500 to $4,000 had been reached. The Habsburg government then approached the State Department in an effort to enlist its help in securing additional compensation for Guertelschmied. Department officials wrote to the governor of Washington about the case, and the governor agreed to approach the two companies for an additional lump sum payment or a small annuity. The companies refused to make any such payments, and the governor and the State Department announced that there was nothing else to be done. The Austrian government accepted this position and resigned itself to supporting a once-productive citizen for the rest of his life.[1]

The Guertelschmied case demonstrates the limits of the Austro-Hungarian government's ability to protect the bodies and property of its citizens living and working in the United States. The Habsburg government had several goals regarding its population in the United States: it wanted to keep money earned by the community flowing back into Austria-Hungary; it wanted to keep its citizens safe while they were in the United States, so they could continue to be productive; and it wanted to make sure its citizens returned to Austria-Hungary after limited sojourns in the United States. Most importantly, the Habsburg government wanted its citizens to maintain their loyalty to the emperor and the Habsburg state. One key way to show that continued loyalty was to retain their Austrian or Hungarian citizenship. Staying safe and returning to Austria-Hungary were goals shared by the majority of the migrants when they set out from

---

[1] For Guertelschmied's case, see file no. 311.631 G96, in NARA.

Europe, but the conditions they faced in the United States caused some to rethink their plans to return and their identities as Austrian or Hungarian citizens loyal to the Habsburgs.[2]

Guertelschmied, like the majority of other Austrian and Hungarian citizens in the United States, worked a job that was physically demanding and dangerous; construction projects, mines, and iron and steel works were the most common sites of employment for these people. These were the types of jobs available to foreign-born workers in a United States committed to laissez faire capitalism and infused with racial prejudice and xenophobia. "New Immigrants" from Southern and Eastern Europe – including Austria-Hungary – were particularly vulnerable to these trends.[3] Because Austrian and Hungarian citizens worked such dangerous jobs, the incidence of on-the-job injuries and deaths was high, leaving workers and their dependents on both sides of the Atlantic extremely vulnerable.[4] Local American officials and corporations wanted to shift the costs of caring for such people to the Habsburg government, whereas the Habsburg government naturally wanted the corporations to pay. The Habsburg government – like other governments whose citizens served in the U.S. labor force – wanted to use its claims to sovereignty over its citizens abroad to pressure the U.S. government and American corporations to compensate deaths and injuries that occurred on U.S. soil.

For the Habsburg government to be successful in its efforts to protect its citizens and get Americans to provide workers' compensation, it needed a large consular presence in the United States. Consuls needed to be located in areas with significant Austrian and Hungarian populations, and they needed to be aware of as many such cases as possible so they could bring the full power of international law to bear in each case to achieve maximum compensation. The presence of Habsburg consuls also helped to maintain citizens' loyalty to the Habsburgs and encouraged them to retain their Austrian or Hungarian citizenship and their plans to return to Europe.

---

[2] On return migration, see Mark Wyman, *Round-trip to America: The Immigrants Return to Europe, 1880–1930* (Ithaca, 1993).

[3] See, among numerous others, Matthew Frye Jacobson, *Whiteness of a Different Color: European Immigrants and the Alchemy of Race* (Cambridge MA, 1998); and David R. Roediger, *Working toward Whiteness: How America's Immigrants Became White* (New York, 2005).

[4] On workplace injury and subsequent legal proceedings, see John Fabian Witt, *The Accidental Republic: Crippled Workingmen, Destitute Widows, and the Remaking of American Law* (Cambridge MA, 2004); Louis Anthes, *Lawyers and Immigrants, 1870–1940: A Cultural History* (Levittown, 2003); and Roediger.

As the Guertelschmied case illustrates, the Habsburg consular service in the United States was not large or well placed enough to meet these goals (see Appendix II). Consuls had to compete with mutual aid societies and other nationally specific organizations, such as the Polish National Alliance, that wanted to assist individuals in these types of situations. These groups were trying to expand their membership and improve conditions for immigrants who were planning to remain permanently in the United States. Habsburg consuls also had to compete with American lawyers and other individuals who were out to make a profit off the immigrants and who were not necessarily committed to scrupulous conduct. As much as national organizations and profiteers undermined Habsburg efforts in the United States, the small consular service was dependent on them for communicating with and protecting many Austrian and Hungarian citizens.

The adverse living and working conditions Austrian and Hungarian citizens faced in the United States and the development of nationalist feeling through voluntary organizations and the ethnic press in the United States did prompt an expansion of the Habsburg consular presence there. However, the expansion began in earnest only in the decade before World War I, which was too late to be effective. An expanded consular service was intended to enforce more effectively Habsburg sovereignty over the bodies of its citizens abroad and to exercise that sovereignty independently of ethnic organizations and private American citizens; it was designed to project the power of the Habsburg state onto U.S. soil. An increasing number of Habsburg authorities – especially those in the Hungarian government – questioned the value of such efforts, given the pervasive hostility of the American environment. They began to advocate large-scale repatriation projects, which were designed to alleviate the problems posed by migration by limiting mobility and privileging territorial sovereignty. In short, they maintained that the Habsburg government could best protect the lives and property of its citizens if those citizens remained on Habsburg soil.

Very little is presently known about the broad contours of the Habsburg consular service. It was created in 1718 – well before the British service was created and before Habsburg rulers embarked on the systematic creation of a central bureaucracy in the 1740s.[5] The American, French, and British

---

[5] The British consular service was founded in 1825. On the Habsburg bureaucracy, see Waltraud Heindl, "Bureaucracy, Officials, and the State in the Austrian Monarchy: Stages of Change since the Eighteenth Century," *AHY* 37 (2006): 35–57; and Waltraud Heindl, *Gehorsame Rebellen: Bürokratie und Beamte in Österreich 1780 bis 1848* (Vienna, 1991).

TABLE 4.1 *Habsburg Consular Posts in the United States*
SECTION A. *Historical List of Habsburg Posts Compiled by Rudolf Agstner*

Consulates–General
New York City, New York
  Consulate: 1819–30
  Consulate general: 1830–45
  Honorary consulate general:
  1845–53
  Consulate general: 1853–71
  Honorary consulate general:
  1871–96
  Consulate general: 1896–1917
Chicago, Illinois
  Honorary consulate: 1871
  Consulate: 1894–97

Consulates
Philadelphia, Pennsylvania
  Honorary vice-consulate: 1841–92
  Honorary consulate: 1892–1911
  Consulate: 1911–17
San Francisco, California
  Honorary consulate: 1850–1911
  Consulate: 1911–17
St. Louis, Missouri
  Honorary vice-consulate: 1855–72
  Honorary consulate: 1872–1913
  Consulate: 1913–17
Pittsburgh, Pennsylvania
  Honorary consulate:1875–94
  Consulate: 1894–1917
Cleveland, Ohio
  Consulate: 1903
Denver, Colorado
  Consulate: 1909
St. Paul, Minnesota
  Consulate: 1912

Honorary Posts
New Orleans, Louisiana: 1837–1917
Boston Massachusetts: 1841–1917
Mobile, Alabama: 1846–1914
Charleston, South Carolina: 1848–1907
Savannah, Georgia: 1849–1917
Apalachicola, Florida: 1849–88
Key West, Florida: 1855 (never activated)
Baltimore, Maryland: 1855–1917
Galveston, Texas: 1855–1917
Richmond, Virginia: 1855–1917
Norfolk, Virginia: 1857–66 (officially closed 1909)
San Juan, Puerto Rico: 1859–1917
Milwaukee, Wisconsin: 1867–1907 (officially closed 1917)
Louisville, Kentucky: 1868–91 (officially closed 1917)
Honolulu, Hawaii: 1869–1917
Cincinnati, Ohio: 1871–88
Pensacola, Florida: 1888–1917
Hazelton, Pennsylvania: 1898–1902 and 1909–12
Charleston, West Virginia: 1903–17
Clarksburg, West Virginia: 1907–11
Proctor, Vermont: 1909–10 (officially closed 1917)
Buffalo, New York: 1909–16
Uniontown, Pennsylvania: 1911–17
Wilkes-Barre, Pennsylvania: 1912–17

Source: Rudolf Agstner, "From Apalachicola to Wilkes-Barre: Austria(-Hungary) and Its Consulates in the United States of America, 1820–1917," *AHY* 37 (2006): 163–80.

SECTION B. *Posts and Districts Listed by the Habsburg Government in 1907*
The U.S. State Department asked the Habsburg government to provide a list of
consular districts in 1907 so that local officials could be reminded of Austro-
Hungarian treaty rights regarding deceased Austrian and Hungarian citizens.
This is the list provided by the Habsburg government.

Active Posts

Mobile Alabama – Consulate
   District: Alabama
San Francisco, California – Consulate
   District: California, Nevada,
   Oregon, Idaho, Utah, Washington,
   Arizona,
   Alaska
Pensacola, Florida – Vice-consulate
   District: Florida
Savannah, Georgia – Vice-consulate
   District: Georgia, South Carolina
Honolulu, Hawaii – Consulate
   District: Hawaii
Chicago, Illinois – Consulate-general
   District: Illinois, Iowa, Nebraska,
     North Dakota, South Dakota,
     Montana,Wyoming, Indiana
   Temporary jurisdiction: Michigan,
     Minnesota, Wisconsin
New Orleans, Louisiana – Consulate
   District: Louisiana, Mississippi
Baltimore, Maryland – Consulate
   District: Maryland, Delaware
Boston Massachusetts – Consulate
   District: Massachusetts, Maine,
   Vermont, New Hampshire
St. Louis, Missouri – Consulate
   District: Missouri, Arkansas,
   Kansas,Colorado, Oklahoma,
   New Mexico
New York City, New York –
Consulate-general
   District: New York, Connecticut,
   New Jersey, Rhode Island

Cleveland, Ohio – Vice-consulate
   District: Ohio
Philadelphia, Pennsylvania –
   Consulate
   District: Eastern Pennsylvania
Pittsburgh, Pennsylvania – Consulate
   District: Western Pennsylvania, West
   Virginia
Manila, Philippine Islands –
   Consulate
   District: Philippine Islands
San Juan, Puerto Rico – Consulate
   District: Puerto Rico
Galveston, Texas – Consulate
   District: Texas
Richmond, Virginia – Consulate
   District: Virginia
   Temporary jurisdiction: Kentucky,
   North Carolina, Tennessee

Vacant Posts
Louisville, Kentucky
Cincinnati, Ohio
Hazleton, Pennsylvania
Norfolk, Virginia
Milwaukee,Wisconsin

Source: "Appendix 2: Austro-Hungarian Consular Officers in the United States," enclosed in
Adee, Circular to State Governors, Washington, 27 June 1907, in *M862: Numerical and
Minor Files of the Department of State, 1906–1910, roll 534, Cases 6830–6851* (Washington,
1972), case no. 6847.

services were initially associated primarily with facilitating overseas trade; the Habsburg Empire has never been famed for its maritime prowess, however, and it is difficult to fathom that overseas trade was the driving force behind the service's creation and expansion. It is possible that a trade facilitation agenda was combined early on with assisting and protecting religious pilgrims abroad. According to Rudolf Agstner, himself a professional consul, the Habsburg consular service included more than seven hundred posts over the course of its two-hundred-year history, but it is not clear exactly where all these posts were or how many of them were honorary rather than official.[6] Historian William Godsey reports that the consular service included 108 official and 364 honorary posts in 1914.[7]

Although the Habsburg consular service expanded over time and increasingly concerned itself with protecting its citizens abroad – just as the American consular service did – its trajectory of professionalization was apparently rather different from its American counterpart. The Habsburg Ministry of Foreign Affairs, of which the consular service was a part, enjoyed a more secure position in Habsburg society than the U.S. State Department. While U.S. politicians clung to a rhetoric of isolationism, international affairs were widely recognized in Austria-Hungary as being of critical importance.[8] The empire occupied an undesirable strategic position in Central Europe; Prussia and later Germany, France, Italy, the Ottoman Empire, and Russia could all pose serious military threats to the

[6] On the number of consulates, see Rudolf Agstner, "From Apalachicola to Wilkes-Barre: Austria(-Hungary) and Its Consulates in the United States of America, 1820–1917," *AHY* 37 (2006): 163–80. Unfortunately, Agstner provides no citations for his figure or his list of U.S. consulates. HHStA records list eighty-four consular posts in its finding guide to their records, but this list is not comprehensive, and it raises questions. The list does not mention any consulates in the United States. However, there are records in the HHStA that pertain to consulates in New York City, Chicago, and other American cities. These records are incomplete as well; not every extant consulate has a file there – for example, Philadelphia is missing – and some cities, such as Detroit, which never had consulates, do have records in the HHStA consular files. See also Rudolf Agstner, "Les services consulaires autrichens (austro-hongrois) entre 1800 et 1914," in *Consuls Et Services Consulaires Au XIXe Siecle = Die Welt Der Konsulate Im 19. Jahrhundert = Consulship in the 19th Century,* ed. Jörg Ulbert and Lukain Prijac (Hamburg, 2010), 175–90.
[7] William D. Godsey, Jr., *Aristocratic Redoubt: The Austro-Hungarian Foreign Office on the Eve of the First World War* (West Lafayette, 1999), 14. Godsey provides no citation for these figures, either.
[8] See Godsey. See also Gerald H. Davis, "The Diplomatic Relations between the United States and Austria-Hungary, 1913–1917" (Ph.D. diss., Vanderbilt University, 1958); A. J. P. Taylor, *The Struggle for Mastery in Europe, 1848–1918* (Oxford, 1954); and F. R. Bridge, *Great Britain and Austria-Hungary, 1906–1914: A Diplomatic History* (London, 1972).

empire. Because of its location, a well-trained, well-supported foreign ministry staff was a must for the empire, and the ministry as a whole consistently employed competent people. By the 1890s, the consular personnel serving in the United States were almost all in possession of titles of nobility; whether those titles were long-standing or the result of more recent bureaucratic service is open to question. Noble families were often in the best position to offer their children the education that would serve them well abroad, including language instruction and exposure to elite social practices. There was also a Consular Academy in Vienna, but it is not clear how many consuls it actually produced, at least among those who served in the United States; its instruction in Oriental languages likely had a positive impact on the consular service in Asia.[9]

Habsburg consuls, like Habsburg diplomats and other foreign ministry personnel, were almost always strong proponents of a supranational, *kaisertreu* identity and were committed to upholding the rule of law.[10] Since the 1867 reorganization of the country that created "Austria-Hungary," subjects of the crown were either Austrian or Hungarian citizens, depending on the half of the country in which they had been born.[11] Language, religion, social class, and other potentially differentiating attributes or identities were not emphasized – and were often actively ignored or suppressed – by the joint ministries of the central government, whereas the equality of all individuals before the law and the political citizenship categories *Austrian* and *Hungarian* were adhered to scrupulously.[12] Employees of the Ministry of Foreign Affairs, including

---

[9] On personnel issues in the MFA and the diplomatic corps, see Godsey. See also Oliver Rathkolb, ed., *250 Jahre: Von Der Orientalischen Zur Diplomatischen Akademie in Wien = 250 Years: From the Oriental to the Diplomatic Academy in Vienna = 250 Années: De l'Académie Orientale à l'Académie Diplomatique à Vienne* (Innsbruck, 2004); and Adam Wandruszka, ed., *Die Habsburgermonarchie in System der Internationalen Beziehungen*, vol. 6, *Die Habsburgermonarchie, 1848–1918* (Vienna, 1989–93).

[10] In English, *kaisertreu* is best rendered as "loyalty to the emperor." See Godsey; James Allan Treichel, "Magyars at the Ballplatz: A Study of the Hungarians in the Austro-Hungarian Diplomatic Service, 1906–1914" (Ph.D. diss., Georgetown University, 1972); Ernst Bruckmüller, "Was There a 'Habsburg Society' in Austria-Hungary?" *AHY* 37 (2006): 1–16; István Deák, *Beyond Nationalism: A Social and Political History of the Habsburg Officer Corps, 1848–1918* (New York, 1990); Heindl, "Bureaucracy"; and Jeremy King, *Budweisers into Czechs and Germans: A Local History of Bohemian Politics, 1848–1948* (Princeton, 2002).

[11] After 1878, the Habsburgs also controlled Bosnia and Herzegovina, whose residents did not fall into these categories.

[12] Officials in the Austrian and Hungarian governments were a less uniform group in terms of adherence to a supranational identity than were officials in the central government. The

diplomats and consuls, were more strongly committed to these political categories and individual rights than just about any other people in the empire. As representatives of the empire abroad, they were uniquely placed to advocate these political categories to other governments, thus reinforcing Habsburg legitimacy in the international community.

Reflecting their supranational Habsburg identity, most consular employees in the United States spoke a number of languages in addition to German and French, which were required.[13] The consuls and consul-generals were sent from Vienna, as were their vice consuls and some of the clerical staff, some members of which would go on to be consuls themselves. In addition to these people from Europe, consuls supplemented their staff with American, Austrian, and Habsburg citizens living near the consulates. When hiring additional staff for the consulates, linguistic skills were a priority; consuls hoped to economize by hiring people fluent in multiple languages. For example, in 1897, Josef Lepša was hired as second clerk at the Chicago consulate; Consul Freyesleben reported that Lepša was fluent in Czech, German, English, Croatian, Polish, and Slovak, making him a definite asset to the consulate.[14] Consuls and ministry staff also had to consider balance between Austrian and Hungarian personnel when making staffing decisions. There was not much official complaint from the Hungarian government on this issue, but the Hungarian press and the Magyar-language press in the United States did register dissatisfaction. For example, one paper, the *Amerikai Nemzetör* (Hungarian-American National Guard), complained about the lack of Hungarians on staff of the New York City consulate-general and, specifically, that the consul appointed in 1894 was not of Hungarian ancestry.[15] Consuls were more concerned with the efficiency of their staff than with their citizenship. Gender was unimportant as well – in addition to good language skills,

Hungarian government was notorious for its nationalist leanings. As World War I approached, linguistic categories were increasingly used to provide certain social services. This was in part a pragmatic choice on the part of the central government, but it contributed to the creation of national identities. On social services, see Tara Zahra, *Kidnapped Souls: National Indifference and the Battle for Children in the Bohemian Lands, 1900–1948* (Ithaca, 2008).

[13] Ministry employees who were Hungarian citizens were also required to know Magyar.
[14] No. LV, Freyesleben to MFA, 19 April 1897, in HHStA, AR, Fach 8 – Konsolate, K. 109 – Konsularsitze Chicago 1880–1918.
[15] No. XXIIIB, Tavera to MFA, 2 June 1894, in HHStA, AR, Fach 8, K. 180 – Konsularsitze New York 1880–1918. On Austrian and Hungarian personnel balance in the ministry, see Godsey; and Treichel.

consuls also looked for people with stenographic and typing skills, and they hired a significant number of women.[16]

To maximize the efficiency and expertise of the consuls, the ministry left its professional consuls at their posts for long periods, just as they did with their diplomats. Whereas American consuls were frequently rotated out of office or discharged based on the outcome of presidential elections, Habsburg consuls served at the pleasure of the emperor. Because Franz Joseph ruled for almost seventy years, there was little pressure for politically motivated staffing changes. Habsburg officials also recognized the advantages that could come from long service: consuls could become experts on the conditions at their posts, and they could cultivate trust and positive relationships with local officials and attorneys. Such relationships were especially important for Habsburg consuls because so much of their work involved representing Austrian and Hungarian citizens in American courts.[17] When Habsburg consular staff in the United States were moved from their positions, it was typically to another post in the United States.[18] Long-serving consuls also enjoyed the trust of their superiors in Vienna, who allowed them considerable discretion in handling local matters independently, without having to seek approval and guidance from Vienna.[19]

On the whole, then, Habsburg consuls enjoyed the advantages of working for a ministry considered politically important, and they were well trained. Like the American consular service, however, the Habsburg service was limited by its allocated budget. Habsburg consuls did, in practice, need an outside income to supplement their salaries in order to support themselves in the style to which they were accustomed. The government, however, did provide funds for running consulates and providing aid for Austrian and Hungarian citizens in trouble – expenses American consuls typically paid from their own pockets.

There was not financial support for expanding the number of professionally staffed consulates in the United States, however. The government

---

[16] See personnel reports in HHStA, AR, Fach 8, K. 110 – Konsularsitze Chicago-Cin 1880–1918.

[17] Consuls also provided legal counsel for citizens charged with crimes, including murder. See, for example, Johann Bartok's case in Adm. CCIII., Silvestri to MFA, 6 June 1911, in HHStA, AR, Fach 8, K. 110.

[18] See, for example, the personnel records located in HHStA, AR, Fach 8, K. 194 – Konsularsitze Pittsburgh 1880–1918.

[19] That autonomy was markedly different from American practices, in which DOS officials in Washington demanded authority.

relied heavily on honorary consuls – that is, unpaid volunteers – to serve its constituents in the United States. In large part, this reflected the traditional trade-focused agenda of consular services and the limited nature of U.S.-Habsburg trade. Many of the honorary consuls were located at port cities on the East and Gulf coasts, including New Orleans, Galveston, Savannah, Charleston, Baltimore, Norfolk, and Boston. The duties at these posts focused primarily on certifying trade goods, and they have left very few records in the Vienna archives.

At some of these ports and other commercially important cities, consuls representing the German Empire also served as honorary Austro-Hungarian consuls.[20] For commercial matters, this arrangement was workable, as the commercial language of the empire was traditionally German,[21] and much of the trade went through North German ports. Over time, however, the use of German consuls began to cause two major problems for the Habsburg government. First, as the consular agenda shifted from commerce to protecting citizens abroad, Austrian and Hungarian citizens had different needs than German citizens. They needed consuls who spoke a broader spectrum of the empire's languages, and they needed the respect that race-conscious German officials were often unwilling or unable to provide them. Second, Americans were not likely to see a difference between Germany and Austria-Hungary, especially since a popular American perception of the empire was that its German speakers dominated the entire country. In addition, developing racialist thought maintained that language was a manifestation of race, suggesting, in this case, that Germans and German-speaking Austrians were really a single community. Mutual representation of Germany and Austria-Hungary reinforced these perceptions and made it difficult for the Habsburg government to present a separate identity later, especially during World War I.[22]

In addition to these commercially motivated posts, the Habsburg government maintained other honorary posts at a variety of locations with small concentrations of Austrian and Hungarian citizens, such as in Proctor, Vermont, where marble quarries provided employment opportunities. These posts were typically maintained only when a well-off Austrian

---

[20] Agstner, "From Apalachicola."

[21] This was changing over time, especially as Italian, Magyar, and Croatian were increasingly in use in the Adriatic.

[22] On American conflation of Austria-Hungary and Germany, see Carol Jackson Adams, "Courting the 'Vassal': Austro-American Relations during World War I" (Ph.D. diss., University of Alabama, 1997).

or Hungarian lived there and wanted the prestige of being able to claim honorary consular status. If he moved or died, the post became vacant and was not refilled. On occasion, these consuls were able to assist citizens in the area or help expand trade, but they did very little to help the empire actively. They may actually have proved detrimental because their existence might have suggested to some in Austria-Hungary that the Habsburg consular presence in the United States was large enough, making expansion unjustified. It is important to note, however, that the placement of consuls was just as important as their numbers: one consul in close proximity to a large population of constituents was more useful than five consuls in places with just a handful of Austrian and Hungarian citizens.

The Habsburgs focused their professional consular presence in the northeastern United States, where the first waves of Austrian and Hungarian citizens concentrated. They maintained consulate-generals in New York City and Chicago and consulates in Philadelphia, Pittsburgh, and Cleveland. Over time, they opened consulates in San Francisco, St. Louis, and Denver, but these later consulates, although staffed by professional consuls, were not frequently consulted by the Habsburg government.[23] They also left a minimal paper trail in the Vienna archives, leaving the scope of their activities and effectiveness in the realm of speculation.

The consulate-general in New York City was the oldest Habsburg post in the United States. It opened in 1819 and was raised to a consulate-general in 1830. From 1845 to 1853, and again from 1871 to 1896, it operated as an honorary post, but it would appear from the extant records that it was honorary in that the consul general was unpaid, although he still did the quality and quantity of work expected from a state-supported professional consul. It was the most prestigious Habsburg consular post in the United States. In the decade before the war, it was headed by Alexander Nuber von Pereked, who had been promoted after several years of important and distinguished service in Chicago.[24]

---

[23] When asking for reports on conditions, it was common practice for the MFA and the embassy in Washington to only ask the five major consulates. It is possible that, in some cases, only the five reported, which does not reflect well on the nonreporting consulates. See, for example, no. 4136a/no. 30 A-C, Hengelmüller to Aehrenthal, 31 August 1908, in HHStA, PA XXXIII – Vereinigten Staaten, K. 100 – USA Liasse I: Rückwander. Aktion.

[24] "Appendix 2: Austro-Hungarian Consular Officers in the United States," enclosed in Adee, Circular to State Governors, 27 June 1907, in *M862: Numerical and Minor Files of the Department of State, 1906–1910, roll 534, Cases 3381–3388* (Washington, 1972), case no. 6847.

The duties of the consular staff in New York City were more diverse than those of other posts, since they had a full commercial agenda at the very busy port, as well as protection and representational duties. The majority of Austrian and Hungarian citizens entering the United States came through New York City, and they needed assistance in getting their bearings in the United States and dealing with immigration officials. Many opted to stay close by in New York, New Jersey, and Connecticut, where they worked in factories, as domestics, or in small businesses.[25] Many people returned to Austria-Hungary via New York City, and the consulate-general aided them as well, helping those who had lost their tickets or who needed financial assistance to get home.[26]

The consul general also had a large number of ceremonial duties in New York, organizing celebrations for events like the emperor's birthday or the arrival of Habsburg naval vessels in New York Harbor, and participating in events organized by various groups of Austrian and Hungarian citizens.[27] The consular staff also reported to the embassy in Washington and the ministry in Vienna on the activities of such organizations that were hostile to the Habsburg government. In addition, they monitored press coverage of Austria-Hungary from the mainstream and ethnic press because many key publications were based in New York City. The Habsburg government obviously could not control U.S.-based newspapers, but its members were understandably interested, given the nationalist rhetoric many of these papers adopted.

After the founding of the New York City consulate-general, the next important post opened in Philadelphia. It began as an honorary vice consulate in 1841, became an honorary consulate in 1892, and was raised to an official consulate only in 1911. Like the New York City consulate-general, the Philadelphia consul's honorary status did not prevent him from performing full consular duties. The Philadelphia consulate had a busy workload, assisting Austrian and Hungarian factory workers in the eastern part of the state, but its importance was quickly eclipsed by the consulate at Pittsburgh, which became the center of protection for Austrian and Hungarian citizens engaged in coal mining and iron and

---

[25] Julianna Puskás, *Ties that Bind, Ties that Divide: 100 Years of Hungarian Experience in the United States,* trans. Zora Ludwig (New York, 2000), 110–12.

[26] On lost tickets and other assistance matters at the New York City post, see HHStA, AR, Fach 8, K. 180.

[27] On plans for the emperor's birthday, see no. CCLXXXIV., Schwegle (?) to MFA, 11 July 1900, in HHStA, AR, Fach 8, K. 110; on the arrival of ships, see various reports in HHStA, AR, Fach 8, K. 180.

steel production. An honorary consulate began in Pittsburgh in 1875, in response to the growing presence of Austrian and Hungarian laborers in the region. It was raised to a full consulate in 1894, serving western Pennsylvania and West Virginia, another important coal mining state.

Pennsylvania could be a very dangerous place in the years between the Civil War and World War I. It was a key mining and industrial center where Andrew Carnegie and other major industrialists operated their businesses. Labor conditions in the state helped spur the development of labor unions, including the Knights of Labor; these unions were originally founded by native-born American citizens.[28] In the 1870s, a series of major strikes began, and Carnegie and others turned to Europe to supply strike-breakers. Many Italian and Hungarian citizens, including many Slovak speakers, answered the call, although many of them did not know that they were being recruited specifically to break strikes.[29] These immigrants faced several problems. First, the jobs they had were dangerous, and they risked serious injury or even death. Second, they were understandably the objects of anger from displaced native-born workers: historian John Higham has characterized Pennsylvania as the place "where militant anti-foreign senti-ment gripped the native working class earliest and most fiercely."[30] Third, depending on exactly how they got their jobs and came to the United States, they could be subject to deportation because they were in violation of contract labor laws.[31] That the companies were actually to blame for such violations rather than the laborers themselves was often overlooked by U.S. legal authorities. Fourth, as the number of immigrants grew and economic conditions changed, many lost their jobs and had problems supporting themselves and any dependents.

As the years went by, immigrant workers became more deeply entrenched in the struggle for improved working conditions. Some became involved in organized labor and therefore were accepted by their native-born co-unionists, whereas other unions continued to maintain a xeno-phobic stance. Employers were increasingly prone to resort to violence as a

---

[28] See Roediger; John Higham, *Strangers in the Land: Patterns of American Nativism, 1860–1925* (New Brunswick, 2002), 57.

[29] Higham, 47; Puskás, 97.

[30] Higham, 47.

[31] From 1864 to 1885, it was legal for employers to recruit laborers abroad and have them sign contracts stating that the company would pay their passage to the United States and, in return, the worker would then be obliged to work for a specific time period. The law was overturned due to pressure from native-born laborers. The practice continued illegally, however.

result of labor dissatisfaction, however. Austrian and Hungarian citizens were involved in all the major labor uprisings in Pennsylvania, including those at Homestead and Hazelton. At Hazelton, in 1897, a loosely organized sheriff's posse opened fire on a crowd of immigrant laborers, killing twenty-one and injuring forty. In another example, in 1906, workers were attacked by police; the consul reported that two Austrian citizens from Galicia had been seriously wounded and that others were interested in returning to the empire to escape the dangerous local conditions.[32]

By 1908, the Austrian and Hungarian population in Pennsylvania was estimated at 157,000.[33] With such a large population and an atmosphere of labor unrest, growing nativism, racism, and xenophobia, as well as boom-and-bust economic cycles, the consulates at Pittsburgh and Philadelphia were kept extremely busy. The Austrian and Hungarian population was also becoming more diverse. The consulates had performed most of their work in German and various Slavic languages, but, by 1904, the Magyar-speaking population had grown to such a degree that the Pittsburgh consulate, supported by the embassy in Washington, was clamoring for a staff member who spoke the language.[34]

For many Austrians and Hungarians in distress in Pennsylvania and West Virginia, their financial circumstances were so grim – or their company's work schedule so demanding – that they could not travel to Pittsburgh or Philadelphia to seek help from the consulates. Consular officials, recognizing the importance of being able to assist Austrian and Hungarian citizens in these areas, opened a series of *expositurs*, or branch offices, to better aid their citizens. The Pittsburgh consulate oversaw such branches in Hazelton, Wilkes-Barre, and Uniontown, Pennsylvania, as well as in Charleston and Clarksburg, West Virginia. The purpose of these branches was to provide Habsburg officials and their citizens with information that was as timely and accurate as possible on local conditions and employment opportunities. Consuls had an interest in knowing which firms were reputable and thus less likely to create problems for Austrian and Hungarian citizens. They also wanted to be on-site in the event of the outbreak of labor- or race-related violence.

---

[32] See Higham, 89–90; and the report in HHStA, AR, Fach 15 – Aus- und Einwanderung, K. 37 – Generalia, 1871–1918, Heimbeförderung.

[33] Batt to the Governor of Pennsylvania, no date [spring 1908], in *M862*, roll 534, case no. 6847.

[34] No. 31B, Hengelmüller to MFA, 20 October 1904, in HHStA, AR, Fach 8, K. 195 – Konsularsitze Pittsburg Plojest (Ploesti) 1880–1918, folder Pittsburgh.

Austrian and Hungarian citizens had first been attracted to the factories of the northeast and the mines of Pennsylvania and West Virginia. They were increasingly drawn farther west, however, to the rapidly growing city of Chicago and beyond. The Habsburg government opened an honorary, trade-focused consulate in Chicago in 1871; by 1894, it was an official, protection-focused consulate. Reflecting the rapid development of the city and its role as the gateway to the American West, the post was quickly upgraded to a consulate-general in 1897. The Chicago office was responsible for not only the state of Illinois, but Iowa, Nebraska, North Dakota, South Dakota, Montana, Wyoming, Indiana, Michigan, Minnesota, and Wisconsin as well.[35] With such a vast jurisdiction, the office staff was kept extremely busy, but, even so, there was no way they could effectively monitor conditions for Austrian and Hungarian citizens in the entire region.

Chicago itself had large populations of Polish and German speakers, many of whom were citizens of the empire, as well as Magyar speakers and other Austrian and Hungarian citizens. When staffing the consulate-general in 1897, Consul General Freyesleben was encouraged by the governments in Vienna and Budapest to employ someone who spoke Magyar and who was also a Hungarian citizen, but he wrote that he preferred to use his funds to hire someone who spoke a Slavic language because the demand for those languages in Chicago was much greater than the demand for Magyar. He did make an effort to meet both demands in a single person, but he reported that "My efforts to find a qualified candidate of Hungarian nationality who is also strong in a Slavic idiom have been unsuccessful."[36] After his initial appointments, Freyesleben and his successors at Chicago repeatedly requested that the ministry send them staff who could speak Magyar and Polish, or at least that the post's budget be increased so that locals could be hired.[37] The workload of the consulate-general was constantly expanding, and the increasing demands were reflected not only in the size of the staff, but also in the expansion of the consulate-general's office space. After 1900, the consulate-general was

---

[35] These states were in its jurisdiction in 1907. At times, other honorary posts had control over some of these regions, notably Wisconsin and Minnesota. Also, Michigan was transferred to the Cleveland consular district in 1912. See "Appendix 2: Austro-Hungarian Consular Officers in the United States," 27 June 1907. On Michigan, see no. CCXII, Ludwig to MFA, 15 April 1912, in HHStA, AR, Fach 8, K. 122 – Konsularsitze Ded-Dortmund 1880–1918.

[36] No. LV, Freyesleben to MFA, 19 April 1897.

[37] See HHStA, AR, Fach 8, K. 110.

located in downtown Chicago, on the eighth floor of the Women's Christian Temperance Building – commonly known as "The Temple" – and it expanded from occupying just one room to six rooms by 1915.[38]

The final major Austro-Hungarian consulate was in Cleveland, Ohio; it opened as an official consulate in 1903. Cleveland had an extensive Magyar-speaking population: by 1920, it had reached approximately 56,000.[39] There were also large numbers of German and Slovak speakers. Consuls were continuously requesting a larger staff with abilities in a growing number of languages.[40] Ohio more generally had an extensive Austrian and Hungarian population, especially in major cities such as Cincinnati, Dayton, and Toledo.[41] Throughout Ohio, work in factories was common, particularly factories that manufactured various products from iron and steel. Cleveland also became a major center of nationalist activity; the Magyar population was especially active in this regard. The consulate kept busy monitoring their events and the local Magyar-language paper, *Szabadság* (Liberty), which grew to be a daily paper with nationwide circulation.[42]

After 1912, the Cleveland consular district also included the lower peninsula of Michigan, with its large Austrian and Hungarian populations in and around Detroit and Flint.[43] That redrawing of consular districts was designed to reduce the Chicago consulate-general's workload, thus rendering the service as a whole more effective. With this change in boundaries and the continued expansion of the Austrian and Hungarian community in Cleveland, Consul Ernst Ludwig advocated the elevation of the post to a consulate-general in 1913. The war began, however, before officials in Vienna acted on his request.[44]

In addition to these five major posts, the Ministry of Foreign Affairs created three new consulates in the five years before World War I. In 1909, a consulate was opened in Denver; its primary function was to serve miners in the Western states and to assist Austrian and Hungarian citizens with

---

[38] On the consulate's offices, see Adm. no. CCCLXI, Hoffmann to MFA, 13 June 1912; Adm. CXLVIII, Silvestri to MFA, 5 April 1913; and Zl. 7194/K-47/A, Silvestri to MFA, 12 April 1915, all in HHStA, AR, Fach 8, K. 109.

[39] Puskás, 109.

[40] See Folder Cleveland in HHStA, AR, Fach 8, K. 111 – Konsularsitze Civ-Cle 1880–1918.

[41] No. XXX-D, Zwiedinek to MFA, 1 March 1913, enclosing Krenner's 7 February 1913 report on the Cincinnati *Amtstag*, in HHStA, AR, Fach 8, K. 110.

[42] Puskás, 164.

[43] No. CCXII, Ludwig to MFA, 15 April 1912.

[44] No. LXXXVI-M, Dumba to MFA, 23 July 1913, in HHStA, AR, Fach 8, K. 112 – Konsularsitze, Cle-Col 1880–1918, folder Cleveland.

the increasingly volatile labor conditions in the region, which were fostered by the presence of the International Workers of the World. The honorary consulate in San Francisco, in place since 1850, became an official consulate in 1911. Finally, in 1913, the honorary consulate in St. Louis was raised to an official post; it had been in place as an honorary vice consulate since 1855 and an honorary consulate since 1872.

These three posts represent the start of the Habsburg government's efforts to expand their official consular presence and make the service more efficient and effective. Their locations also reflect the movement of Austrian and Hungarian citizens beyond the Northeast and into the West and Midwest. For reasons that will be discussed later, the South was a low priority. Unfortunately for the Habsburg government – and, arguably, for many Austrian and Hungarian citizens – the war abruptly ended the expansion efforts of the Habsburg consular service throughout the United States.

Even with the addition of the Denver, San Francisco, and St. Louis posts, however, there were significant populations of Austrian and Hungarian citizens who lacked local consular representatives. The consuls themselves lobbied most vociferously for posts in Cincinnati and Detroit.[45] By 1913, Cincinnati had a population of more than 25,000 Austrians and Hungarians, and there were many more in the surrounding area, including Dayton, Middletown, and Hamilton.[46] The local lawyers who did work for the consulate also supported the idea of opening a consulate in Cincinnati, since "quick action is vital" in cases involving the protection of Austrian and Hungarian citizens, and waiting for correspondence to travel between the lawyers and the consulate and Cleveland took too long.[47]

Consuls also advocated the creation of a consular post in Detroit. Cleveland Vice Consul Pelényi reported that Detroit had 10–15,000 Hungarians and somewhere between 25–40,000 Poles.[48] The Poles had

---

[45] See, for example, no. CCXCI, Ludwig to MFA, 13 May 1912, enclosing no. 15955, Pelényi to Ludwig, 13 May 1912, in HHStA, AR, Fach 8, K. 110; and Folder Detroit, in HHStA, AR, Fach 8, K. 122. The Pacific Northwest would likely have been another location for expansion if the war had not arrived; there was a significant Croatian-speaking population engaged in logging in the region. See Kristofer Allerfeldt, *Race, Radicalism, Religion, and Restriction: Immigration in the Pacific Northwest, 1890–1924* (Westport, 2003).

[46] No. XXX-D, Zwiedinek to MFA, 1 March 1913.

[47] Ibid.

[48] No. LXI-H, Hengelmüller to MFA, 15 July 1912, enclosing no. 17621, Pelényi to Ludwig, 15 June 1912, in HHStA, AR, Fach 8, K. 110.

been there for quite some time; they had built a number of churches, and some among them had become lawyers and local officials.[49] The city as a whole had seen its immigrant population rise by more than 60 percent between 1900 and 1912, "as a result of favorable commercial conditions and the automobile industry." Pelényi observed that "A large increase in the size of the colony here is expected in the near future, and it is high time an Expositur was designated here."[50]

To meet the demand for consular assistance in Cincinnati and Detroit, Habsburg consuls from Cleveland and Chicago held *Amtstage*, or "office days."[51] On a designated and well-advertised day, one or two members of the Cleveland or Chicago consular staff traveled to Cincinnati or Detroit and held office hours in a local institution, such as a bank. Austrian and Hungarian citizens could then avail themselves of the consul's services. *Amtstage* were usually held two to four times per year in each city, and they were frequently held on Sundays so that constituents would not have to miss work to attend. Consuls were usually available for at least ten hours per *Amtstag*. Reports indicate that the lines for services were always extremely long.[52] Because of the continued high attendance at *Amtstage*, the consuls in charge always used them as an opportunity to tell Vienna that a consulate or at least an expositur needed to be opened. Vice Consul Pelényi argued that opening a post would be cheaper than continuing to hold *Amtstage*, which were expensive because of the costs of travel, rent, and advertising.[53]

In addition to assisting constituents with business matters, *Amtstage* often included meetings, dinners, or receptions with local organizations of Austrian and Hungarian citizens and clergy members, as consuls sought positive relationships with these institutions. These groups often echoed the consuls' desire to open new consulates because they felt that having a consulate would be a useful symbol of the community's prestige and its importance to the Habsburg government. Consuls were always sure to pass along these requests in their reports to Vienna.[54] *Amtstage* were also frequently combined with visits to local officials, especially judges, district

---

[49] No. CCXII, Ludwig to MFA, 15 April 1912.
[50] No. LXI-H, Hengelmüller to MFA, 15 July 1912.
[51] No. XXX-D, Zwiedinek to MFA, 1 March 1913; on Detroit, see no. LXI-H, Hengelmüller to MFA, 15 July 1912.
[52] See Folder Detroit, in HHStA, AR, Fach 8, K. 122.
[53] No. CCXCI, Ludwig to MFA, 13 May 1912.
[54] See, for example, no. XXX-D, Zwiedinek to MFA, 1 March 1913.

attorneys, and coroners.[55] Habsburg consuls worked to cultivate relationships with these people so that they were more likely to inform the consulate of cases involving Austrian or Hungarian citizens. Consuls also met with local attorneys so they could decide if those attorneys should be recommended to local Austrian or Hungarian citizens in need of legal assistance. These personal relationships facilitated consuls' important protection duties.

Habsburg consuls were charged with protecting the lives and property of Austrian and Hungarian citizens abroad. From the perspective of the Habsburg consuls and the Ministry of Foreign Affairs more generally, the politically based, legal citizenship categories of *Austrian* and *Hungarian* were the only salient identity categories; language, religion, or other potentially differentiating identities were ignored when it came to protecting the rights of their citizens. All citizens were therefore entitled to the consular service's best efforts. Habsburg consuls protected Austrian and Hungarian citizens in the United States – and those considering coming to the United States – by keeping them appraised of local conditions, opportunities, and frauds. They also offered assistance to workers who had been injured on the job, and they actively pursued their treaty rights to take charge of the property of deceased Austrian and Hungarian citizens and to represent overseas dependents of the deceased in American courts. Through these efforts, they sought to maintain a healthy population of Austrian and Hungarian citizens in the United States who could support themselves and their dependents in the United States and in Austria-Hungary, and, in the event of death, to protect the property rights of Austrian and Hungarian citizens residing in the empire.

The Habsburg government, on the whole, was interested in having its citizens go to the United States for only temporary stays. Temporary residence was the plan of the majority of the people who came from Austria-Hungary to the United States: they hoped to earn enough money in a few years of work to be able to return to the empire and improve their financial situation and that of their families. With the money they earned in the United States, these sojourners bought land in the empire – usually adding to existing holdings – built more substantial and modern houses, bought additional livestock and farming technology, and settled debts and back taxes, among other things.[56]

[55] No. LXI-H, Hengelmüller to MFA, 15 July 1912.
[56] See Wyman; Puskás.

The Habsburg government was definitely interested in maintaining the flow of money back to the empire. For Hungary alone, that flow has been estimated at $80 million between 1880 and 1914, and such funds were certainly welcome to the government in terms of general economic development.[57] Habsburg officials provided circulars and other information in multiple languages to aid people in sending money back to Austria-Hungary.[58] Habsburg officials, however, were also concerned that men laboring in the United States would continue to support their dependents in the empire, who would otherwise become a public expense. U.S. officials were typically willing to assist the Austro-Hungarian government in cases in which men deserted their wives. For example, in one case, Mrs. Mary Výborná visited the U.S. consulate in Prague in 1913 to report that her husband had deserted her two years previously, right before the birth of their child. He had gone to the United States with a young woman, who was apparently living with him there. Mrs. Výborná was able to supply the consulate with their address in Cleveland, and she asked if her husband could be deported. Consul Joseph Britton was sympathetic, noting that "Many similar cases of desertion are reported to the consulate." Immigration officials seized the opportunity to reunite Mrs. Výborná with her rightful husband back in Austria; within six weeks of the State Department receiving notice of the case, Mr. Výborná, the other woman, and the woman's mother had all been deported.[59]

This cooperation between the U.S. and Habsburg governments reflects the fact that, ultimately, both U.S. and Habsburg authorities – and much of the general public, especially in the United States – would have preferred that Austrian and Hungarian citizens not go abroad to find work. From the U.S. perspective, if people were going to come to the United States, they should bring their families or acquire families in the United States and become permanent, rooted Americans; indeed, the myth of the United States as a melting pot or a land of immigrants entirely erases the phenomenon of return migration.[60] From the Habsburg perspective, migration was more complicated. Money generated in the United States and sent

---

[57] Puskás, 73. It was likely higher for Austria.
[58] See various reports in HHStA, AR, Fach 15, K. 54 – Aus und Rückwanderung 1880–1918, Amerika 18, 22–46; and Austrian Commerce Ministry, "Wie soll ein Auswanderer sein erspartes Geld nach Hause schicken?" enclosed in no. 93.140/8a 1909, in HHStA, AR, Fach 15, K. 54.
[59] No. 239, "Mary Výborná deserted by her husband," Britton to SecState, 21 May 1913, file no. 311.632 V99, in NARA.
[60] See Wyman.

back to the empire was a good thing, but it became increasingly clear to Habsburg authorities that the human and political costs of laboring in the United States were very high – perhaps too high.

To keep people apprised of the risks, the Habsburg consular service, along with the Habsburg embassy in Washington, served as an important conduit of information about conditions in the United States. The transatlantic community was filled with rumors about opportunities and dangers in the United States. In Europe, agents for the ship lines talked up the allegedly endless opportunities for profits in the United States in an effort to sell tickets. Husbands in the United States – even those who were having a terrible time – often wrote about the excellent conditions and opportunities the United States offered in efforts to assuage concerns at home or to convince their families to come and keep them company.[61] American corporations advertised jobs in Europe and facilitated immigration, and railroad companies publicized the availability of land and business opportunities along their lines. Added to all this were the voices of other boosters who played up the notion of America as the land of opportunity and stressed get-rich-quick schemes associated with the discovery of gold and silver in the American West and Alaska.[62]

These positive voices were easy to hear in Europe, as well as in the United States, where even native-born Americans were often seduced by the idea of starting over and achieving success out West. The negatives of life in the United States could be harder to discover outside the realm of first-hand experience. Some historians have argued that those who had been in the United States and returned home rarely talked about their negative experiences. Injuries and fatalities, so prominent in the consular agenda, were downplayed by many members of the public in Europe and taken as signs of personal weakness or defects.[63] Ministry of Foreign Affairs records demonstrate that the Austro-Hungarian government, however, was not so quick to rationalize these injuries and deaths. Officials were clearly aware of the frequency of such incidents, and the Hungarian government often asked Habsburg consuls in the United States to report on general conditions and specific allegations of wrongdoing and poor

[61] Puskás, 80–87.

[62] On Western boosterism, see, among others, Patricia Nelson Limerick, *The Legacy of Conquest* (New York, 1987); Victoria E. Dye, *All Aboard for Santa Fe: Railway Promotion of the Southwest, 1890s to 1930s* (Albuquerque, 2005); and David M. Wrobel, *Promised Lands: Promotion, Memory, and the Creation of the American West* (Lawrence, 2002).

[63] Puskás, 85–87.

conditions.[64] The press in the empire and the ethnic press in the United States frequently commented on poor conditions in the United States – undoubtedly right alongside glowing reports of opportunity – and, in some cases in which significant groups of their co-nationals were injured, they protested loudly and typically blamed the Habsburg consuls for not performing their protection duties adequately.[65]

In an effort to preserve Austrian and Hungarian lives and their own reputations, Habsburg officials in the United States did their best to provide accurate information on local conditions. The embassy staff, drawing in part on consular reports, transmitted copies of federal laws and regulations to Vienna. They sent copies of laws about who could be deported or denied entry and why, as well as copies of congressional debates, newspaper editorials, and proposed legislation surrounding immigration and labor questions.[66] They sent a 339-page publication from the U.S. government entitled "Circular from the General Land Office showing the Manner of Proceeding to Obtain Title to Public Lands under the Homestead, Desert Land, and Other Laws."[67] They sent information about immigrating to U.S.-controlled Cuba and the Philippines.[68] They sent directions on how to get to the Klondike in Alaska, where gold had been discovered.[69]

In addition to keeping track of laws and U.S. government-sponsored opportunities, consuls also submitted reports about which private employers were genuine. For example, consular staff in Chicago made a list of companies in the Great Lakes region that actually existed and were

---

[64] See reports in HHStA, AR, Fach 15, K. 36 – Generalia 1871–1918, Heimbeförderung; and no. LXIV.N., Ambrózy to MFA, 22 October 1907, in HHStA, AR, Fach 15, K 54.

[65] See, for example, no. LXV., Hengelmüller to MFA, 28 October 1906, in HHStA, AR, Fach 8, K. 181 – Konsularsitze New York 1880–1918. See also the substantial collection of such press reports in HHStA, AR, Fach 15, K. 36.

[66] No. 10631/1, Hengelmüller to Root, 17 December 1907, in M862, roll 739, case no. 10631. See also no. DCXXXIII, Grivičić to MFA, 8 June 1905, in HHStA, AR, Fach 15, K. 36.

[67] No. 7233, Hengelmüller to MFA, 1904, in HHStA, AR, Fach 15, K. 53 – Aus und Rückwanderung 1880–1918, Amerika 1–21.

[68] No. XXI F, Riedl to MFA, 20 June 1899, in HHStA, AR, Fach 15, K. 53.

[69] No. LXVIII E, Hengelmüller to MFA, 27 November 1897, in HHStA, AR, Fach 15, K. 53. For other reports and information on laws, see, among others, no. 5 D, Hengelmüller to Gołuchowski, 16 February 1903; and no. 7 A-D, Hengelmüller to Gołuchowski, 13 March 1903, both in HHStA, K. 43 – BWV 1903; no. LIV 9, Tavera to MFA, 24 December 1891; no. IV C, Tavera to MFA, 27 January 1899; no. 8356, John M. Francis to Pasetti, 4 April 1885; no. 17 C, Tavera to Kálnoky, 27 April 1893; and no. XVI, Hengelmüller to MFA, 7 March 1896, all in HHStA, AR, Fach 15, K. 52 – Aus und Rückwanderung 1880–1918 C – Amerika 1; see also the files in HHStA, AR, Fach 15, K. 54.

currently in operation.[70] Without such information, people accepted jobs from imaginary or defunct companies or spent their savings to travel to places where there were merely rumors of jobs. When they arrived and discovered the truth, they were left in dire straits and in need of consular assistance. Consuls tried to prevent such situations, rather than having to pick up the pieces afterward.

Consuls conducted many investigations themselves, but they also called on the U.S. government to look into certain situations.[71] Such investigations could be awkward and contentious because U.S. officials were often involved in swindles. In one 1911 case, Franz Sorin, an Austrian citizen newly arrived in New York City, was told by immigration authorities that there was definitely work to be had in Larned, Kansas. The mayor of Larned, Mr. Frizell, had informed the New York authorities that there was employment available; Sorin said he had been given "almost a written guarantee" of the availability of work. Sorin and several other immigrants made the lengthy trek to Larned, only to find that there was, in fact, no work there for them. Sorin complained to the Austro-Hungarian embassy, and embassy staff referred the case to the State Department and asked for an investigation. Following proper procedure, the department passed the request on to the Department of Commerce and Labor, which investigated the actions of its own immigration agents, in addition to Frizell and Sorin. The Commerce and Labor investigators decided that Sorin was troublesome and hard to please, and that Frizell had an excellent reputation for employing immigrants and others in need of work; the fault in the situation lay with Sorin, not Frizell. Habsburg officials did not pursue the case further, choosing not to fight this particular battle, but they likely encouraged those Austrian and Hungarian citizens they came in contact with not to venture to Larned.[72]

Habsburg consuls had similar reservations about the South as a whole, as the region offered a unique combination of opportunity and danger to Austrian and Hungarian citizens. Habsburg records include a great many statements from Southern politicians and newspapers that were part of an initiative to attract more immigrants, and Habsburg consuls duly reported to Vienna on this potential opportunity. The motivation behind Southern

[70] Z.VIII, Chicago consulate to MFA, 26 May 1911, in HHStA, AR, Fach 15, K. 55 – Aus und Rückwanderung 1880–1918, Amerika 47–108.
[71] See, for example, Folder 18 – Marcus Braun, in HHStA, AR, Fach 15, K. 54; HHStA, AR, Fach 15, K. 55; and no. 66970, 28 July 1909, in HHStA, AR, Fach 8, K. 181.
[72] Lowenthal to Knox, 28 September 1911, file no. 311.631 S06, in NARA.

efforts was suspect, though. One newspaper headline summed up the plan well: "Calls for Immigrants to Replace Negroes."[73]

Consul Grivičič was invited to attend a conference of Southern governors in Chattanooga, Tennessee in 1906 on the subject of encouraging immigration. Grivičič reported that the South would welcome "all desirable white immigrants," and that, contrary to a widely circulated rumor, the South would gladly welcome working-class immigrants. The governors also promised "to use the resources of the country to help those who have talent adapt to local circumstances."[74]

Despite the governors' efforts, the South was not a popular destination for Austrian and Hungarian citizens. The primary occupation there was farming, and most Austrian and Hungarian citizens were uninterested in acquiring property and thus permanent roots in the United States. Some did find work as agricultural laborers, but wages were extremely low; Consul Hindermann in New Orleans reported that, in 1906, sugar plantation workers along the Gulf Coast were making only 80 cents a day.[75]

Given the small number of Austrian and Hungarian citizens who attempted to farm – estimated at less than 1 percent of these immigrants[76] – the large number of Austrian and Hungarian victims of agricultural swindles is surprising. Perhaps the most famous such case is that of Gusztáv Weber. Weber set up a scheme in which Magyar-speaking immigrants just arriving in New York City were persuaded to buy land for farming in a community in Florida. They put all their money into buying the land and getting to Florida. When they got there, they found that the land they had bought was not Weber's to sell; they were destitute and stuck in Florida. The Habsburg government ultimately sent a naval vessel to Florida to repatriate the victims, and officials in the United States and the empire actively followed the legal proceedings against Weber.[77]

In another case, Habsburg consuls helped a group of Hungarians in Alabama bring charges against the Jackson Lumber Company. The company was accused of "conspiracy to commit peonage," which, in practical terms, meant that it was requiring its employees to work very long hours at arduous tasks for almost no compensation; Ambassador Hengelmüller

---

[73] No. LXVI F, Hengelmüller to MFA, 14 October 1905, in HHStA, AR, Fach 15, K. 53; see also Higham, 113–14.
[74] No. VIII Ff, Hengelmüller to MFA, 5 February 1906, enclosing an excerpt from Grivičič's report, in HHStA, Fach 15, K. 53.
[75] No. 104, Hindermann to MFA, 25 July 1908, in HHStA, AR, Fach 15, K. 37.
[76] Puskás, 113–14.
[77] Folder 18 – Marcus Braun; see also Puskás, 114.

likened it to slavery. The honorary consuls in Mobile, New Orleans, and Pensacola banded together to help these people, and, ultimately, they requested help from the embassy. The embassy arranged for a New York City lawyer to go to Alabama to take the case. That lawyer was counsel for the Austro-Hungarian consulate-general in New York, and he was the most trusted member of the Habsburg consular service's network of American lawyers. The consul at Pensacola evacuated the Hungarians to Florida and made arrangements for yet another Habsburg vessel to arrive and repatriate them at government expense.[78]

Poor wages, potential frauds, and the permanency of farming convinced Habsburg consuls that the South was not a particularly good place for Austrian and Hungarian citizens. Southern politicians quickly agreed: as more and more immigrants actually came to the region – many from Italy – Southerners began to rethink the desirability of having an immigrant population. Although the immigrants had originally been recruited to help solve the South's race problems by bolstering the number of white people, the racial rhetoric quickly shifted at the expense of immigrants. Especially after the massive influx of immigrants in 1907, some Southerners began to argue that Europeans from around the Mediterranean had African blood and therefore were not genuinely white.[79] Habsburg consuls were not going to debunk these long-standing beliefs any time soon – especially since there were so few professional consuls in the South – and so they responded by repatriating Austrian and Hungarian citizens in trouble and discouraging further emigration to the region.

Although there were few Austrian and Hungarian citizens who ventured south, those in the rest of the country kept Habsburg consuls occupied in dealing with the effects of on-the-job injuries and deaths. Racial and class prejudices and xenophobia kept most Austrian and Hungarian citizens in the most unattractive and dangerous jobs and living conditions that the United States had to offer. Božo and Filipp Čorak, Croatian speakers living in Salt Lake City, observed to the Habsburg government that Austrians and Hungarians in the United States "only get work when there are no workers of other nationalities at hand. They are only used for the dangerous work, and if one has an accident, the injured man will receive no compensation."[80]

---

[78] No. LXV., Hengelmüller to MFA, 28 October 1906; see also no. 7649, Hengelmüller's telegram to MFA, 2 October 1906, in HHStA, AR, Fach 8, K. 181.

[79] See Jacobson, *Whiteness;* Roediger; and Higham, 159, 164.

[80] Z. 81322/1852, Božo and Filipp Čorak to the Austro-Hungarian government, 28 July 1915, in HHStA, AR, Fach 15, K. 36.

The occurrence of on-the-job injuries and deaths was high, both for Austrian and Hungarian citizens and for other workers, including the native born. Prevailing legal attitudes, especially in the decades between the U.S. Civil War and the end of the century, favored employers over employees, who worked at their own risk.[81] To mention just a few examples of incidents involving Austrian or Hungarian citizens, Louis Zubich, who worked on a construction crew for the Milwaukee Railway Company in Iowa, sustained permanent injuries: "His back is dislocated so that he is absolutely helpless." A Croatian-speaking employee of the U.S. Department of the Interior in Alaska died after his skull was fractured while he was cutting railroad ties. Frederick Decsenyi lost an arm while working for the Erie Railroad Company.[82]

Vice Consul Pelényi commented on general labor conditions in the United States after a 1912 *Amtstag* in Detroit. He noted that the automobile factories in Detroit provided rare favorable working conditions. He and a local doctor inspected forty-nine men that day to determine if they were fit for military service; twenty-four of the forty-nine were considered fit. Pelényi observed that, "For American circumstances, this is an exceptionally extraordinarily good result. It can be attributed to the relatively light work in automobile and other factories and healthy housing conditions."[83] In other parts of the country, labor conditions were more extreme, rendering many people unsuitable for military service, if they did not actually maim or kill the workers. Pelényi mentioned "the flat feet ... and varicose veins of the miner, the hernias of the iron worker, the obesity of the brewer, ... [and] the vertigo of the cement worker," as well as tenement-induced trachoma as common ailments for Austrian and Hungarian citizens in the United States.[84]

Habsburg consuls made a concerted effort to involve themselves in the settlement of workplace injury cases. Consuls had multiple motivations for getting involved that went beyond general humanitarian concern for the fate of their constituents. One concern was the cost of supporting disabled workers and their dependents. If the injured person remained in the United States and had no family or friends to care for him, he became the financial responsibility of the county or municipality in which he lived; in American

---

[81] See Witt.

[82] See, respectively, Drees to Lansing, 1 July 1915, file no. 311.63/5, in NARA; file no. 311.63/18, in NARA; Decsenyi to DOS, 4 October 1911, file no. 311.631 D35, in NARA.

[83] No. LXI-H, Hengelmüller to MFA, 15 July 1912.

[84] Ibid.

terms, he became a "public charge." Local American officials did not want to assume these costs, and they were under no strict legal obligation to provide quality care. They frequently tried to get injured people deported back to Europe; their attempts could be successful if the request for deportation came within a person's first two years in the United States.[85] If an injured person was deported, or if he elected to return to Austria-Hungary, as many did, the costs of his upkeep shifted to the Habsburg government, which was willing to assume the responsibility of supporting injured workers and their dependents, but less than enthusiastic about the prospect. In addition, by being directly involved in compensation cases, Habsburg consuls could usually secure higher compensation payments than individuals acting alone because they could say with authority what other companies had paid in comparable situations.[86] They could also, on occasion, heighten the seriousness of the situation because of their official status. Cases were no longer about an individual worker and his or her employer – they now operated at the level of international politics, and, at times, the U.S. government could be persuaded to get involved, as in the Guertelschmied case.

The preferred Habsburg solution for dealing with injured workers was to seek compensation from American employers. Some Habsburg consuls went so far as to express an interest in working to reform American labor laws. After a handful of states had passed workers' compensation laws, the U.S. Senate began considering federal legislation in 1911. The law allowed for dependents in the United States, Mexico, and Canada to collect compensation payments, but dependents residing in other countries were excluded. Consul Generals Silvestri and Nuber in Chicago and New York, respectively, advocated lobbying the White House, the State Department, and Congress to extend benefits to dependents in all countries; they also considered a public campaign. Their efforts were stymied by the embassy in Washington, however, because the ambassador was committed to upholding the norm of the Great Power System that stressed nonintervention in the domestic affairs of another state.[87]

---

[85] See, for example, Drees to Lansing, 1 July 1915; and no. DCXXXIII, Grivičič to MFA, 8 June 1905.

[86] See, for example, file no. 311.631 G96; see also the file on Rechtsschutzkrediten in HHStA, AR, Fach 8, K. 112, folder Cleveland.

[87] Hyde to Silvestri, 12 May 1913, in HHStA, AR, Fach 8, K. 110; and no. XCII-N, Dumba to MFA, 8 August 1913, in HHStA, AR, Fach 8, K. 109. See also Witt. According to Dumba, Consul Ernst Ludwig was friends with the governor of Ohio and other politicians

The embassy advocated a more typical approach, which was to deal with corporations on a case-by-case basis. Habsburg consuls discovered that the best method was to employ an American lawyer to approach the corporation. Employers preferred to deal privately with lawyers rather than going to court or dealing publicly with Habsburg officials; companies were generally eager to avoid public scrutiny, which might result in more widespread demands for workers' compensation.[88] Some companies went so far as to send their attorneys overseas to compensate families privately in an effort to avoid the Habsburg consulates altogether.[89]

To pursue compensation cases, Habsburg consuls had a network of American lawyers. Some of these lawyers practiced in close proximity to the consulate, and Habsburg officials were confident that they could be trusted because they were personal acquaintances of the consuls themselves. For those lawyers whose practices were farther away, there was a greater element of risk for the consuls and their citizens. Habsburg consuls made an effort to meet local lawyers whenever they traveled so they could provide sound recommendations to their citizens in legal trouble.[90] The consuls had not been everywhere, though, and at times they had not met the lawyers entrusted with compensation cases. In these instances, consuls could be vulnerable to criticism for recommending a bad lawyer, and they stood to lose the loyalty both of those poorly served and the people to whom the victim related his or her situation. In other cases, the consul was unable to make a recommendation before a local lawyer had inserted himself into the case. Consuls and trusted lawyers complained about these cases that fell "into unfamiliar hands" because they often resulted in unsatisfactory settlements and irate or disappointed constituents.[91] The problem of finding trustworthy lawyers to take Austrian and Hungarian

and was therefore "invited to be present at the meetings of the committee in which the law concerning the liability of the employer for injuries sustained while at work was discussed." See Konstantin Dumba, *Memoirs of a Diplomat*, trans. Ian F. D. Morrow (Boston, 1932), 279.

[88] Adm. CCLV, Silvestri to MFA, 23 June 1911, in HHStA, AR, Fach 8, K. 110.

[89] No. 83, "Article XVI of the Consular Convention concluded July 11, 1870, between the United States and Austria-Hungary," Hotschick to Assistant SecState, 30 July 1909; and no. 70, Phillips to Hotschick, 2 September 1909, both in *M862*, roll 534, case no. 6847. In this case at least, the U.S. consuls in the empire were involved because they were called on to notarize documents. The consul at Trieste refused to sign, as he – rightly – felt that the consular treaty was being violated. The DOS staff in Washington ignored his protest.

[90] No. LXI-H, Hengelmüller to MFA, 15 July 1912.

[91] No. XXX-D, Zwiedinek to MFA, 1 March 1913.

citizens' cases in the United States was another issue that could have been lessened by the presence of a larger number of well-placed consuls.

Habsburg consuls also wanted to be involved in compensation cases because they hoped to maintain the loyalty of their constituents. The Habsburg government wanted to be the agent of aid to its citizens.[92] It paid the legal fees of Austrian and Hungarian citizens who required assistance, especially in personal injury and accidental death cases.[93] The relative lack of consuls, combined with the presence of numerous competitors, including national organizations and individual profiteers, made it difficult for consuls to be the sole source of such aid, however. Consul General Silvestri in Chicago reported that most of the cases that found their way to the consulate were fatalities, because others could get to the injured more quickly than the consuls.[94] Vice Consul Krenner observed that "crafty people" could seize the opportunity presented by a lack of consuls to declare themselves the protector of poor immigrants and make a considerable profit.[95]

National organizations could be helpful to Habsburg consuls, but, more often, they were problematic because they competed with consuls and typically worked toward different goals. The organizations were popular, however: in the face of hostile American conditions, some Austrian and Hungarian citizens, along with immigrants from other countries, banded together to offer each other financial assistance, social support, camaraderie, and, among some groups, to try to improve American perceptions of the recently arrived populations. These people formed all sorts of voluntary associations, from mutual aid and insurance societies to political organizations to gymnastic and choral groups. For the current discussion, these organizations can be seen as falling into three categories. First, there were a handful of organizations that offered assistance to all citizens of the empire and promoted a pro-Habsburg, supranational identity. Second, there were ever increasing numbers of organizations that aimed at improving conditions in the United States for foreign-born permanent residents and their families; they were invested in helping immigrants make permanent lives for themselves in the United States. Finally, there were organizations that were primarily concerned with promoting political change in

---

[92] The importance of Habsburg state services to maintaining citizen loyalty is convincingly presented in Maureen Healy, *Vienna and the Fall of the Habsburg Empire: Total War and Everyday Life in World War I* (New York, 2004).

[93] Adm. CCLV, Silvestri to MFA, 23 June 1911.

[94] Ibid. See also no. XXX-D, Zwiedinek to MFA, 1 March 1913.

[95] No. XXX-D, Zwiedinek to MFA, 1 March 1913.

Europe. They found the United States a more conducive place in which to pursue their European-based agendas, but they did foster the return of migrants to Europe in order to spread their ideas. The line between these latter two types of groups was not always clear; certain groups and their individual members pursued both types of agendas.[96] In addition to these organizations, an ethnic press and a clergy serving the foreign-born developed. These institutions occasionally helped the Habsburg agenda but tended to mostly undermine it at other times.

From the perspective of Habsburg consuls, the existence of all of these organizations and institutions – except, of course, for the few supranational aid societies – was highly problematic. They were almost all organized around categories of racial nationalism: few groups were open to all citizens of the empire, but there were plenty of organizations available to those willing to identify themselves as Poles, Czechs, Slovaks, Germans, Croatians, Italians, Ukrainians, Magyars, or Romanians. These identity categories helped build national communities at the expense of the supranational, political citizenship categories expounded by the Habsburg government and its overseas representatives. These organizations competed with Habsburg consuls for the loyalty of migrants from the empire. They also typically advocated the acquisition of U.S. citizenship, which was directly at odds with Habsburg goals. Habsburg consuls repeatedly advocated the expansion of the consular presence in the United States to combat the effects of such groups. In the meantime, the relative lack of consuls meant that the consular staff had to rely on the networks developed by these organizations to communicate with Austrian and Hungarian citizens in the United States.

Habsburg consuls offered their ardent support for the few empire-wide organizations that did exist. Ministry records provide the most information about the aid society in Chicago. Consul General Silvestri observed, "I constantly give this group my fullest attention." He and the vice consul regularly attended the society's meetings and offered opinions as to the types of activities the group should pursue and how those activities should be carried out. The society included forty or fifty members from the Chicago area. In addition to helping Austrian and Hungarian citizens in legal or financial trouble, it contributed approximately $300 a year toward

<hr>

[96] For other examples of nationalist movements on foreign territory, see Jonathan W. Gantt, *Irish Terrorism in the Atlantic Community, 1865–1922* (New York, 2010); and Michelle A. Stephens, "Black Transnationalism and the Politics of National Identity: West Indian Intellectuals in Harlem in the Age of War and Revolution" *AQ* 50, 3 (1998): 592–608.

the operation of the consulate-general. The society also organized dinners and other social events for visiting Austro-Hungarian dignitaries.[97] The ministry and the central government in general advocated the creation of more such organizations that would work closely with consular officials and promote loyalty to the Habsburg government.[98]

The second type of organization – those aimed at improving conditions in the United States for foreign-born permanent residents – was obviously more of a problem for Habsburg consuls. In the face of prejudice and harsh conditions in the United States, these organizations aimed to provide financial, legal, and social assistance to particular linguistic, religious, or cultural communities. They often developed in conjunction with a newsletter or newspaper in the language of use. Some organizations provided essentially the same services as the consular service, including legal assistance, notary services, and assistance transferring money to the empire.[99] By organizing people along linguistic lines – which were often perceived as being interchangeable with racial lines – the organizations' membership could and often did consist of people from multiple countries. For example, German groups could easily involve people with Austrian, Hungarian, German, Swiss, or Russian citizenship, thus building ties among racial or cultural groups rather than among holders of the same political citizenship.

Some of these organizations explicitly hoped to counter American prejudices. For example, the Magyar Betegsegélyző Egyletek Szövetsége (American Hungarian Aid Society), an umbrella organization for Magyar societies, was founded in Bridgeport, Connecticut, in 1892. Members articulated their goals at the first meeting: to assist Magyars, to counter Pan-Slavism, and "to win the Americans' respect and honor for the thousand-year-old glorious Magyar name!"[100] Magyars and other groups felt compelled to argue for the prestige of their people in the face of American criticism, thus fueling nationalism.

One way to improve conditions for the foreign-born was for them to become naturalized U.S. citizens and therefore voters. Many national organizations adopted this strategy. They reiterated the idea that the

---

[97] Z. CCLVI, Silvestri to MFA, 23 June 1911, in HHStA, AR, Fach 8, K. 110.
[98] See, for example, no. LXI-H, Hengelmüller to MFA, 15 July 1912; and no. 34.813/3, Circular from Gołuchowski to Consuls, 1 May 1905, in HHStA, AR, Fach 15, K. 37.
[99] The general development of such groups is discussed in Puskás, 131–79; see also Charles Thomas Johnson, *Culture at Twilight: The National German-American Alliance, 1901–1918* (New York, 1999).
[100] Cited in Puskás, 143.

American nation could assimilate newcomers, who would then go on to be active, informed participants in American representative government.

Nationalist organizations concerned with American problems also catered to American perceptions of the meaning of immigration to the United States. The idea of the United States as a city on a hill, an exemplary society of political freedom and economic opportunity, free from European problems, was exceptionally pervasive. Immigrants were typically seen as "voting with their feet": in the American myth, they were drawn to the American political system and were actively escaping or rejecting European monarchical oppression. From the American perspective, immigrants were choosing to be part of an exceptional American state. These immigrants, recognizing the obvious superiority of the United States, would become permanent residents and would naturally seek to renounce their previous citizenship in favor of self-evidently more desirable U.S. citizenship. Whole families would come, severing all ties with their land of origin. They would acquire land in the United States and make their own way, very likely on the all-important frontier; that experience would make them Americans and help keep the American nation vital. They were freely choosing the United States, consenting to membership, reaffirming the social contract.

For many arrivals – including the majority of those from Austria-Hungary – this myth did not hold true. Many immigrants were single men who were interested in working in the United States for a limited time and then, when they had amassed funds, returning to Europe to take up permanent residence there. Their long-term goals were in Europe, not in the United States, and so U.S. citizenship was not a priority. Habsburg consuls supported this position – they wanted people to go back, and they preferred that their constituents preserve their Austrian or Hungarian citizenship while they were in the United States. In part, it was about maintaining sheer numbers. A large population theoretically translated into the number of people who could be used in military conflict. In less concrete terms, a growing population was viewed as a sign of success, vitality, and progress, whereas a declining population was a mark of failure – or at least of serious problems.

Although some organizations wanted people to become U.S. citizens in order to prove their ability to assimilate into American society, others wanted their members to become U.S. citizens so they could return to Europe and become nationalist agitators, entitled to the legal protections that derived from U.S. citizenship. Some groups counted on the European circulation of newspapers and ideas committed to paper on American soil.

Other groups paid the passage for their members to return to Europe to spread the word. Vice Consul Pelényi noted, in 1912, that this was a common strategy of the Pan-Germanists. He observed that the leaders of the Pan-German movement in Cincinnati had been born Hungarian citizens and that the Hungarian government's Magyarization policies were responsible for their emigration and their nationalism. To combat Pan-Germanism in Cincinnati, and therefore in the empire, Pelényi advocated the opening of a consulate in the city. He remarked, "clearly, establishing an office in Cincinnati is in Austrian and without doubt in dynastic interests."[101] After an *Amtstag* in Detroit, he expressed a similar sentiment, noting that "It would definitely be in the strong interests of the home government to have an effective state representative here, who could tactfully and with the help of the good elements of the colony promote patriotic feeling and calm national passions."[102]

These European-focused groups were dangerous to the Habsburg government, especially when they advocated territorial changes. Ministry records contain numerous reports on Polish organizations in the United States, especially those that called for the creation of an independent Polish state.[103] Vice consuls Pelényi and Krenner also stressed the need for a consulate in Cincinnati to counter the effects of Romanian nationalism there. Alexander Landesco, a Romanian-speaking Jew who had been expelled from Austria-Hungary, spoke publicly in Cincinnati about the inefficiencies and ineptitude of the empire's officials in the United States and claimed that they abandoned poor emigrants, who were then at the mercy of Americans, who would exploit them. His solution was to ask the Romanian government to open a consulate in Cincinnati, which would be responsible for all ethnic Romanians, regardless of their political citizenship.[104]

Victor Krenner, the consular official who reported on Landesco's activities, thought there was little chance of the Romanian government

---

[101] No. CCXCI, Ludwig to MFA, 13 May 1912.
[102] No. LXI-H, Hengelmüller to MFA, 15 July 1912.
[103] For reports on Polish national activity, see, for example, no. 1363, Berchtold to Zwiedinek, 31 March 1913; and no. 3, Zwiedinek to Berchtold, 6 February 1913, both in HHStA, PA XXXIII, K. 51 – Berichte und Weisungen 1913–14 und Varia 1914; no. 1209/IIA, Dumba to MFA, 31 March 1915, in HHStA, PA XXXIII, K. 52 – Berichte, Varia 1915–1917, Weisungen 1916–17, folder Berichte 1915; no. 6D, Ambrózy to Aehrenthal, 15 March 1910; no. 13, Loewenthal to Aehrenthal, 20 May 1910; and no. 14, Loewenthal to Aehrenthal, 1 June 1910, all in HHStA, PA XXXIII, K. 49 – BWV 1910, folder Berichte.
[104] No. XXX-D, Zwiedinek to MFA, 1 March 1913.

honoring the request, as the population of Cincinnati Romanians was not large. Perhaps, more importantly, most were expelled Jews and thus not likely to interest the Romanian government.[105] But Krenner used Landesco's activities to point out to the ministry that the empire needed an official presence in Cincinnati to protect both its citizens and its reputation. That citizens of the empire would call on their racial brethren in other states to assist them was indeed threatening to the Habsburg state.

Vice Consul Pelényi also mentioned the Cincinnati Romanian community's request to the Romanian government for a vice consulate in Cincinnati. Whereas Krenner had downplayed the possibility of a post actually opening, Pelényi painted a bleaker picture: "Since most of the Romanians there are from Hungarian provinces and of an irredentist mind, it is that much more important to have an official Austro-Hungarian presence here. Should the Romanians put an office here, we must prepare ourselves for conditions like those that prevail in Pittsburgh, where the notorious Pan-Slav P. V. Rovnianek was named Vice Consul."[106]

Pan-Slav groups did attract some Austrian and Hungarian citizens in the United States, and many Americans were sympathetic to their cause, and especially to the cause of Czech nationalism. Indeed, historian Ernest Spaulding has observed that Czech nationalism and the Czech state were "quite clearly 'made in America.'"[107] Pan-Slav rhetoric about the empire furthered the popular conception in America that the (Catholic) Germans in Austria oppressed and dominated the Czechs. The Hungarian domination of the Slovaks, Croatians, and Serbs was also a common theme in the Pan-Slav press, but that idea did not resonate as well among Americans because of their long-standing approval of a Hungary and its valiant 1848 freedom fighters, especially Lajos Kossuth. The Czechs benefited from the fact that Americans already thought the Austro-Germans oppressed the Hungarians; the South Slavs countered that well-ingrained narrative and thus had a more difficult time rallying support for their cause.

Adding to the constellation of interests surrounding national identity and citizenship were the clergy and the ethnic press. The clergy could often be a conservative force in harmony with Habsburg goals, and Habsburg consuls cultivated relationships with them. One consul noted, "The

---

[105] Ibid.
[106] No. CCXCI, Ludwig to MFA, 13 May 1912.
[107] Ernest Wilder Spaulding, *The Quiet Invaders: The Story of the Austrian Impact upon America* (Vienna, 1968), 79.

numerous national clergy, who often make pronouncements about various local affairs, are constantly treated with particular courtesy and a standing contact is preserved."[108] Many clergy members advocated the continued use of European languages and the continuation of traditional practices. With these ideas, they contributed to a continued sense of community with the European homeland, which in turn fostered the maintenance of economic ties and kept return a solid option. Many clergy members were sent to the United States by European-based churches, and others were even funded by the Hungarian government. Their ideas and loyalties were in Europe. As the United States developed its own dioceses and other religious leadership infrastructures, however, there was more room for the clergy to promote integration into the American environment and thus more opportunity for conflict.[109]

The clergy could also directly counter the Habsburg agenda. They needed money to build churches and fund activities – and provide their own livelihood – and money was best produced by people who put down roots in the United States and were not sending money "home." Formal religious observance could also be upheld more effectively among a settled population. Churches built community among their members, and, often, that sense of community was couched in nationalist rather than religious terms. One consul remarked that churches were where nationalist feeling "crystallized" in the United States.[110] Church-based organizations could also be used for nationalist political proposes. Habsburg consuls were especially concerned about the Lutheran Church's Missouri Synod and its ties to Pan-Slav movements.[111]

The ethnic press could also be a help or an infernal nuisance to Habsburg consuls. Habsburg consuls could use the papers to reach a wide audience, informing them of *Amtstage*, frauds, and opportunities.[112] Many had wide circulation and were therefore invaluable for reaching populations that did not have a consulate in the vicinity. Newspapers also created an important sense of community among their readership.[113] Habsburg consuls tried to tap into those networks, but they ran into problems because there was no

---

[108] Z. CCLVI, Silvestri to MFA, 23 June 1911.
[109] See Higham; Puskás; and Spaulding.
[110] No. CCXCI, Ludwig to MFA, 13 May 1912.
[111] Zl. 449/res., Pelényi to Ludwig, 30 July 1915, in HHStA, AR, Fach 8, K. 122.
[112] On advertising *Amtstage*, see no. XXX-D, Zwiedinek to MFA, 1 March 1913; and no. LXI-H, Hengelmüller to MFA, 15 July 1912.
[113] Benedict Anderson, *Imagined Communities: Reflections on the Origin and Spread of Nationalism*, revised ed. (New York, 1991).

single newspaper that could reach all of the empire's citizens; to print a paper in so many languages would have been prohibitively expensive. The Habsburg and Hungarian governments did occasionally subsidize papers that were sympathetic to their goals, but there was nothing like an official Habsburg newspaper in the United States.[114]

Newspapers – like the national organizations they worked so closely with – could be a double-edged sword for communities of foreign-born U.S. residents, too. On the one hand, having a community newspaper could be taken as a sign of their compatibility with American governmental institutions. A free press was often touted as being essential to democracies and republics. Those favoring immigration restriction favored a literacy test to keep the undesirable out; having a newspaper demonstrated the development and intelligence of the group in question as a whole.[115] On the other hand, they could be signs of the existence of an exclusive community, a "foreign colony" on U.S. soil. An editorial in the *New York Times* remarked that "It is a well-nigh invariable rule that a few aliens excite interest and liking rather than antagonism, wherever they may be, but if they become numerous, and especially if they group closely and form a more or less independent community of their own, a contrary feeling develops at once." The writer went on to add, "Of course there are advantages for them in being with people of their own customs and language, but these are more than balanced by the inevitable disadvantages that follow. Safety for the foreigner lies in scattering and assimilating. If he has constitutional and unconquerable objections or inabilities for assimilation, he had better remain at home. He is sure to get into trouble sooner or later if he doesn't."[116]

It is vitally important to remember that American newspapers – be they mainstream or ethnic – were business endeavors, and therefore they were

---

[114] The Habsburg government limited its activities to support for Croatian-language papers that were favorable to the monarchy; it is likely that these subsidies were designed at least in part to build Croatian opposition to Magyar nationalism and thus make the Hungarian government easier for the central government to manage. On Croatian-language papers, see Faszikel 1, in HHStA, PA XXXIII, K. 101 – Liasse I: Varia. On Hungarian support of papers, see Faszikel 3, in HHStA, PA XXXIII, K. 101.

[115] On the literacy test, see Jeanne Petit, "Breeders, Workers, and Mothers: Gender and the Congressional Literacy Test Debate, 1896–1897," *JGAPE* 3, 1 (2004): 35–58; and Hans Vought, "Division and Reunion: Woodrow Wilson, Immigration, and the Myth of American Unity," *JAEH* 13, 3 (1994): 24–50.

[116] "Topics of the Times: Colonies, Not Aliens, Are Persecuted," *NYT*, 24 February 1909, p. 8. See also Neil Larry Shumsky, "'Let No Man Stop to Plunder!' American Hostility to Return Migration, 1890–1924," *JAEH* 11, 2 (1992): 56–75.

interested in printing what would sell. Controversy is always good for the newspaper business, and turn-of-the-century papers were largely collections of invective editorials interspersed with a few facts and a lot of advertisements. From day to day – or even from page to page – the opinion expounded by the papers' writers could change. For example, in 1910, Baron Ambrózy indicated that a key aspect of the "emigration problem" was "the attitude of the Hungarian-American press and their perfidious agitation against Hungary." He observed that, "On the one hand, they daily drag the Hungarian homeland through the mud, and on the other hand, they seek to win the sympathy of the local Hungarian population by infallibly effective means, by evoking the glory of the 48ers and enveloping them in unadulterated Austro-phobia."[117] In short, the press could not be counted on to take either a strictly anti-Habsburg or pro-Habsburg line. It was a vehicle for mixed messages. Historian Ernest Spaulding noted that "These papers produced a babel of demands and pleas and points of view that, on the whole, contributed but little to the Austrian cause."[118]

As much as Habsburg consuls disliked the press and nationalist groups and the national identities they fostered, the consuls were reliant on them to help with the task of protecting Austrian and Hungarian citizens. Consul Silvestri observed from Chicago in 1911, "We are resigned to the fact that our point of contact with these people [Austrian and Hungarian citizens in the United States] is through the national clergy and the press."[119] By using nationally organized groups, the Habsburg consuls were ultimately supporting the very identity categories they were working to oppose. With a greater state-sponsored consular presence, they might have been able to do more to counter emerging nationalist sentiments, but the necessary growth in the institution did not occur.

Habsburg consular efforts to promote a supranational identity among Austrian and Hungarian citizens in the United States were complicated not only by conditions in the United States, but also by the Hungarian government. Some Habsburg consuls blamed Magyarization efforts for the development of national identity among German, Slovak, Croatian, and Romanian speakers and the emigration of those groups. Many members of the Hungarian government, however, were quite pleased with the fact that so many non-Magyars were leaving. Just as many Americans were

[117] No. 10 (4979/a), Ambrózy to Aehrenthal, 1 April 1910, in HHStA, PA XXXIII, K. 100.
[118] Spaulding, 78.
[119] Z. CCLVI, Silvestri to MFA, 23 June 1911.

concerned about the American or Anglo-Saxon nation's ability to assimilate newcomers, the Hungarian government was concerned about the Magyar nation's ability to assimilate Hungary's non-Magyar population. As Hungarian undersecretary of state Count Kuno Klebelsberg wrote in 1902, "For the institution of national statehood it is absolutely necessary that the ruling race – which has been called to uphold the national state and populate it – increase accordingly and thus after a while become the majority of the population. This increase can be brought about artificially, via assimilation. Nevertheless, as the smaller ethnic groups have recently been awakening to an ever increasing national consciousness, it is hardly possible to count any further on more extensive assimilation."[120] By allowing emigration – or even encouraging it with Magyarization policies – the Hungarian government was hoping to achieve a more homogeneous, more Magyar population.

In 1904, the Hungarian government went so far as to sign a contract with the Cunard Line. If Cunard promised to process emigrants and repatriates through the Hungarian port of Fiume, and thus help build the Hungarian economy there, the Hungarian government would guarantee Cunard at least 30,000 outbound passengers a year. The contract was certainly controversial in both Europe and the United States. The American press in particular was hostile to Hungary's export of immigrants, as was Marcus Braun, a high-ranking official in the Bureau of Immigration.[121] He accused the Hungarian government of conspiring to unload its most undesirable citizens on the United States, a comment that provoked considerable editorial comment on both sides of the Atlantic.[122]

After the turn of the century, Hungarian officials gradually became more concerned about emigration, in part because it was now Magyar speakers who were leaving in response to economic troubles in the empire. The year of the largest emigration was 1907, and that exodus prompted a number of legislative changes in Hungary. On the one hand, the government attempted to make it harder to leave the country. In 1909, a law came into effect that required those individuals who wished to leave Hungary to apply for a permit from the government.[123] The Hungarian government's limited ability to enforce the law muted its effects, however.

---

[120] Cited in Puskás, 90.
[121] On the Cunard agreement, see ibid., 91.
[122] See, for example, "Braun to the Hungarians," *NYT*, 1 July 1905, p. 4.
[123] No. 93.414-11-1914, Note Verbalé of the Ministry of Foreign Affairs to the American Embassy in Vienna, 6 December 1914, Vienna, in HHStA, AR, Fach 15, K. 55.

On the other hand, the government also took steps to make returning easier. In October 1907, Emperor Franz Joseph granted "an inclusive amnesty for people who have neglected their military service." The Hungarian minister president wrote to the foreign minister and asked him to have the news published in the United States. He observed, "The amnesty is supposed to make it easier for people to return, which is desirable from a national economic standpoint, and so it would be advisable to make the amnesty known to as many concerned persons as possible."[124] The Hungarian government also adjusted its naturalization laws so that former holders of Hungarian citizenship could request an immediate reinstatement of their Hungarian citizenship upon their return, rather than having to wait ten years, as was required by the previous law.[125]

In addition to these legal changes, the Hungarian government began to consider launching a large-scale repatriation program in 1907. Officials there were concerned about the number of returnees coming home in dire financial straits or with serious injuries, and they were also concerned more generally about adverse conditions in the United States. The Hungarian government wanted to promote national feeling among the emigrants and foster the desire to come home.[126] The repatriation program would also benefit Hungary by revitalizing and developing certain regions of Hungary that had been hard hit by emigration. It would, however, repopulate the distressed areas with Magyars, rather than with the non-Magyar Hungarian citizens who had left, thus helping to build a stronger, more Magyar nation at home.

The desired returnees were those "who will build the Hungarian nation" and Magyar speakers. The government was especially interested in repatriating Magyar-speaking Roman Catholics. Hungarian officials were also happy to accept Magyar-speaking members of the Reformed (Calvinist) and Greek Catholic (Uniate) churches, but they were less than enthusiastic about the members of these churches who were not Magyars. People with Pan-Slavic tendencies were definitely not welcome, and the government expected that no Germans would want to come back – reinforcing the consuls' opinion that a Magyarizing Hungarian government was inadvertently promoting a reactionary Pan-German nationalism.[127]

---

[124] No. 3855/a, Übersetzung der ungarischen Note des kgl. ung. Ministerpräsidiums vom 24./II. 1908, Z. 271, in HHStA, PA XXXIII, K. 100.

[125] No. 10631/1, Hengelmüller to Root, 17 December 1907.

[126] No. 3531a, Übersetzung einer Note des kgl. ung. Ministerpräsidenten an den kgl. ung. Ackerbauminister, vom 6. Juli 1907, Z. 3269, in HHStA, PA XXXIII, K. 100.

[127] Ibid.

The government grappled with how a repatriation should be achieved. Its members felt that the United States in general would be upset by a large-scale repatriation program if it was government sponsored; Americans would likely reject such a flagrant statement of the failure and undesirability of the American environment. Hungarian officials thought that its citizens in the United States might be exposed to even stronger prejudices and possibly even violence if the Americans were provoked with a repatriation program, and the government was concerned that its citizens would become "paralyzed." In hopes of diffusing American protests, the Hungarian government hoped to have the repatriation program handled by a private organization.[128]

The repatriation was supposed to be one large event, rather than a piecemeal return of individuals. Such an orchestrated effort would require extensive organization and coordination among Hungarians throughout the United States. The government planned to use the Magyar-language press to get the word out – convenient, since it only wanted Magyar speakers to come back. The government also thought it should advertise the repatriation at home, so the relatives of people in the United States could help exert pressure to get people to return.[129]

In addition, the Hungarian government thought the clergy might assist with the effort. Some clergy were already paid by the Hungarian government, so they could likely be counted on for support. In general, the clergy were strong supporters of maintaining the use of European languages and keeping religious beliefs and cultural practices alive in the United States. The government did note, however, that some clergy in the United States would not welcome the reduction in the size of their flock in the United States, especially because it would be that much harder to maintain their churches financially. The government was considering offering clergy a sum of money for each person they helped to repatriate.[130]

The Hungarian government was keenly aware that creating or fostering a desire to come home was different from making it actually possible for people to return home. The government had sent several agents to the United States to report on conditions among Hungarian citizens, and those reports had indicated that many Hungarians lacked the means to return

---

[128] Ibid.
[129] Ibid.
[130] Ibid.

home at their own expense.[131] The government estimated that it would have to pay approximately half the costs of each individual repatriation. It hoped to start a bank in the United States – a private bank, of course – that people would use to save money for their return home. It hoped to use already existing organizations, including the Országos Gazdaszövetség and Julian-Verein, to help get things started, and they asked Ambassador Hengelmüller and the consuls in the United States to sound out opinion in their districts and identify people who might help.[132]

Members of the government knew that they would need to advertise where in Hungary repatriates would be settled and what economic opportunities were available there. From their perspective, the point of the repatriation was to bolster the Magyar or Magyarized population of the kingdom and thus minimize the political impact of non-Magyar populations. They did realize, at some level, that emigration had been prompted by economic conditions, and so they wanted to spread the word that there was ample opportunity back in Hungary.[133]

When Hengelmüller received word of the Hungarian government's emerging repatriation plan and its request for information, he was just concluding his own report on the voluntary repatriation of Austrian and Hungarian citizens. His report was prompted by earlier requests from the Hungarians to investigate conditions in the face of popular and press reports of huge waves of Hungarian citizens returning to Europe in destitution. Hengelmüller argued that such reports needed to be taken "with a grain of salt." After inquiring in New York City, he reported that those who returned to Austria-Hungary were actually taking significant funds home with them: on just one ship, Austrian citizens had taken $76,000 back to the empire, whereas Hungarian citizens were returning with a total of $64,000.[134] Hungarian officials later reported that Hengelmüller's

---

[131] The Hungarian government sent Baron Ambrózy on more than one tour. See, for example, no. 18A-C (4476/a), Ambrózy to Aehrenthal, 18 May 1909, in HHStA, PA XXXIII, K. 100.

[132] No. 3531a, Übersetzung ... 6. Juli 1907.

[133] Ibid. See also no. 111, Francis to Root, 6 December 1906, in M862, roll 315, case no. 3388. Francis reported on newspaper coverage of a speech Hengelmüller had made to the Hungarian government. According to Hengelmüller, "There is no doubt, and it can be proved by statistical data, that emigration from Austria to America is far less than it is from Hungary. In my opinion the reason for this lies in the fact that Austria is a manufacturing country and gives greater opportunities for its population to find employment."

[134] No. 3812a/no. 1 A-E, Hengelmüller to Aehrenthal, 2 January 1908, in HHStA, PA XXXIII, K. 100. There is no information on how many people were returning on this ship, so a per capita figure cannot be determined.

findings did not align with their experiences at Fiume; it is likely that the truth lies somewhere between the two accounts.[135]

Hengelmüller was cool toward the Hungarian repatriation plan, undoubtedly seeing it as a nationalist measure and therefore not in the interests of the empire as a whole. He dutifully asked the consuls to report on local possibilities, however. The consuls and Hengelmüller certainly took their time pondering the Hungarian government's request: Hengelmüller did not submit their collective report for almost a year.[136]

The consuls in the Northeast reported little enthusiasm in their districts for the proposed mass repatriation. A few consuls submitted names of people who might help, but they generally reported that local clergy were hostile to the plan. The consuls did report that it would cost $1,500 to $2,000 to place advertisements in the Magyar-language papers for a year. From Chicago, Consul General Silvestri cautioned the government against using the newspapers to advertise the plan, however, because it would invite editorial comment from the papers, which he implied would be opposed to the plan or at least make the repatriation more complicated than it needed to be.[137]

In this report, and on most other occasions when they were asked to report on return migration, Habsburg officials in the United States always pointed to two major factors: the economic and the psychological.[138] When economic conditions were bad, people were interested in going home – especially at state expense. When things were going well, the urge to return was far less pronounced. Psychological factors included American prejudices, but also people's memories of home. The Hungarian government was casting things in national terms, wanting people to come home to benefit the glorious Hungarian nation. Habsburg consuls, however, pointed out that people in the United States were not yearning for Hungary as a whole. Instead, they missed their specific villages or regions. To call for a repatriation in nationalist terms would perhaps motivate Magyar nationalists, but there was little reason for them to have left Hungary in the first place. To get Hungarian citizens to go home, the consuls said, nationalist rhetoric would not work.[139]

---

[135] No. 4108/a, Übersetzung der ungarischen Note des kgl. ung. Ministeriums des Innern von 12./VIII. 1908, in HHStA, PA XXXIII, K. 100.

[136] 4136a/no. 30 A-C, Hengelmüller to Aehrenthal, 31 August 1908.

[137] Ibid.

[138] For one invocation of this idea, see no. 40 (4242/a), Hengelmüller to Aehrenthal, 16 November 1908, in HHStA, PA XXXIII, K. 100.

[139] 4136a/no. 30 A-C, Hengelmüller to Aehrenthal, 31 August 1908. See also King, *Budweisers*; and Spaulding.

The Hungarian mass repatriation plan did not come to fruition, but it did result in a smaller scale program wherein individual Hungarian citizens pledged to return to Hungary; the government set up a fund to help facilitate their return. The program did not work out exactly as planned, however. The Hungarian government had to send numerous requests to Habsburg consuls, asking them to locate individuals who had promised to return but had not yet done so. In some cases, consuls reported that the individuals did not have enough money to return, but they refused to take charity, so their return would be delayed until they could earn the money. Others had made the pledge when they were out of work, but had since found jobs that they did not want to leave. Still others said they had changed their minds about returning or asserted that their promise was nonbinding.[140]

The Hungarian government's interest in repatriation gradually spread to the Austrian and central governments as well. From at least 1909, the Ministry of Foreign Affairs provided a form to consulates so they could collect statistics on returnees.[141] Those statistics were distributed to the Austrian and Hungarian interior ministries, the joint war ministry, the joint finance ministry, the provincial governments along the Adriatic coast, and the ministry of commerce and labor. Once World War I began – but before the United States entered – the War Ministry was especially interested in such statistics.[142] As the war progressed, a growing number of officials in the Austrian, Hungarian, and central governments began planning for expected waves of postwar returnees. The wartime increases in the virulence of American prejudices and race-related violence was considered the major factor that would prompt Austrian and Hungarian citizens to return.[143]

Habsburg consuls in the United States did not offer much support for large-scale repatriation plans, but they did support the repatriation of smaller groups of needy, injured, and defrauded Austrian and Hungarian citizens at government expense. Before 1905, such repatriations were done at the discretion of individual consuls and were funded through charitable donations, the consulate's budget, the ministry's budget, or consuls' personal funds. These pre-1905 cases are not well documented in the extant

---

[140] Folder Publikationen – Amerika, in HHStA, AR, Fach 15, K. 37.
[141] The earliest form in the HHStA is dated 1909. See HHStA, AR, Fach 15, K. 36.
[142] Ibid.
[143] On postwar return, see the various reports in HHStA, AR, Fach 15, K. 56 – Aus und Rückwanderung 1880–1918, Amerika 98, 109–116 and Argentinien 3–11.

ministry archives. After 1905, however, the ministry developed a set process for repatriations that involved consuls reporting on many of the cases they handled. Foreign Minister Gołuchowski issued a circular in May 1905 in an effort to standardize the process and shift the costs to the Austrian and Hungarian interior ministries.[144]

In the circular, Gołuchowski stressed that government assistance was only to be given to proven Austrian and Hungarian citizens who were genuinely and legitimately in need. Professional beggars and those who were disinclined to work were to be weeded out, as were "politically unpleasant elements," such as anarchists and nonfugitive criminals. Consuls were especially encouraged to assist women, orphans, the sick, and those injured on the job. Gołuchowski stressed that, before considering repatriation, consuls should do all they could to help those in need find work. That would likely involve asking local Austro-Hungarian aid societies for assistance in locating employers. He advocated founding Austro-Hungarian aid societies in areas that did not have them. Ideally, Gołuchowski said that those who were repatriated should eventually reimburse the state for their trip. To reduce government costs, Habsburg ships should be used for repatriating people. For sending Hungarian citizens to the empire from North America, the Cunard line was supposed to be used.[145]

To get the interior ministries to pay, Gołuchowski observed, consuls needed to establish the recipients' citizenship and attest to their inability to find work or suitable living conditions. Only Austrian and Hungarian citizens were to be repatriated at state expense. This opened the question of how to prove citizenship status when most people traveled without passports or other identity documents. The favored method was to see documents issued by the Habsburg state; passports and birth certificates would certainly be accepted, but so would a variety of other government documents, including work cards. For such papers that included physical descriptions, the consul was supposed to match that description against the person in possession of the documents. Signature comparisons could also be used, as well as unspecified "other expedient ways."[146]

If documents were not available, consuls were supposed to ask questions about local conditions and landmarks at the person's place of residence in the empire and consider the person's linguistic abilities and

[144] No. 34.813/3, Circular from Gołuchowski to Consuls, 1 May 1905.
[145] Ibid.
[146] Ibid.

dialect. Gołuchowski pointed out that "the lack of ... documents itself is no reason to refrain from the repatriation, if, as indicated, the nationality of the applicant can be determined without doubt from other clues." It is not clear from Gołuchowski's directions exactly what should happen in a case in which someone could be proved to be a member of a national group represented in the empire but could not prove his or her legal citizenship; it is possible that some noncitizens could and did pass for Polish- or Italian-speaking Austrian citizens, for example, even when they did not legally hold Austrian citizenship. In the case of Hungary, Gołuchowski maintained that knowledge of the Magyar language was sufficient to prove Hungarian citizenship to the Hungarian interior ministry.[147]

To facilitate payment by the interior ministries – and subsequent repayment by repatriates – consuls had to provide reports on assistance given. They were to record expenses for Austrian and Hungarian citizens separately and also list residents of Bosnia and Herzegovina as a distinct group. Repatriates were obliged to provide the consuls with an address in the empire where they could be reached following their return.[148] On receipt of this information, consuls could provide repatriates with money for rail and ship tickets, the application fees for travel documents, and basic necessities such as food and clothing.

The exact number of Austrian and Hungarian citizens that Habsburg consuls helped to repatriate is unknown, but scattered evidence has survived. In July 1909, the consulate-general in New York City issued a report about the number of people it had helped secure reduced-fare ($10) steamship tickets between May 1908 and April 1909. The consulate had provided such assistance to 218 people, of whom 47 were Austrians, 167 were Hungarians, and 4 were Bosnians.[149]

Consular reports about other specific cases also exist. The Gusztáv Weber and Jackson Lumber Company cases have already been mentioned. In 1908, Consul Hindermann in New Orleans reported on local conditions along the Gulf Coast. Members of the local Austrian and Hungarian population, primarily from Trieste and Istria, had written to their relatives and the government back in Europe and "describ[ed] the local conditions in the darkest colors," saying that people were dying from starvation. Hindermann was dispatched to investigate, and he found conditions bad, but not so dire as they had been painted in those letters. He did, however,

---

[147] Ibid.
[148] No. 34.813/3, Circular from Gołuchowski to Consuls, 1 May 1905.
[149] No. LXXIV G, Ambrózy to MFA, 14 July 1909, in HHStA, AR, Fach 15, K. 37.

consider thirty-four cases serious enough to merit state-assisted repatriation.[150]

Also in 1908, the consul at Pittsburgh reported that, due to long periods of unemployment, "On every day around 200 Bosnians and Hercegovenians arrive at the consulate, all of whom want to go home or be supported." He observed that many in need of assistance were young people who were homeless and had not eaten in days. In a more poetic assessment than one typically finds in consular reports, he noted that "Misery and desperation looked out of their eyes." The consul immediately gave the neediest $1 each and then proceeded to make arrangements for groups to return to the empire.[151]

In this situation, the consul noted that he only found out about the long-term unemployment of this group when they arrived at the consulate and asked for help. Had they not sought consular assistance, it is likely that Habsburg authorities would never have known of their problems unless a member of the community had actually died and thus come to the attention of U.S. authorities. One can only speculate – as the Habsburg consuls undoubtedly did – as to how many such cases escaped consular notice, either because there was no consul nearby or because a competing national organization reached those in need first.

Although a great many injury cases undoubtedly escaped the notice of Habsburg consuls, who could not be everywhere at once, the consuls did have slightly better results when workers were actually killed because local American officials had to determine what was to become of the deceased's property. There were quite a number of deaths. Many were the result of industrial labor conditions, but there were an assortment of other situations as well. One was killed after being struck by a train on the Missouri Pacific line, a handful died while serving in the U.S. military, and at least one died while being processed at Ellis Island.[152]

According to the U.S.-Habsburg consular conventions of 1848 and 1870, Habsburg consuls or their designated representatives were entitled to represent the overseas dependents of their deceased citizens in American courts, and American consuls had reciprocal privileges in the empire. As one consul observed to American judges, "in the administration of estates

---

[150] No. 104, Hindermann to MFA, 25 July 1908.
[151] No. CDXLIX, Bornemisza to MFA, 25 April 1908, in HHStA, AR, Fach 15, K. 37.
[152] On deaths of Austrian and Hungarian citizens in the United States, see file no. 363.1143, in NARA. U.S. consuls in the Habsburg Empire also dealt with the deaths of U.S. citizens in the empire; on those cases, see file 363.113, in NARA.

of foreign subjects, great injustice has frequently been wrought, because irresponsible strangers have improperly administered the estates on behalf of the decedent's mother, or widow, or children, or heirs, who could not appear in court to protect their own interests against the stranger or interloper, because they lived across the sea."[153] Acting in all these cases could be a huge job: in Pennsylvania alone, an estimated 3,000 Austrian and Hungarian citizens died every year.[154] The consular service wanted to be involved in them all, however, so it could demonstrate the Habsburg government's commitment to its citizens and therefore its continued legitimacy.

To make this system work, consuls had to be made aware of the death. Local American officials were supposed to notify the consul assigned to their part of the country. Such an arrangement was not unique to Austria-Hungary; Belgium, Germany, Great Britain, Greece, Guatemala, Italy, the Netherlands, Romania, Serbia, and Spain all had comparable treaties. Austria-Hungary, however, had more problems securing its treaty rights than most other countries. State Department official Alvee Adee observed in 1907 that "Italy and Austria-Hungary are the only governments which have complained that any of the various states of the Union have failed to comply with those provisions."[155] Ambassador Hengelmüller wrote to the State Department and requested that local officials be reminded of the treaty. The department, ever mindful of international law, complied, notifying all governors and asking them to transmit the request to the judges in their state or territory.[156]

Local officials gradually complied with the law, although not without some grumbling. Wilmer R. Batt, the state registrar of Pennsylvania, protested that the sheer number of Austrian and Hungarian deaths in the state made it unreasonable for state officials "to comply literally with the provisions of the Consular Convention."[157] After more than a year of dragging his heels, Batt was finally forced to comply with the treaty by a directive from the governor.[158] In 1910, Hengelmüller had to complain

---

[153] Ernst Ludwig, "Treaty Rights of Austro-Hungarian Consuls," enclosed in no. CCXII, Ludwig to MFA, 15 April 1912.

[154] Batt to the Governor of Pennsylvania, no date [spring 1908].

[155] No. 6847/17, Adee to the governor of West Virginia, 21 August 1907, in *M862*, roll 534, case no. 6847.

[156] No. 1087, Hengelmüller to Root, 30 May 1907; and no. 257, Root to Hengelmüller, 8 June 1907, both in *M862*, roll 534, case no. 6847. To reach the territorial governors, the DOS wrote to the Interior Department.

[157] Batt to the Governor of Pennsylvania, no date [spring 1908].

[158] Batt to Root, 11 January 1909, in *M862*, roll 534, case no. 6847.

again, this time specifically about unreported deaths in the Denver consular district.[159]

Deaths in Michigan also often went unreported, which contributed to the transfer of the Lower Peninsula of the state to the Cleveland consular district from the overworked Chicago consulate in 1912. Cleveland Consul Ludwig had a booklet printed at his own expense for distribution to Michigan judges entitled "Treaty Rights of Austro-Hungarian Consuls." In the booklet, he made sure to point out that U.S. consuls had the same rights to protect the property of U.S. citizens who died in the empire, and he backed up his argument with pages of references to American and international law and court decisions.[160]

One section of Ludwig's booklet is especially striking and quite probably reflects the root of the problem. Ludwig felt compelled to write that "*Austrian* subjects include the following national groups: German Austrians, Bohemians, Moravians, Poles, that is Galician Poles, Ruthenians, ... Italian-Austrians from Dalmatia, Triest or Tyrol, etc. *Hungarian* subjects include the following groups: Magyars, German Hungarians, Croatians, Roumanian-Hungarians, Slovaks, Servian Hungarians, etc."[161]

To mention these national or racial categories was anathema to Habsburg consuls, who clung passionately to the political labels *Austrian* and *Hungarian*. If compelled to differentiate among their citizens more precisely, Habsburg consuls invoked language, but combined it with political citizenship. For example, they might discuss a Polish-speaking Austrian or a Croatian-speaking Hungarian. Michigan judges, by contrast, were apparently conditioned to think in racial terms, rather than to consider the political citizenship of the foreign-born. That judges did not think of people as Austrians or Hungarians likely contributed to their not thinking to contact the Austro-Hungarian consulate in estate cases. To get local American officials to comply with international law, Habsburg consuls had to use American terminology, despite the fact that such terminology undermined the sovereignty of the Habsburg government.

Ideally, Habsburg consuls wanted to be involved in the settlement of all workplace injury and fatality cases in the United States that involved

---

[159] No. 108, Hengelmüller to Knox, 17 January 1910, in M862, roll 534, case no. 6847. Deaths in the territories of Arizona and New Mexico were the specific problem. These were not yet states, suggesting that the problem may have been at the Interior Department.
[160] Ludwig, "Treaty Rights of Austro-Hungarian Consuls."
[161] Ibid.

Austrian or Hungarian citizens. By being involved, they could work for maximum compensation and avoid problems created by the involvement of "irresponsible strangers." They would have a more accurate understanding of the scope of the problem and might therefore be able to effect change in U.S. or international law. They could also ensure that dependents were provided for, and they could reinforce the ties between the Habsburg government and its citizens. In reality, the consuls were involved in only a fraction of such cases and were thus only partially effective. The size and placement of the Habsburg consular service in the United States contributed significantly to this problem, but Habsburg consular efforts were also thwarted by the prevalence of racialist thinking and xenophobia in the United States. These ideas found their way into various local and federal government institutions, especially the U.S. Bureau of Immigration, encouraging many Americans – including Michigan judges – and Austrian and Hungarian citizens in the United States to think in racial terms rather than politically based citizenship categories. This racial thinking undermined the legitimate sovereignty of the Habsburg government and planted the seed for later American recognition of race-based nation-states in Central Europe.

5

Racial Identity and Political Citizenship

American Challenges to Habsburg Sovereignty

When U.S. consuls working in the Habsburg Empire tried to exercise
sovereign jurisdiction over the bodies of U.S. citizens, they were generally
successful, in large part because they exercised their sovereignty within the
well-established Habsburg legal and bureaucratic system, which was full
of officials dedicated to the rule of law. When Habsburg consuls posted to
the United States tried to protect their citizens, however, they were working in a much more complex environment. What made the United States so
much more troublesome was the pervasiveness of racial nationalism and
xenophobia. Racial prejudice, backed up by scientific proclamations, and
xenophobia were not simply the province of the American private sphere –
they were also deeply entrenched in many aspects of American local, state,
and federal government. The pervasive climate of prejudice kept Austrian
and Hungarian citizens in dangerous jobs and, at times, made their persons
and property targets of racially motivated violence. When Austrian and
Hungarian citizens were involved in legal proceedings in American courts,
the possibility of receiving a fair trial could be slim. Most important,
however, the U.S. Bureau of Immigration's use of racial identity categories
to label immigrants undermined Habsburg sovereign claims to politically
based citizenship and conditioned many Americans – and immigrants – to
think in racial terms.

Habsburg Ministry of Foreign Affairs personnel, including diplomats,
consuls, and central office staff, were strong proponents of a supranational, *kaisertreu* identity, and they adhered scrupulously to the political
citizenship categories *Austrian* and *Hungarian* when dealing with their
fellow Habsburg subjects. These categories downplayed other potentially
differentiating attributes or identities including language, religion, and

social class. In their position as representatives of the empire abroad, Habsburg Ministry of Foreign Affairs personnel were in a position to advocate these political categories to other governments, thus reinforcing Habsburg legitimacy in the international community.

Habsburg officials in the United States repeatedly pressed the U.S. government to use the political categories *Austrian* and *Hungarian* to refer to inhabitants of the empire, but their efforts were unsuccessful outside of the State Department. This was a significant defeat for the Habsburg government. During World War I and at the subsequent peace conference, years of thinking of racialist terms manifested themselves in the actions of the American delegation and ultimately resulted in the break-up of the Habsburg Empire.

Given its diverse population at home and its lack of an overseas empire, the Habsburg central government was not a major player in the development of racialist science. The government did ask Austrian and Hungarian citizens to self-identify on the census and for access to some other state services by declaring their *Umgangsprache*, or language of everyday use.[1] As we will see, the broader Euro-American community tended to view language as a marker of race, but it did not have that same salience among the vast majority of Austrian and Hungarian citizens or government officials. It should be noted, however, that, after 1867, there were three governments in the Habsburg Empire: the Austrian government, over which Franz Joseph ruled as emperor; the Hungarian government, of which he was king; and the central government, which comprised the foreign, finance, and war ministries. The central government was most resistant to racial-nationalist categories, whereas the Hungarian government was most responsive to them. The Hungarian government employed ideas about language and assimilation in an effort to bolster Magyar political power at the expense of other groups within the kingdom; its Magyarization plans were very much in keeping with nationalization efforts in other parts of Europe, the United States, and the British settler colonies.[2]

---

[1] Emil Brix, *Die Umgangssprachen in Altösterreich zwischen Agitation und Assimilation: Die Sprachenstatistik in den zisleithanischen Volkszählungen, 1880 bis 1910* (Vienna, 1982). See also Gerald Stourzh, *Die Gleichberechtigung der Nationalitäten in der Verfassung und Verwaltung Österreichs, 1848–1918* (Vienna, 1980); and Benno Gammerl, "Subjects, Citizens and Others: The Handling of Ethnic Differences in the British and the Habsburg Empires (late Nineteenth and Early Twentieth Century)," *European Review of History* 16, 4 (2009): 523–49.

[2] István Deák, *Beyond Nationalism: A Social and Political History of the Habsburg Officer Corps, 1848–1918* (New York, 1990); William D. Godsey, Jr., *Aristocratic Redoubt: The*

In the Habsburg context, several key elements blunted the edges of the census categories. First and foremost, Austrian and Hungarian citizens self-reported their *Umgangsprache*, rather than having an official of the state determine what identity category to put them in.[3] It should be noted, however, that the state did determine which languages to offer as choices, which limited individual choice. Most important, Yiddish was not one of the languages available, despite the interest of some Jews in adding it to the list.[4] Although one could argue that the omission of the language from the list of identity possibilities was detrimental to Jews in the Empire, one could also make the case that the state was aiming to maintain Judaism as a strictly religious category.

Austrian and Hungarian citizens could also change their official *Umgangsprache* over time and in different contexts. This made identification with a particular language group opportunistic, rather than static. With so many languages spoken throughout the Empire, many people were at least bilingual, if not multilingual, and scholars have demonstrated that it was quite common for people to use one language at home and another language in their place of business, as well as possessing some level of familiarity with the languages of administration in the Empire – German in the Austrian half, and, in the latter decades of the nineteenth century, Magyar in the Hungarian half.[5] The fluidity of identity and the ability of an

---

Austro-Hungarian Foreign Office on the Eve of the First World War (West Lafayette, 1999); James Allan Treichel, "Magyars at the Ballplatz: A Study of the Hungarians in the Austro-Hungarian Diplomatic Service, 1906–1914" (Ph.D. diss., Georgetown University, 1972); Andrew C. Janos, *The Politics of Backwardness in Hungary, 1825–1945* (Princeton, 1982); and Marilyn Lake and Henry Reynolds, *Drawing the Global Colour Line: White Men's Countries and the International Challenge of Racial Equality* (Cambridge, 2008).

[3] In the United States, census enumerators determined identity categories. On the imprecision in that process, see Martha A. Sandweiss, *Passing Strange: A Gilded Age Tale of Love and Deception Across the Color Line* (New York, 2009).

[4] Gabriele Kohlbauer-Fritz and Lee Mitzman, "Yiddish as an Expression of Jewish Cultural Identity in Galicia and Vienna," *Polin* 12 (1999): 164–76; and Gerald Stourzh, "The Age of Emancipation and Assimilation: Liberalism and Its Heritage," in *Österreich-Konzeptionen und jüdisches Selbstverständnis. Identitäts Transfigurationen im 19. Und 20. Jahrhundert*, ed. Hanni Mittelmann and Armin A. Wallas (Tübingen, 2001), 11–28.

[5] See, among numerous others, Jeremy King, "The Nationalization of East Central Europe: Ethnicism, Ethnicity, and Beyond," in *Staging the Past: The Politics of Commemoration in Habsburg Central Europe, 1848 to the Present*, ed. Maria Bucur and Nancy M. Wingfield (West Lafayette, 2001), 112–52; Tara Zahra, *Kidnapped Souls: National Indifference and the Battle for Children in the Bohemian Lands, 1900–1948* (Ithaca, 2008); and Fred Stambrook, "National and Other Identities in Bukovina in Late Austrian Times," *AHY* 35 (2004): 185–203. See also Rogers Brubaker and Frederick Cooper, "Beyond 'Identity,'" *Theory and Society* 29, 1 (2000): 1–47.

individual person to identify with more than one linguistic community over time and even on a daily basis was decisively at odds with the notion of racial identity that was developing in the United States and other parts of Europe, which posited that each individual person had a single racial identity that was ultimately manifested in the language he or she spoke.

The Habsburgs were an exception, however, when it came to the nineteenth-century development of racialist thought. Scholars have long debated whether theories of race and racism traveled from the United States to Europe or vice versa – after all, there is a great deal of blame to be assigned if there is a clear origin – but, in general, it is best to view the development of racialist thinking as a product of a transatlantic community.[6] Conceptualizing racial difference has its origins in the colonial process, but to understand the way in which racial difference came to be understood as a product of science, we should look to the eighteenth- and nineteenth-century scientific community's interest in categorization and taxonomy.[7] Identifying and classifying new species was central to scientific practice during this time period. Scholars have demonstrated the constructed nature of these categories, noting that the line between one species and another is arbitrarily determined.[8] It should not be surprising that scientists, philosophers, and politicians opted to apply this interest in classification and hierarchy to the human population. Not only was the language of classification popular in and of itself, but there was tremendous political power to be gained – or lost – by applying ideas of biological difference and hierarchy to human beings.

Americans, with the assistance of European colonial powers, especially the British settler colonies, became particularly adept at drawing the color line between whites and nonwhites over the course of the nineteenth century. For Europeans, this was largely done through the creation of

---

[6] Audrey Smedley, *Race in North America: Origin and Evolution of a Worldview*, 3rd ed. (Boulder, 2007).

[7] On conceptions of race and the colonial process, see Anthony Pagden, *The Fall of Natural Man: The American Indian and the Origins of Comparative Ethnology* (Cambridge, 1982); Joyce E. Chaplin, *Subject Matter: Technology, the Body, and Science on the Anglo-American Frontier, 1500–1676* (Cambridge MA, 2001); Winthrop D. Jordan, *White over Black: American Attitudes Toward the Negro, 1550–1812* (Chapel Hill, 1968); and Lake and Reynolds.

[8] John S. Haller, Jr., *Outcasts from Evolution: Scientific Attitudes toward Racial Inferiority, 1859–1900*, rev. ed. (Carbondale, 1995); Eric D. Weitz, "Race and Nation: An Intellectual History," in *A Century of Genocide: Utopias of Race and Nation* (Princeton, 2003), 16–52; and Matthew Frye Jacobson, *Barbarian Virtues: The United States Encounters Foreign Peoples at Home and Abroad, 1876–1917* (New York, 2000).

overseas empire, whereas in the United States context, it was done through westward expansion – a term that disguises the American imperial process in an effort to keep the United States out of the ranks of imperial powers. However, U.S. dealings with Native Americans and, after 1898, the Philippines, Puerto Rico, and Guam, were clearly imperial. American and European colonizers created a language of difference that they then attached to racial categories that allowed them to see native populations as inferior, uncivilized, and unfit for self-government, thus allowing the colonizers to take their lands and, in many cases, their lives.[9]

In addition to using categories of race to claim land, white Americans also developed racial claims that allowed them to justify slavery and then the denial of civil rights to African Americans. Here, the problem was the Declaration of Independence, with its crucial statement that "all men are created equal." Much American discourse on racial difference came from a need by some to justify the practice of slavery. The connection of science with racial ideas began most effectively in the 1830s, when slavery was increasingly under attack from Northern and British abolitionists. Before the Civil War, these ideas could be dismissed as contemptible Southern attempts to hold on to the "peculiar institution," but, during the Civil War, Northern scientists, using the laboratory conveniently provided to them by the large Union Army, began to conduct scientific studies to measure racial difference, and their findings helped give national legitimacy to the idea of African-American inferiority. In the immediate aftermath of the Civil War, radical Republicans who had been abolitionists before the war insisted on extending full citizenship and civil rights to newly freed African Americans, but as the reconstruction process dragged on and was not particularly successful, most Northerners conceded the idea of African-American inferiority, choosing to reconcile with white Southerners by accepting the color line, rather than by continuing the campaign for civil

---

[9] Lake and Reynolds; Paul A. Kramer, "Power and Connection: Imperial Histories of the United States in the World," *AHR* 116, 5 (2011): 1348–91; Kramer, *The Blood of Government: Race, Empire, the United States, and the Philippines* (Chapel Hill, 2006); Sam Erman, "Meanings of Citizenship in the U.S. Empire: Puerto Rico, Isabel Gonzalez, and the Supreme Court, 1898 to 1905," *JAEH* 27, 4 (2008): 5–33; Reginald Horsman, *Race and Manifest Destiny: The Origins of American Racial Anglo-Saxonism*, rev. ed. (Cambridge MA, 1986); Allison L. Sneider, *Suffragists in an Imperial Age: U.S. Expansion and the Woman Question, 1870–1929* (New York, 2008); and Rose Stremlau, "'To Domesticate and Civilize Wild Indians': Allotment and the Campaign to Reform Indian Families, 1875–1887," *Journal of Family History* 30, 3 (2005): 265–86. Racial difference was also salient for many American anti-imperialists; see Eric T. L. Love, *Race Over Empire: Racism and U.S. Imperialism, 1865–1900* (Chapel Hill, 2004).

rights.[10] As Northerners shifted their attention away from the South after 1876, African Americans continued to demand access to public spaces and the rights and obligations of citizenship, and in many – although certainly not all – cases, the federal courts found in their favor, necessitating the creation of Jim Crow laws in the South if whites were going to continue to try and exclude African Americans from the body politic. Segregation, disfranchisement, the development of sharecropping, and lynching all combined to separate white from black and relegate African Americans to second-class status.[11]

As immigration from China picked up in the 1860s and '70s, many Americans in the Western states became interested in developing a new color line to exclude Chinese and other Asians from U.S. citizenship and economic opportunities. Although the Fourteenth Amendment and U.S. naturalization laws allowed whites and blacks access to U.S. citizenship, the courts determined that Chinese were neither, and the category of "ineligible to citizenship" was born, paving the way for the 1875 Page Act, the 1882 Chinese Exclusion Act, and, eventually, in 1917, the "barred Asiatic zone" that prohibited immigration from Asia.[12]

Americans were crucial in developing a global color line between whites and nonwhites, whereas European governments and scientists concerned with domestic developments focused more of their attention on drawing categories of difference among whites. They used similar techniques, focusing on physical manifestations of difference, including cranial capacity and phrenology. Alphonse Bertillon's system for identifying

[10] Haller; Louis Menand, *The Metaphysical Club* (New York, 2001); Heather Cox Richardson, *The Death of Reconstruction: Race, Labor, and Politics in the Post-Civil War North, 1865–1901* (Cambridge MA, 2001); Lloyd E. Ambrosius, "Woodrow Wilson and The Birth of a Nation: American Democracy and International Relations," *Diplomacy & Statecraft* 18, 4 (2007): 689–718; T. J. Boisseau, "White Queens at the Chicago World's Fair, 1893: New Womanhood in the Service of Class, Race, and Nation," *Gender & History* 12, 1 (2000): 33–81; Bluford Adams, "World Conquerors or a Dying People? Racial Theory, Regional Anxiety, and the Brahmin Anglo-Saxonists," *JGAPE* 8, 2 (2009): 189–215.

[11] Barbara Young Welke, "When All the Women Were White, and All the Blacks Were Men: Gender, Class, Race, and the Road to 'Plessy,' 1855–1914," *Law & History Review* 13, 2 (1995): 261–316; R. Volney Riser, *Defying Disfranchisement: Black Voting Rights Activism in the Jim Crow South, 1890–1908* (Baton Rouge, 2010); Stephen Kantrowitz, *Ben Tillman & the Reconstruction of White Supremacy* (Chapel Hill, 2000); and Michael Perman, *Struggle for Mastery: Disfranchisement in the South, 1888–1908* (Chapel Hill, 2001).

[12] Erika Lee, *At America's Gates: Chinese Immigration during the Exclusion Era, 1882–1943* (Chapel Hill, 2003); and Lucy Salyer, *Laws Harsh as Tigers: Chinese Immigrants and the Shaping of Modern Immigration Law* (Chapel Hill, 1995).

individuals based on a host of physical characteristics and Cesare Lombroso's application of anthropology and psychology to determine innate criminality helped to focus the attention of state officials on physical manifestations of internal character.[13]

As migration from Europe to the United States intensified from the 1870s, and especially after the 1890 census revealed that a greater percentage of those immigrants were coming from southern and Eastern Europe – much of which was under Habsburg jurisdiction – rather than from the "traditional" northern and Western European countries, native-born Americans became even more interested in differentiating and ranking among whites.[14] Scientists, anthropologists, and other racial theorists began to stress the link between language and race in the service of differentiation among whites. As the popular author Madison Grant wrote in the preface to a colleague's book, there was a scholarly

desire to trace the connection existing between linguistic areas in Europe and the subdivision of the continent into nations. The endeavour has been made to show that language exerts a strong formative influence on nationality because words express thoughts and ideals. But underlying the currents of national feeling, or of speech, is found the persistent action of the land, or geography, which like the recurrent motif of an operatic composition prevails from beginning to end of the orchestration and endows it with a unity of theme. Upon these foundations, linguistic frontiers deserve recognition as the symbol of the divide between distinct sets of economic and social conditions.[15]

With this, the author was trying to work out the relationship among language, race, physical location, and political culture, and as a host of writers dealt with these issues, they came to see language as a manifestation of race, as well as the hereditary nature of culture. By arguing that certain races were genetically predisposed to democratic institutions and freedom whereas others were not, scientific racism was developing another powerful tool for limiting access to political participation.

Key in American debates was whether the American or Anglo-Saxon race could assimilate others. For some, including the powerful Senator

---

[13] Haller; Peter D'Agostino, "Craniums, Criminals, and the "Cursed Race": Italian Anthropology in American Racial Thought," *Comparative Studies in Society and History* 44, 2 (2002): 319–43; and Simon A. Cole, *Suspect Identities: A History of Fingerprinting and Criminal Identification* (Cambridge MA, 2001).

[14] John Higham, *Strangers in the Land: Patterns of American Nativism, 1860–1925* (New Brunswick, 2002); Adams, "World Conquerors."

[15] Leon Dominian, *The Frontiers of Language and Nationality in Europe* (New York, 1917), vii. See also William Z. Ripley, *The Races of Europe: A Sociological Study* (New York: D. Appleton and Company, 1899).

Henry Cabot Lodge of Massachusetts, racial purity was necessary for the proper functioning of government, and he advocated immigration restriction to prevent the Anglo-Saxon body politic from becoming polluted.[16] This line of thinking also produced the development of eugenics, which, when adopted by some states, resulted in forced sterilization of "undesirables"; African-American women were the most common targets, although certainly not the only ones.[17] For others, including Theodore Roosevelt, Woodrow Wilson, and Frederick Jackson Turner on their best days, it was possible to become an American by renouncing previous loyalties and practices and behaving like a "real" American.[18] The first camp advocated exclusion, whereas the second demanded that individuals conform with social norms, potentially at the expense of their individual preferences.

People in both the racial-nationalist camp, like Lodge, and the civic nationalist camp, like a mature Wilson, questioned the ability of democratic institutions to function in a diverse society. Here, a sense of changing generations is important. The antebellum abolitionists who had ultimately produced the Civil War – although many of them were too old to have actually fought in it, if they were men – had generally positive hopes for the ability of blacks and whites to exist in a single political community.[19] Those who actually fought in the war or were of age to have done so tended to take more diverse, yet nuanced positions, often valuing reconciliation and the rejection of absolute moral positions that produced dramatic conflict, as the war had.[20] Then there was a generation of social reformers who, in many cases, had been too young to fight in the war – Theodore Roosevelt among them – and they began their political careers with a sense that assimilation was possible and desirable. But, as their efforts to reform society and integrate immigrants met with failure, they tended to shift the blame for those failures away from the flaws in their programs and on to those they were trying to reform, coming to the

---

[16] Haller; Adams, "World Conquerors."

[17] Paul A. Lombardo, ed., *A Century of Eugenics in America: From the Indiana Experiment to the Human Genome Era* (Bloomington, 2011); and Barbara Young Welke, *Law and the Borders of Belonging in the Long Nineteenth Century United States* (New York, 2010).

[18] Ambrosius; and Gary Gerstle, "Theodore Roosevelt and the Divided Character of American Nationalism," *JAH* 86, 3 (1999): 1280–307.

[19] Leslie Butler, *Critical Americans: Victorian Intellectuals and Transatlantic Liberal Reform* (Chapel Hill, 2007); and Frank A. Ninkovich, *Global Dawn: The Cultural Foundation of American Internationalism, 1865–1890* (Cambridge MA, 2009).

[20] Menand; Kristin Hoganson, *Fighting for American Manhood: How Gender Politics Provoked the Spanish-American and Philippine-American Wars* (New Haven, 1998).

conclusion that something – some biological characteristic – in those people prevented them from conforming.[21] Finally, we have the generation born in the 1880s and 1890s who grew up constantly immersed in racialist rhetoric, with its separation of civilized and barbarous people and its calls for American imperial expansion; for them, seeing biological racial difference was commonplace.[22] Most of the men whom Wilson and House selected to work at the Inquiry crafting policy recommendations for the postwar world were of this youngest generation.[23]

As the number of immigrants rose, reaching a peak of approximately one million arrivals in 1907, restrictionists were gaining ground, and Congress created the Dillingham Commission to investigate immigration and offer policy suggestions about how best to control it. Austrian and Hungarian citizens – identified primarily in racial terms – were the subject of a significant amount of the commission's work, which was published in a forty-volume study in 1911.[24] Habsburg consular officials faced increasing challenges in protecting their citizens in an American environment that was increasingly hostile to the presence of Austrian and Hungarian citizens in the United States.

These increasingly potent ideas about race produced numerous obstacles for Habsburg consuls serving in the United States. Consuls themselves had difficulty establishing relationships with American elites – relationships that would have helped the consuls to protect Austrian and Hungarian citizens more effectively. Austrian and Hungarian citizens also faced violence and unfair legal proceedings. Most important, the legitimacy of the Habsburg government itself was actively undermined.

As individuals, Habsburg consuls in the United States occupied a unique and unenviable social position. Because of their official position and their personal titles of nobility, they should have been accepted in elite American

[21] Welke, *Law*; Douglas C. Baynton, *Forbidden Signs: American Culture and the Campaign against Sign Language* (Chicago, 1998); Sneider; Michael Willrich, *City of Courts: Socializing Justice in Progressive Era Chicago* (Cambridge, 2003); and Kyle E. Ciani, "Hidden Laborers: Female Day Workers in Detroit, 1870–1920," *JGAPE* 4, 1 (2005): 23–51.

[22] Brian Rouleau, "Childhood's Imperial Imagination: Edward Stratemeyer's Fiction Factory and the Valorization of American Empire," *JGAPE* 7, 4 (2008): 479–512; Gail Bederman, *Manliness and Civilization: A Cultural History of Gender and Race in the United States, 1880–1917* (Chicago, 1995); and John Pettegrew, *Brutes in Suits: Male Sensibility in America, 1890–1920* (Baltimore, 2007).

[23] On the Inquiry, see Chapter 6.

[24] Higham; Jeanne Petit, "Breeders, Workers, and Mothers: Gender and the Congressional Literacy Test Debate, 1896–1897," *JGAPE* 3, 1 (2004): 35–58; and Mae M. Ngai, *Impossible Subjects: Illegal Aliens and the Making of Modern America* (Princeton, 2004).

social circles, especially in newer cities like Cleveland and Chicago. Their position in a transnational upper class should have resulted in their personal social acceptance in the United States, and, in some cases, it did. However, Habsburg consuls were also representatives of a country whose population many Americans considered to be racially, culturally, and socially inferior to American Anglo-Saxons. As Consul Silvestri pointed out in Chicago in 1911, "only a few isolated countrymen in the United States have improved their station. In Chicago, for example, there are no Austrians or Hungarians today who are fully accepted in the first American circles."[25]

Silvestri and other consuls struggled with the question of how best to "serve the reputation of the monarchy and the interests of the whole," as well as the needs of individual Austrian and Hungarian citizens. One option was to be closely involved with Austrian and Hungarian citizens in the United States, helping them with their problems and possibly helping them improve their economic position and therefore their social position. This approach had two major drawbacks. First, it required that the consul spend a great deal of time with his constituents. Such frequent interaction caused American elites to see the consul as a person as undesirable as his constituents, and, as a result, they shunned him. That, in turn, limited his ability to interact with local leaders and officials to effect changes that would improve conditions. Silvestri observed that "the consul is isolated here: He cannot have much personal interaction with his countrymen without losing his reputation in the eyes of the Americans. If he does, the Americans will think that the social standing of an Austro-Hungarian consul is not very high."[26] Second, if Austrian and Hungarian citizens improved their standard of living in the United States, they were more likely to become permanent residents of the United States and potentially even U.S. citizens. In a culture that frequently invoked population size as a measure of a country's strength and prestige, the loss of citizens was certainly undesirable. If Austrian and Hungarian citizens put down permanent roots in the United States, they were also more apt to stop sending money back to the empire, which was not to the country's economic advantage.

At the other extreme, consuls could opt to have no interaction with their constituents – they would leave that to their subordinates – and instead

---

[25] Z. CCLVI, Silvestri to MFA, 23 June 1911, in HHStA, AR, Fach 8 – Konsulate, K. 110 – Konsularsitze Chicago-Cin 1880–1918.
[26] Ibid.

cultivate their personal acceptance among American elites. The thinking behind this approach was that an individual consul could prove his own ability to behave in a "civilized," socially acceptable manner. As a representative of his race or people, such behavior would prove to native-born Americans that his people were ultimately capable of civilized behavior as well, and therefore Americans might raise their opinion of the whole country. That improved opinion would then result in a general reduction in prejudice and a bettering of conditions for the foreign-born in the United States. Silvestri reported that some consuls from other countries had elected this approach.[27]

This position also had its downside. Most important, it gave the impression that the consul was uninterested in his constituents. Some European consuls undoubtedly were uninterested; they shared the prejudices of their American hosts and believed in their own personal or racial superiority. This attitude does not, however, seem to have been common among Habsburg consuls in the United States. If the consuls did decide not to interact with their constituents, they risked the loyalty of those constituents. If there had been no other options than seeking out consular officials for help, then this strategy might have been a more reasonable option; regardless of how consuls treated them, Austrian and Hungarian citizens in trouble would nonetheless have to go to them for help. In reality, however, consuls did not have a monopoly on providing assistance. Consuls had to compete with nationally organized societies and American lawyers and profiteers for the privilege of representing Austrian and Hungarian citizens in trouble. If the consul refused to deal with those citizens, they would look elsewhere for help, their loyalty to the Habsburg government would be eroded, and they would be more apt to apply for U.S. citizenship.

Silvestri wrote, "I do not sanction either of these extremes and go a middle route."[28] Such a balancing act was undoubtedly difficult. Unfortunately for Habsburg consuls, the situation did not improve with time: American ideas about the hereditary and therefore immutable nature of culture only solidified as World War I approached, making the goal of the social acceptance of Austrian and Hungarian citizens even more elusive. Race thinking also contributed to nationalist sentiments among Austrian and Hungarian citizens, who increasingly turned to nationally

[27] Ibid.
[28] Ibid.

organized institutions rather than Habsburg consuls to improve their position in the United States.

Habsburg consuls occupied a precarious social position in the United States, but they could typically rest assured that they themselves would not be an object of physical violence. Other Austrian and Hungarian citizens in the United States could not say the same. Race- and labor-related violence was relatively commonplace in the United States at the time, and Austrian and Hungarian citizens were frequent victims, suffering property damage, physical injury, and occasionally even death. For example, a major wave of strikes broke out in the Colorado coal mines in 1914. In May 1914, John Schwager, the Habsburg consul at Denver, reported that "[a]bout 40 percent of strikers in Southern and 20 percent in Northern Colorado [are] citizens of Austria-Hungary." In an incident that has come to be known as the Ludlow Massacre, the governor of Colorado, at the behest of mine owner John D. Rockefeller, called out the National Guard to deal with the strikers, who had set up a tent city at Ludlow. The guardsmen opened fire into the crowds, and the makeshift settlement caught fire; twenty-five people, including twelve children, were killed. Also among the casualties were two Austrians, Luke Vrhovnik and Giovanni Bortolotti. In such conditions, local authorities were supposed to keep the peace and protect the lives and property of people in the vicinity. According to the consul, he had "ascertained [that the] life and property of our people among strikers and strikebreakers [was] not sufficiently protected before arrival of federal troops. Considerable personal property of Austrians and Hungarians destroyed."[29]

In South Omaha, Nebraska, in February 1909, race riots swept the area after a Greek national shot and killed a patrol officer who was trying to arrest him. Although citizens of Greece were the primary target of the ensuing riots, citizens of the Ottoman Empire and Austria-Hungary were among the victims, and they suffered considerable property damage.[30] All three governments approached the State Department to seek

---

[29] Telegram from the Austro-Hungarian consul in Denver to the Austro-Hungarian Embassy, 2 May 1914, file no. 311.631 C71, in NARA; see also [Article 3 – No Title], *NYT*, 29 May 1914, p. 5. On Ludlow, see Thomas G. Andrews, *Killing for Coal: America's Deadliest Labor War* (Cambridge MA, 2010).

[30] Furse to DOS, 26 February 1910, file no. 311.631 So8/26, in NARA. In its coverage, the *NYT* noted that the non-Greek victims were "Italians and Roumanians, who were mistaken for Greeks." The Italian and Romanian governments did not protest, however, suggesting that the victims were likely Italian- or Romanian-speaking citizens of Austria-Hungary and the Ottoman Empire. "South Omaha Mob Wars on Greeks," *NYT*, 22 February 1909, p. 1.

compensation from the state of Nebraska. Local officials denied any responsibility and stressed that the foreigners lived in such poor conditions that their possessions were not worth anything anyway.[31] The complaining governments thought otherwise: the Greek government asked for $153,533 in damages, whereas the Ottomans and Habsburgs asked for $1,984 and $5,981.50, respectively. After six long years of deliberation, the State Department determined that the Greek government should receive $40,000, the Ottomans $230, and the Habsburgs $800.[32]

Occasionally, Habsburg consuls met with more success. In September 1913, the consul general in Chicago sent a telegram to the governor of Illinois:

A delegation of Austrian and Hungarian citizens of Benton, Franklin County, Illinois, request me to appeal to your Excellency to provide immediate protection of foreign population of Benton, where anti-foreign feeling is running very high since the murder of two Americans which occurred last Sunday. Local authorities seem unable to cope with the situation. In the name of humanity and justice I most ardently appeal to your Excellency to protect the life and property of Austrian and Hungarian citizens in Franklin County against mob violence.[33]

The consul general also notified the embassy in Washington about his request, and Ambassador Dumba took it up with Secretary of State William Jennings Bryan. Bryan also telegraphed the governor, echoing the Habsburg officials.[34] The governor called out the National Guard "immediately upon receipt" of the consul general's telegram and pledged that "Illinois will protect Austrian . . . subjects thoroughly."[35]

On the whole, Habsburg officials had a mixed record when counting on state and local officials in the United States to stop racial and xenophobic violence against Austrian and Hungarian citizens. The governor of Illinois likely considered the importance of the immigrant vote in state politics, whereas authorities in Colorado and Nebraska apparently were not as concerned. When Habsburg officials dealt with the federal Justice Department, however, they were not likely to meet with success. For example, a violent "disturbance" broke out on 25 December 1913 in Miami, Arizona, when some members of the population raised the

---

[31] Furse to DOS, 11 March 1910, file no. 311.631 So8/28; and Bennet to DOS, 4 March 1910, enclosing a letter from a South Omaha attorney, file no. 311.631 So8/27, both in NARA.
[32] Adee to Allen, 14 January 1916, file no. 311.631 So8/31, in NARA.
[33] Dumba's telegram to Bryan, 27 September 1913, file no. 311.631 B44, in NARA.
[34] Bryan's telegram to Dunne, 29 September 1913, file no. 311.631 B44, in NARA.
[35] Dunne's telegram to Bryan, 30 September 1913, file no. 311.631 B44/1, in NARA.

Austrian flag. The Department of Justice declined to act. The assistant attorney general reported, "As I read the correspondence and affidavits, the matter appears to have been merely a racial trouble arising out of differences in regard to the Balkan War, and the Greek and Roman Catholic Churches, and is not, therefore, one which should be taken up by this Department."[36] He considered racial violence outside the Justice Department's jurisdiction and not worthy of intervention.

The Justice Department's complacency about racial prejudice and its consequences was also reflected in courtrooms across the United States. Baron Bornemisza, the Habsburg consul in Pittsburgh, was so disturbed by what he had witnessed in Pennsylvania courts that he wrote a lengthy report on the subject; the report caught the eye of Ambassador Hengelmüller, and he considered it important enough to send to the foreign minister in Vienna.[37] In the report, Bornemisza explained the process of jury selection for criminal trials in American courts. Attorneys for both the defense and the prosecution had a certain number of preemptory challenges, through which they could prevent individual people from serving on the jury without stating why they objected. In addition to those preemptory challenges, attorneys could challenge potential jurors for cause; it was then up to the presiding judge to determine if the cause was valid. Bornemisza wrote about the numerous occasions when a foreign-born citizen was the defendant and potential jurors were asked if they were prejudiced against foreigners. More often than not, the potential juror answered in the affirmative. The defense attorney naturally objected for cause in these situations. Bornemisza reported that he had never once seen a judge accept the objection, and, as a result, juries were full of people who openly acknowledged their prejudices, thus seriously jeopardizing the possibility of a fair trial.[38] That Pennsylvania judges allowed openly prejudiced people to serve on juries affirmed the ideas of several prominent race thinkers, including Nathan Shaler, who

---

[36] Assistant Attorney General to SecState, 28 January 1914, file no. 311.631 M58, in NARA.

[37] No. IX.B., Hengelmüller to MFA, 31 January 1909, in HHStA, AR, Fach 15 – Aus- und Einwanderung, K 54 – Aus und Rückwanderung 1880–1918 – Amerika 18, 22–46.

[38] Ibid., enclosing an excerpt from Bornemisza to Ambrózy, Pittsburgh, 30 December 1908. Bornemisza went on to note that admissions of prejudice could be much more specific if need be: if the potential juror was also foreign-born or of a different nationality than the defendant, he had to be asked if he was prejudiced against "Hungarians or Italians or Russians, etc." In these cases as well, prejudice was not considered appropriate grounds for challenge.

argued that race hatred was natural and essential to the preservation and progress of the nation.[39]

As these examples demonstrate, race thinking and prejudice were widespread in the American population and among individual government employees. The U.S. Bureau of Immigration as a whole also embraced race thinking, and its adherence to allegedly scientific race-based identity categories had serious, negative effects on the Habsburg government's claims to legitimate sovereignty. The Habsburg government – and particularly Ministry of Foreign Affairs employees – recognized its citizens only as either Austrian or Hungarian. In the Great Power System, such assertions on the part of a recognized, legitimately sovereign government should have been respected by all other states in the system. The U.S. State Department, scrupulously adhering to the system's norms, did recognize all those from Austria-Hungary as either Austrian or Hungarian citizens. The U.S. Bureau of Immigration, however, operated differently. Because individuals did not typically travel with passports or other identification documents, their claims to citizenship or identity could be questioned whenever an individual crossed an international border. The U.S. Bureau of Immigration rejected Habsburg identity categories and instead used racial categories that directly competed with Habsburg-sanctioned categories, thus undermining Habsburg legitimacy and fostering the development of exclusionary racial nationalisms.

The U.S. Bureau of Immigration – indeed, the entire federal government – became a factor in the immigration process relatively late in the game. Before the Fourteenth Amendment was ratified in 1868, federal citizenship was a function of state citizenship, and states determined what immigration procedures were and what obligations and privileges applied to noncitizen residents. The Fourteenth Amendment flipped the relationship between federal and state citizenship, basing state citizenship on federal citizenship in a Radical Reconstruction effort to extend the full rights and obligations of citizenship to emancipated African Americans. As migration to the United States increased in volume and became more controversial, the federal government developed a stronger role in determining immigration policy. Congress passed the Page Act in 1875, the Chinese Exclusion Act in 1882, and the Immigration Act of 1882, all of which barred categories of people from entering the country. In particular,

---

[39] Haller, 185. Shaler was a professor of the natural sciences at Harvard; he had been a student of Louis Agassiz. He was also an active participant in the Immigration Restriction League.

Chinese were identified as a specific racial group that was "ineligible to citizenship" because its members were considered neither white nor black, although access to U.S. territory was granted or denied via a constellation of racial, class, and gendered elements, rather than strictly race. The federal government still lacked an enforcement mechanism, however, and states remained responsible for processing migrants. The rising numbers of migrants and the growing complexities of the restrictions prompted Congress to create the Bureau of Immigration within the Treasury Department via the Immigration Act of 1891. Immigration restrictions continued to proliferate, but the number of migrants continued to grow, reaching a peak of approximately one million in 1907.[40]

Because the Bureau of Immigration was founded late in the nineteenth century, it was particularly responsive to the popular political and intellectual trends of the time, including statistics and racialist theories. The bureau gradually developed statistical categories for describing and counting immigrants that privileged racial identity over political citizenship. The process of learning to categorize migrants from the Habsburg Empire along racial-national lines followed a similar pattern to Immigration efforts to identify people with physical disabilities and sexual "deviants." It took government officials quite a while to articulate a taxonomy, and, as they did so, they helped to make those categories into social reality, encouraging – or forcing – those they were sorting to conform and identify with the emerging categories.[41] Immigration officials' efforts to create clear boundaries among individuals also echoed Bureau of Indian Affairs attempts to use a "blood quantum" to determine tribal membership; judges' grappling with the presence or absence of whiteness among Puerto Ricans, Syrians, and Armenians; and clerks' and judges' efforts to determine racial status in miscegenation cases.[42]

---

[40] On the impact of the Fourteenth Amendment, see Welke, *Law*. On immigration policy and enforcement, see Paul R. Spickard, *Almost All Aliens: Immigration, Race, and Colonialism in American History and Identity* (New York, 2007); Margot Canaday, *The Straight State: Sexuality and Citizenship in Twentieth-Century* America (Princeton, 2009); and Douglas C. Baynton, "Defectives in the Land: Disability and American Immigration Policy, 1882–1924," *JAEH* 24, 3 (2005): 31–44. On the impacts of Chinese exclusion, see Lee; and Adam McKeown, "Ritualization of Regulation: The Enforcement of Chinese Exclusion in the United States and China," *AHR* 108, 2 (2003): 377–403.

[41] Canaday; James C. Scott, *Seeing Like a State: How Certain Schemes to Improve the Human Condition Have Failed* (New Haven, 1998); Baynton, "Defectives"; and McKoewn.

[42] Eva Marie Garroutte, "The Racial Formation of American Indians: Negotiating Legitimate Identities Within Tribal and Federal Law," *American Indian Quarterly* 25, 2 (2001): 224–39; Ariela J. Gross, *What Blood Won't Tell: A History of Race on Trial in*

The racial-national categories for Europeans developed by officials of the Bureau of Immigration had the greatest effect on Austria-Hungary, the most diverse of the European states, because the political borders of the country were most out of alignment with the perceived racial boundaries of populations. Table 5.1 shows a portion of the categories used by bureau officials in their 1894 annual report. These categories differed from Habsburg categories in two significant ways. First, they included a separate category for people from Bohemia, one of the crownlands of the Austrian half of the country. It is unclear whether Immigration officials intended this category as a territorial category or a racial category. Bohemia was a distinct portion of Austria, but its population consisted primarily of German and Czech speakers; many members of the population were bilingual.[43] It was common practice among U.S. officials – including State Department personnel – to refer to the Czech language as

TABLE 5.1 *Citizenship Categories from the Bureau of Immigration's 1894 Report**

Austria-Hungary
Bohemia
Hungary
Other Austria (except Poland)
Germany
Poland
Russia (except Poland)

* This is a partial listing. Source: No. 16667, "Immigration and Passenger Movement at Ports of the United States during the Year Ending June 30, 1893: Report of the Chief of the Bureau of Statistics," U.S. Treasury Department, 1894, in HHStA, AR, Fach 15, K. 52.

America (Cambridge MA, 2008); Erman; Sarah Gualtieri, "Becoming 'White': Race, Religion and the Foundations of Syrian/Lebanese Ethnicity in the United States," *JAEH* 20, 4 (2001): 29–58; Earlene Craver, "On the Boundary of White: The 'Cartozian' Naturalization Case and the Armenians, 1923–1925," *JAEH* 28, 2 (2009): 30–56; and Peggy Pascoe, *What Comes Naturally: Miscegenation Law and the Making of Race in America* (New York, 2010).

43 On identity in Bohemia, see especially Gary B. Cohen, *The Politics of Ethnic Survival: Germans in Prague, 1861–1914*, new ed. (West Lafayette, 2006); Jeremy King, *Budweisers into Czechs and Germans: A Local History of Bohemian Politics, 1848–1948* (Princeton, 2002); and King, "The Nationalization of East Central Europe: Ethnicism, Ethnicity, and Beyond," In *Staging the Past: The Politics of Commemoration in Habsburg Central Europe, 1848 to the Present*, ed. Maria Bucur and Nancy M. Wingfield (West Lafayette, 2001), 112–52.

"the Bohemian language,"[44] and so it is possible that, in 1894, workers at the Bureau of Immigration meant only Czech speakers when they referred to "Bohemians." Regardless of whether the distinction was territorial or racial, it opened up an additional identity category for Austrian citizens. The category could also be invoked by Czech nationalists who advocated autonomy for Czechs within the Habsburg Empire or even an independent Czech state.

Second, the 1894 statistics included a separate category for Poland, despite the fact that no independent, citizenship-granting Polish state existed at the time. Bohemians were listed as a subgroup of Austro-Hungarian citizens, but Poland got its own category as a country, on par with Austria-Hungary itself. Poles who were Russian citizens were included in the numbers for Poland, but the third partitioning power, Germany, apparently did not have its Polish-speakers counted separately.[45] By giving "Poland" its own statistical category, the Bureau of Immigration made it virtually impossible for Habsburg and Russian officials (and subsequent scholars) to get an accurate count of Austro-Hungarian and Russian emigration to the United States.[46] Far more important, however, the use of the category signaled American acceptance of an independent Polish state and fostered the identification of Polish speakers with that state, rather than with a more cosmopolitan Austrian identity. Habsburg Ministry of Foreign Affairs staff underlined the separate Polish statistics on their copy of the report, making sure those who saw the report took notice of this potentially dangerous categorization.[47]

The next year, in 1895, the Bureau of Immigration produced a much more elaborate annual report, complete with fold-out color charts that documented certain trends in immigration. The report also included a

[44] See, for example, "Imprisonment of Zdenek Bodlak," Hoover to SecState, 10 March 1915, file no. 363.112 B63/3, in NARA.

[45] The Polish-Lithuanian Commonwealth was partitioned in 1772, 1793, and 1795; the Prussians and Russians took territory in all three partitions, whereas the Austrians participated in only the first and third partitions.

[46] Scholarship on Central and Eastern Europeans in immigration history has, to date, largely conformed to the racial-national categories employed by the Bureau of Immigration. To the best of my knowledge, there are no published works on emigration to the United States from the Habsburg Empire as a whole. On the statistics problem, see Mark Wyman, *Round-trip to America: The Immigrants Return to Europe, 1880–1930* (Ithaca, 1993).

[47] No. 16667, "Immigration and Passenger Movement at Ports of the United States during the Year Ending June 30, 1893: Report of the Chief of the Bureau of Statistics," U.S. Treasury Department, 1894, in HHStA, AR, Fach 15, K. 52 – Aus und Rückwanderung 1880–1918 C, Amerika 1.

TABLE 5.2 *"Immigrants Arrived during 25 Years, 1871–1895"**

ANGLO-SAXONS, CELTS, AND WELSHMEN
England, Scotland, Wales
IRISH
Ireland
TEUTONS
Austria, Germany, and the Netherlands
LATINS
Belgium, France, Italy, Spain, and Portugal
SCANDINAVIANS
Denmark, Norway, and Sweden
CZECHS, MAGYARS, AND SLAVS
Bohemia, Hungary, Poland
SWISS
Switzerland
OTHER EUROPE
Greeks, Turks, etc.

* Source: No. 56965, "Immigration and Passenger Movement Ending June 30, 1895," U.S. Treasury Department, 1895, in HHStA, AR, Fach 15, K. 52, folder Nord-Amerika 1.

series of statistics for the preceding twenty-five-year period, not just the 1894–95 fiscal year. One of the charts in the report attempted to align racial categories with specific countries (see Table 5.2). The table listed Austria as a place of residence for "Teutons," along with Germany and the Netherlands. The Swiss, often considered Germanic, were listed as an entirely separate race here. Also included was the curious racial category "Czechs, Magyars, and Slavs," which encompassed one semisovereign and two nonexistent countries: Hungary, Bohemia, and Poland. That Czechs were not considered Slavs is interesting, as is the fact that the word *Czech* was used instead of *Bohemian*; Immigration officials quickly reverted to *Bohemian* in subsequent years. Nationally conscious Magyar-speaking Hungarians would have been appalled to find themselves lumped in with the Slavic peoples, to whom they considered themselves superior. A glaring omission stands out on the table as well: Russians, often looked to as heading the Pan-Slavic movement, were not listed at all.[48]

---

[48] No. 56965, "Immigration and Passenger Movement Ending June 30, 1895," U.S. Treasury Department, 1895, in HHStA, AR, Fach 15, K. 52, folder Nord-Amerika 1.

TABLE 5.3 *1900: "Races and Peoples Represented*
by Those from Austria-Hungary" *

Bohemian & Moravian
Bulgarian, Servian & Montenegrin
Croatian & Slovenian
Dalmatian, Bosnian & Hercegovinian
French
German
Hebrew
Italian, north
Italian, south
Lithuanian
Magyar
Polish
Romanian
Russian
Ruthenian or Russniak
Slovak
Syrian

---

* Source: U.S. Treasury Document no. 2208 (Immigration
Statistics for the fiscal year ending 30 June 1900), in no. LII B,
Hengelmüller to MFA, 20 December 1900, in HHStA, AR,
Fach 15, K. 53.

By 1900, the categories in use had become even more extensive and
racialized. Table 5.3 shows the "Races and Peoples Represented by
Those from Austria-Hungary." *Austrian* and *Hungarian* are no longer
even possibilities in this scheme. The inclusion of *French* and *Syrian* as
categories – not groups commonly associated with Austria-Hungary –
suggests that Immigration personnel ignored naturalized citizens' self-
elected status in favor of allegedly more natural, persistent, and relevant
racial identities.

Hebrew was also listed as a separate category, reflecting the ambiguity
surrounding the question of whether Jews were a separate racial group or
merely a distinct religious community.[49] Bureau of Immigration officials'
inclusion of the category clearly indicates their stance on the issue. By

---

[49] This question was contentious in other countries, as well as among Jews themselves. In the
Habsburg Empire, Judaism was legally recognized as a religion. Yiddish was not recognized as a potential *Umgangsprache* on the census, which meant that the government did
not view Jews as a separate national or ethnic group. See, among others, Stourzh, "Age of
Emancipation."

reinforcing the idea of Jews as a separate racial group, Immigration officials contributed to the popular notion that Jews could not be assimilated into an Anglo-Saxon United States – or into other national states. Had they been simply a religious group, their right to practice their religion would have been protected by the U.S. Constitution, and their claims to participation in U.S. politics would have been more readily honored.

Religion was also a likely factor in other categorizations included by the Bureau of Immigration. Immigration personnel could have listed Serbians, Bulgarians, Slovenes, and Croatians as four separate "races or peoples." Instead, they opted to pair Serbians and Bulgarians and Slovenes and Croatians, suggesting that these groups were similar enough not to be considered distinct groups. From a twenty-first-century vantage point, we might expect Serbians, Slovenes, and Croatians to be combined, as they would later be constituent nations of Yugoslavia. Just combining Serbians and Croatians also seems likely, as the language spoken by both groups is now called "Serbo-Croatian." Bureau of Immigration personnel were likely thinking in religious terms when they made their pairings, however: the majority of Serbians and Bulgarians were Orthodox Christians, whereas Slovenes and Croatians were Roman Catholics.[50] These categorizations reflect the inclusion of cultural criteria in definitions of biological, racial categories.

The Habsburg central government, through its foreign ministry, protested the Bureau of Immigration's methods to the State Department. The Habsburg government argued that the only relevant categories were *Austrian* and *Hungarian*, but if the U.S. government insisted on racial categories, it should at least use them in conjunction with the more important political categories. The State Department passed the Habsburg request on, but Bureau of Immigration officials, without giving any reasoning for their position, announced that they were unable to change the system.[51]

Ten years later, Immigration personnel offered an explanation for their categories. According to the U.S. Immigration Commission, *Austrian* was "not a race name.... It has no significance as to the physical race or language.... The term 'Austrian' simply means an inhabitant or native

---

[50] My thanks to Prof. Alison Frank for drawing my attention to this point.
[51] No. XXXII.D, Hengelmüller to MFA, 4 August 1900, in HHStA, AR, Fach 15, K. 53 – Aus und Rückwanderung 1880–1918 – Amerika 1–21.

of Austria."[52] "An inhabitant or native of Austria" was exactly what Habsburg consuls wanted *Austrian* to mean, but the Bureau of Immigration considered the nonracial term unimportant.

These various Bureau of Immigration reports demonstrate the fluidity of allegedly scientific racial categories in the decades before World War I. Habsburg authorities could not convince the Bureau of Immigration to use the political categories *Austrian* and *Hungarian*, but the bureau itself had also not settled on a definite set of alternative categories. On the one hand, the multiplicity of categories in use opened up many possibilities for personal and national identity. On the other hand, the use of racial categories over political categories conditioned Americans to think of Central and Eastern Europeans – and themselves – in racialized terms, belying their traditional rhetoric about democracy, inclusion, and assimilation. Versions of those racialized categories found their way onto the map of Europe in 1919 because Habsburg diplomats and consuls were silenced during the war, whereas scientifically informed academics and nationalists had a monopoly on President Wilson's attention.

---

[52] Cited in Ernest Wilder Spaulding, *The Quiet Invaders: The Story of the Austrian Impact upon America* (Vienna, 1968), 3. Spaulding observes that the Swiss and the Belgians were also not considered separate racial groups by the Bureau of Immigration in 1910. The Inquiry's Leon Dominian noted in his *Frontiers of Language* that the Belgians had become a distinct people because they had developed their own national poetry.

6

Giving Up on Austria-Hungary

The End of the Great Power System
and the Shift to the Nationalist Successors

While the United States was still officially neutral in World War I, President Wilson made two important decisions that dramatically affected the possibility of continued Habsburg sovereignty after the conclusion of the war. First, he chose to declare the Austro-Hungarian ambassador to the United States, Konstantin Dumba, persona non grata in September 1915. He then refused to receive Dumba's successor, Count Adam Tarnowski, who arrived in the United States on 1 February 1917, just as Wilson had broken diplomatic relations with Germany over the resumption of unrestricted submarine warfare. In refusing to receive Tarnowski and then balancing the U.S.-Habsburg relationship by recalling Ambassador Penfield from Vienna, Wilson severed the diplomatic tie that had reinforced U.S. recognition of Habsburg sovereignty, and the Great Power System was no more.

After those clear decisions, tracking an official U.S. policy toward Austria-Hungary becomes extremely challenging. Certainly, to speak of a single policy is not accurate. A number of different people were engaging in activities and making decisions that had significant implications for Habsburg sovereignty and the political fate of Central Europe, but there was no coordinated U.S. policy working toward a resumption of Habsburg sovereignty, an alternative multinational Central European state, or a collection of successor states conceived in racial-national or any other terms. This lack of a coordinated policy made it easier for deeply ingrained American thinking about racialist categories to manifest itself; people making decisions tended to fall back on the categories they had become familiar with as part of more than twenty years of American

debates on immigration and scholarship about race, rather than seeking a
clearer understanding of the realities of Habsburg society and political
culture. The competitors for Habsburg sovereignty were able to use that to
their advantage, making claims to Wilson and his advisors for the legitimacy of their leadership by invoking a race-based sense of self-
determination. Given the pervasiveness of the terms "self-determination"
and "national self-determination" and its popular association with
Wilson, it is not surprising that they thought that was what he wanted to
hear. For the people on the ground in the Habsburg Empire, those categories became more attractive, too, since they thought adopting the popular
rhetoric of Wilsonianism would produce an end to the blockade and thus
the arrival of desperately needed relief supplies. It was easy for Wilson and
his advisors to interpret those claims as exclusively domestically produced,
despite the importance of earlier American policies and rhetoric that had
helped to create the necessity of such demands in the first place.

The U.S.-Habsburg relationship was in jeopardy when Konstantin Dumba
arrived in the United States in 1913 to replace Hengelmüller. Neither the
newly elected Wilson nor his secretary of state, William Jennings Bryan,
were supporters of the diplomatic culture of the Great Power System, and
Dumba did nothing to change their assessment. In many ways, he conformed to the negative stereotypes many Americans held about diplomats:
he was arrogant and condescending, and he demanded deference to his
diplomatic rank and compliance with the rules of diplomatic culture because
they gave him personal power and prestige, rather than because he was
committed to maintaining the underlying community of the system.[1] His
insistence on his personal importance and abilities was likely fed by the fact
that he was one of the few non-noble members of the Austro-Hungarian
diplomatic corps; his Macedonian family had made its fortune in trade and
had translated that into a position of considerable influence in Viennese
society, but they were not fully accepted by the older aristocracy.[2]

---

[1] This assessment of Dumba is supported by his comments throughout his memoirs.
Konstantin Dumba, *Memoirs of a Diplomat*, trans. Ian F. D. Morrow (Boston, 1932).

[2] William D. Godsey, Jr., *Aristocratic Redoubt: The Austro-Hungarian Foreign Office on the
Eve of the First World War* (West Lafayette, 1999), 30. Dumba was also one of the few non-
Catholics in the diplomatic corps; he was Greek Orthodox. See ibid., 87. On Dumba and his
career, see also Gerald H. Davis, "The Diplomatic Relations between the United States and
Austria-Hungary, 1913–1917" (Ph.D. diss., Vanderbilt University, 1958), 41; and Carol
Jackson Adams, "Courting the 'Vassal': Austro-American Relations during World War I"
(Ph.D. diss., University of Alabama, 1997).

Despite his flaws, he was generally well liked by his Austro-Hungarian colleagues; historian Gerald Davis has observed that "He was respected (perhaps without justification) as one of the shrewdest members of the diplomatic corps."[3] He served on the staff at several major posts, including London, Paris, Rome, and St. Petersburg. He worked under men who later went on to become foreign ministers, and these early personal relationships undoubtedly helped his career.[4] Foreign Minister Aehrenthal promised him an embassy, but the minister died before he could make good on his promise. Dumba had to wait more than three years before Aehrenthal's successor, Berchtold, appointed him to Washington. Although it was an embassy, it was not in Europe, and Dumba was not entirely enthusiastic. Aehrenthal had thought it was a good place to keep the pro-German Dumba out of the way, however, and Berchtold agreed.[5] Dumba held many of the common stereotypes about Washington, thinking that it was an unimportant post and that Americans did not understand the norms of proper diplomatic interaction. He was pleased, however, that the post was of little interest to Berchtold, which meant that Dumba would have a much freer hand to do as he pleased without much interference from Vienna.[6]

He took it upon himself on more than one occasion to lecture the U.S. secretary of state about how things should be done, irritating the secretary and overstepping his orders from Vienna in the process.[7] Hengelmüller had been so successful in Washington because he made friends and largely stayed out of politics; Dumba was unwilling or unable to do the same. Although he thought American diplomats were often bulls in the china shops of European courts, he failed to realize that Washington was a china shop of its own, where tact was just as important as it was at other posts, even if the behavior considered tactful was somewhat different. Dumba could not make the right Americans like him, and therefore his government and his country's reputation in the United States – already precarious – was weakened further.

---

[3] Davis, "Diplomatic Relations," 41.
[4] See Adams, "Courting"; Dumba.
[5] Dumba, 155–57. Dumba, naturally, did not phrase it in this way. He wrote that his close friendship with German officials and diplomats caused Aehrenthal concern because the minister wanted to maintain an independent Austro-Hungarian foreign policy, and Dumba could not be trusted to keep things from his German friends.
[6] Ibid., 277–78.
[7] See, for example, Dumba to Lansing, 26 May 1914, file no. 663.113CSO/110, in NARA. Lansing was acting secretary of state at the time.

Dumba's presence in Washington meant that U.S.-Habsburg relations were already strained when Archduke Franz Ferdinand was assassinated in Belgrade, Serbia, on 28 June 1914. They only grew worse as the subsequent war rapidly expanded from a bilateral Austro-Hungarian-Serbian conflict to a European and then a world war.[8] In some ways, the war was very, very modern, and in other ways it was very typical of the eighteenth century. There were questions about how new technologies such as submarines, chemicals, automobiles, and telephones could be used legitimately in warfare, as well as how enlarged state bureaucracies, industrial economies, and advertising – or propaganda – techniques could be deployed.[9] The Great Power System had relied on rules to keep it going,

---

[8] Austria-Hungary declared war on Serbia on 28 July 1914 after the Serbian government failed to comply with an Austro-Hungarian ultimatum. The expectation among many people in Europe was that it would be a short war of limited scope, but it quickly spiraled into a much larger, system-altering war. Russia came to Serbia's defense, and on 1 August Germany declared war on Russia. Because of the alliance between Russia and France, German military leaders had planned to fight a two-front war; according to the Schlieffen Plan, to beat Russia, Germany had to invade Belgium and then France quickly before the Russian military could mobilize. Therefore, on 3 August, the German government declared war on France, and on 4 August, German troops marched into Belgium. Britain and France had previously guaranteed Belgian independence, and so they declared war on Germany. After a short delay to be sure their naval forces were ready, Britain and France declared war on Austria-Hungary on 12 August. German colonial and economic endeavors in the Far East competed with the Japanese, and so on 23 August, the Japanese government declared war on Germany. The Ottoman government entered the war on the side of the Central Powers on 29 October 1914. Although Italy had a defensive alliance with Germany and Austria-Hungary, the Italian government opted to stay out of the war at first. Italy ultimately joined the Allies and declared war against Austria-Hungary on 23 May 1915; it did not declare war against Germany until 28 August 1916. The Romanian government was persuaded to join the Allies as well and entered the war on 27 August 1916. The United States stayed out until April 1917, when Congress declared war on Germany; a declaration of war against Austria-Hungary followed in December 1917. The literature on how and why the war began is extensive and includes William Mulligan, *The Origins of the First World War* (Cambridge, 2010); Samuel R. Williamson, *Austria-Hungary and the Origins of the First World War* (New York, 1991); James Joll, *The Origins of the First World War* (Harlow, 1984); Fritz Fischer, *Germany's Aims in the First World War* (New York, 1967); F. R. Bridge, *Great Britain and Austria–Hungary, 1906–1914* (London, 1972); Zara S. Steiner, *Britain and the Origins of the First World War* (New York, 1977); J. F. V. Keiger, *France and the Origins of the First World War* (New York, 1983); Stephen Kern, *The Culture of Time and Space, 1880–1918* (Cambridge MA, 1983); D. C. B. Lieven, *Russia and the Origins of the First World War* (New York, 1983); Mustafa Aksakal, *The Ottoman Road to War in 1914: The Ottoman Empire and the First World War* (Cambridge, 2008); and Justus D. Doenecke, *Nothing Less Than War: A New History of America's Entry into World War I* (Lexington, 2011).

[9] On modern warfare, see, among others, Christopher Capozzola, *Uncle Sam Wants You: World War I and the Making of the Modern American Citizen* (New York, 2008); Robert D. Cuff, *The War Industries Board: Business-Government Relations during World War I*

but there were very few, if any, rules surrounding these new methods and technologies. Thus, the war very quickly turned into an environment in which anything was possible – not entirely unlike the lack of restraint that had allowed seventeenth- and eighteenth-century governments to remove neighboring sovereign governments from the international system. Diplomacy also retreated to a style more typical of the eighteenth century, when diplomats maintained alliances, but did not communicate across them. Consular activity continued through the good offices of neutral countries, but the ceremonial affirmation of community and legitimate territorial sovereignty that diplomats had provided ceased.

Because the United States was not officially in the war at the start, its government could and did maintain diplomatic relations with the governments of both the Allied and Central Powers. In the context of this new style of war, however, the rights and responsibilities of neutrality were not entirely clear, and President Wilson and many Americans pursued courses of action that were difficult to interpret as neutral; most blatantly favored the Allies. One of the wartime Austro-Hungarian foreign ministers, Count Stephan Burián, observed, "from the beginning of the war the United States had practiced the duties of neutrality in a manner which did not appear to us to be quite in harmony with the spirit of international law and tradition, while the increasing scale on which our enemies were unfairly favoured aroused our growing resentment."[10] The Wilsonian definition of neutrality prompted several conflicts between the U.S. and Austro-Hungarian governments, including disputes over the rights of neutral citizens to travel on the seas, the right of companies in neutral countries to supply belligerents, and the ability of diplomats representing belligerent governments in neutral countries to communicate with their governments.[11] These conflicts ultimately resulted in the recalls of Dumba and

(Baltimore, 1973); Mark E. Grotelueschen, *The AEF Way of War: The American Army and Combat in World War I* (Cambridge, 1980); John Whiteclay Chambers II, *To Raise an Army: The Draft Comes to Modern America* (New York, 1987); Guy Hartcup, *The War of Invention: Scientific Developments, 1914–18* (London, 1988); and Daniel R. Headrick, *The Invisible Weapon: Telecommunications and International Politics, 1851–1945* (New York, 1991).

[10] Stephan, Count Burián, *Austria in Dissolution, Being the Personal Recollections of Stephan, Count Burián, Minister of Foreign Affairs for Austria and Hungary 1915–1917 and 1918*, trans. Brian Lunn (New York, 1925), 115.

[11] For more on the submarine and munitions issues, see Nicole M. Phelps, "Sovereignty, Citizenship, and the New Liberal Order: U.S.-Habsburg Relations and the Transformation of International Politics, 1880–1924" (Ph.D. diss., University of Minnesota, 2008); and Davis, "Diplomatic Relations."

Penfield and a "peculiar" and "very unstable" U.S.-Habsburg relationship that was "halfway between friendliness and unfriendliness."[12]

The most important of these problems was the issue of diplomatic communication.[13] Early in the war, the British navy had cut the Central Powers' telegraph cables that connected Europe and North America. There were two wireless stations in New Jersey and Long Island that were owned by German companies, but Wilson ordered one completely shut down and the other closely monitored to make sure no communications were sent that violated U.S. neutrality; members of the Wilson administration were concerned that the stations might be used to signal German ships, thus making the stations naval bases. With the official cables cut and these stations disrupted, the diplomatic representatives of the Central Powers in the United States could no longer send secure communications to their governments through their own channels. They were left with two options: they could use the State Department cable, but to do that, they had to provide a copy of the outgoing message to the department; or they could ask the representatives from Brazil, Sweden, or other neutral countries to use their cables, but these legations put strict limitations on the volume of messages that could be sent.[14] Representatives of the Central Powers complained frequently, especially because the U.S. government did not place any restrictions on Allied communication. Penfield reported that "The Foreign Office believes it has a bona fide grievance against the American Government, preventing the Teutonic representatives from telegraphing by wireless in secret to their Governments, while the Entente representatives have every facility of peace times."[15] Communication was further restricted because regular mail and even allegedly sacred diplomatic mail pouches traveled aboard ships: with the British blockade, as

---

[12] Robert Lansing, *War Memoirs of Robert Lansing* (Westport, 1935), 246.

[13] On this issue in U.S.-Habsburg relations, see Rudolf Agstner, "From Apalachicola to Wilkes-Barre: Austria(-Hungary) and Its Consulates in the United States of America, 1820–1917," *AHY* 37 (2006): 163–80; Arthur J. May, "Woodrow Wilson and Austria-Hungary to the End of 1917," in *Festschrift für Heinrich Benedikt*, ed. Hugo Hantsch and Alexander Novotny (Vienna, 1957), 213–42; Adams, "Courting"; Davis, "Diplomatic Relations"; Dumba; and Burián.

[14] Davis, "Diplomatic Relations," 115. Later, the *agrément* for Tarnowski stipulated that he could send ciphered messages over the DOS cable as long as the department had a copy of the cipher book. See no. 2230, Penfield to SecState, 24 November 1916, file no. 701.6311/ 255, in U.S. DOS, *FRUS: 1916 Supplement – The World War* (Washington, 1929), 806–7; and Davis, "Diplomatic Relations," 240–41.

[15] Penfield to SecState, 4 November 1915, file no. 763.72/2251½, in U.S. DOS, *FRUS: The Lansing Papers, 1914–1920*, 2 vols. (Washington, 1939), I:639–42, esp. 640.

much of that correspondence as possible was read by the Allies and often destroyed before it reached its intended destination. Because of these disturbances, representatives of the Central Powers were desperate to find channels of communication.[16]

Some of the Central Power representatives in the United States did have secret things to say. Although the wartime atrocities and intrigues of the Germans were often exaggerated in British-dominated news and other propaganda, there is evidence that they did have a series of plans that came to various degrees of fruition to create conditions in the United States that were favorable to the Central Powers. For example, representatives of the German government set up a series of dummy corporations to buy raw materials in an effort to control supply – their thinking was that, even if goods could not get to Germany, at least they would not get to the Allies, either.[17] The chief architect of these plans was Franz von Papen, a German military attaché, and the plans were almost exclusively conceived and implemented by Germans.[18]

Although these German plans might not stand up to evaluation on an absolute moral scale, it is important to realize that all sides – including the allegedly neutral United States – were engaged in morally questionable activities that were possible because of the new, unregulated tactics and methods that were becoming available at the time. The Allies, and especially the British, had effectively monopolized communications from Europe to the United States, and they flooded the American press with propaganda that flattered the Allies and denigrated the Central Powers.[19]

---

[16] On the communications issue, see Davis, "Diplomatic Relations," 115–16. See also Berchtold to Dumba, no date [1914], in HHStA, PA XXXIII, K. 51, folder Varia 1914.

[17] Davis, "Diplomatic Relations," 143–47. On German war efforts in the United States, see, among others, Martin Kitchen, "The German Invasion of Canada in the First World War," *International History Review* 7, 2 (1985): 245–60; Robert B. Spence, "K. A. Jahnke and the German Sabotage Campaign in the United States and Mexico, 1914–1918," *Historian* 59, 1 (1996): 89–112; Felice A. Bonadio, "The Failure of German Propaganda in the United States, 1914–1917," *Mid-America* 41, 1 (1959): 40–57; and David Welch, *Germany, Propaganda, and Total War, 1914–1918: The Sins of Omission* (New Brunswick, 2000).

[18] Von Papen was later chancellor of Germany, and he was indicted – but acquitted – at the Nuremberg trials after World War II for his participation in the Nazi regime.

[19] Propaganda efforts have received extensive scholarly attention. See, among numerous others, George T. Blakey, *Historians on the Homefront: American Propagandists for the Great War* (Lexington, 1970); Carol S. Gruber, *Mars and Minerva: World War I and the Uses of the Higher Learning in America* (Baton Rouge, 1975); J. Lee Thompson, *Politicians, the Press & Propaganda: Lord Northcliffe & the Great War, 1914–1919* (Kent, 1999); and Stephen Vaughn, *Holding Fast the Inner Lines: Democracy, Nationalism, and the Committee on Public Information* (Chapel Hill, 1980).

Much of that "news" consisted of outright lies. But because there were no explicit rules or even tacit norms against it, they used propaganda to their best advantage. The Central Powers could not compete in that realm, and so they turned to other strategies that were not explicitly forbidden either.

Wilson also used questionable tactics. He tapped the power of the ever-expanding federal government, ordering the Secret Service, under the leadership of Treasury Secretary William G. McAdoo, to monitor the diplomatic and consular representatives of the Central Powers to make sure that they did not violate U.S. neutrality in any way. Their phones were tapped, and they were followed everywhere. In July 1915, Secret Service agents went so far as to steal the briefcase of one German embassy staff member. McAdoo and Lansing personally went through the briefcase and selected documents from it for publication in the press.[20] Allied representatives were not subject to such surveillance, making this yet another instance of Wilson's non-neutral neutrality policies. Neither Lansing, nor McAdoo, nor many other high-ranking government personnel were above direct involvement in efforts to sabotage the Central Powers.

In the summer of 1915, William Warm, the editor of the Cincinnati-based, Magyar-language newspaper *Szabadság* (Liberty), approached Dumba with an idea. He argued that, since U.S. companies continued to produce munitions despite diplomatic protests, perhaps it was time to attempt to stop or at least hinder production through alternative means. Warm said that, with some help, he could organize a strike of steel workers in Bethlehem, Pennsylvania and in factories throughout the Midwest, where most of the workers were either Austrian or Hungarian citizens or had been before their naturalization. Dumba thought the plan a good one – even if it did not have much effect on the output of the munitions industry, it might succeed in improving working conditions for Austrian and Hungarian laborers. The German government had encouraged its citizens to quit their jobs if their companies were helping the Allies, and German representatives in the United States ran an assistance and employment bureau to help those individuals who complied with their government's request; Dumba thought Austria-Hungary might do something similar. Before he made any concrete arrangements with Warm, however, he needed to secure permission and funding from the government in Vienna.[21]

[20] Davis, "Diplomatic Relations," 126–27.
[21] See ibid., 114–55; and Dumba, 256–69.

A few days after Warm's proposal, Bernstorff, the German ambassador, hosted a dinner in New York City on the occasion of Emperor Franz Joseph's birthday at which Dumba was the guest of honor. Among the guests was James F. J. Archibald, an American citizen and one of the few American journalists openly opposed to the Allies. He was sailing for Europe in two days, and he volunteered to carry any letters Bernstorff and Dumba might want to send. At the dinner, Dumba declined, but the next day he changed his mind, having realized the potential value of this opportunity to communicate with his government. He quickly wrote a letter to Foreign Minister Burián about the potential strike plans and rushed to get it to Archibald before his ship sailed.[22]

As might be expected, things went wrong. Archibald's ship, the *Rotterdam*, was stopped by the British navy and forced to dock at Falmouth for a search.[23] Archibald's papers, including the letter from Dumba, were discovered, and the journalist was arrested and held for one night before being allowed to proceed to Amsterdam. The British government gave Dumba's letter to the U.S. ambassador in London, Walter Hines Page, and, two days later, on 5 September 1915, it appeared in the *New York World*. As historian Gerald Davis notes, "The contents of Dumba's letter fully merited the sensation they created," and many American newspapers demanded that Wilson and Lansing take action.[24]

Unfortunately for Wilson and Lansing, there was no evidence against Dumba that the strike plans were actually moving forward, and so they opted to frame the issue as the misuse of an American passport: Dumba had used an American citizen to carry official diplomatic correspondence, and that was against the rules of both neutrality and diplomacy. Archibald was also punished for the abuse of his passport.[25] Dumba did not help the situation by appearing upset that he got caught rather than sorry for breaking the rules. He insisted that U.S. policies regarding diplomatic communication had necessitated the use of Archibald as a private courier.[26]

---

[22] Dumba to Burián, 20 August 1915, enclosed in no. 2732, Page to SecState, 1 September 1915, file no. 701.6311/141, in U.S. DOS, *FRUS: 1915 Supplement – The World War* (Washington, 1928), 932–33.

[23] May claims the British stopped the ship specifically to look for Archibald on a tip from Czech agents. See May, "Woodrow Wilson," 220.

[24] Davis, "Diplomatic Relations," 129, 131–32.

[25] When Archibald arrived in Amsterdam, he learned that the DOS had cancelled his passport except for his return to the United States, where he faced legal charges for misusing his passport. See Davis, "Diplomatic Relations," 135–36.

[26] Ibid., 132, 137. See also Dumba.

Wilson certainly believed that Dumba – who Wilson described in dramatic terms as "the king pin in this structure of intrigue" – would have to go, but it seemed that Dumba's departure solved only part of the problem.[27] He wrote to House that he wanted to get rid of Bernstorff, too: "If Dumba goes, why not Bernstorff also? Is there any essential difference?"[28] The essential difference was that there was evidence that Dumba had overstepped the rules by using a private American citizen as a diplomatic courier, whereas Bernstorff had not, despite the fact that the German representatives in the United States were actively involved in clandestine efforts to hinder American commerce. This was not the right moment to be rid of German diplomats in the United States, and so Wilson had to settle for Dumba alone.

Wilson insisted that Dumba be recalled. His instructions were telegraphed to Ambassador Penfield and concurrently released to the press on 8 September 1915.[29] Burián was not eager to comply, however. A recall was serious business: in this case, it was an admission that Dumba had broken the rules of diplomatic practice, and the blame could be assigned to the Austro-Hungarian government as a whole, which could, in turn, trigger a breach of diplomatic relations. There was no question in Vienna that Dumba should be permanently removed from Washington – the issue was how that removal was going to be effected. Burián said that he would not recall Dumba until the ambassador was allowed to report on the situation, either by telegraph or in person. Lansing denied Dumba the use of the State Department's cable, so he could not telegraph. To report in person in Vienna would require that Lansing approach the British and French governments to secure Dumba's safe passage, which Lansing refused to do until Dumba had been officially recalled. Lansing's other choice was to give Dumba his passports, which was the Great Power System way of kicking a diplomat out of the host country. Lansing did not want to do that either – he wanted the Austro-Hungarian government to recall Dumba and thereby make an admission of guilt. Finally, on 4 November 1915, Burián agreed to Dumba's recall in a single communication; he did not use the word again in relation to Dumba, but Lansing

[27] Wilson to Lansing, file no. 701.6311/151½, 15 September 1915, in *FRUS: Lansing Papers*, 1:83.

[28] Wilson to House, 7 September 1915, *PWW*, 34:426.

[29] No. 887, Lansing's telegram to Penfield, 8 September 1915, file no. 701.6311/145a, in *FRUS: 1915 Supplement*, 933–34.

seized the small victory Burián had handed him, and Dumba's passage to Europe was secured.[30]

In response to the Dumba situation, and as a general protest of the U.S. practice of neutrality, the Austro-Hungarian government declined to send another ambassador to the United States to replace Dumba immediately.[31] The embassy was left in the capable hands of Baron Erich von Zwiedinek, who Lansing thought was scrupulously honest, if not politically savvy.[32] Lansing thought Zwiedinek alone fully grasped the significance of events: "I think he felt that it was a disastrous moment for his country because he realized better than others of his countrymen what the result would be on the future of the Empire which he represented."[33] Not trying to send another ambassador then may have been the Austro-Hungarian government's biggest mistake of the war. Austro-Hungarian officials did not gain U.S. compliance with any of their demands regarding communications, and by the time that they did try to send another ambassador, Wilson's opinion of Austria-Hungary had soured even further.

That new ambassador, Count Adam Tarnowski, had the bad luck to arrive in the United States on 1 February 1917, just as the German diplomatic and consular staff, headed by Bernstorff, was departing for home. Wilson had just severed diplomatic relations with the German government over the resumption of unrestricted submarine warfare. The Habsburg government had secured an *agrément* from Wilson before Tarnowski sailed, but now Wilson reneged and refused to receive him, rendering Tarnowski powerless.[34] Without presenting his credentials to Wilson, he could not officially take up his duties as ambassador. He could not try to repair the damage Dumba had done, he could not advocate for the continued value of Habsburg sovereignty or of Austria-Hungary in general in the international political system, and he could not use his office to gain the hearing of other American leaders who might restrain or overrule Wilson. In addition – and perhaps most crucially – by refusing to receive Tarnowski, Wilson was refusing to participate in the credentials ceremony, which would have

---

[30] No. 106,067/2, Burián to Penfield, 8 November 1915, enclosed in no. 932, Penfield to SecState, 10 November 1915, file no. 701.6311/196, in *FRUS: 1915 Supplement*, 947. See also Davis, "Diplomatic Relations," 138–41.

[31] See, for example, no. 967, Penfield to SecState, 18 November 1915, file no. 124.636/20, in NARA. Penfield reported that Burián told him that the Dumba case and the communications issue was closed but "not forgotten."

[32] Lansing, *War Memoirs*, 359–60.

[33] Ibid., 253.

[34] See Lansing's telegram to Penfield, 28 March 1917, file no. 124.63/19a, in NARA.

signaled the U.S. government's continued acceptance of Habsburg sovereignty. By not receiving Tarnowski, Wilson created an opportunity for the recognition of an alternate sovereignty in Central Europe.

Tarnowski's position was unenviable. Wilson's treatment of him was an affront to Tarnowski personally and to his government and his country. Tarnowski was also under considerable pressure from Foreign Minister Count Ottokar Czernin, who was anxious to preserve the diplomatic channels between the United States and Austria-Hungary. The minister kept asking why Tarnowski had not yet presented his credentials, since Ambassador Penfield in Vienna had promised that Tarnowski would be received, and Wilson had accepted him by *agrément*.[35] Tarnowski had to explain that the president had changed his mind and that the ambassador had been unsuccessful in convincing those near Wilson to work to change the president's opinion. Tarnowski did what he could to make the best of the situation. He was allowed to hold several unofficial conversations with Secretary of State Lansing in an attempt to secure his reception and to improve U.S.-Habsburg relations, but these conversations produced no positive results for the Habsburg government. Finally, in April 1917, he sailed for home, telling Lansing that he would happily return at any point when Wilson was ready to receive him.[36]

Allegedly to avoid the awkwardness created by uneven staffing in U.S.-Habsburg relations, Wilson recalled Ambassador Penfield from Vienna with the intention of reducing U.S.-Habsburg relations to the care of chargés d'affaires.[37] In practice, Penfield's recall was a severance of diplomatic relations without an official statement. Penfield, still attached to U.S. neutrality, fond of Austria-Hungary, and dedicated to his impressive war work, told the Austro-Hungarian foreign minister that he was taking a leave of absence – he hoped to return when the immediate conflict was over.[38] In his opinion, Austria-Hungary would still be there when he returned.[39]

---

[35] Czernin to Tarnowski, 6 February 1917, cited in Davis, "Diplomatic Relations." On Tarnowski's appointment, see ibid., 238–41. Davis's work provides a document-by-document chronicle.

[36] Lansing, *War Memoirs*, 255.

[37] Wilson to Lansing, 27 March 1917, file no. 701.6311/271, in *FRUS: Lansing Papers*, 1:633–34.

[38] See no. 12700, Penfield to Czernin, 6 April 1917, in HHStA, AR, Fach 7 – Fremde Missionen, K. 46 – Staaten Nordamerika 1880–1918; and Penfield's telegram to Lansing, 1 April 1917, file no. 124.63/19, in NARA. See also Davis, "Diplomatic Relations," 264–65.

[39] This was a widely held opinion among European policymakers, with only Nicholas II of Russia frequently asserting at this early stage that the empire would not last through the

Before Penfield could leave Vienna, however, the U.S. Congress declared war on Germany at Wilson's request. Germany's allies – Austria-Hungary, the Ottoman Empire, and Bulgaria – severed diplomatic relations with the United States as a result. There was a general repatriation of diplomatic and consular staff between the United States and the Central Powers. With the break in U.S.-Habsburg diplomatic relations, the Great Power System was officially at an end. The mutual recognition of legitimate sovereignty that the exchange of diplomats had symbolized was over, and the international communication that had been filtered through the stylized language of diplomats in the field now happened primarily by more direct communications between foreign office personnel and heads of government in their capital cities. In the United States, Wilson went even further, minimizing the role of the State Department in favor of the private diplomacy of his political confidant, "Colonel" Edward House, and the research and policy planning efforts of the Inquiry.[40]

With the declaration of war against Germany, the Wilson administration's top priority was mobilizing Americans for the war effort. Wilson explained repeatedly in his public speeches that the German government's autocratic nature – the antithesis of American democracy – was ultimately to blame for the start of the war. Austria-Hungary was also presented as having a problematic government, although its faults were more complex than in the German case: not only was it autocratic, according to Wilson, but it oppressed not just a single nation, but a host of them. Despite the apparent strength of the Habsburg government to maintain an iron grip on so many, Wilson also presented it as a vassal of the German government, weak and incapable of acting independently. Indeed, Wilson argued that it was Austria-Hungary's "vassal" status that necessitated a U.S. declaration of war against the country in December 1917: the integration of the German and Habsburg militaries – under German direction, Wilson stressed – meant that U.S. soldiers were in a position to kill and be killed by Austrians and Hungarians, an awkward legal situation that prompted Wilson to seek a declaration of war from

war. See Wilfried Fest, *Peace or Partition: The Habsburg Monarchy and British Policy, 1914–1918* (New York: St. Martin's Press, 1978).

[40] The most recent in a long line of Wilson-House studies is Godfrey Hodgson, *Woodrow Wilson's Right Hand: The Life of Colonel Edward M. House* (New Haven: Yale University Press, 2006).

Congress.[41] The United States government never declared war on the other two Central Powers, Bulgaria and the Ottoman Empire.

To achieve the stable peace Wilson envisioned, both the German and Habsburg governments would have to go. In Germany, which Wilson perceived as a homogenous national community, achieving democracy would be easy: remove the autocracy, and the German people would naturally select a democratic government. For Austria-Hungary, it was unclear what exactly needed to happen: would getting rid of the Habsburgs be enough? Or, would the various clearly defined national groups that Wilson saw there need to be separated into independent states? To help determine a policy on the fate of Austria-Hungary and on the numerous other questions that would be involved in the peace settlement, Wilson turned away from the State Department, with its commitments to international law and Great Power System norms, and to a new institution created specifically to apply scientific reason and expertise to international politics in an effort to secure a lasting peace: the Inquiry.[42]

Wilson had a penchant for like-minded souls, so members of the Inquiry had to be committed to his specific vision of the postwar world. The American Historical Association's National Board for Historical Service, whose members included Wilson's close friend Frederick Jackson Turner, helped Col. House select the members of the Inquiry. More than half came from Harvard, Yale, Columbia, Princeton, the University of Chicago, and the ranks of the American Geographical Society. The majority of those selected were young, in their twenties or thirties, although service with the Inquiry was also attractive to men who were too old to serve in the military.[43]

As historian Lawrence Gelfand has pointed out, enthusiasm for the cause – and personal connections – were far more important for securing a position with the Inquiry than any actual expertise in modern history or

[41] Woodrow Wilson, "Address to a Joint Session of Congress Calling for War with Austria-Hungary," 4 December 1917, *PWW*, 45: 194–202. See also Arthur S. Link, *Wilson*, 5 vols. (Princeton, 1947–65); and Binoy Kampmark, "'No Peace with the Hohenzollerns': American Attitudes on Political Legitimacy Towards Hohenzollern Germany, 1917–1918," *DH* 34, 5 (2010): 769–91.

[42] On the Inquiry and its relationship to the DOS, see Jonathan M. Nielson, "American Historians at the Versailles Peace Conference, 1919: The Scholar as Patriot and Diplomat" (Ph.D. diss., University of California – Santa Barbara, 1985); and Lawrence E. Gelfand, *The Inquiry: American Preparations for Peace, 1917–1919* (New Haven, 1963).

[43] See Gelfand; Nielson, chapter 3.

international relations.[44] In part, this reflected the state of American – and European – higher education at the time, in which modern history and languages were rarely part of a curriculum that focused instead on classics and medieval history. But there was also a conscious effort to select people who could be counted on to support the president's program and keep the Inquiry a secret. In keeping with these priorities, the Inquiry's first leader was Sidney E. Mezes, Colonel House's brother-in-law. Mezes was a philosopher of religion, and he had significant administrative experience, first at the University of Texas and then as president of the City College of New York.[45]

From its inception in September 1917 until its partial transformation into the American Commission to Negotiate Peace in January 1919, the Inquiry employed approximately 150 people. None were experts on Austria-Hungary. A handful had proficiency in some of the empire's languages, but none had made the empire as a whole his or her object of study. One of the few true, relevant experts on the Inquiry was Robert Lord, a historian of Poland who was fluent in the language and had studied in Vienna, Berlin, and Moscow. Lord was in his early thirties during the war, and his one publication at that point was his Ph.D. thesis on the Second Partition of Poland in 1793 – the only partition that had not involved the Habsburg government.

Inquiry staff were therefore largely reliant on the writings of British experts when it came to understanding Austria-Hungary. The British pool was certainly not large either, and its members were strongly biased. The two major British experts on Austria-Hungary were Robert Seton-Watson and Henry Wickham Steed. Seton-Watson taught at Oxford. He sympathized with the Hungarian revolutionary cause until 1905, when he traveled to the empire for the first time and realized that there was a significant gap between Hungarian liberal rhetoric and the Magyarization policies actually in place in the country.[46] Although Seton-Watson was a bona fide academic, Steed was primarily a

---

[44] In *The Inquiry*, Gelfand is quick to point out that the collective expertise of the Inquiry was seriously overrated, but many scholars have bought into the Inquiry's self-assessment of its superior intelligence. See, for example, Margaret Macmillan, *Paris 1919: Six Months that Changed the World* (New York, 2002); and Frederick Dumin, "Self-Determination: The United States and Austria in 1919," *Research Studies* 40, 3 (1972): 176–94.

[45] Gelfand, 32–78, esp. 38.

[46] On Seton-Watson, see Fest; G. H. Bolsover, *Robert William Seton-Watson, 1879–1951* (London, 1959); Hugh Seton-Watson and Christopher Seton-Watson, *The Making of a New Europe: R. W. Seton-Watson and the Last Years of Austria-Hungary* (Seattle, 1981); John Bruce Robinson, "Robert William Seton-Watson and the Yugoslavs" (MA thesis,

newspaper man. He had served as *The* (London) *Times*'s correspondent in Vienna from 1902 until 1913. During his stay in Vienna, Steed produced a book, *The Habsburg Monarchy*, which emerged from research and writings Steed had done in anticipation of providing coverage of Franz Joseph's death; he began writing in 1905, but the emperor did not die until 1916. The book was influential in English-speaking circles because it was one of very few English-language sources of information available on the empire.[47] Its utility was questioned by contemporaries, however: for example, an American consul stationed in Trieste wanted to buy it for the consulate to use as a reference, but the State Department did not deem it sufficiently useful to spend money on it.[48]

Despite the fact that they wrote about Austria-Hungary, the driving goal of Steed and Seton-Watson's work was not actually focused on Austria-Hungary at all, but rather on Germany. As staunch supporters of the British Empire, Steed and Seton-Watson resented German economic and colonial competition and were anxious to find a way to limit or even destroy German power. They were strong proponents of the argument that the Austro-Hungarian government was a vassal of the German government. By portraying the Habsburg government as ethnically and culturally German and asserting that German speakers within the monarchy controlled the country, they could argue that the government in Berlin was ultimately responsible for the oppression of the Slavs in Austria-Hungary. They wanted to either remake Austria-Hungary into a tripartite state, in which the Slavs could block German aggression and expansion, or else break up the empire entirely so Berlin did not have added strength through its control over all the non-Germans in Austria-Hungary.[49]

Just as Wilson had looked to American academics to supply staff for the Inquiry, the British government employed a number of experts and academics in various aspects of war work. During the war, both Steed and

Ohio State University, 1974); and Mark Robert Baker, "A Tale of Two Historians: The Involvement of R. W. Seton-Watson and Lewis Namier in the Creation of New Nation-States in Eastern Europe at the End of the First World War" (MA thesis, University of Alberta, 1993).

[47] Henry Wickham Steed, *The Habsburg Monarchy* (London, 1913). On Steed, see Fest; and Peter Schuster, *Henry Wickham Steed und die Habsburgermonarchie* (Vienna, 1970).

[48] No. 20, Busser to SecState, 16 March 1914; and no. 14, Carr to Busser, 28 April 1914, file 125.9452/10, both in NARA.

[49] See, among others, Steed, *Habsburg Monarchy*; R. W. Seton-Watson, *German, Slav, and Magyar: A Study in the Origins of the Great War* (New York, 1916); Seton-Watson, *The Rise of Nationality in the Balkans* (London, 1917); and Seton-Watson, *The Southern Slav Question and the Habsburg Monarchy* (London, 1911).

Seton-Watson worked for numerous British government agencies, and an important part of their work was authoring considerable amounts of anti-Habsburg propaganda for distribution in Britain, the United States, and Central Europe. They were the founders of a weekly journal called *New Europe*, which was the primary anti-Habsburg English-language publication. Inquiry members, who were translating their own claims to expertise into political power without qualms, had no reason to doubt what they read from the pens of Steed and Seton-Watson.

The Inquiry was limited in its treatment of Austria-Hungary by its members' lack of expertise, and, as Gelfand notes in his study, it was also limited in its effectiveness by its lack of a clear mandate, list of priorities, or clear organization. This lack of organization was repeated at the Paris Peace Conference itself. Ultimately, Inquiry members compiled approximately 2,000 reports, made 1,200 maps, and assembled an impressive library. They aimed primarily at amassing facts, rather than providing analysis, and they hoped to organize the facts in such a way that they could be called up quickly and in no particular order.[50]

The basic organization they finally decided on, the type of data they collected, the way they chose to present that information, and their basic assumptions about identity made it a foregone conclusion that the American delegation would advocate the break-up of the Habsburg Empire into smaller nation-states. The fundamental idea that Inquiry members were hoping to capture in the postwar settlement was that peace could be achieved only if the states of the system were democracies. Secretary of State Lansing also supported that basic position, noting that "No people on earth desire war, particularly an aggressive war. If the people can exercise their will, they will remain at peace. If a nation possesses democratic institutions, the popular will be exercised."[51] However, Inquiry members also coupled this idea with the notions that democratic government was only possible in racially homogeneous societies and that each individual clearly belonged to a single racial group.

For Central Europe, Inquiry members maintained that creating homogeneous nations that could then pursue democratic governance should be achieved by adjusting territorial boundaries. As geographer and Inquiry member Leon Dominian wrote, "an ill-adjusted boundary is a hatching

---

[50] Gelfand; Nielson.
[51] Lansing to House, 8 April 1918, file no. 763.72119/1562a, in *FRUS: Lansing Papers*, 2:118–20.

oven for war. A scientific boundary, on the other hand, prepares the way for permanent goodwill between peoples."[52] This focus on the territorial was reinforced by the large number of geographers employed by the Inquiry.[53] Dominian and his colleagues believed that the best way to determine an individual's racial makeup, and hence what nation he or she belonged to, was to know what language the individual spoke. For Dominian, language was a product of both biological raw material and the physical environment, and it reflected whether a people or a nation could progress or adapt, or whether it was static and uncivilized. He argued that "every language has a home of its own upon the surface of the earth," and that "language is little more than the expression of [a man or nation's] character."[54]

Dominian's key assumption – which was also held by other Inquiry members and Wilson – was that individuals spoke only one language. That, of course, meant that they could indeed be divided neatly into nation-states with other individuals who spoke the same language and were thus of the same biological stock. This assumption – that every individual had a single identity derived from the biological and manifested in the use of a single language – was completely at odds with reality in the Habsburg Empire, where individuals spoke multiple languages and selected identities opportunistically. Neither Inquiry members nor Wilson ever seemed to grasp that point, however, and they did not antici-pate the complexities of applying their ideas.[55] In their planning and even at the peace conference, when evidence to the contrary was piling up, they continued to assume the existence of clear social borders between racial-national groups and that it would be possible to connect those social borders to specific territory.

The abundance of geographers working for the Inquiry definitely rein-forced this interpretation. In November 1917, Inquiry headquarters moved from the New York Public Library to the headquarters of the American Geographical Society, and the president of the Society, Isaiah Bowman, took an active role in the organization, ultimately taking over leadership from Mezes. Inquiry members wanted to be able to express all

---

[52] Leon Dominian, *The Frontiers of Language and Nationality in Europe* (New York, 1917), vii.
[53] See Neil Smith, *American Empire: Roosevelt's Geographer and the Prelude to Globalization* (Berkeley, 2003); Charles Seymour, *Geography, Justice, and Politics at the Paris Conference of 1919* (New York, 1951); and Dominian.
[54] Dominian, 1, 2. Dominian repeatedly referred to nations as men.
[55] On similar British thinking, see Fest, 16–17.

kinds of economic, political, and social data on overlaying maps, and that goal required data that could be presented in two-dimensional form. In the case of Austria-Hungary, its population maps were drawn to show distinct geographical areas inhabited by speakers of a single language. According to the maps, there were no areas of overlap, and therefore all that needed to be done was to carve up the territory along those clear linguistic lines.

The large numbers of geographers also contributed to the way Inquiry staff framed their tasks. The Inquiry's subcommittees were organized by geography: there was an Eastern European Division, a Balkan Division, and an Austro-Italian Division – among others for other parts of the world – but there was no committee that dealt with Central Europe or Austria-Hungary as a whole. From the very beginning, then, the Inquiry was dealing with the Polish question, the Balkan question, and the Italian question, and never with "the Austro-Hungarian question." The Paris Peace Conference adopted a similar organization, and so there was no pressure for the American delegation to think about the fate of Central Europe in anything other than national and geographic terms.[56]

The Inquiry also contributed decisively to the postwar settlement and American policy toward Austria-Hungary through its participation in the drafting of President Wilson's famous Fourteen Points. The Inquiry, of course, was supposed to provide the president with expert advice, but Inquiry members were asked to make recommendations for the Fourteen Points before any research had begun – indeed, before a significant number of staff members had even been hired. That did not stop the executive committee of the Inquiry from making two sets of recommendations to the president, one in late December 1917 and the other in early January 1918.[57] With some minor adjustments from the president, the Inquiry's unresearched recommendations became Wilson's Fourteen Points, which in turn provided a basis for the armistice and peace settlement.

Four of the Fourteen Points had direct bearing on Austria-Hungary, and they largely reflected both the geographic focus that the Inquiry was haphazardly adopting and an underlying logic of racial nationalism. Point IX held that "a readjustment of the frontiers of Italy should be effected along clearly recognizable lines of nationality." For the Inquiry,

---

[56] Gelfand. See also Bruce F. Pauley, "The Patchwork Treaties: St. Germain and Trianon Reconsidered," *Rocky Mountain Social Science Journal* 9, 2 (1972): 61–70.

[57] Inquiry Document no. 887, "The Present Situation: The War Aims and Peace Terms It Suggests," 22 December 1917, in U.S. DOS, *FRUS: 1919 – The Paris Peace Conference*, vol. 1 (Washington, 1942), 41–53; see also Gelfand, 136.

those lines were indeed "clearly recognizable," a statement consistent with the idea that racial groups had distinct borders. They had suggested to Wilson that Trieste should be a free city, because the city's population was "exclusively Italian," in contrast to the Slavic population in the surrounding countryside and along the Dalmatian coast.[58] Had they consulted the State Department, they would have known that the city was hardly purely Italian – the consulate staff as a whole needed to be able to function in not only Italian, but German, Croatian, French, and Magyar as well.

Point XI applied to the Balkans. It was vague enough to allow for the possibility of some sort of Yugoslav state or for independent nation-states in the region. Point XIII called for "an independent Polish state … which should include the territories inhabited by indisputably Polish populations." Inquiry members believed that the Polish question was "by far the most complex of all problems to be considered."[59] The complexity stemmed from two contradictory imperatives: the principle of nationality, and Wilson's insistence that all countries should have access to the sea. To give Poland sea access would mean including significant numbers of ethnic Germans in the Polish state, and that would clearly bring problems. The initial Inquiry position was that internal discord within Poland must be kept to a minimum in order for Poland to be an effective block against future German expansion or aggression.[60] In his speech, Wilson opted to include both demands, putting off the need for a concrete decision until some point in the future.

Finally, the Inquiry made a recommendation regarding Austria-Hungary: "Towards Austria-Hungary the approach should consist of references to the subjugation of the various nationalities, in order to keep that agitation alive, but coupled with it should go repeated assurances that no dismemberment of the Empire is intended, together with allusions to the humiliating vassalage of the proudest court in Europe."[61] In his tenth point, Wilson altered this quite a bit, stating that "The peoples of Austria-Hungary, whose place among the nations we wish to see safeguarded and assured, should be accorded the freest opportunity to autonomous development."[62] One interpretation of this statement was that

[58] Woodrow Wilson, "Address to a Joint Session of Congress on the Conditions of Peace," 8 January 1914, *PWW* 45:534–39; see also Inquiry Document no. 887; and Gelfand, 141–42.

[59] Wilson, "Conditions of Peace"; Inquiry Document no. 887; and Gelfand, 146–47.

[60] Gelfand, 148.

[61] Inquiry Document no. 887; and Gelfand, 143.

[62] Wilson, "Conditions of Peace."

Austria-Hungary would continue to exist, but it would be pressured to make changes to the structure of its government. This was Burián's understanding. He wrote in his memoirs, "We were at least justified in expecting that Wilson, while logically trying to carry out his ideas, would inevitably be forced to advocate our right to existence. He required us to carry out certain reforms. In order to do so it was necessary that we should continue to exist."[63] The statement also left the possibility of a break-up into nation-states in place, however. Either way, Wilson referred to the inhabitants of the Habsburg Empire not as Austrian and Hungarian citizens, but rather as "peoples," implying the existence of multiple, distinct groups that even a liberal government would not be able to turn into a single community.

In practice, however, Wilson employed the Inquiry's recommendation with regard to Austria-Hungary and did not commit to either the break-up of the empire or the recognition of national governments to replace the empire. The British government adopted a similar, contradictory policy. Both U.S. and British officials hoped to be able to use Austria-Hungary to defeat Germany, but they did not want to commit to turning an intact Austria-Hungary against Germany or to destroying Austria-Hungary and thus eliminating Germany's major ally. That policy led Wilson and the British government to pursue a secret diplomatic settlement with Austria-Hungary while also courting hopeful successor governments and planning for future Central European nation-states. Among Inquiry members, the preference was strongly in favor of nation-states, with their ideal homogeneous populations and peace-promoting democratic governments. Secretary of State Lansing shared this view; he wrote shortly after Wilson gave his speech that "I think that the President will have to ... require the separation of Austria and Hungary. This is the only certain means of ending German power in Europe."[64] When their attempts at a separate peace failed, Wilson and the British government moved firmly into this camp as well.

Approximately four months before the United States entered the war, on 21 November 1916, Emperor Franz Joseph died, ending his sixty-eight-year reign. Since his only son, Rudolf, had died in 1889, and the next man in line for the throne, Archduke Franz Ferdinand, had been killed in 1914,

[63] Burián, 399.
[64] Robert Lansing, "Private Memorandum on the President's Statement of War Aims on January 8, 1918, which are Open to Debate," 10 January 1918, Lansing Confidential Files, Lansing Manuscript Collection, Library of Congress; cited in Gelfand, 152. He expressed a similar sentiment in his *War Memoirs*, 261.

the crown was passed to Karl, a grandnephew of Franz Joseph. Just under thirty years of age when he inherited the throne, Karl and his young wife, Princess Zita of Parma, were popular in Vienna and much of the empire because they were friendly and visible to the public; they could often be seen out walking along the Ringstrasse with their young children. Karl had not been particularly well prepared for inheriting the throne, however. Before Franz Ferdinand's death, it had seemed unlikely that Karl would ever have to assume such responsibilities, and even when he was the heir presumptive, he was sent to serve in the armed forces on the Italian and Russian fronts, rather than learning the process of governing in Vienna.[65]

With Franz Joseph's death, there was potential to change the dynamics of the war, and all the participants realized that. The German government hoped to make the Austro-Hungarian government more compliant with its own wishes. To accomplish that, the Germans wanted a new Austro-Hungarian foreign minister. Count Stephan Burián had occupied the position since January 1915, and the German government disapproved of his insistence on maintaining a separation between Germany and Austria-Hungary. Emperor Wilhelm II traveled in person to Vienna to speak to the new emperor about it, and Karl complied, replacing Burián with Count Ottokar Czernin, who was an ardent supporter of the Austro-German alliance.[66]

Members of the British and French governments thought that, with Franz Joseph's death, there might be an opportunity to negotiate a separate peace with Austria-Hungary. In particular, many of the French had considered it impossible to do such a thing when Franz Joseph was alive because they believed he would not be willing to abandon the German alliance.[67] With the change in leadership, however, they thought there might be a chance. The British government sent South African General

---

[65] For a glowing account of Karl's life and career, see Gordon Brook-Shepherd, *The Last Habsburg* (New York, 1968). This is a very sympathetic account written by a journalist, but Brook-Shepherd's work is important because he had access to unique sources, including Habsburg family papers and the British royal family's archives; he also interviewed Zita. For a more recent, but flawed, biography see Elisabeth Kovács, *Untergang oder Rettung der Donaumonarchie? Die österreichische Frage: Kaiser und König Karl I. (IV.) und die Neuordnung Mitteleuropas (1916–1922)*, 2 vols. (Vienna, 2004). For a particularly negative account of Karl, see Count Ottokar Czernin, *In the World War* (London, 1919), esp. 56–57.

[66] See Burián, 234. In his memoirs, Czernin asserted that Karl wanted to be rid of Burián. See Czernin, 114. German pressure was likely stronger than Karl's dissatisfaction. See also Fest, 49–50.

[67] Fest, 45–51; Brook-Shepherd, 63.

Jan Smuts to Switzerland for a secret meeting with Count Mensdorff, the former Austro-Hungarian ambassador to Britain. Smuts sounded out Mensdorff on the subject of a separate peace. Smuts told Mensdorff that he believed the empire could remain intact, with slight adjustments to its borders with Italy and Romania and a political reorganization that would likely improve the position of the Czechs in the government. Mensdorff insisted that a peace without all the Central Powers was not possible, but Smuts believed that Mensdorff would convey the Allied ideas to the government in Vienna, where they might bear fruit.[68]

The Austro-German alliance was of fairly long standing, having been negotiated in 1879. It was not without its problems, however, since the longer term relationship between the Hohenzollern rulers of Prussia and the Habsburgs had been exceptionally rocky. The two dynasties had struggled for dominance among the various German states since the mid eighteenth century. After a war against one another in 1866, Prussia had assumed the dominant position among the smaller German states, which were united to form the German Empire under Hohenzollern rule in 1871. The Habsburgs contented themselves with their more diverse, non-German holdings. The 1879 alliance was part of Bismarck's grand plans for German security in the face of an emerging Franco-Russian alliance.[69] Burián noted that the alliance was generally welcome among the people of Austria-Hungary, although not because they felt a strong attachment to Germany or German policy per se: "the feeling of the general public for the alliance was, with the possible exception of pan-German elements in Austria-Hungary, free from any extravagance. It was just felt to be a useful and convenient arrangement expressing the sentiment of the vast majority."[70]

Many Europeans and Americans considered the alliance logical or even natural, given the racial and cultural ties they perceived between the German people and the German speakers of Austria, who included the royal family. The common wartime perception in the United States – fueled by Wilson's speeches – was that Austria-Hungary was dominated by German speakers, who ruled over other national groups. In reality,

---

[68] For detailed accounts of this meeting, see Fest, 160–77; and Adams, "Courting," 231–33. See also Czernin.

[69] See Charles W. Ingrao, *The Habsburg Monarchy, 1618–1815* (Cambridge, 1994); Robert A. Kann, *A History of the Habsburg Empire, 1526–1918* (Berkeley, 1974); A. J. P. Taylor, *The Habsburg Monarchy, 1809–1918* (Chicago, 1948); and Taylor, *The Struggle for Mastery in Europe, 1848–1918* (Oxford, 1954).

[70] Burián, 122.

German speakers made up far less than half the population of the country and shared the responsibilities of government with non-Germans as well. That the Austro-German alliance was perceived as natural became a considerable stumbling block for the Habsburg government: the Habsburg government desperately wanted to be seen as independent from Germany and therefore as a government that should legitimately exist after the war. The war brought the Austro-German alliance to a new and uncomfortable level, however. After a series of defeats on the Eastern Front in the fall of 1914, the German military effectively took over control of the Austro-Hungarian army and the war planning of the alliance.[71] Burián tried to maintain a separation, and Karl was interested, too, worrying that Austria-Hungary would lose its power to Prussia.[72] With Burián out of office, however, the pro-German Czernin worked to tie the two states ever closer together, especially in light of political developments in Russia.[73]

Despite Czernin's pro-German efforts, Karl worked to maintain Austria-Hungary's freedom of action and to end the war. He continued secret talks with Allied and Associated representatives in Switzerland throughout the summer of 1917, although those talks did little to advance the two sides toward peace. In addition to these talks, Karl also chose to pursue peace through familial channels. On 24 March 1917, he wrote to his brother-in-law, Prince Sixtus de Bourbon-Parma, who was then serving in the Belgian army.[74] In this letter, Karl expressed his belief that the repeatedly controversial province of Alsace-Lorraine should be returned to France, which had lost it to Germany in the Franco-Prussian War of 1870–71.[75] Karl's statement was significant in many ways. First, Karl was the head of the House of Lorraine, the dynasty that had ruled Lorraine until a mid-eighteenth-century rearrangement of Europe, and, as such, his opinion on the fate of the province carried significant weight in some circles – and with the current French president

[71] Davis, "Diplomatic Relations," 58.
[72] Brook-Shepherd, 158.
[73] Adams, "Courting," 243. See also Czernin; August Demblin and Alexander Demblin, *Minister gegen Kaiser: Aufzeichnungen eines österreichisch-ungarischen Diplomaten über Aussenminister Czernin und Kaiser Karl* (Vienna, 1997); and Ladislas Singer, *Ottokar Graf Czernin: Staatsman einer Zeitenwende* (Graz, 1965).
[74] The Bourbons, who had previously been the royal family in France, were forbidden from holding public offices, including military posts, in France.
[75] On the letter and Karl's goals for peace, see Robert A. Kann, *Die Sixtusaffäre und die geheimen Friedensverhandlungen Österreich-Ungarns im Ersten Weltkrieg* (Munich, 1966); and Brook-Shepherd, 63–67.

Raymond Poincaré, who was an Alsatian.[76] The fate of Alsace-Lorraine was also of paramount importance to both the French and German governments. To illustrate the depth of feeling of some Germans on the subject, Czernin recounted one anecdote: "A German official of high standing said to me in the spring of 1918: 'I had two sons; one of them fell on the field of battle, but I would rather part with the other one too than give up Alsace-Lorraine,' and many were of the same opinion."[77] Alsace-Lorraine would be a major point of controversy in any peace settlement. That Karl, as the head of the Germans' chief ally, took a pro-French position meant that the German government might possibly be persuaded to give up the province, and it also demonstrated a potential fissure in Austro-German relations.

Karl and Sixtus had an agreement that Sixtus would show the letter to Poincaré in an effort to secure an end to the war. Karl did not tell Foreign Minister Czernin about the specific contents of the letter, especially his comments on Alsace-Lorraine. The French government shared the letter with the British, and, eventually, these Allies discussed the matter with the Italian government, which wanted nothing to do with a separate peace with Austria-Hungary because such a peace would likely limit the territorial concessions from Austria-Hungary the Italians coveted.[78]

The matter might have ended with the Italian rejection and therefore without any real help or hindrance to the Austro-Hungarian cause. However, in April 1918, the issue exploded with disastrous consequences. In a public statement, Foreign Minister Czernin hinted that he had spoken with French prime minister Georges Clemenceau about a potential peace, and the only thing that stood in the way of a settlement was the French claim to Alsace-Lorraine. Clemenceau, not wanting to appear weak in front of his constituents, his allies, or his enemies, denied that the conversation with Czernin had ever taken place and stated that Karl himself favored French control of Alsace-Lorraine. To back up his claim, Clemenceau had the text of Karl's letter to Sixtus printed in the newspapers for all to see.[79]

This was an unmitigated disaster for Karl and his government. It altered perceptions of the Austro-Hungarian government in Germany, Britain,

---

[76] Maria Theresa married Francis Stephen, the Duke of Lorraine, in 1736. See also Brook-Shepherd, 67.

[77] Czernin, 71.

[78] On the discussion with the Italians, see Fest, 64–76.

[79] Adams provides the most detailed English-language account of the Sixtus Affair; see Adams, "Courting," esp. 243. See also Fest, 64–76; Kann, *Sixtusaffäre*; and Kovács.

and the United States and paved the way for a new set of policies that seriously jeopardized Habsburg sovereignty. First, Karl had to placate the German government. He disavowed the letter and publicly pledged his support for Germany and the Austro-German alliance.[80] He traveled to Spa to meet personally with Wilhelm II to discuss the issue. Wilhelm and other members of the German government saw this as a golden opportunity to bind Austria-Hungary much more closely to Germany, which they did by forcing Karl to agree to a long-term political and military alliance.[81] Lansing rightly observed that Clemenceau's action "has thrown Austria bodily into the arms of Germany. The Austrian Emperor has no other course now but to eat his words and affirm in the most unequivocal terms his loyalty to his domineering ally and the aims of his ally."[82]

The Allied governments, especially the British, who were the strongest proponents of a potential separate peace with Austria-Hungary, were now convinced that such a peace was entirely impossible. They changed their policy and now began to offer support to various national groups that proposed to replace the empire with a series of smaller nation-states. When taken all together, these concessions severely limited the possibility of maintaining Habsburg sovereignty and Austro-Hungarian territorial integrity after the war.

American perceptions of the Austro-Hungarian government and American policy toward Austria-Hungary also changed in the wake of the Sixtus affair. Foreign Minister Czernin resigned his post on 13 April 1918 as a result of the emperor's actions, and Karl returned the veteran Burián to office.[83] Lansing found this personnel change especially troublesome, and it cemented his already strong opposition to the Habsburg government and the continued existence of Austria-Hungary. For reasons that are not entirely clear – although he was likely influenced by the personal opinions of Ambassador Dumba – Lansing believed Czernin to be "liberal" and progressive, which Lansing thought was vital to Austro-Hungarian survival.[84] In contrast to Czernin, Lansing believed Burián to

---

[80] Brook-Shepherd, 142–48.
[81] Adams, "Courting," 250–51.
[82] Lansing is quoting from a memo he penned on 12 April 1918; see Lansing, *War Memoirs*, 265.
[83] On problems between Czernin and Karl, see Demblin and Demblin; and Singer.
[84] Lansing, *War Memoirs*, 264. Dumba may have fed Lansing's opinion. He was pro-German, and he described Burián as an "incorrigible doctrinaire and pedant." See Dumba, 310.

be a backward, reactionary conservative "of the old school" and "a pro-German imperialist."[85]

Lansing's perceptions of the two men were almost entirely wrong. Burián advocated the independence of the Austro-Hungarian state from Germany and, as we have seen, worked to maintain Austro-Hungarian freedom of action. Burián was committed to the continued existence of a – possibly reformed – Austria-Hungary that continued to respect the rule of law and foster diversity and compromise. He was good friends with the Hungarian prime minister, Count István Tisza, and he therefore worked to maintain the constitutional and legal provisions that called for Hungarian involvement in policy making, although he did not allow his friendship with Tisza to overpower his commitment to a supranational Habsburg state.[86] Czernin, on the other hand, was staunchly pro-German and advocated a closer connection between the two states – a closeness that Wilson and Lansing would later claim to abhor. Czernin was quite fond of Wilhelm II, describing him as "full of good intentions" and "a thoroughly kind and good man"; the foreign minister believed that "the Germans just wanted their place in the world."[87] He was also strongly opposed to the Hungarians, observing that "Hungary is firmly linked to us, but like a stone a drowning man has tied around his own neck."[88] Lansing was apparently willing to overlook the fact that "Czernin was in a measure pro-German."[89] Had the Austro-Hungarian government managed to maintain diplomatic ties with the United States, it might have succeeded in presenting Lansing with a more accurate view of its opinions and policies. Lansing chose to believe what he wanted, however, and when Burián returned to office, he decided that Habsburg-ruled Austria-Hungary was irrevocably illiberal and pro-German. Lansing and Wilson's hopes for a separate peace with Austria-Hungary were extinguished, and they too began to move toward open support for nationalist groups, whose rhetoric aligned with Inquiry planning.[90]

Even as the Americans and the British were pursuing a secret separate peace with the Habsburgs, they were also making commitments to support

---

[85] Lansing, *War Memoirs*, 264, 266–67.

[86] See Burián; and Davis, "Diplomatic Relations," 57. For a critical account, see Czernin, 134–35.

[87] Czernin, 69, 3.

[88] Ibid., 138. Czernin is labeled a "Magyarphobe" in Godsey, 149.

[89] Lansing, *War Memoirs*, 267.

[90] See ibid., 245, 248, 266–67; and May, "Woodrow Wilson," 225.

the political aspirations of certain nationalist leaders and various changes to Austria-Hungary's territorial borders. The changes favored by Wilson and the Inquiry and those favored by the British government were not the same, however: the Americans favored the creation of an independent Poland and then a Czech state, whereas the British had made treaty commitments to Italy and Romania and were also in favor of the creation of a South Slav state in the Balkans. If all of these goals and commitments were to be honored, the Habsburg Empire would have to be reduced to the hereditary Austrian lands and a fraction of the Kingdom of Hungary, reducing the Habsburg state by so much that it would no longer be recognizable – or acceptable to the Habsburg government. The Inquiry and then the peace conference were organized around these commitments, rather than around an examination of Austria-Hungary as a whole, thus making the creation of new states legitimized via racial claims the most likely outcome of the planning and peace processes. Although the Inquiry lacked clear instructions, it did have a very energetic staff and the enthusiasm of Wilson and House – an enthusiasm that U.S. attempts at a separate peace with the Habsburgs had lacked. Although Wilson refused to commit publicly to the idea of breaking up the empire, the choices he and his advisors and allies made on related issues gradually made the recognition of new states conceived in racial-national terms the most likely outcome.[91]

Wilson's first commitment was to an independent Poland. He was encouraged in this by Colonel House, who arranged for Polish nationalist leaders to visit Wilson at the White House; Robert Lord, the Inquiry's expert on Polish history; and George Jan Sosnowski, a Polish American activist who wrote to Wilson frequently after one of Wilson's college friends opened the correspondence.[92] There was also significant domestic interest in the Polish cause, as various Polish American voluntary associations and charitable organizations had made humanitarian relief to Polish-inhabited Eastern Europe a national mission, and Wilson had used the issue in his 1916 reelection campaign.[93]

[91] See, for example, Wilson, "Conditions of Peace"; and "Address to a Joint Session of Congress Calling for War with Austria-Hungary." On the British, see Fest.

[92] See, for example, Sosnowski to Wilson, 8 August 1917 in *PWW*, 44:4–6.

[93] M. B. Biskupski, "The Diplomacy of Wartime Relief: The United States and Poland, 1914–1918," *DH* 19, 3 (1995): 431–51; Louis L. Gerson, *Woodrow Wilson and the Rebirth of Poland, 1914–1920: A Study in the Influence on American Policy of Minority Groups of Foreign Origin* (New Haven, 1953); Jan Karski, *The Great Powers & Poland, 1919–1945:*

Historian Seth Tillman has observed that the American government "displayed excessive tenderness for the ambitions of the reborn Polish state," and historian Louis Gerson has concurred, noting that "a united, independent, and free Polish nation and state could not have been resurrected without the intervention of the United States and President Wilson."[94] An independent Poland was a profoundly American cause: not only had the Polish state been destroyed through the "Old Diplomacy" that Wilson presented to the public as a contributing factor to the war, but Polish military leaders had served with distinction in the American Revolution.

The Polish question was complicated by the fact that there were significant numbers of Poles living in three countries: Germany, Austria-Hungary, and Russia. Although there was sympathy for Polish nationalism among all three sets of Poles, they had been part of different political communities for more than a century and therefore had different goals and interests. In particular, the Austrian Poles – who were concentrated in the province of Galicia – were the most content with their government; they enjoyed greater rights and local power than the Poles of Germany or Russia, who were often the objects of prejudice and persecution. As a result, a significant number of Poles favored remaining within the Habsburg Empire; the German and Habsburg governments had even reached an agreement to expand the Polish region of Austria at German and Russian expense at the end of the war. There were ethnic Poles in London during the war – including a former governor of Galicia – who advocated the maintenance of the Habsburg state, which they argued would be strong and staunchly independent after the war, having learned the perils of an alliance with Germany.[95]

The British and French governments could not support the idea of an independent Poland while they remained allied with tsarist Russia, since the tsar governed a considerable number of Poles and controlled territory that would likely be part of any new Polish state. The Allies therefore advocated the creation of an autonomous Polish territory within Russia.

From Versailles to Yalta (Lanham, 1985); Kay Lundgreen-Nielsen, "The Mayer Thesis Reconsidered: The Poles and the Paris Peace Conference, 1919," *International History Review* 7, 1 (1985): 68–102; and Carole Fink, "The Paris Peace Conference and the Question of Minority Rights," *Peace and Change* 21, 3 (1996): 273–88.

[94] Seth P. Tillman, *Anglo-American Relations at the Paris Peace Conference of 1919* (Princeton, 1961), 404.

[95] Fest, 156–61. The Germans would be compensated for their losses by receiving control of the Romanian economy.

When Russia left the war, the French and British governments gave up any commitment to an independent or autonomous Polish state. They believed that forcing the German and Habsburg governments to accept an independent Poland would prolong the war considerably, and they were not willing to spend their resources to achieve a "liberation" of the Poles.[96] Wilson continued to insist, however, and he went so far as to include an explicit demand for Polish independence in his Fourteen Points. He continued his support through the peace conference, thus emerging as Poland's strongest advocate.

The other strong American commitment was to the creation of an independent Czechoslovak state; the Czecho-Slovak National Council first found support for full independence, rather than autonomy, in the United States. Support for a Czechoslovak state was the result first and foremost of the skills of the council's leaders, Tomáš Masaryk and Edvard Beneš, who were adept at making friends in the United States and in the Allied countries and winning support for their cause. Masaryk had an especially valuable friend in Robert Seton-Watson, who secured a lectureship at King's College, Oxford, for Masaryk and, more important, "grossly exaggerated Masaryk's backing inside Bohemia so as to attract the attention of the government to Masaryk's ideas about 'the future of Bohemia.'"[97]

The Czecho-Slovak National Council also benefitted from the particular constellation of perceptions Wilson, Lansing, and the Inquiry staff held about Central Europe. Ambassador Dumba expressed this cynically in his memoirs when he wrote that "The utter ignorance of facts and geography displayed by Wilson ... were the Czechs' best allies."[98] Czech nationalists could point to the industrial development of Bohemia and the success – and assimilation – of Bohemian Americans in the United States. Czech nationalists and Pan-Slav rhetoric about the empire furthered the popular conception in the United States that the (Catholic) Germans in Austria oppressed and dominated the Czechs.

---

[96] Fest, 15–20, 156–60.
[97] Ibid., 37. On the Czechoslovaks, see Victor S. Mamatey, *The United States and East Central Europe 1914–1918: A Study in Wilsonian Diplomacy and Propaganda* (Princeton, 1957); Dagmar Perman, *The Shaping of the Czechoslovak State: Diplomatic History of the Boundaries of Czechoslovakia, 1914–1920* (Leiden, 1962); and Betty Miller Unterberger, *The United States, Revolutionary Russia, and the Rise of Czechoslovakia* (Chapel Hill, 1989).
[98] Dumba, 223.

Perhaps most importantly, however, the Czechoslovak nationalists were able to appeal to racialist science to support their cause. Somehow, the Czecho-Slovak National Council had to argue that Bohemians and Moravians – Czechs – and Slovaks belonged in the same nation-state. An appeal to history would not have been effective here: the Czechs had been part of the Kingdom of Bohemia and then the post-1867 Austrian half of the empire, whereas Slovakia had been part of the Kingdom of Hungary for almost a thousand years. An appeal to science would work, though. They could argue – especially to an audience that knew no better – that the Czech and Slovak languages were so similar as to be almost identical. From there, they could assert that the two groups were racially similar and therefore the two groups must be in possession of common political aspirations. This logic was met with considerable support among Inquiry members. Leon Dominian skillfully used the passive voice to bolster the Czechoslovak cause, writing that "Community of national aspirations, under the leadership of the Bohemian element, is generally ascribed to these three Slavic groups [Bohemians, Moravians, and Slovaks]." He also observed that "The Czech linguistic area presents homogeneity of composition which is seldom encountered in other parts of Austria-Hungary. Intermingling of Slavic and Teutonic elements has been slight in this advanced strip of Slavdom." This was, of course, patently false, but it supported the idea that each individual had a single identity, and that was useful to the Czechoslovak nationalists.[99] Dominian applied the story of Habsburg oppression and Wilsonian self-determination to the Czechoslovak cause, arguing that "Bohemia's national enfranchisement, if carried out on a linguistic basis, will rescue the old lands of the Bohemian crown, namely Bohemia, Moravia, and the Slovak districts of northwestern Hungary, from Teutonic rule. The historical validity of Bohemia's claims to independence and the failure of centuries of Germanization to deprive the Bohemian of his individuality establish the country's right to a distinct place in a Europe of free and harmonious nations. The Bohemian has his own objects in self-development and the achievement of his independence should be no disparagement to the aims and pursuits of other nations."[100]

---

[99] On language politics, see Alexander Maxwell, "Why the Slovak Language Has Three Dialects: A Case Study in Historical Perceptual Dialectology," *AHY* 37 (2006): 141–62.

[100] Dominian, 142, 153.

The members of the Czecho-Slovak National Council were brilliant at telling Wilson, House, and Lansing exactly what they wanted to hear. They stressed the oppressive and Germanic or Teutonic nature of the Habsburg government and promised a Czechoslovak state that would be democratic, based on the consent of the governed, and a product of an orderly, liberal revolution that would take 1776 as its model. These arguments did not resonate as well with the British and French governments, and especially with the Italian government, which did not want the Czechoslovaks to set a precedent that might be seized on by the South Slavs. However, as the war progressed, the Czecho-Slovak National Council was able to adopt a position that the French especially found useful.[101] The process of obtaining Allied support for the Czecho-Slovak National Council will be discussed in the next chapter. Before the summer of 1918, however, the Czechoslovaks found their greatest allies in the Wilson administration.

While Wilson supported the Polish and Czechoslovak causes for ideological reasons, the British and French governments supported Italian and Romanian claims against the empire for short-term military purposes. These claims had been written into secret treaties, and those treaties were used to bring Italy and Romania into the war on the Allied side. For Italy, joining the Allies meant an outright reversal of the Italian government's 1882 treaty with the German and Habsburg governments that had pledged mutual aid in the event of attack. The Italians had already violated that treaty by remaining neutral in 1914, but they had at least not become active belligerents in the war. By secretly promising that Italy would gain the Tirol, Trieste, and the Dalmatian coast – all areas where the Italian language was in use alongside others – the British and French governments were able to secure Italian participation.[102]

The Italian claims were partially about bringing ethnic Italians into the Italian nation-state, but the territories they asked for went beyond Italian-inhabited regions and were designed to make Italy a stronger and more imperialist country, particularly by expanding Italian interests – and hegemony – into the Balkans. For this reason, the Tsarist government was never particularly supportive of the Italian claims. The

[101] Fest, 15; Mamatey, *United States*; and Tomáš G. Masaryk and Henry Wickham Steed, *The Making of a State: Memories and Observations, 1914–1918* (New York, 1927). Steed publicly advocated the creation of a South Slav kingdom, an autonomous Russian Poland, and an independent or home-ruled Czechoslovakia from April 1916.
[102] For a detailed description of the Italian claims, see Nielson, 143–46.

Russians were not interested in replacing one pro-Catholic competitor in the region – the Habsburg Empire – with another. They did agree to the 1915 Treaty of London, however, in large part because that treaty was to remain secret. The British and French also appreciated the secrecy of the treaty, since it gave them the freedom to back out of the agreement in the future. Surely, three Great Powers could convince an upstart Italy to reduce or abandon its claims if circumstances made that desirable for the Allied cause as a whole?

The Romanian government followed the Italian lead and set a high price for its participation in the war. In their secret treaty, Romanian officials asked for approximately two-thirds of the Kingdom of Hungary – a claim beyond the acquisition of Transylvania, which included many Romanian speakers – and the Bukovina. Steed was absolutely thrilled when he heard the details of the Romanian treaty. He wrote that "the intervention of Romania signs the death-warrant of Hungary, begins the necessary partition of Austria, and foreshadows the reconstruction of Europe on the basis of ethnically-complete states." Historian Wilfried Fest concurs with Steed on the decisiveness of the treaty, but he criticizes the British officials who thought that the Habsburg government could meet the Romanian demands and remain in power. For Fest, the Romanian treaty demonstrated "the scanty knowledge in the Foreign Office which seemed entirely uninformed about the territorial extension of the Kingdom of Hungary and its constitutional rights concerning the treatment of minorities."[103]

The Romanian claims were diffused fairly quickly: by December 1916, the Central Powers had defeated Romanian forces and taken over Bucharest. The Romanian government left the war and adjusted its aspirations considerably, hoping that the Allies would choose to insist on the status quo ante bellum as part of any future peace settlement.[104] When the peace conference finally occurred, the Romanian government benefitted from the American embrace of racial nationalism and received Transylvania.

The Italian claims were a different matter. As long as they remained secret, they could be adjusted or abandoned at minimal cost to the Allied governments. The treaties became public in the spring of 1918, however, when the newly communist Russian government left the war. In the spirit

[103] Steed quote: Memorandum of 4 August 1916, Steed Papers, Printing House Square, cited in Fest, 36. Fest quote: p. 55.
[104] Fest, 166.

of Wilsonian "New Diplomacy," tempered by a considerable measure of vindictiveness, Lenin argued that all treaties should be made public. With the publication of the treaties, the British and French governments now faced three major problems. First, Wilson was upset with them because they had engaged in "Old Diplomacy," making behind-the-scenes agreements for territorial change that had been kept secret from the public and that did not consider the desires of the people who inhabited the territory in question. Wilson was not necessarily opposed to the Italian claims, but he was upset that Allied action was not fully aboveboard, as Wilson had assured the American public.[105] Second, the British public turned against the Italian alliance. They argued – correctly – that Italian claims went beyond nationality and entered the realm of imperialism. They insisted that it was pointless to continue to spend British lives and money to secure Italy's unreasonable aspirations.[106]

Third, the Habsburg government could hardly find the concessions to the Italians agreeable, and it made the government that much more committed to staying in the war until a more favorable moment. Emperor Karl particularly disliked the Italian government, and the prospect of ceding territory to it was especially unpalatable. Foreign Minister Czernin noted in his memoirs that the publication of the secret treaties made the Habsburg government even more distrustful of the Allies' goals for the empire. It was crystal clear at that point that the very survival of the empire was definitely at stake, and the Habsburg government was convinced that the Allies planned to break up the country if they won, despite the fact that Allied leaders had never publicly committed to that position.[107] The problems that came with the Italian claims notwithstanding, the British government remained firmly committed to honoring its treaty commitments in some fashion. In short, the British were going to give Italy something, even if they could not meet the full demands laid out in the Treaty of London. They therefore looked to apply the nationality principle and to give Italy the advantage whenever possible.[108]

Italian claims also made support for a South Slav state in the Balkans more difficult. The British government – along with Steed and Seton-Watson – supported the idea of such a state from very early in the war,

---

[105] Gelfand, 11–12.
[106] Fest, 181–82.
[107] Czernin, 192. See also Burián.
[108] Fest supports the idea of British insistence on honoring Italian claims.

however. The British hoped to stabilize the Balkans and also to remove the Ottoman presence as much as possible. Members of the British government could not decide on which of two major options they preferred, though: the Serbs could be in charge of the new state, or it could be a Yugoslav endeavor, with Slovenes and Croatians sharing power alongside the Serbs. In both cases, the foundational idea of the state was that the various Slavic peoples of the Balkans were sufficiently close to one another in terms of race, language, and political aspirations to form a legitimate and viable state; to outsiders, it was going to be, first and foremost, a Slavic state.[109] Lloyd George and the Russian government preferred the Serbian option. The Russians preferred this to the Yugoslav solution because they wanted to maintain the power of the Orthodox Church in the Balkans, and they believed a Yugoslav solution would invite too much Roman Catholic influence into the region. The Serbian cause was also advocated in London by members of the Serbian Society, a voluntary association headed by a British peer.[110]

The Yugoslav solution was initially favored almost exclusively by a small group of ethnic Croatians, but they gradually gained wider support for their cause.[111] They had a representative in London, and the U.S.-based South Slavic National Council arranged for European leaders of the Yugoslav movement to have an audience with President Wilson at the White House. That audience was made possible through the efforts of House and Lansing, who were initially more enthusiastic about the Yugoslav cause than was President Wilson. In part, Wilson's coolness – and that of some British authorities – resulted from his belief that the Slavs of the Balkans fell too low on the hierarchy of races to be capable of self-government.[112] Yugoslav tales of Magyar oppression also ran counter to the post-1848 American sympathy for the Hungarians as liberal revolutionaries who were themselves oppressed by the Germans of Vienna.

[109] For an elucidation of this argument, see Dominian.
[110] Fest, 19–20, 26–27.
[111] In particular, they reached an agreement with certain Serbs in the summer of 1917. Known as the Declaration of Corfu, this agreement brought a critical mass of Serb leaders around to supporting the Yugoslav state, rather than a Greater Serbia. Fest, 209–10. On Yugoslavia, see Ivo J. Lederer, *Yugoslavia at the Paris Peace Conference: A Study in Frontiermaking* (New Haven, 1963); and Dragan R. Zivojinovic, *America, Italy, and the Birth of Yugoslavia (1917–1919)* (New York, 1972).
[112] Fest, 94, 165.

The South Slovak National Council won the president over by telling him what he wanted to hear. When requesting an audience with the president for the Yugoslav leaders, council members wrote that the purpose of the visit was "to thank the President of the United States for his expressions of sympathy for the small nations, and to explain to him the work of the Committee and the aspirations of the Jugoslav [sic] race." They went on, informing the president that "The Slavs have been the most steady admirers of the policies of the President, and look upon him as the great champion of liberty of the small oppressed races of Europe," and that the Yugoslavs were visiting the United States "for the purpose of urging the members of these races to exert their utmost efforts in behalf of the United States during the present war."[113] Wilson could hardly resist: the council reinforced his self-perception as "the great champion of liberty," and their insistence on the oppressive nature of the Habsburg government, the importance of racial unity, and support for the war effort echoed his own rhetoric.

As with the Czecho-Slovak National Council, the Yugoslavs sought support internationally for a cause that did not yet have much support at home. Frano Supilo, the Yugoslav representative in London, admitted that a plebiscite on the creation of Yugoslavia would likely fail. In particular, many ethnic Croatians and Slovenes who were Austrian or Hungarian citizens preferred inclusion in the Habsburg Empire to membership in a Yugoslav state that would likely be too weak to block Italian attempts at regional hegemony.[114]

If the U.S. and Allied governments honored all the rhetorical and formal commitments they had made to the Poles, Czechoslovaks, Italians, Romanians, and South Slavs, there would be little left of the Habsburg Empire, save the hereditary lands – "Austria," in its narrowest definition – and a part of the Kingdom of Hungary. The American and Allied commitments certainly favored the break-up of the empire. With the publication of the Sixtus Letter and the official end of hopes for a separate peace with Austria-Hungary, Lloyd George gave Steed and Seton-Watson free rein to launch a massive propaganda campaign aimed at inciting nationalist revolution in the empire.[115] At an inter-

---

[113] South Slavic National Council to SecState, 22 September 1917, file no. 033.6311/9, in NARA.
[114] Fest, 55, 118, 207; see also Lederer.
[115] On propaganda efforts, see Mark Cornwall, *The Undermining of Austria-Hungary: The Battle for Hearts and Minds* (New York, 2000); Fest; Seton-Watson and Seton-Watson;

Allied propaganda conference in February 1918, Allied representatives planned for a "Congress of Oppressed Races," which was supposed to bring nationalist leaders and Allied propaganda in line with one another. It was also supposed to convince Austrian and Hungarian citizens that they were indeed oppressed and that they needed to find their salvation in Habsburg-free national states.

The main obstacle to this plan was the continued lack of Italian support for either Yugoslavia or Czechoslovakia. Steed worked personally on fixing this situation. Through personal negotiations with Italian and Yugoslav leaders, he managed to achieve a rapprochement between the Italian government and the Yugoslav nationalists. In part, he managed to do this by convincing the Italian government that a German victory would result in the German Empire taking over the Tirol and a strip of land that would give Germany access to the Adriatic, thus making Germany and Italy direct neighbors, without the buffer zone of the Habsburg Empire. Representatives of the Italian government and the Yugoslav movement signed the so-called Pact of Rome on 7 March 1918 – an event orchestrated and witnessed by Steed and Seton-Watson.[116] It was an important propaganda victory for the Italians, who were slowly regaining British popular support, and for the Yugoslav movement.

The path was now clear for the proposed Congress of Oppressed Races. To capitalize on the Italians' improved place in British public opinion, the conference was held in Rome. For four days in April 1918, representatives of the Polish, Czechoslovak, Yugoslav, Romanian, and Italian nationalist movements met to discuss their common problems and aspirations. The title of the conference reinforced the racialist thinking of the time and again asserted the existence of Czechoslovak and Yugoslav "races." Following the advice of Steed and Seton-Watson – who were, of course, present for the event – the congress adopted three resolutions that reaffirmed the story Steed, Seton-Watson, and Wilson had been telling about Austria-Hungary and the postwar world. First, they resolved that all the represented groups would receive "full political and economic independence" after the war, a nod to Wilsonian insistence on democracy and capitalistic free trade. Second, they stated that

and Henry W. Steed, *Through Thirty Years, 1892–1922: A Personal Narrative*, 2 vols. (Garden City, 1924).
[116] Fest, 209–14. See also Steed, *Through Thirty Years*; and Sterling J. Kernek, "Woodrow Wilson and National Self-Determination along Italy's Frontier: A Study of the Manipulation of Principles in the Pursuit of Political Interests," *Proceedings of the American Philosophical Society* 126, 4 (1982): 243–300.

the Austro-Hungarian monarchy was "the instrument of German domination," directly reaffirming how Wilson, Steed, and Seton-Watson had been describing the empire throughout the war – and how they would describe it after the war. Finally, the members of the congress resolved to cooperate with one another against the Habsburgs, giving weight to the idea that a nationally divided Central Europe would be a peaceful and cooperative place where the will of the people reigned supreme.[117]

On 29 May 1918, Lansing publically announced the U.S. government's "great interest" in the congress and expressed its sympathies with the Czechoslovak and Yugoslav causes in particular.[118] Lansing made the announcement on the advice of Czechoslovak leader Edvard Beneš, who argued that such an announcement of support from the United States would provide important moral support for revolutionaries in Bohemia who were anxiously awaiting the military defeat of the Austro-Hungarian army so that they could begin their – orderly, democratic, and noncommunist – revolution.[119] The *New York Times* reported on the congress and Lansing's statement in positive terms, downplaying the fact that it was really a statement of American support for revolutions in Central Europe. The *Times* observed that, even if it was a statement that incited revolutions abroad, it was only "a detail in the general democratic policy of freedom."[120]

Reports from the field and subsequent historical analysis indicate that the propaganda campaign and the Congress of Oppressed Races had little effect on the inhabitants of Austria-Hungary.[121] They did, however, bring British and American government officials fully around to the idea that the break-up of the Habsburg Empire was somehow inevitable. British and American officials began to support the nationalists publicly.

After the conference, Steed managed to get the various national committees to declare their independence, and he also worked to secure Allied recognition of their claims to independence. On 3 June 1918, the British, French, and Italian governments recognized the Czechoslovak National Council as "the supreme organ of the Czechoslovak movement in Allied

---

[117] On the congress, see Fest, 220–30; and Adams, "Courting," 252–53.

[118] No. 1363, SecState to Page, 29 May 1918, file no. 763.72/10108, in U.S. DOS, *FRUS: 1918 Supplement 1 – The World War*, vol. 1 (Washington, 1933), 1:808–9.

[119] See no. 62, Frazier to SecState, 28 May 1918, file no. 763.72119/1690, in *FRUS: 1918 Supplement 1*, 1:807–8.

[120] "America for the Slavs," *NYT*, 31 May 1918, p. 12.

[121] See Cornwall; Fest.

countries."[122] The Allied and Associated governments stopped short of making pledges to secure that independence, though. As historian Wilfried Fest has argued, the British leaders were focused on the short term, and they believed that they still had the option of backing away from these national governments. Steed, however, was thinking in the long term, and he rightly believed that the recognition of that independence would be difficult to ignore in the future.[123]

By the summer of 1918, then, it was clear that, if the Central Powers were defeated, there would be an independent Poland, Czechoslovakia, and Yugoslavia, as well as an augmented Italy and Romania. The Allied and Associated governments accepted these states in principle, but as of yet they had no concrete plans for what territory these states might possess, and they had not extended any sort of formal, legal recognition of any successor government's legitimate sovereignty. The process of defining territories and populations and recognizing legitimate sovereignty would be a gradual one, as would the creation of domestic support for these alternative Central European states.

[122] Eduard Beneš, *My War Memoirs* (Boston, 1928), 376.
[123] Fest, 219–20.

7

Establishing Sovereignty

The Process of Aligning Race, Place, and Citizenship

By the summer of 1918, the Allied and Associated governments had given up on the idea of a separate peace with Austria-Hungary and were committed to the idea of the empire's break-up into nation-states that were based on racial nationalism. They had not yet recognized any new sovereign governments in Central Europe, however, nor had they determined which territories the new states would comprise or which individual people would become their citizens. The process of granting this recognition and establishing these borders was gradual; it began in the summer of 1918, when the Czecho-Slovak National Council was given the right to raise an army, and ended in the fall of 1921, when the Swedish consular staff stopped protecting Austrian and Hungarian citizens – Habsburg subjects – and diplomatic relations were established between the United States and the last of the successor states. Creating domestic support for the new states and striving to reach the goals of democracy, capitalism, and homogeneous and nationally conscious populations took much longer and prompted considerable international and civil violence in post-1919 Europe.

Allied and Associated commitment to the national states and abandonment of the Habsburg government and the idea of a postwar multinational Central European state roughly coincided with the Bolshevik Revolution in Russia and the new Soviet Union's decision to leave the war in the spring of 1918. In the chaos of the Russian situation, ethnic Czechs held in Russian prisoner of war camps liberated themselves and began fighting against the communists in Russia as they began the trek to the Pacific coast, where they hoped to be rescued by the Allies.[1] The Allies, and especially the Americans, feared communism because it went against the concept of private property, which they held sacred. Wilson was also particularly concerned that Lenin might attract more followers to the modern, communist cause than he could to his modern, liberal cause.[2]

The terms of the war shifted: not only were the Allied and Associated powers fighting against the evils of German autocracy, they were now also battling the evil forces of Soviet communism. The Czecho-Slovak National Council used this situation to their best advantage. Building on the growing anticommunist reputation of the Czech Legion in the Soviet Union, they approached the French government about the possibility of receiving French permission to raise an independent Czechoslovak army. Such permission would be an important step toward recognition of full, legitimate sovereignty because state governments were supposed to have a monopoly on international violence.[3]

The Czecho-Slovak National Council was wise to start this program in France. The French were strongly in favor of an independent Czecho-Slovak state because they wanted to check potential German aggression by establishing a series of small states in Central Europe that would block German expansion. The French were also concerned about the severity of present French losses along the Western front and were receptive to anything that would help ease the military burden; that support for the Czechoslovaks came with a shadowy possibility of a new Eastern front was particularly attractive. In response to Czechoslovak requests, the French government announced in August 1917 that it would support the principle of the Czechoslovaks forming their own army, and it made its approval formal on 16 December 1917. On 29 June 1918, the French also pledged support for Czecho-Slovak independence over unspecified "historic territories."[4] Beneš, who had been stationed in Paris for most of the war, then traveled to Italy to try to obtain similar concessions while his friends in London worked on securing British support as well.[5]

---

[1] See Victor S. Mamatey, *The United States and East Central Europe 1914–1918: A Study in Wilsonian Diplomacy and Propaganda* (Princeton, 1957); Betty Miller Unterberger, *The United States, Revolutionary Russia, and the Rise of Czechoslovakia* (Chapel Hill, 1989); and Blanka Sevcik Glos and George Ernest Glos, *Czechoslovak Troops in Russia and Siberia during the First World War* (New York, 2000).

[2] See especially Arno J. Mayer, *Political Origins of the New Diplomacy* (New Haven, 1959).

[3] On the Czechs, see Unterberger; and Mamatey, *United States*.

[4] Wilfried Fest, *Peace or Partition: The Habsburg Monarchy and British Policy, 1914–1918* (New York: St. Martin's Press, 1978), 240.

[5] Ibid., 232–34.

On 9 August 1917, the British government adopted a resolution Steed had drafted, recognizing the Czecho-Slovak National Council as the "present 'trustee' of the future Czecho-Slovak government." Again, that recognition came with no specific territory. In response, the Habsburg government strongly considered recognizing the independence of Ireland, Egypt, and India, but were blocked by the German government. On 2 September 1918, the U.S. government followed the French and British lead, recognizing the Czecho-Slovak National Council as a "defacto belligerent government." Italy was the major Ally holding out; its leaders did not want to set a precedent with the Czecho-Slovaks that they might be expected to follow in regard to the Yugoslavs.[6]

This recognition of partial Czechoslovak sovereignty was a unique event in international history at the time. It was only possible because the diplomatic culture of the Great Power System had been destroyed earlier in the war. The recognition greatly vexed Habsburg leaders, who were aware of how little support the Czechoslovak movement had in the empire itself. Burián noted that Czechs were still in the Austrian government when this recognition occurred, which meant that the Czech people as a whole – if there even was such a thing – were not in a state of war and that the Czecho-Slovak National Council did not speak for all the Czechs. He also wrote in his memoirs that there should have been a plebiscite in Slovakia because they likely would have voted against Czech rule.[7] Dumba wrote that "The Czech State arose by a sort of miracle."[8] The Czecho-Slovak National Council had achieved partial international recognition as a sovereign government, however, and that international recognition proved stronger than the need for domestic support. The recognition did help generate that support; many residents of Bohemia believed that a Czecho-Slovak government that was supported by the Allies and the

---

[6] On the British statement, see Henry W. Steed, *Through Thirty Years, 1892–1922: A Personal Narrative*, 2 vols. (Garden City, 1924), 2:232. For the U.S. statement, see Lansing's "Memorandum on the Recognition of the Czecho-Slovaks as a Nationality," 23 August 1918, in U.S. DOS, *FRUS: 1918 Supplement 1 – The World War*, vol. 1 (Washington, 1933), 824; see also Mamatey, *United States*, 309. On Italy's policy, see Dragan R. Zivojinovic, *America, Italy, and the Birth of Yugoslavia (1917–1919)* (New York, 1972); Ivo J. Lederer, *Yugoslavia at the Paris Peace Conference: A Study in Frontiermaking* (New Haven, 1963); and Fest, 241–42.

[7] Stephan, Count Burián, *Austria in Dissolution, Being the Personal Recollections of Stephan, Count Burián, Minister of Foreign Affairs for Austria and Hungary 1915–1917 and 1918*, trans. Brian Lunn (New York, 1925), 413.

[8] Konstantin Dumba, *Memoirs of a Diplomat*, trans. Ian F. D. Morrow (Boston, 1932), 223; and Ernest Wilder Spaulding, *The Quiet Invaders: The Story of the Austrian Impact upon America* (Vienna, 1968), 79. See also Mamatey, *United States*.

United States would be able to end the blockade that kept food and other vital supplies from reaching the Habsburg Empire's population.[9]

Given this recognition of the Czechoslovaks and the "material and spiritual" exhaustion of continued warfare and lack of supplies, Karl moved to take Austria-Hungary out of the war independently; the country officially left the war on 3 November 1918.[10] Karl also moved to reorganize Austria-Hungary, introducing a version of federalism.[11] This was an effort to change the empire into a country that would be more palatable to the United States and the Allies, since it would allow political action based on national categories. In U.S. and Allied opinion, this was too little, too late, and it did nothing to alter their views on the fate of Habsburg sovereignty. As chaos took hold in Central Europe, Karl made the decision to leave the imperial and royal thrones on 11 and 13 November, respectively. This was not the end of the Habsburg government, however: it was still being represented abroad in consular cases by the Swedish government, which continued to exercise Habsburg sovereignty by protecting citizens of the former empire in the United States until the summer of 1921.

With Karl's departure from government, there was now a vacuum in Central Europe. The inhabitants of Austria-Hungary were not at all sure what the victors – or even the Germans – had in store for them.[12] The Allied and Associated governments had certainly indicated that national states with democratic governments would be the wave of the future, but they had not recognized any specific territorial boundaries or commented on what would happen in areas of mixed population – areas that Wilson, Lansing, and the Inquiry in particular did not believe to exist.

Adopting a course of action that they believed the Americans at least supported, a group in Vienna moved in November 1918 to declare the existence of an Austrian Republic; then, a popular vote was held in which the Austro-Germans elected to join Germany. They firmly believed that this was what the Americans wanted: having been told for years that Austro-Germans were racially German and that each race should have its own nation-state, they opted to join their nation-state, which had recently switched from a monarchy to a republic at Wilson's request.

---

[9] On the effects of the blockade, see Maureen Healy, *Vienna and the Fall of the Habsburg Empire: Total War and Everyday Life in World War I* (New York, 2004).

[10] Burián, 9.

[11] Helmut Rumpler, *Das Völkermanifest Kaiser Karls vom 16. Oktober 1918. Letzter Versuch zur Rettung des Habsburgerreiches* (Vienna, 1966).

[12] German military forces invaded the Tirol. See Gordon Brook-Shepherd, *The Last Habsburg* (New York, 1968).

The fact that there had been a vote should have been icing on the cake for Wilson because it was both democratic and an example of self-determination in action. By doing exactly what the Americans said they had wanted – getting rid of the Habsburgs, establishing a race-based nation-state, and supporting a democratic government – the Austro-Germans hoped to end the blockade and be allowed to concentrate on rebuilding and finding their place in the new international order.[13]

The Americans, however, had not yet recognized the new German government, and they refused to commit to the idea of an *Anschluss* – a union between Germany and the hereditary lands of Austria – or to recognize the Austrian vote. They opted instead to wait for the peace conference to figure out what to do on this question and numerous others. This policy, which was also followed by the Allied governments, meant that Central Europeans were left in limbo for months while they waited for the delegates at the peace conference to make decisions; the blockade remained in place.

According to historian Lawrence Gelfand, members of the Inquiry did not see any problem with this state of affairs: "There was a tacit assumption that while the peace engineers went about their tasks of manipulating and directing the institutional changes, the existing nations and societies would remain stable, pliable, accepting these changes without complaints. That the peoples of east-central Europe, the Middle East, Africa, and elsewhere would not acquiesce and readily approve the design offered by the engineers was never given serious consideration."[14]

Events in Central Europe did not simply grind to a halt, however. The national governments worked to build support among their likely future constituents, and fighting continued as new governments tried to establish control over as much territory as possible. They hoped that they could create a situation on the ground that was favorable to them, and that the peace conference would merely recognize the legitimacy of that situation.

---

[13] On the German-Austrian actions, see John W. Boyer, "Silent War and Bitter Peace: The Revolution of 1918 in Austria," *AHY* 34 (2003): 1–56; Frederick Dumin, "Self-Determination: The United States and Austria in 1919," *Research Studies* 40, 3 (1972): 176–94; Gerald Stourzh, "Ethnic Attribution in Late Imperial Austria: Good Intentions, Evil Consequences," in *The Habsburg Legacy: National Identity in Historical Perspective*, ed. Ritchie Robertson and Edward Timms (Edinburgh, 1994), 67–83; and Alfred D. Low, *The Anschluss Movement, 1918–1919, and the Paris Peace Conference* (Philadelphia, 1974). On Germany, see, among numerous others, Klaus Schwabe, *Woodrow Wilson, Revolutionary Germany, and Peacemaking, 1918–1919: Missionary Diplomacy and the Realities of Power* (Chapel Hill, 1985).

[14] Lawrence E. Gelfand, *The Inquiry: American Preparations for Peace, 1917–1919* (New Haven, 1963), 158.

The Paris Peace Conference itself was highly disorganized, so it essentially provided an opportunity to reaffirm basic principles that had already been established – such as the importance of democracy, capitalism, and racial nationalism – and to provide some, but not all, of the concrete details around which the new states of Central Europe could be built.[15] In terms of formerly Habsburg Central Europe, the peace conference was important in that it eventually provided full legal recognition of the successor governments and clarified the territory over which they were sovereign.

During the conference, the U.S. government as a whole signaled its recognition of the Czechoslovak and Polish governments by establishing diplomatic missions at the rank of envoy in Prague and Warsaw. A diplomatic mission to Yugoslavia at the rank of envoy came in July 1919, shortly after the conclusion of the conference. By contrast, the U.S. government withheld diplomatic recognition from Germany, Austria, and Hungary until 1921, when all three states had finally established governments that were acceptable to the United States.

The Hungarians also felt the dissatisfaction of the delegates at Paris. Not only did Hungarians continue fighting after the armistice in an effort to retain Slovakia and Transylvania, they also adopted a series of governments that were unacceptable to Wilson and the other delegates at Paris. Wilson and Allied leaders had feared that the combination of wartime uncertainty and the existence of the Soviet Union would prompt a series of communist revolutions in Europe. Their fears came true in the cases of Germany and Hungary. Several soviets, or workers' councils, were established in southern Germany, competing with the liberal Weimar government while a communist government led by Belá Kun came to power in Hungary in 1919. At that point, most American sympathy for the Hungarian cause – in place since 1848 – was eclipsed by the stronger American opposition to communism.[16]

---

[15] On the disorganization of the conference, see especially Harold Temperley, ed., *A History of the Peace Conference of Paris*, 6 vols. (London, 1920–24); Harold Nicolson, *Peacemaking, 1919* (New York, 1933); and F. S. Marston, *The Peace Conference of 1919: Organization and Procedure* (London, 1944).

[16] James M. Smallwood, "Banquo's Ghost at the Paris Peace Conference: The United States and the Hungarian Question," *East European Quarterly* 12, 3 (1978): 289–307; Peter Pastor, "The Hungarian Revolution's Road from Wilsonianism to Leninism, 1918–19," *East Central Europe* 3, 2 (1976): 210–19; Francis Deák, *Hungary at the Paris Peace Conference: The Diplomatic History of the Treaty of Trianon* (New York, 1942); Alfred D. Low, *The Soviet Hungarian Republic and the Paris Peace Conference* (Philadelphia, 1963); and George W. Hopkins, "The Politics of Food: United States and Soviet Hungary, March-August 1919," *Mid-America* 55, 4 (1973): 245–70.

After Kun's government fell, however, the situation was far from resolved. Admiral Miklos Horthy came to power and used the title "regent," implying a continuation of the Hungarian kingdom. In addition, royalists in Hungary assisted Karl in two attempts to regain the Hungarian throne, demonstrating the continued popularity of monarchy – and, indeed, Habsburg monarchy – among a noteworthy segment of the Hungarian population. Only after Karl was exiled to the island of Madeira in 1921 and Regent Horthy's government agreed to accept sovereignty over a sizably reduced territory was the Treaty of Trianon finally signed, officially ending World War I as far as Hungary was concerned.[17] The Hungarian government received U.S. diplomatic recognition in December 1921.

The delegates at the Paris Peace Conference also worked on determining the borders of the new Central European states. Establishing those borders took almost two full years, however. Much of the difficulty stemmed from American and British efforts to create states that included the smallest number of minorities possible, whereas the French government aimed at granting the new states militarily defensible frontiers.[18] The boundaries they finally decided on left a considerable number of individuals on the "wrong side" of the various borders. Delegates at the Paris Peace Conference sought to deal with this by requiring the successor states to make formal agreements to protect their minorities, but such agreements contradicted the main idea that Wilson and American and British delegates had repeatedly stressed; namely, that national homogeneity was essential.[19] The treaties also reinforced the idea of unbridgeable difference between the majority and minority populations, thus making cooperation and true equality more difficult to achieve. The successor states were more inclined to work to create that homogeneity through laws, forced repatriations, and eventually "ethnic cleansing" and genocide programs than they were to protect minority groups.

---

[17] Karl died in 1922.

[18] On the establishment of borders at the conference, see Temperley; Edward M. House and Charles Seymour, eds. *What Really Happened at Paris: The Story of the Peace Conference, 1918–1919* (New York, 1921); and Dagmar Perman, *The Shaping of the Czechoslovak State: Diplomatic History of the Boundaries of Czechoslovakia, 1914–1920* (Leiden, 1962), esp. 142–43.

[19] On minority treaties, see Temperley; Carole Fink, *Defending the Rights of Others: The Great Powers, the Jews, and International Minority Protection, 1878–1938* (New York, 2004); Carole Fink, "The Paris Peace Conference and the Question of Minority Rights," *Peace and Change* 21, 3 (1996): 273–88; and Eric D. Weitz, "From the Vienna to the Paris System: International Politics and the Entangled Histories of Human Rights, Forced Deportations, and Civilizing Missions," *AHR* 113, 5 (2008): 1313–43.

The inhabitants of Central Europe were not the only ones who had to find a way to carry out the broad directives spelled out by Allied and Associated leaders during the war and at the Paris Peace Conference. Various agencies of the U.S. government, the Swedish consular service, and the successor states also had to reach some sort of effective, practical consensus on what to do with the Austrian and Hungarian citizens who had been interned or arrested in the United States as "enemy aliens" during the war. The Swedish legation operated on the understanding that the U.S. government would want each deportee or repatriate to be sent to the nation-state that matched his or her racial identity. However, the departments of State, Justice, and Labor could not agree on how to match their own policies with the Swedish interpretation of Wilsonian principles, despite their earlier work in creating those principles and the racial-national categories that corresponded to the new states. In processing the former enemy aliens, U.S. officials helped to clarify the new territorial and population borders of Central Europe, aiding the process of nation-state building there.

Approximately 2,300 Austrian, Hungarian, and German civilians and an additional 4,000 prisoners of war were held at four camps in the United States, with most of the civilians at Fort Oglethorpe in Georgia and Fort Douglas in Utah. All enemy aliens had to register with U.S. authorities, and many, including most women, who were suspected of dangerous activity were jailed or held in Immigration detention centers, rather than sent to internment camps. The camps were run by the U.S. Army, but the Justice Department had jurisdiction over civilian cases.[20]

During the war, the internees worked with the Swedish legation to improve their living conditions and, most importantly, to try to make their cases to the U.S. government as to why they had been wrongly imprisoned. In general, before the armistice, the Justice Department refused to release internees, usually on vague claims that the individuals posed a threat to the

---

[20] On the circumstances that landed civilians in the camps and their experiences once there, see Nicole M. Phelps, "'A Status Which Does Not Exist Anymore': Austrian and Hungarian Enemy Aliens in the United States, 1917–1921," in *From Empire to Republic: Post-World War I Austria*, Contemporary Austrian Studies 19, ed. Günter Bischof, Fritz Plasser, and Peter Berger (New Orleans, 2010), 90–109; Jörg A. Nagler, *Nationale Minoritäten im Krieg. »Feindliche Ausländer« und die amerikanische Heimatfront während des Ersten Weltkriegs«* (Hamburg, 2000); Nagler, "Enemy Aliens and Internment during World War I: Alvo von Alvensleben in Fort Douglas, Utah. A Case Study," *Utah Historical Quarterly* 58, 4 (1990): 388–405; and Gerald H. Davis, "'Orgelsdorf': A World War I Internment Camp in America," *Yearbook of German-American Studies* 26 (1991): 249–65.

United States. Most of the internees had been arrested due to the popular explosion of racial prejudice, 100 percent Americanism, and wartime hysteria, rather than for cause, and the Justice Department's normal practice was to intern people first, then conduct investigations. Some were paroled to supervised jobs, but most requests for release were denied.

The partial recognition of Czechoslovak sovereignty in the fall of 1918, along with the American establishment of diplomatic relations with the Czechoslovak government, created new confusion and new possibilities among the Austrian and Hungarian internees. In March 1919, Frank Daniš, an internee at Fort Oglethorpe, wrote to the State Department "as spokesman of the internees of Slavic nationality," asking for release on the grounds that those internees born in Bohemia and Moravia were now citizens of the "Tsechco-Slovakian Republic," which had been recognized by Allies. "They have been interned as Austrians," he wrote, "a status which, in their particular case, does not exist anymore." He added that he and his fellow internees wished to stay in the United States "for the time being at least" and that "not a single one has been indicted for an offence against the United States."[21] Daniš wrote for the group again a few days later, this time sending an excerpt from a *New York Times* article on "Britain's Interned Aliens." According to the article, of Britain's 18,607 interned enemy civilians, approximately 6,000 had been repatriated, and 113 had been released from the camps; two-thirds of this latter number were released "on being duly recognized as Czechoslovaks and therefore ceasing to be enemies."[22] Daniš observed, "As we presume you are going to treat subjects of the Czecho-Slovak Republic similarly we trust you will recognize our present status."[23]

In answering these communications from the State Department, a Justice Department official wrote that his department "has informed the internees that in the absence of any notice from you [the State Department] that the status of natives, citizens, denizens or subjects of a hostile nation or government has been changed they must still be considered alien enemies."[24] When

---

[21] Daniš et al. to DOS, 9 March 1919, file no. 311.63/436, in NARA.
[22] "Britain's Interned Aliens," *NYT*, 16 March 1919, quoted in Daniš et al. to DOS, 21 Mach 1919, file no. 311.63/449, in NARA.
[23] Daniš et al. to DOS, 21 Mach 1919.
[24] O'Brien to Lansing, 27 March 1919, file no. 311.63/450; see also O'Brien to Lansing, 3 April 1919, file no. 311.63/457, both in NARA. In a similar case, an ethnic Romanian from Transylvania was denied release because Transylvania was still considered enemy territory, despite the fact that it had passed into the possession of Allied Romania. See O'Brien to Lansing, 24 February 1919, file no. 311.63/430, in NARA.

put to the Office of the Solicitor at the State Department, official opinion held that, although the Czecho-Slovak National Council had been recognized as "a de facto belligerent government clothed with proper authority to direct the military forces of the Czecho Slovaks," no specific territorial rights came with that recognition. Therefore, the territory of Bohemia retained its status as enemy territory, and the internees were still enemy aliens.[25] The State Department solicitor was still operating on the nineteenth-century principle of territorial sovereignty. Daniš again wrote to the State Department, encouraging its officials to notify the Justice Department of their change in status. He argued that,

ever since [the Czecho-Slovak Republic's] establishment we unequivocally considered ourselves citizens of the New State. We were born in districts which undoubtedly compose the Czecho-Slovak Republic, our nearest relatives are living there, some of whom have meanwhile become official members of Boards instituted by the new Czech authorities, we own property and business there, and some of us have there permanent residence there. In the present state of affairs we know of no other reasons which could prove our present status as citizens of the Czecho-Slovak Republic more clearly since we cannot be citizens of Austria-Hungary which does not exist anymore, and therefore also ceased to be technical alien enemies.[26]

Daniš managed to get out on parole after an investigation of his particular circumstances, but the others in his group were still interned. Their new spokesman was Erich Posselt, and he wrote to both the State Department and Justice Department several times over the following months. He repeated their arguments about the fact that Austria-Hungary no longer existed and thus could not have citizens and again drew attention to the recognition of the Czechoslovak government by the Allies and Czechoslovak participation in the peace negotiations. He went further with his arguments, stating that he and those he represented had all taken out their first citizenship papers, thus demonstrating their intention to become U.S. citizens. He again requested that the State Department inform the Justice Department of their change in status.[27] Admitting a desire to stay in the United States may have hurt Posselt's case, as the Justice Department was keen to repatriate or deport as many internees as possible. A claim on U.S. citizenship also undermined his claim to Czechoslovak citizenship.

---

[25] DOS Solicitor to Coffin, "Memorandum," 7 January 1919, file no. 311.636/6, in NARA.
[26] Daniš et al. to DOS, ca. 9 April 1919, file no. 311.63/458, in NARA.
[27] Posselt to DOS, 4 June 1919, file no. 311.63/515; see also Posselt to DOS, 23 May 1919, file no. 311.63/504, both in NARA.

By August, Posselt was writing on his own behalf.[28] He wrote to the Swedish Legation:

In view of the fact that it is my intention to become a citizen of this country – I have taken out my so-called First paper more than five years ago – I respectfully ask you once more to intervene in my behalf to bring about my discharge from the internment camp. As I have pointed out before I happen to be born in, and am still a subject of Bohemia. As you know Bohemia, under the protection of the Allied powers, and more especially under the protection and with the aid of the United States, has become an independent republic even now represented in Washington. I have never had any connections with German or Austrian subjects who were in the pay of the respective Governments, and have never received any [sic] penny out of any German or Austrian fund. I am far from being an anarchist or a believer in the doctrins [sic] of bolshevism. I am not a propagandist. And I know myself absolutely innocent of any overt act against this country. I am a married man, and my wife is living here. I have no near relatives abroad, and have no business interests in Europe. It is my wish to stay permanently in the U.S., and I am willing to give any guarantee required for my bona fide intentions. May be these points, if presented by you to the proper authorities, will help to finally settle my case in my favor.[29]

The State Department, apparently ignoring previous correspondence from the Justice Department that told them the issue of release from camps for such persons depended on a statement from the State Department, forwarded Posselt's letter on to the Justice Department. This time, however, the Justice Department's story changed. Rather than laying the blame for continued internment at the State Department's door, the Justice Department responded that, "while it is fully cognizant of certain appealing aspects in Mr. Posselt's case, it has thus far, notwithstanding a most careful review of the record of his activities in this country, not deemed it expedient to release him. The Department will, however, give Mr. Posselt's case further attention."[30]

In November 1919, Posselt changed his story. He had an interview with a Justice Department representative, who informed him that the department believed him to have been engaged in espionage, a charge that Posselt hotly denied. He asked for a trial on those charges.[31] He did not wait for a

---

[28] It is not clear from the available records what became of the others represented in this correspondence.

[29] Posselt to the Swedish Legation, 2 August 1919 (forwarded to DOS on 14 August 1919), file no. 311.63/534, in NARA.

[30] Creighton to SecState, 10 September 1919, file no. 311.63/543, in NARA.

[31] Posselt's letter, enclosed in no. 4500/21, Ekengren to DOS, 8 November 1919, file no. 311.63/559, in NARA.

response before writing again. In this next letter, he announced that his wife was ill, without funds, and thus in need of his assistance and release.[32] In the past, an appeal based on the need to support dependents residing in the United States had helped to secure some other internees' release. It did not provoke a quick response in Posselt's case, however, and he wrote again in December 1919, this time saying that he had "instructed my lawyers to start habeas corpus proceedings ... as it is contrary to all national and international law to hold in confinement without legal charge any person. (See Article-Amendment VI of the Constitution)."[33] This letter, and, more importantly, the passage of time, yielded the desired results, and Posselt was paroled on 8 January 1920.[34] The combination of a desire to remain in the United States, presumed espionage activities, and the State Department's decision not to announce to the Justice Department that the status of Czechoslovaks had changed kept people in internment camps for more than a year past U.S. recognition of the Czecho-Slovak Republic and the end of all hostilities. It did not change their status as enemy aliens as far as the Justice Department was concerned, though – Posselt and others like him were paroled, not given complete liberty, and their postwar citizenship status remained unclear.

At least one internee was successfully able to claim Czecho-Slovak citizenship, however. Felix Zweig wrote to the State Department in May 1919 that "Under date of April 21st, 1919 I have been informed by my lawyer ... that the Czecho-Slovak Minister has recognized me as a citizen of his country and that he has stated this fact to the State Department. I am asking you herewith to kindly officially notify the Justice Department of said change in my status."[35] Shortly thereafter, a New York City attorney wrote to the State Department requesting a passport for Zweig, as the Justice Department had agreed to his release.[36] Apparently, the combination of official Czecho-Slovak recognition and the desire to leave the United States were enough to secure release.

On the whole, however, the successor states were in no rush to claim responsibility for the internees. In March 1919, the Swedish Legation

---

[32] Posselt's letter, enclosed in no. 4581/21, Ekengren to DOS, 11 November 1919, file no. 311.63/560, in NARA.

[33] Posselt to DOS, 7 December 1919, file no. 311.63/567, in NARA.

[34] Hanna to DOS, 9 January 1919, file no. 311.63/574, in NARA.

[35] Zweig to Adee, 9 May 1919, file no. 311.63/495, in NARA. Note that his letter is filed under Austria-Hungary, not Czechoslovakia. A search of the Czechoslovak protection of interest files yielded no documents relating to internment.

[36] Wachtell to DOS, 31 May 1919, file no. 311.63/509, in NARA.

informed the State Department that relief payments to internees and their families, which had been funded by the Habsburg government, had to stop, "since the Governments of the various states of the former Austro-Hungarian Monarchy are not disposed to furnish the necessary funds." The Swedish Minister went on to request the immediate release of internees with families to support, or, failing that, to adjust the powers of the private, New York City-based War Prisoners Relief Committee under the 1917 Trading with the Enemy Act so that they could provide relief payments in lieu of those from the Austro-Hungarian government.[37] The Justice Department replied that the release of all such internees was "not deemed advisable," but a half a dozen were released under this initiative, and the Relief Committee was allowed to provide funds.[38]

Not only were the successor states unwilling to make relief payments, they were also generally unwilling to accept repatriates or deportees from the United States, although the American determination to send these people back ultimately prevailed. By repatriating internees and deporting others who had been arrested, officials of the U.S. government hoped to align individuals' racial identity, political citizenship, and physical location, thereby achieving the homogeneity and order that was supposed to produce lasting peace. Various agencies of the U.S. government were not firmly united on how best to achieve this aim, however. In particular, the Department of Labor, which handled immigration and deportation issues at the time, had not fully embraced the principles advocated by Wilson and affirmed at the Paris Peace Conference. Their lag in applying these categories to former Austrian and Hungarian citizens was ironic, given the department's important role in shaping those principles in the first place.

At least three dozen former Austrians and Hungarians were awaiting deportation on anarchy charges between 1919 and 1921. The Department of Labor had jurisdiction over deportees – as opposed to those who were being repatriated – and their approach to sending people away from the United States differed from that of the Justice Department. Justice Department officials were content to wait to hear from the State Department regarding changes in enemy aliens' status, and the staff of the State Department was waiting for a resolution from Paris. Rather than trying to hold out for a clearly defined peace treaty, however, the

[37] No. 1011/21, Swedish Legation to SecState, 19 March 1919, file no. 311.63/447, in NARA.

[38] O'Brien to SecState, 9 April 1919, file no. 311.63/455, in NARA.

Department of Labor began actively deporting people into the confusion that was Central and Eastern Europe.

The heart of the problem was this: the official diplomatic name of Austria-Hungary while it existed was *Austria*, so when people had given their place of birth to Immigration officials before the war, they usually named a town, a province, and then Austria, or, in many cases, merely Austria. Thus, when immigration officials wanted to deport people after the war, they planned on sending all these people back to where they came from: Austria. However, most of these deportees had not come from the territory that was now the independent Republic of Austria; at least one-third were from the province of Galicia, which was now part of Poland, and, ethnically, they were either Polish or Ruthenian (Ukrainian). The government of the new Austrian republic did not want to accept the anarchists, nor did it want them traveling through Austrian territory en route to other locations.[39]

For example, one potential deportee, Mike Podolak, was identified as "a native and subject of Austria, . . . of the Ukrainian race, [who] gives his place of birth as Sambor, Lonevich, Galicia, Austria."[40] To the Swedish Legation, the most relevant part of that statement was either *Galicia*, which meant that he should be sent to Poland, or *Ukrainian*, which meant he should be sent to Ukraine, which was occupied by Soviet forces at the time. The Labor Department, however, kept focusing on *Austria*, much to the dismay of the government of the Austrian republic. Ultimately, what was most important to Immigration officials was *Sambor*, but they did not clearly convey that to either the Swedes or the Austrians. Given this confusion, the Swedish Minister wrote to the State Department "to request the kind intermediary of the Secretary of State with a view that the Department of Labor, before issuing the warrants for deportation, may kindly establish positively the present citizenship of subjects of the former Austro-Hungarian Monarchy, in order that they be deported to the State of which they are subjects at the present time, and that the deportation of subjects of the former Austro-Hungarian Monarchy be held in abeyance until their present citizenship has been positively ascertained."[41]

---

[39] See file 311.6324.
[40] All anarchist deportations are filed under 311.6324. The classic historical work on the deportations is Robert K. Murray, *Red Scare: A Study in National Hysteria, 1919–1920* (Minneapolis, 1955).
[41] No. 1986/21, Ekengren to DOS, 1 May 1920, file no. 311.6324B86/2, in NARA.

The Labor Department would not be deterred, however. Officials did not stop the deportations, and they insisted that the people would be returned to the specific place from whence they had come. Louis F. Post, assistant secretary of labor, wrote, "It seems immaterial whether the homes of these aliens are included in States other than Austria under the geographical rearrangement effected in Europe, and notwithstanding they were ordered deported to Austria, the Commissioner at Ellis Island invariably secures transportation in deportations at Government expense to the aliens' respective homes, and it would seem that this is all that is necessary under the present unsettled conditions."[42] Post apparently did not realize that the deportations were contributing to the "unsettled conditions"; the Labor Department's focus on returning people to the specific town they had originally come from undermined the efforts of President Wilson and the American delegation at Paris to create racially homogenous nation-states in Central and Eastern Europe. That focus on the town, however, reinforced the concept of purely territorial sovereignty that had been at the heart of the Great Power System.

The U.S. government as a whole, however, was committed to returning internees to Europe. This was not a pleasing prospect to many internees. One Austrian internee, Louis F. Schulze, wrote to request that he be allowed to go to Mexico, where he had been living for several years before the U.S. invasion in 1914.[43] He wrote:

I have no desire whatsoever of being thrown into what I take to be chaotic economical and political conditions such as exist in Europe today. Considering that I left Austria as far back as 1902, without having returned, nor had any desire to return to the old country, except perhaps for a short visit. . . . I wish to state with emphasis that I own real estate, mining interests, etc., valuated at $25000.00, in which I have invested my life's savings, providing for my old age, which I wish to spend in quiet and comfort, and I cannot see how you can possibly repatriate me against my wishes. I am nearly 50 years of age and cannot start life anew, my health being very poor, so that I could not possibly stand the strain of all the turmoil nor the stress of a new departure would cause me, besides I have my Interests in Mexico and I do not wish, nor can you possibly expect me to allow Other people to liquidate my property.[44]

---

[42] Post to DOS, 30 July 1920, file no. 311.6324P26/2, in NARA; see similar statements from Post: Post to DOS, 21 May 1920, file no. 311.6324B49/4; and Post to DOS, 9 July 1920, file no. 311.6324R96/2, both in NARA.

[43] Wilson had deployed U.S. troops to Vera Cruz, Mexico in opposition to Victoriano Huerta's government.

[44] Schulze to DOS, 27 May 1919, file no. 311.63/516, in NARA.

His request was denied: the need to align racial identity, political citizenship, and physical location was stronger than the U.S. government's willingness to honor the wishes of individual people. That disregard for individual choice regarding nationality and citizenship became a hallmark of the post-1919 international system, which privileged group identity and rights over those of individual people.[45]

---

[45] Weitz, "From the Vienna to the Paris System"; and Linda K. Kerber, "The Stateless as the Citizen's Other: A View from the United States," *AHR* 112, 1 (2007): 1–34. The work of Hannah Arendt is also extremely important in this regard.

Conclusion

After the Peace

The ability of the U.S. government to repatriate enemy aliens to Central Europe against their will and against the wishes of the successor governments reflects the strength it had achieved, both domestically and internationally. Wilson and his advisors had been able to achieve many of their aims: the culture of diplomacy that had governed European relations before the war had ended, although that culture had little in common with the "Old Diplomacy" Wilson had described; they had made it more difficult for individuals to cross international borders, thus altering the process of immigration to the United States; and they had removed the Habsburg government from power and helped to create nation-states in Europe, signaling their belief in the importance of racial homogeneity to the proper functioning of democracy.

Although members of Congress did not accept Wilson's full program for "New Diplomacy," they did contribute significantly to building a new culture of diplomacy for the post-1919 world. Many senators rejected the League of Nations because they felt it infringed on national sovereignty, but they did choose to support programs of reform aimed at the diplomatic corps and consular service. With the Rogers Act of 1924, the diplomatic corps and consular service were merged into a new entity, the U.S. Foreign Service. Professionalization measures were adopted, including entrance exams and merit-based promotions.[1]

[1] See Robert D. Schulzinger, *The Making of the Diplomatic Mind: The Training, Outlook, and Style of United States Foreign Service Officers, 1908–1931* (Middletown, 1975); Richard Hume Werking, *The Master Architects: Building the United States Foreign Service, 1890–1913* (Lexington, 1977); and Warren Frederick Ilchman, *Professional*

The presence of U.S. Foreign Service personnel meant something different from the presence of Great Power System diplomats, however. Foreign Service Officers were expressions of national sovereignty: they marked – indeed, celebrated – the fundamental, unbridgeable difference between "us" and "them" that Great Power System diplomats had minimized or even overlooked. The professionalized U.S. Foreign Service rotated its members out of office every three years, reinforcing the ideas that one post was the same as another and that it was the office itself, rather than its specific occupant, that mattered. Holding to the American tradition of amateur diplomacy, approximately half of the chief of mission positions were reserved for political appointees, and personal connections outweighed suitability for the job for these positions.[2]

Finally, the U.S. government gradually expanded on its emerging use of the ambassadorial rank. In the Great Power System, the ranks had meaning, reflecting the underlying hierarchy of the system and two countries' mutual understanding of the importance of their relationship. By the 1940s, the U.S. government had almost entirely stopped using any other rank besides that of ambassador. American rhetoric announced that embassies were a mark of equality and respect, but American policies rarely reflected those qualities.[3] The symbolism of the post-1919 diplomatic culture did not align with the distribution of power in the international system, giving it a hollow, hypocritical feel that has done little to promote pro-U.S. feeling or a true sense of international cooperation.

Congress also took measures to shore up territorial sovereignty, align racial identity and political citizenship, and curtail international mobility. The U.S. government – and most European governments – kept wartime passport regulations in place after the war, requiring people to carry documentation of their citizenship status when they traveled internationally.[4] A peacetime visa system allowed for official documentation of the length of a person's stay abroad. Passport and visa requirements went a

---

 Diplomacy in the United States, 1779–1939: A Study in Administrative History (Chicago, 1961).

[2] See U.S. DOS, *Principal Officers of the Department of State and United States Chiefs of Mission, 1778–1990* (Washington, 1991). See also Martin Florian Herz, ed., *Diplomacy: The Role of the Wife: A Symposium* (Washington, 1981). Various contributors to the volume grapple with the issue of post-1924 political appointees.

[3] On the imperialistic symbolism of American embassy buildings, see Ron Theodore Robin, *Enclaves of America: The Rhetoric of American Political Architecture Abroad, 1900–1965* (Princeton, 1992).

[4] See John Torpey, *The Invention of the Passport: Surveillance, Citizenship and the State* (Cambridge, 2000); see also Mae M. Ngai, *Impossible Subjects: Illegal Aliens and the Making of Modern America* (Princeton, 2004).

long way toward alleviating the problems consular officials dealt with prior to the war: they made international travel more difficult by requiring individuals to obtain travel documents before they embarked on their journeys, and they clearly identified individuals' citizenship status. These documents alleviated much of the conflict between sovereign claims based on territory and those based on citizenship.

Passports and visas proved to be insufficient for addressing another major American problem, however: they did not curb immigration to the United States as effectively as many Americans would have hoped. Congress addressed this issue by adopting a race-based quota system for immigration that dramatically reduced the annual number of immigrants and blocked much of the allegedly undesirable "New Immigrants" from Central and Eastern Europe, along with Asians. The Immigration Act of 1924, like the World War I peace settlements, was designed to be "scientific," and the people charged with determining the size of the quotas faced problems similar to those faced by the Inquiry and the Paris Peace Conference delegates. Both groups relied on scientific theories of race that proved impractical when applied to real people. Both the Paris Peace Conference participants and the designers of the quota system did go a long way toward achieving their goal of creating national populations that were increasingly homogeneous, although the peace that they hoped to achieve through such measures has certainly proved elusive.[5]

The Wilson administration had also achieved the removal of the allegedly autocratic and oppressive Habsburg Empire from Central Europe and its replacement with states that conformed more thoroughly with their vision of the ideal state. The successor states had democratic governments and were allegedly based on the will of "the people," although we have seen that international recognition was absolutely vital for the creation and success of the new states. They were capitalist – immediately after World War I, communism failed to take hold in Europe, much to the relief of Wilson and the Allied governments. The new states also aimed at being racially homogeneous, a goal that Wilson and his advisors had insisted was vital to a successful democracy. By giving each of the European "peoples" their own state, Wilson and his supporters believed that fewer people

---

[5] On the 1924 act, see Mae M. Ngai, "The Architecture of Race in American Immigration Law: A Reexamination of the Immigration Act of 1924," *JAH* 86, 1 (1999): 67–92. For a contrasting interpretation that emphasizes the shorter term political environment produced by the debate over U.S. entry into the League of Nations, see Kristofer Allerfeldt, *Beyond the Huddled Masses: American Immigration and the Treaty of Versailles* (London, 2006).

would have a need to seek new opportunity in the United States, leaving Americans free to pursue the creation of their own Anglo-Saxon nation.

Redrawing the map of Central and Eastern Europe did not bring about the peace Wilson and many of his contemporaries had hoped for, however. A major motivating factor for the Nazis and their allies in World War II was, of course, a desire to readjust the territorial boundaries of Europe in an effort to rectify the perceived wrongs of the Paris treaties. Allied victory in World War II meant that the 1919 territorial borders largely remained in place throughout the twentieth century. Far more important, however, the new post-1919 governments worked to adjust the social borders of their nations. Nazi policies are perhaps the most famous: they worked to remove Jews permanently from the German nation through the Holocaust; massacred Poles, Russians, and other Slavs they deemed racially inferior; and further "refined" the German nation by using force to crush political dissent.

The Nazis were not the only ones who attempted to create a racially pure nation. Despite the minority protections that were included in the Paris treaties, the Polish and Czechoslovak governments worked to minimize minority involvement in the new nations and, especially in the immediate aftermath of World War II, forcibly "repatriated" sizeable numbers of ethnic Germans to Germany. Czech leaders sought at times to dominate the Slovaks and at other times to assimilate them, belying the racial unity they had insisted existed during the war; Czech efforts strengthened a sense of Slovak nationalism and ultimately resulted in the break-up of the country's territorial borders in 1993. The Yugoslav state, again based on the idea of a fundamental racial unity among its members, also witnessed almost a century of violence and then genocide as groups with different visions of "the nation" sought to make their goals into reality.[6] The Wilsonian rhetoric of World War I and the Paris Peace Conference gave governments in the post-1919 international system authorization to create homogeneous nation-states and to base that homogeneity in racial terms.

Since World War I, Europe has witnessed assimilation programs, mass emigrations, forced repatriations, murders, and genocides in an effort to create homogeneous populations within largely static territorial borders.

---

[6] See, among numerous others, Eric D. Weitz, *A Century of Genocide: Utopias of Race and Nation* (Princeton, 2003); Weitz, "From the Vienna to the Paris System: International Politics and the Entangled Histories of Human Rights, Forced Deportations, and Civilizing Missions," *AHR* 113, 5 (2008): 1313–43; and Daniel E. Miller, "Colonizing the Hungarian and German Border Areas during the Czechoslovak Land Reform, 1918–1938," *AHY* 34 (2003): 303–17.

The United States has not escaped nationalist violence either: lynchings, race riots, the Red Scares of 1919–20 and the 1950s, and hate crimes have served to enforce the – often changing – social borders of the American nation. Over the course of the century and continuing into the present, the national imperative of the post-1919 system has spread throughout the world, prompting both domestic and international violence.[7] In an effort to create nation-states – and especially nation-states that are capitalist and "democratic" – individual choice – true self-determination – has often been suppressed or destroyed.

With the end of the peace conference in 1919, American and British academics who had put their intellectual talents to work for their governments during the war returned to the academy and began to write. They wrote their memoirs, and they wrote reports on what had happened at the conference. Some – most famously, John Maynard Keynes – wrote scathing indictments of the settlement and worked to distance themselves from it, especially as Europe and the rest of the world descended into economic depression, fascism, and war.[8]

When writing about Austria-Hungary, Anglo-American peace conference participants began to write themselves out of the story of the country's break-up almost immediately. In their accounts of the conference, they wrote that continued fighting in Central Europe after the armistice was what set the territorial borders of the empire's successor states; the treaties were merely a fait accompli.[9] Subsequent scholars of the conference and the treaties were more interested – quite understandably – in finding the World War I-era roots of World War II and the Cold War. That the Paris peace treaties contributed to both of these unpleasant events did not encourage many American historians to embrace American agency in their construction, and the extensive scholarship on the Big Four themselves suggests that both professional and amateur historians – and their

---

[7] This point is well-explored in Erez Manela, *The Wilsonian Moment: Self-determination and the International Origins of Anticolonial Nationalism* (New York, 2007).

[8] For an excellent bibliography of participants' memoirs, see *Margaret Macmillan, Paris 1919: Six Months that Changed the World* (New York, 2002). See also John Maynard Keynes, *The Economic Consequences of the Peace* (London, 1920).

[9] For fait accompli arguments, see especially the various reminiscences and commentaries in Harold Temperley, ed., *A History of the Peace Conference of Paris*, 6 vols. (London, 1920–24); and Edward M. House and Charles Seymour, eds., *What Really Happened at Paris: The Story of the Peace Conference, 1918–1919* (New York: C. Scribner's Sons, 1921). For a scholarly account that takes this perspective, see Victor S. Mamatey, "The Disintegration of the Habsburg Monarchy: Legalizing the Collapse of Austria-Hungary at the Paris Peace Conference," *AHY* 3 (1967): 206–37.

audiences – have been more comfortable singling out specific individuals to blame, rather than looking to the larger society that so many more people had a role in shaping.

The Anglo-American peace conference participants – and the later generations of students they advised and influenced – also wrote histories of the Habsburg Empire that argued that it had been collapsing from the weight of internal problems: unbridgeable conflicts among the empire's constituent national groups, oppressive, autocratic government, and economic stagnation. The rhetoric of decline, twilight, eclipse, fall, and backwardness pervades these accounts. Central European scholars writing histories to bolster the sovereign claims of the successor governments echoed these themes, writing of decades or even centuries of Habsburg oppression and the equally long-standing sense of community among members of national groups.[10] Those national groups were presented as naturally occurring – no human agency was involved in their genesis and persistence.

In the United States, the directions that the professions of history and political science took after World War I reinforced this narrative about Austria-Hungary and the lack of outside involvement in its demise. European and American history were separate fields, and the rhetoric of American isolation from European affairs operated to keep many scholars from studying transatlantic connections and commonalities. Historians working in European history typically focused on a single national community. Historians studying immigrants in the United States also usually chose a single national or ethnic group to study – a choice facilitated or even dictated by the ways in which the Bureau of Immigration kept its statistics.[11] These choices helped to reify and naturalize national categories that actually had their roots in the racialist thought of the nineteenth century. Political scientists did their part to naturalize the nation-state as the basic unit of international affairs, and the assertion by many that the

---

[10] Representative works include Oscar Jászi, *The Dissolution of the Habsburg Monarchy* (Chicago, 1929); Josef Redlich, *Emperor Francis Joseph of Austria: A Biography* (London, 1929); A. J. P. Taylor, *The Habsburg Monarchy, 1809–1918* (Chicago, 1948); C. A. Macartney, *The Habsburg Empire, 1790–1918* (New York, 1969); Alexander Gerschenkron, *An Economic Spurt that Failed: Four Lectures in Austrian History* (Princeton, 1977); Steven Beller, *Francis Joseph* (London, 1996); Solomon Wank, "Some Reflections on the Habsburg Empire and Its Legacy in the Nationalities Question," *AHY* 28 (1997): 131–46; and Robin Okey, *The Habsburg Monarchy: From Enlightenment to Eclipse* (New York, 2001).

[11] On the history of the American historical profession, see Peter Novick, *That Noble Dream: The 'Objectivity Question' and the American Historical Profession* (Cambridge, 1988).

rules of international politics were timeless helped to erase the reality of the nation-state system's recent birth.[12]

The nation-state system is historically contingent, however, and human beings – including many Americans – were essential agents in its creation. It is a product of long-term debates over sovereignty, identity, and diplomatic culture and the specific circumstances of World War I. The outbreak of World War I, coupled with Wilson's election, brought people to the fore who were willing to change and created the opportunity for change to occur. The diplomatic culture of the Great Power System was shut down and advocates of the Habsburg government abroad were silenced, creating the opportunity to change both the diplomatic culture and the political organization of Central Europe. The experience of consular officials in the decades before the war and especially during the war made a significant group of foreign policy makers willing and indeed enthusiastic about making changes that would reduce the consular workload by clearly marking citizenship and limiting mobility. And, of course, Wilson himself was desirous of changed. He wanted to be the instrument of creating a new international order in which all states conformed with his ideal vision of America: they were democratic and they were capitalist, and to be democratic, they first had to be racially pure.

The specific circumstances of the war brought all of these forces together, and the world emerged from the war fundamentally altered. Wilson's ideas carried the day, and there was no longer room for Austria-Hungary. The Habsburg central government's commitment to diversity, consensus, and political citizenship had no place in a Wilsonian world of conformity and immutable and all-important racial identity.

---

[12] See, for example, Hans J. Morganthau, *Politics Among Nations: The Struggle for Power and Peace* (New York, 1948); Kenneth N. Waltz, *Theory of International Politics* (Reading, 1979); and Alexander Wendt, *Social Theory of International Politics* (New York, 1999).

Index

abolitionists, 52n, 201, 204
Adams, John Quincy, 42
Adee, Alvee, 194
Aehrenthal, Count Alois, 34, 221
African Americans, 5, 171, 201–202, 204, 211
  as slaves, 5
agrément, 75, 77–80, 86–87, 224n14, 229–230
agriculture and farming. See Southern states, U.S.
Agriculture, U.S. Department of, 111
Alabama, 171–172, See also Mobile
Alaska, 73, 168, 169, 173
Allied (Entente) Powers. See specific countries
Alsace-Lorraine, 242–243
Ambrózy, Baron Ludwig, 184, 188n131
American Commission to Negotiate Peace, 233, See also Paris Peace Conference
American Geographical Society, 232, 236
American Historical Association, 232
Americanization. See assimilation
Amtstage, 165–166, 173, 180, 182
anarchists, 191, 268, 270–271
Anglo-Saxon, 5, 6, 11, 91, 104, 185, 203–204, 206, 217, 278
Anschluss, 262
Anti-Federalists, 42
anti-Semitism, 79, 216–217, See also Jews and Judaism
Archibald, James F. J., 227
archives, 31, 34

Habsburg, 153n6, 157, 158, 190–191
U.S., 81, 129n92, 129, 143
Argentina, 93, 113
Arizona, 103, 195n159, 209–210
Armenians, 212
armies, 18
  Czechoslovak, 259, See also Czech Legion
  Habsburg, 21, 130, 131n102, 135, 137, 190, 231, 240, 242, 256
  U.S., 51, 103, 193, 201, 265
  see also military service
Asia, 5, 23, 154
assimilation, 278
  Americanization, 118, 179, 183, 185, 203–205, 218
  Czechs and Slovaks, 248, 278
  Jews and, 203–205
  Magyarization, 118, 180, 185, 198, 233
associations and societies, 147, 150, 159, 165, 176–181, 183, 188, 191, 193, 207
  Magyar, 67, 178, 188
  Polish, 246
  Serbian, 253
  see also specific associations
Athens, U.S. legation, 96, 123
attorneys. See lawyers
Ausgleich, 3, 74, 75, 124 , 198
Australia, 5, 6
Austria, First Republic, 261–262, 271
autocracy, 80, 232, 259

Balkan Question, 237, *See also* Yugoslavia
Baltimore, Maryland, 157
Bar Harbor, Maine, 89
Barbary States, 113
Batt, Wilmer R., 194
Bayard, Thomas F., 76, 77–85
Beelen-Bertholff, Baron F. E. F. de, 41
Belgium, 94, 139, 143, 194, 218n52, 222n8, 242
Beneš, Edvard, 248, 256, 259
Berchtold, Count Leopold, 221
Bernstorff, Count Johann Heinrich, 227, 228, 229
Bertillon, Alphonse, 202
birth certificates. *See* citizenship documentation
Bismarck, Prince Otto von, 241
blockade of Central Powers, 220, 224, 261, 262
blood quantum, 212
Bohemia, 31, 124
    as identity category, 124n68, 195, 215
    commerce and industry, 111, 115–116
    see also specific cities, Czech nationalism
Bonaparte, Prince Victor, 94
Bornemisza, Baron, 210
Bosnia and Herzegovina, 154n11, 192, 193
Boston, Massachusetts, 157
Bowman, Isaiah, 236
Braun, Marcus, 185
Brazil, 50, 93, 113, 224
Britain and the British, 20, 62, 222n8
    ambassadors, 37, 77, 92
    Foreign office, 24–25, 37
    Great Power status, 3, 22–23, 95
    internnes in, 266
    Paris Peace Conference and, 264
    relations with Habsburg Empire, 40–41, 59, 62, 227, 228, 243
    relations with U.S., 42, 43, 53, 68–69, 73, 77, 92, 108, 194
    U.S. protection of interests, 139, 143
    see also specific successor states; Sixtus Affair; Treaty of London; Treaty of Bucharest
Britton, Joseph, 115, 167
Bryan, William Jennings, 99–100, 209, 220
Buchanan, James, 49, 50–51, 55
Budapest, consulate general, 112–113, 115, 116–117, 120, 123n67, 123, 139–144, *See also* military service

Bulgaria and Bulgarians, 217, 231, 232
Buol-Schauenstein, Count Karl, 67
bureaucracy, 18, 222
    Habsburg, 21–22, 133, 150, 197
Burián, Count Stephan, 223, 227, 228–229, 239, 240, 241, 244–245, 260
Busser, Ralph, 113, 114, 119, 128, 140

cadastres and surveys, 14, 18
calls, social, 29, 31–32
Canada, 5, 6, 52, 53, 122
capitalism, 255, 258, 263, 277, 279, 281
Carlsbad, consulate, 112, 116, 117, 120–123, 142
Carnegie, Andrew, 160
Cass, Lewis, 55, 57, 58–59, 63
Catholics, Roman, 3, 14, 44, 63, 69, 78, 83, 94–95, 100, 186, 210, 217, 251, 253
    U.S. anti-Catholicism, 44, 67, 95, 181, 248
    see also Vatican
censuses, 18
    Habsburg, 198, 199, 216n49
    U.S., 199n3, 203
Central Powers. *See* specific countries
Charleston, South Carolina, 161
Chattanooga, Tennessee, 171
Chicago, consulate general, 155, 158, 162–163, 165, 169, 174, 176, 177, 189, 195, 209
Chicago, Illinois, 125, 135, 206
Chilean consular service, 145
Chinese Exclusion Act, 202, 211–212
Christianity, 20, 44, 79, *See also* specific denominations
Cincinnati, Ohio, 94, 163, 164, 180–181, 226
citizenship, 281
    determining for enemy aliens, 12, 258, 265
    determining for Habsburg protection cases, 90, 191–192
    determining for U.S. protection cases, 10, 11, 110, 111, 130, 131, 132–133, 135, 142, 276–277
    dual, 110, 131, 134–136, 146
    encouraging retention of Austrian or Hungarian, 148, 149, 177, 179, 207
    Habsburg categories, 4, 6–7, 11, 74, 154–155, 166, 177, 195, 197–198, 211, 212, 239, 281

in the Great Power System, 4, 14
office holding and, 16, 56, 155, 162
U.S. limitations on, 5, 11, 123, 201–202
see also Fourteenth Amendment;
expatriation; naturalization
citizenship documentation, 107, 109, 131,
142, 211
birth certificates, 135, 191
naturalization papers, 104–105, 132, 133,
142
passports, 6, 10, 110, 111, 112,
132, 133, 140, 146, 191, 227–228,
269, 276
visas, 6, 10, 111, 146, 276
civil service reform, U.S., 25, 49, 76
Civil War, U.S., 39, 68–69, 70, 72, 73, 93,
160, 173, 201–202, 204
civilization, 81, 85, 201, 205, 207, 236
diplomacy and, 5, 39, 91–92
Clay, Henry, 60–61
Clayton, John M., 56, 58, 59, 60, 62, 67
Clemenceau, George, 243, 244
clergy, 135, 165, 177, 181–182, 184, 187,
189
Cleveland, consulate, 158, 162n35, 163,
164–165, 195
Cleveland, Grover, 75, 76, 77–78, 82, 85,
91, 99, 100
Cleveland, Ohio, 167, 206
Coffin, William, 133, 142, 143, 144
colonialism. *See* imperialism
Colorado. *See* Ludlow Massacre. *See also*
Denver
Commerce and Labor, U.S. Department of,
170
communism, 8n18, 54, 251, 258–259, 263,
277
Congress of Oppressed Races, 255–256
Congress of Vienna, 3–4, 13–14, 22–24,
35–36, 95
Congress, U.S., 11, 49, 62, 64, 92, 94, 101,
136, 140, 169, 174, 205, 211–212, 231,
232, 275–277, *See also* Senate, U.S.
Connecticut, 100, 159, 178
Consular Conventions, U.S.-Habsburg
(1848 and 1870), 166, 175n89,
193–195
consular service, Habsburg, 47, 90, 108,
149–158, 164, 168–170, 195–196,
197, 205–208, 226
Consular Academy, 154

employment of women, 157–158
honorary consuls, 153, 156–158, 159,
162, 164, 172
see also specific posts
consular service, U.S., 48, 106, 108,
109–111, 116–117, 140, 150, 153, 275,
281
honorary consuls, 118
see also specific posts
consular services, 4, 11, 107–109, 115
British, 108, 113, 139n133, 150–153
citizenship requirements, 16, 56
French, 113, 150
German, 113, 157
see also neutrality, specific countries
convict labor, 116–117
Counter-Reformation, 21n25
Cowan, Edgar, 73
credence, letter of, 30–31, 33, 73
Crimean War, 13n1
Croatia and Croatians, 54, 117, 119, 138,
155, 181, 184, 195, 217, 238
in U.S., 164n45, 172, 173, 177, 183n114
see also assimilation, Yugoslavia
Cunard Line, 185, 191
Czech language, 3, 115, 124n68, 124, 155,
213–214, 249
Czech Legion, 258–259
Czech nationalism, 124
desire for Triple Monarchy, 124, 241
in U.S., 57, 124–125, 177, 181
see also Czecho-Slovak National Council
Czecho-Slovak National Council, 254
racial nationalim and, 249
recognition and internees, 266–269
recognition of, 256–257, 258–261, 263
Wilson and, 7, 246, 248–250
see also Congress of Oppressed Races
Czechoslovakia, 278, *See also* Czecho-
Slovak National Council
Czernin, Count Ottokar, 230, 240, 242,
243, 244–245, 252

Dalmatia, 195, 238, 250
Declaration of Corfu, 253n111
Declaration of Independence, U.S., 2, 201
Deedmeyer, Frank, 115
democracy, 7, 8, 37, 183, 218, 231, 232,
250, 255–256, 258, 261–262, 263, 279
racial homogenity and, 5, 203–204, 235,
239, 275, 277, 281

Democratic Party, 39, 48–49, 51, 52, 55–56, 57, 59, 61, 67, 76, 78, 87, 88, 94, 98, 100, 102, 134
Democratic Republicans, 42
Denver, consulate, 158, 163–164, 195, *See also* Ludlow Massacre
deportation, 10, 160, 167, 169, 174, 265, 267, 270–273
Detroit. *See* Michigan
Dillingham Commission, 205
diplomatic culture, 8, 97, 223, 275–276, 281
  ceremonial and social activities in, 13, 26–27, 59, 63, 65, 74–75, 76, 86, 87, 89, 96, 98–99, 121, 159, 165, 178
  credentials ceremony, 29–32, 229
  formal protest in, 60, 62, 64, 97–98, 217
  funding for, 27–28, 36, 49–50, 101, 145, 156–157, 177, 190
  origins of, 15–18
  rank of post, 30, 35–37, 43, 46, 49, 65, 67, 68, 88, 91–93, 113, 163, 276
  recall of diplomats, 95–97, 223, 228–229
  rotation in office, 16, 36, 42, 46–49, 89, 156, 276
  separation of functions in, 4, 10, 11–12, 24–26, 57–58, 141, 145, 223, 258
  social class in, 27–28, 35, 36, 42, 76–77, 84, 87, 88, 94, 100, 121, 154, 157, 205–206, 220
  stylized language, 28–29, 33–35, 71–72, 111–112
  U.S. criticism of, 4–5, 7, 15, 29, 37–38, 39, 51, 76, 87, 88, 92, 95, 98, 99–100, 153, 220, 275
  see also neutrality
disability, 212
divine right theory, 19–20
Dominian, Leon, 218n52, 235–236, 249, 253n109
Dumba, Konstantin, 30n56, 99, 102, 174n87, 209, 219, 223, 226–229, 244, 248, 260
Dutch Republic. *See* Netherlands

Egypt, 100, 107, 260
Ellis Island, 193, 272
enemy aliens. *See* internment
espionage, 15, 17
  during World War I, 225, 268–269
estate cases, 112, 193–196
ethnicity. *See* racial nationalism

eugenics, 204, *See also* racial nationalism
Everett, Edward, 67
expatriation, 10, 131, 136–138
expositurs, 161
  demand for, 164–165
extradition, 41, 116

Farewell Address. *See* Washington, George
Federalists, 42
filibusters, 39, 52
Fillmore, Millard, 60, 62, 63, 64–66
Fiume, 117, 185, 189
Fiume, consulate, 112, 116, 117–120, 129n92, 143
Florida, 171, 172
Flourney, Richard W., Jr., 134
Foote, Thomas, 67
Foreign Affairs, I & R Ministry of the I & R House and, 24, 50, 53, 56, 77, 96–97, 98, 111, 133, 148, 153–154, 159, 166, 190, 198, 217
Foreign Service, U.S., 275–276
Fort Douglas, 265, *See also* internment
Fort Oglethorpe, 265, 266, *See also* internment
Fourteen Points, 8, 237–239
Fourteenth Amendment, 202, 211
France and the French, 94
  Great Power status, 3, 22–23, 95, 153
  influence on diplomatic culture, 17–18, 24, 35, 37, 76–77
  relations with Ottomans, 61–62
  relations with U.S., 40–42, 92, 108
  support for successor states, 247–251, 256–257, 264
  U.S. protection of interests, 139, 143
  see also Czecho-Slovak National Council, Louis Napoleon, Sixtus Affair
Francis, Charles, 31n58, 83–84, 85, 96
Franco-Prussian War, 242
Frankfurt Parliament, 52
Franklin, Benjamin, 40
Franz Ferdinand, 222, 239–240
Franz II/I, 22
Franz Joseph, 31, 32, 36n73, 47, 65, 69, 72, 73, 74–75, 100, 127n83, 137, 156, 186, 198, 227, 234, 239–240
French language, 30, 155, 238
  as identity category, 216
Freyesleben, Ferdinand, 155, 162

Galicia, 88, 103–104, 130n96, 143, 161,
195, 247, 271, *See also* Poland and
Poles
Galveston, Texas, 157
genocide, 264, 278
geography and geographers, 9, 235–237,
248
influence on race, 203
see also Inquiry
Georgia, 51, 157, *See also* Fort Oglethorpe
German language, 3, 88, 100, 103, 113, 124,
162, 163, 199, 213
in diplomacy, 30, 115–116, 118–119,
121, 155, 161, 238
press in U.S., 85
Germany and Germans, 144, 214
anti-Americanism, 121–122
criticism of, 121–122, 126, 231–232, 259
Great Power status, 3, 95
identity categorization and, 195, 215, 250
Nazi policies, 278
Poland and, 238, 247–248
relations with Habsburg Empire, 77, 153,
157, 221, 240–244, 260
relations with Italy, 250, 255
relations with U.S., 92, 194, 219, 229,
263, 265
steamship ports, 119
Weimar Republic, 263
see also espionage during World War I,
Anschluss
Gołuchowski, Count Agenor, 88, 90, 97,
191–192
Grant, Frederick, 105–106
Grant, Madison, 203
Grant, Ulysses S., 48, 75
Grant-Smith, Ulysses, 138
Great Power System, 2, 3, 7, 8, 9, 13, 23, 53,
68, 76, 87, 90, 97, 102, 111, 211, 219,
222, 231, 232, 276, 281, *See also*
Congress of Vienna, diplomatic culture
Greece and Greeks, 107, 113, 194,
208–209, *See also* Athens
Greek Catholic Church, 186, 210
Grivičič, Georg von, 171
Grund, Francis, 57, 63
Guatemala, 93, 194

Habsburg government
as as "vassal" of German government,
157, 231, 234, 238, 242, 244, 256

as oppressor of nationalites, 2, 157, 198,
231, 234, 238, 249–250, 254, 255, 277
services provided by, 2, 21, 148, 195–196,
270
U.S. criticism of, 80–81, 127, 133
U.S. recognition of, 3, 4–5, 8, 40, 43, 53,
61, 75, 88, 99, 101–102, 111, 132, 196,
197–198, 219, 229–231
see also citizenship, revolutions
Halstead, Albert, 122
Hazelton, Pennsylvania, 161
Hebrew, as racial category, 83, 216–217, *See
also* Jews and Judaism
Hengelmüller von Hengervár, Baron
Ladislaus, 34, 87–91, 96–97, 101, 171,
188–189, 194, 210, 220, 221
Hindermann, Franz, 192
Hobbes, Thomas, 19, 24
Holmes, Oliver Wendell, Sr., 72–73
Holocaust, 278
Holy Alliance, 44
Holy Roman Empire, 22
Holy See. *See* Vatican
honor, 33, 72–73, 85, 115, 178
Hoover, Charles, 120–121, 125–128, 142
Horthy, Miklos, 264
House of Representatives, U.S. *See* Congress,
U.S.
House, Edward, 205, 228, 231, 232, 233,
246, 250, 253
Hülsemann, Johann von, 45–46, 53, 58–60,
61, 62–67, 68
Hungary and its government, 110, 112,
117–118, 133, 143–144, 155, 181, 182,
183, 215, 233, 239, 245, 246, 253, 254
1848 revolution, 52–68
1867 coronation, 72, 74–75
emigration, 120, 168, 184–185
see also assimilation; repatriation; Kun,
Belá; Treaty of Trianon (1921); specific
cities

Illinois, 209, *See also* Chicago
immigration laws, U.S., 119, 169
1882, 211
1891, 212
1921, 11
1924, 11, 277
contract labor, 160
see also Chinese Exclusion Act
immigration to U.S., 5, 220, 275

immigration to U.S., (cont.)
   "New Immigrants", 110, 119, 149, 203,
     277
   corporate-sponsored, 168
   inspections, 119–120
   quota system, 11, 146, 277
   restriction, 5, 183, 204, 205, 211n39
   Southern states and, 170–172
Immigration, U.S. Bureau of, 6, 10–11,
   159, 167, 170, 185, 196, 265,
   270–272
   use of racial categories, 197, 211–218
imperialism, 6, 93, 200–201, 205, 250
impressment. *See* military service
India, 260
Indian Affairs, Bureau of, 212
Indians, American. *See* Native Americans
Industrial Workers of the World, 164
injury and death, workplace, 109, 147–149,
   160, 166, 168–169, 172–176, 186,
   190–191, 195–193, 208
Inquiry, The, 8–9, 205, 231, 232–239,
   245–246, 248–249, 261, 262, 277
Interior, U.S. Department of the, 173,
   195n159, *See also* Indian Affairs,
   Bureau of
internment, 10, 12, 265–273
Ireland, 260
Italian government, 139, 153
   citizens in U.S., 174, 196
   demand for ambassadors, 37
   early modern diplomacy, 15–17
   Keiley controversy, 77–78
   nationalism and, 52
   see also Congress of Oppressed Races,
     Treaty of London
Italian language, 3, 113, 117, 118, 157n21,
   192, 195, 238, 250

Jackson Lumber Company, 171, 192
Jackson, Andrew, 39, 49
Japan and Japanese, 5, 23, 139, 202,
   222n8, 277
Jefferson, Thomas, 39, 115n32
Jenifer, Daniel, 45
Jews and Judaism, 3, 21n25, 103n2, *See also*
   anti-Semitism; Hebrew; Holocaust;
   Keiley, Rebecca; Landesco, Alexander;
   Yiddish
Johnson, Andrew, 72–73
Joseph II, 22

journalists, 54–55, 70, 100, 227, 234, *See
   also* newspapers and the press
jury selection and prejudice (U.S.), 210–211
Justice, U.S. Department of, 11, 209–210,
   265–270

Kálnoky, Count Gustav, 78–80, 81, 82, 83,
   84, 86–87, 88, 105
Kansas, 170
Karl I, 32, 240, 244, 252, 261, 264
   abdication, 9, 11, 12, 261
Keiley, Anthony, 75, 77–79, 81, 87
Keiley, Rebecca, 79, 80, 81, 82, 83
Keynes, John Maynard, 281
Klebelsberg, Kuno, 185
Klementine, Princess, 94
Knights of Labor, 160
Knox, Philander, 89
Kossuth, Lajos, 51, 54–55, 61, 62–64,
   67–68, 181
Krenner, Victor, 176, 180–181
Kun, Belá, 54, 263–264

Labor, U.S. Department of, 11, 265,
   270–272
LaGuardia, Fiorello, 119–120
Landesco, Alexander, 180–181
Lansing, Robert, 123, 136, 145, 226, 227,
   230–229, 235, 239, 244–245, 248, 250,
   253, 256, 261
Latin, 17
Latin America, 23, 42n6, 52, 69, 93, *See also*
   specific countries
lawyers, 112, 147, 150, 156, 164–165, 172,
   175–176, 207, 210, 256
League of Nations, 275
Lederer, Baron Karl von, 68
Lenin, V. I., 252, 259
Leopold II, 22n29
Lepša, Josef, 155
Liberec. *See* Reichenberg, consulate
Lincoln, Abraham, 69, 75
Lloyd George, David, 253, 254
Locke, John, 2, 19–20
Lodge, Henry Cabot, 135–136, 204
Lombroso, Cesare, 203
London Times, 57
London, U.S. legation/embassy, 42, 92,
   100, 227
Longchamps, Charles Julien de, 41
Longworth, Nicholas, 94, 95

Lord, Robert, 233, 246
Louis Napoleon, 69
Louis XIV, 17
Lowrie, Will, 120–121
loyalty, 16
    questioned in U.S., 131, 137, 204
    to emperor, 4, 20–21, 47–48, 130,
        148–149, 154n10, 175, 176, 177, 178,
        204, 207
Ludlow Massacre, 208
Ludwig, Ernst, 163, 174n87, 195
lynching, 202, 279

Magyar language, 3, 54, 88, 118–119,
    162–163, 192, 199, 215, 238
    press in U.S., 155, 163, 187, 189, 226
Magyarization. *See* assimilation
mail, 125–126, 140
    wartime disruptions to service, 114, 127,
        129n92, 143, 224
Mallett, Frank E., 129n92, 141, 142, 144
Mann, A. Dudley, 56–57, 58, 59–60, 61, 62,
    67
Marbois, Barbé de, 41
Mareschall, Baron Wenzel von, 44, 45
marriage. *See* Keiley, Rebecca; Storer, Maria
    Longworth Nichols
    citizenship and, 132n104
    desertion, 109, 167
    diplomats and, 32n61, 32
Martini, Orestes de, 114
Masaryk, Tomáš, 124n68, 248
Maximilian I of Mexico, 69–71
McAdoo, William G., 226
McCurdy, Charles, 64–65, 66–67
McDuffie, George, 51
McKinley, William, 33, 90–91, 92, 94
M'Crackin, George, 72–73
Mensdorff-Pouilly-Dietrichstein, Count
    Albert, 241
mercantilism, 15n6
Metternich-Winneburg, Prince Clemens, 22,
    44–45, 52, 115
Mexican War, 52, 104
Mexico, 5, 53, 69–72, 73, 93, 174, 272n43,
    272
Mezes, Sidney E., 233, 236
Michigan, 55, 153n6, 162n35, 162, 163,
    164–165, 173, 180, 195–196
migration. *See* specific types
military service

amnesty, 186
impressment, 109, 112–113, 123,
    128–139
    requirements in Habsburg Empire, 71,
        130, 173
    U.S., 104, 126n78, 232
Minnesota, 124, 162
minority treaties, 264, 278
miscegenation, 212
Missouri, 117, *See also* St. Louis
Mobile, Alabama, 172
Monroe Doctrine, 69, 70–72
Monroe, James, 42n6, 42, 69
Montenegro, 139
Moravia, 124, *See* Bohemia
Morris, Gouverneur, 42
Motley, John Lothrup, 68–75
Muhlenberg, Henry, 29n53, 44–45, 115
multilingualism, 3, 9, 199
munitions, 223, 226
Muslims, 3

Napoleonic Wars, 13n1, 14, 20, 22, 42
Nash, Paul, 128
Native Americans, 5, 6, 103, 201
natural rights, 2, 18, 19–20
naturalization
    as protection for nationalists, 179–180
    Hungarian law, 186
    U.S., 104, 131–132n104, 133–134,
        178
Naturalization Act of 1907, U.S., 136
Naturalization Convention, U.S.-Austro-
    Hungarian (1870), 105, 106, 110,
        131–132, 134–136
navies, 18
    Austro-Hungarian, 131n102, 159, 171
    British, 69, 108, 224, 227
    U.S., 51, 62–63
Nebraska, 162, 208–209
Netherlands, 14n4, 27, 42, 194, 215
neutrality
    protection of interests and, 57–58, 111,
        139, 141, 145, 223
    U.S. during World War I, 122, 219,
        223–226, 227, 229
New Jersey, 104, 159, 224
New Mexico, 103, 195n159
New Orleans, Louisiana, 157, 171–172,
    192–193
New York City, 62, 63, 119, 170, 188, 227

New York City, consulate general, 66, 155, 158–159, 172, 174, 192
New York Evening Post, 86
New York Times, 70, 82, 183, 256, 266
New York World, 227
New Zealand, 5, 6
newspapers and the press, 34, 54, 57, 59, 61, 63, 64, 66, 70, 78, 82, 84, 85–86, 90, 92, 95, 96, 98, 99, 159, 170, 185, 225, 227, 228, 243
    foreign language in U.S., 85, 124–125, 150, 155, 159, 169, 177, 182–184, 189, 226
    in the Habsburg Empire, 126, 155, 169, 188
    see also specific papers
Nicholas II, 230n39
Norfolk, Virginia, 157
note verbalé, 33, 71
Nuber von Pereked, Alexander, 158, 174

Ohio, 37, 93–94, 163, *See also* specific cities
Orthodox Christianity, 3, 217, 220n2, 253
Ottoman Empire, 113, 117n42, 126, 153, 208–209, 222n8, 231, 232, 253

Pact of Rome, 255
Page Act. *See* Chinese Exclusion Act
Page, Walter Hines, 227
Pan-German nationalism, 177, 178, 179–180, 184, 186
Pan-Slavism, 178, 181, 182, 186, 215, 248
Papen, Franz von, 225
Paris Peace Conference, 2, 7–8, 10, 11, 12, 14, 145–146, 198, 236, 248, 251, 262–264, 270, 272, 275–281
    organization, 235, 237, 263
parliaments in the Habsburg Empire, 21, 47, 74
    Reichsrat, 91, 98
Passport Control, U.S. DOS Bureau of, 134
passports. *See* citizenship documentation
Pelényi (Vice Consul), 165, 173, 180–181
Penfield, Anna Weightman Walker, 100
Penfield, Frederick Courtland, 31, 32, 87, 88, 100–102, 112, 113, 122–123, 127n83, 128, 135, 140, 214, 219, 224, 228, 230–231
Pennsylvania, 41, 44, 74, 100, 160–162, 181, 194, 210–211, 226, *See also* specific cities

persona non grata, 67, 219
Philadelphia, consulate, 153n6, 158, 159, 161
Philippines, 169, 201
Pierce, Franklin, 67
Pinckney, Thomas, 42
Pittsburgh, consulate, 158, 159–161, 193, 210
Poincaré, Raymond, 242–243
Poland and Poles, 138, 162, 192, 271, 278
    in U.S. immigration statistics, 214
    Polish Question, 237, 238, 246–248
    U.S. recognition of, 263
    see also Galicia, Congress of Oppressed Races
Polish and Lithuanian Commonwealth, 15
Polish language, 3, 116, 155, 162, 195
Polish National Alliance, 7, 150, 180
Polk, James K., 49, 51
Portugal, 36, 42
Post, Louis F., 272
Prague, consulate, 112–113, 115–116, 116–117, 121, 123–128, 167
    post-WWI legation, 263
prisoners of war, 10, 130, 265, *See also* Czech Legion
Proctor, Vermont, 157
propaganda, 222, 225–226, 234–235, 254–256
property. *See* estate cases. *See also* assimilation, expatriation
Protestants, 3, 14, 21n25, 67
Prussia. *See* Germany and Germans
Puerto Rico, 201

racial nationalism, 107, 177, 181, 237, 255
    as foundation of post-1919 international system, 3, 7–8, 10, 11, 196, 198, 219–220, 246, 251, 258, 261–262, 263, 270, 272–273, 275–281
    diplomats and, 122–123, 205–208
    discrimination and, 149, 161, 172, 253, 266
    language and, 3, 9, 157, 178, 198, 200, 203, 236, 249, 253
    science and, 5–6, 9, 91, 172, 197, 198, 200–205, 235–236, 249
    U.S. legal system and, 195, 211
    violence and, 7, 161, 190, 197, 208–210
    see also assimilation; Immigration, U.S. Bureau of; democracy

reaccredidation, 32–33
Regelmént of 1815, 35–37
Reichenberg, consulate, 112, 116–117
Reichsrat. *See* parliaments in the Habsburg
  Empire
relief payments
  by U.S. consuls, 139, 143
  to U.S. internees, 269–270
  see also repatriation
religion. *See* Keiley, Rebecca; clergy; and
  specific denominations
repatriation, 264, 278
  Habsburg assisted, 171–172, 190–193
  Hungarian program, 150, 186–190
  of internees in U.S., 10, 265, 267, 270, 275
  U.S. facilitated, 105–106, 142–143
Republican Party, 39, 52, 72, 74, 75–76, 83,
  91, 94, 98, 99
return migration, 6, 106, 110, 167–168,
  176–177, 179, 185
revolutions, 20, 40, 44, 69, 250, 254, 256
  American, 20, 40, 45, 247
  in 1848, 52–53, 74
  see also Hungary, Russia
Rijeka. *See* Fiume
Ripley, William Z., 203n15
Rockefeller, John D., 208
Rogers Act, 107n12, 275
Romania and Romanians, 139, 194, 222n8,
  255, 266n24
  borders, 241, 246, 254, 257
  in Hungary, 3, 54, 118, 184
  in U.S., 177, 180–181, 208n30
  see also Treaty of Bucharest
Rome, diplomatic posts
  Habsburg, 221
  U.S., 27n47, 77, 92
Roosevelt, Theodore, 31n58, 33, 88, 89, 92,
  94–96, 97, 98–99, 204
Root, Elihu, 94, 95–97, 98
Rousseau, Jean-Jacques, 19
Rudolf, Crown Prince, 239
Russia and Russians, 3, 16, 22, 44, 73, 95,
  153, 215, 278
  Bolshevik Revoluion, 242, 248, 251,
  258–259
  German-speaking, 178
  Hungary and, 52, 56, 65–66
  in World War I, 130, 222n8, 240
  Polish-speaking, 214, 247
  U.S. protection of interests, 139, 142–143

Yugoslavia and, 250–251, 253
Russia, diplomats in
  French, 77
  Habsburg, 77, 221
  U.S., 42, 49, 92
Ruthenians. *See* Ukraine and
  Ukrainians

Salt Lake City, Utah, 172
San Francisco, consulate, 158, 164
San Marino, 139
Schaeffer, Baron Ignaz von, 79–84
Schwager, John, 208
Schwarz (Consul), 56
Schwarzenberg, Prince Karl, 58, 59–60, 62,
  64–66
scientific racism. *See* racial nationalism
Secret Service, U.S., 226
self-determination, 7, 220, 249, 262, 279
Senate, U.S., 49–51, 57–61, 73–74, 78, 98,
  174, *See also* Congress, U.S.
separate peace. *See* Sixtus Affair
Serbia and Serbs, 130, 139, 181, 194,
  217, 222
  and a South Slav state, 253
  see also Yugoslavia
Serbo-Croatian, 3
Seton-Watson, Robert, 233–235, 248, 252,
  254–256
Seward, William, 69, 71, 72–73
Shaler, Nathan, 210
Silvestri, Hugo, 174, 176, 177, 184, 189,
  206–207
Sixtus Affair, 242–244
Slavs, 215, 234, 278, *See also* Czecho-Slovak
  National Council, Yugoslavia
Slocum, Clarence Rice, 118–119
Slovakia and Slovaks, 3, 54, 118,
  124n69, 155, 160, 163, 177, 181,
  184, 195, 263, *See also* assimilation,
  Czecho-Slovak National Council
Slovenia and Slovenes, 3, 217, *See also*
  Yugoslavia
Smuts, Jan, 240–241
Solicitor, U.S. DOS Office of the,
  266–267
Sosnowski, George Jan, 246
South Africa, 5, 6, 240
South Slavic National Council, 7,
  254
South Slavs. *See* Yugoslavia

Southern states, U.S., 43, 58, 83, 164, 170–172, 201–202, *See also* specific states

sovereignty, 2–12, 13, 18–20, 31, 33, 42, 57, 110, 195, 197, 211, 257, 259, 281
diplomats and, 17, 28, 35, 58, 76, 81, 223, 276
territorial, 14–15, 23, 24, 106–107, 123, 149, 150, 267, 272, 276–277
see also Habsburg government, Czecho-Slovak National Council

Soviet Union. *See* Russia and Russians

Spain and the Spanish, 5, 37, 42, 68, 69, 90, 91, 93n163, 94, 141, 145, 194

Spanish-American War, 90

special tobacco agents, U.S., 43–44

Spokane, Washington, 147–148

St. Louis, consulate, 158, 164

Stanton, Benjamin W., 37

State, U.S. Department of, 8–10, 32, 49–50, 115, 125, 143, 148, 153, 198, 211, 217, 231, 232, 238, 266–270, 271

Steed, Henry Wickham, 233–235, 251, 252, 254–257, 260

Stiles, William H., 51, 55, 56

Stone, William J., 116

Storer, Bellamy, 91, 92, 93–99

Storer, Maria Longworth Nichols, 91, 94–95, 97, 99

Sumner, Charles, 73

Supilo, Frano, 254

Sweden and Swedes, 11, 42, 224, 258, 261, 265, 268

Switzerland and Swiss, 16, 145, 178, 215, 218n52, 241, 242

Syrians, 216

Taft, William Howard, 88

Talleyrand-Périgord, Charles Maurice de, 22

Tarnowski, Count Adam, 8, 219, 224n14, 229–230

Taylor, Zachary, 51, 55–56, 58–60, 62, 67

telegraph, 133, 140, 142
in diplomatic culture, 25, 87
wartime disruption of, 144, 224, 228

Thirty Years' War, 14

Tisza, Count István, 245

tobacco, 43–44, 50, 109n17, 114–115

trade. *See* tobacco, specific consular posts and countries

Trading with the Enemy Act, 270

Transylvania, 251, 263, 266n24. *See* Treaty of Bucharest (1916)

travel, 6, 10, 27, 57, 106, 109, 110, 113, 119, 120, 125, 134, 136, 223, 277, *See also* citizenship documentation

treason cases. *See* Prauge, consulate

Treasury, U.S. Department of the, 116–117, 212, 226

Treaty of Bucharest (1916), 246, 251

Treaty of Commerce and Navigation, U.S.-Habsburg (1829), 43, 58, 114

Treaty of London (1915), 246, 251, 252

Treaty of Trianon (1920), 264

Trieste, 192, 237–238, 250

Trieste, consulate, 43, 112–114, 116–118, 128, 137, 140, 175n89, 234

trust
in diplomatic culture, 16–18, 26, 48, 156
in Habsburg protection cases, 156, 172, 175–176
in U.S.-Habsburg relations, 97, 132, 252

Tucker, Randolph, 78

Turner, Frederick Jackson, 204, 232

Ukraine and Ukrainians, 3, 177, 271

Umgangsprache, 198, 199, 216n49

Uniate churches. 186. *See* Greek Catholic Church

Vatican, 36n73, 37n74, 78, 94

Victor Emmanuel II, 78

Victoria, 92

Vienna, consulate general, 43, 56, 104, 112–113, 116–117, 123, *See also* military service

Vienna, U.S. diplomatic post, 17n17, 44, 112, *See also* specific diplomats

visas. *See* citizenship documentation

Waller, George P., Jr., 122–123

War of 1812, 43

War Prisoners Relief Committee, 270

war, declaration of
U.S. against Austria-Hungary, 231–232
U.S. against Germany, 111, 231

Warm, William, 226–227

Washington Post, 89

Washington, diplomatic post, 159, 161, 168, 174, 209
as hardship post, 45, 48, 77, 88, 221
rank of, 46, 91–92

Washington, George, 41–42, 53, 58, 70, 86
Watts, Henry, 74
Webb, James Watson, 59
Weber, Gusztáv, 171, 192
Webster, Daniel, 60, 61, 63–67
Welsersheimb, Count Rudolf, 105
West Virginia, 161–162
Westphalian system, 13, 14–15, 17, 24, 25, 27, 40
Whig Party, 39, 42, 52, 55–56, 59, 61
Wilhelm II, 240, 244, 245
Wilson, Woodrow, 4, 7–9, 31, 32, 88, 99–100, 134, 204, 205, 218, 219–220, 223–224, 226, 227–232, 234,

237–236, 241, 245–252, 253–254, 255–256, 259, 261–262, 263, 264, 270, 272n43, 272, 275
workers' compensation. *See* injury and death, workplace
World War II, 23n33, 278

Yiddish, 3, 199, 216n49
Young, Wallace, 121–123
Yugoslavia, 113n26, 181, 217, 246, 250, 252–256, 257, 260, 263, 278

Zita, Princess, 240
Zwiedinek, Baron Erich von, 229